From Here to Denmark

Endorsements

'The authors, armed with years of experience as practitioners of development policy, take a deep dive into what makes for success in development. They zero in on good governance as a key determinant. They recognize that governance is difficult to define and there are no simple solutions of achieving it. What needs to be done may vary across countries and also take many years to yield results. But without good governance throwing money at the problem will not help—it can even make it worse. Strongly recommended for anyone who wants to understand the challenges of development.'

—Montek Singh Ahluwalia, Distinguished Fellow, Centre for Social and Economic Progress (CSEP), New Delhi; Former Deputy Chairman, Planning Commission, India

'Why do some countries take off while others stall? Nag and Kohli's new book is a far-ranging investigation of this age-old question. Drawing on diverse sources, from formal economics to political science, through fascinating case studies, covering all continents, to their own experience as policymakers, this book is an unexpected page-turner.'

—Kaushik Basu, Professor of Economics and Carl Marks Professor of International Studies, Cornell University; Former Chief Economist, World Bank

'By authoring *From Here to Denmark*, the Nag–Kohli duo has rendered yeoman's service. A superbly researched volume, it reflects the rich experiences of two ace development practitioners. The blend of key takeaways that development is more than GDP; economic growth must improve human capital through better health and education; and this inevitably needs good governance is significant. A must-read book for everyone desirous of living in a better world.'

—Rajiv Bhatia, Distinguished Fellow, Gateway House, Indian Council on Global Relations; Former Ambassador, Author and Columnist, India

'With a deep understanding of the challenges faced by countries in building strong institutions, Nag and Kohli have written a very realistic and yet optimistic book about the journey to Denmark. Realistic that there is no silver bullet and that it takes long to make this journey, perhaps even centuries. And, optimistic that a successful journey is indeed possible, even if very challenging. A most relevant read by policymakers, practitioners, and interested citizens.'

—*Bambang Brodjonegoro, Former Minister of Finance and Former Minister of National Development Planning, (BAPPENAS), Research and Technology, Indonesia*

'Nag and Kohli argue that strong institutions, the hallmark of Denmark, are key to ensure good governance and as such a fundamental pillar of a long-term development strategy that reconciles economic growth objectives with macroeconomic stability, social equity, and environmental sustainability criteria. While recognizing that there is no unique or easy path to move in that direction, the book is ultimately optimistic: "the arc of justice does bend towards Denmark". In this endeavour the authors present a well-argued case on the importance of joint coordinated actions between governments, market institutions, and the community. It is indeed an ambitious, creative, and enjoyable book.'

—*Enrique Garcia R., Former President of CAF-Development Bank of Latin America; Former Minister of Planning and Coordination, Bolivia*

'Nag and Kohli correctly identify weak institutions as a principal cause of poor governance around the world. Drawing on insights from behavioural economics, focal points, and game theory, and boldly identifying ten global megatrends which will increase pressures for good governance, they eloquently make the case for human agency and active participation by the community in the journey to Denmark. A fascinating, thought-provoking book.'

—*Abdoulie Janneh, Executive Director, Mo Ibrahim Foundation; Former UN Under-Secretary General and Executive Secretary, UN Commission for Africa*

From Here to Denmark

The Importance of Institutions for Good Governance

RAJAT M. NAG

Distinguished Fellow, Emerging Markets Forum

HARINDER S. KOHLI

Founding Director and Chief Executive of Emerging Markets Forum and Founding Director, President, and CEO of Centennial Group International

Dear Mr. Friedman:

With the hope that our children, if not we, will get to "Denmark".

With best wishes.

Rajat Nag

Synapse @ Gurgaon
Feb 24/2024

OXFORD
UNIVERSITY PRESS

OXFORD
UNIVERSITY PRESS

Great Clarendon Street, Oxford, OX2 6DP,
United Kingdom

Oxford University Press is a department of the University of Oxford.
It furthers the University's objective of excellence in research, scholarship,
and education by publishing worldwide. Oxford is a registered trade mark of
Oxford University Press in the UK and in certain other countries

Published in the United States of America by Oxford University Press
198 Madison Avenue, New York, NY 10016, United States of America

British Library Cataloguing in Publication Data

Data available

Library of Congress Control Number: 2023942432

ISBN 978-0-19-889310-3

DOI: 10.1093/oso/9780198893103.001.0001

Printed and bound in India by Replika Press Pvt. Ltd.

To
The Girl Child,
May she find a fairer, kinder world to grow up in

"Where the mind is without fear,
and the head is held high. . .

. . . Where the mind is led forward by thee
Into ever-widening thought and action
Into that heaven of freedom, my Father,
let my country awake."

Rabindranath Tagore, (1861–1941)
Nobel Laureate in Literature 1913

Preface

In over four decades of our work in development practice, we have spent much of our time trying to bridge the gaps between paper and reality, between desires and resources, between what and how. We have had the privilege of meeting and working with citizens, politicians, bureaucrats, activists, community organizers, members of the civil society, academics, and professionals in the non-governmental organizations as well as colleagues in different parts of the world. We have been humbled by their sense of commitment, sincerity, competence, and perseverance against all odds in trying to make the world a better, kinder, fairer, cleaner, and a more just place to live in.

We have been equally inspired and educated by stories of their successes. It is no mean achievement that all over the world, be it in Asia or Africa or elsewhere, people now live longer, are more literate, and are richer today than they were only a generation back. Hundreds of millions have been lifted out of poverty within our lifetime. Undoubtedly, there is much to applaud in the successes of the past half century. But there is much to worry too, if not despair.

In this book, while we celebrate such successes, we also underline that not all is well with the state of the world. Inequalities remain high and is in fact growing in many societies. Rapidly worsening climate challenges pose an existential threat to humanity. The little girl to whom this book is dedicated starts her life with many unfair challenges and unfortunately often has to continue fighting those throughout her lifetime. Economic and social deprivations haunt millions around the world. Many more are subjected to crushing discrimination, indignities, and injustices, be it because of their poverty, gender, religion, sexual orientation, ideology, or for just being in the wrong place at the wrong time.

Any number of diagnostics on why our world still faces so many ills highlight one major conclusion: poor governance. That is hardly surprising, but it leads to an obvious question: how to achieve better governance? Amongst the plethora of ideas, solutions, and advice, there is one consistent thought: the need for good, strong institutions.

Like several other well-intentioned development practitioners, we also freely and passionately extolled the virtues of good governance and strong institutions to our counterparts and colleagues in the developing world. To add weight to our words, we often made references to 'Denmark', the aspirational ideal of good governance.

In many cases, if not most, we were preaching to the converted.

Many of the political leaders and policymakers, to whom we patronizingly gave such diagnosis and advice, did not need to be convinced. They saw bad governance all around them. They knew the vicious and deleterious effects of corruption. Most wanted to change and bring in good governance. They could write books on why their countries needed better governance. Their real concern was the what and the how. They asked two very simple questions: how do we get to Denmark? What do we do? Two earnest, straightforward questions that left us fumbling for answers. We did attempt to give some answers then, but we knew that they were inadequate. Our hosts were usually too gracious to say what they thought of our advice.

These seemingly simple questions have gnawed at us during our careers and our research. This book is our honest attempt to give better answers than we did then. In writing this book, we have appreciated just how complex and multidimensional the issues are. We have often felt completely overwhelmed by the sheer volume of work of many brilliant scholars, academics, and committed practitioners in this space. Their work provided us a deeply rich repository of wisdom and advice. We have drawn on their work most liberally and stood on their shoulders. We acknowledge that in many ways our answers are still inadequate and at best only partial, but we hope that they are at least a more considered and nuanced response to the questions our hosts had asked us

Ours is not an academic work. Rather, it is the story of a journey of two students in the forest of development who are still struggling to map the way to Denmark. We recognize that the path will neither be well-paved nor necessarily unique. Perhaps Denmark will not even be reached, at least not for a very long time. But so long as we reach a better world—a fairer, kinder, more prosperous, less unequal world, then the journey will have been worthwhile.

We invite you to join us on that journey.

Acknowledgements

This book was born of an idea posed—first informally and later more formally—by the Oxford University Press, India (OUP) that we write a book on "governance" based on our decades of work on emerging economies worldwide. Having struggled with this topic during our long years at the Asian Development Bank and the World Bank and more recently at the Emerging Markets Forum, we knew how complex the issues were. So, initially we were not so sure that we wanted to take on this project. But the then Director, Global Academic Publishing, OUP, India Sugata Ghosh, and Rekha Natarajan, Head of Commissioning, OUP India persisted. Taking their invitation as both a challenge and a compliment, we finally accepted though with some trepidation. We are grateful to Sugata and Rekha for their confidence in us. Luckily for us, despite a subsequent major corporate restructuring at the OUP, India, the organization has continued to enthusiastically support this book and was very ably steered by Dhiraj Pandey and his team, both in India and at Oxford. Without Dhiraj's commitment, able leadership and gentle, yet firm prodding, we would have fallen even further behind on finishing this book.

It will be obvious to the readers that the philosophical foundation and inspiration of this book derives from India's first Nobel Laureate, poet Rabindranath Tagore. We owe an immense debt of intellectual gratitude to another, more recent, Indian Nobel Laureate, Amartya Sen who has heavily influenced most of our generation and beyond on key issues such as the care for the poor and the marginalized and social justice. In this context, we also acknowledge and thank dozens, if not hundreds, of scholars and intellectuals whose works we have also generously drawn upon. They are too numerous to name individually but are referenced in the book appropriately. We thank our many colleagues, both at our workplaces and in the many countries we have worked in, in the governments, businesses and civil society for generously sharing their own experiences and their perspectives on the challenges of governance and institutions. But most important of all, we express our deep gratitude to the thousands of common people in small towns and villages who shared with us their real-life stories in their full range of raw emotions and tribulations of how poor governance and injustices, big and small, affected them in their daily lives. If it were not for such voices, our own perspectives on governance would surely have been even more incomplete than they perhaps still are.

This book would not have been possible without the constant support of many colleagues. Harpaul Kohli's support with facts and figures was indispenasable as was Ieva Vilkelyte's excellent research and analytic work. She also provided critical support in the final editing, and formatting of the manuscript and prepared the cover. Laura Shelton and Leo Zucker provided much needed research support. Bernadette Buensuceso helped shape numerous initial draft chapters into a cohesive single document and put together the bibliography. If writing the early drafts were challenging, reading, rereading and editing them were even more so. Shradha Biyani undertook this task with great enthusiasm and made us revisit our writing (and often our thinking) with gentle (but firm) persuasion. Suneethi Raja did an excellent job of preparing the index in record time. We are grateful to them all.

Rajat wishes to thank Shikha for her constant support, encouragement, and patient hearing of many obscure and inane points which he believed were brilliant, but which then fell on her to convince him otherwise. Diya, Navaz and Rohit were similarly constructive but 'gentler' critics and even more importantly, together with Shikha and his extended family, a constant source of support, particularly when the promised 'last draft' always turned out to be far from it. Their relief at the Final Draft being sent to OUP was genuine, perhaps more so because they were despairing that it would never happen.

Harinder wishes to thank his two children Harpaul and Monica for their constant emotional support and encouragement, especially during the past few years, without which this and other major projects would not have been possible.

Finally, our sincere thanks to Ayshwarya Ramakrishnan, and her team of editors, on behalf of OUP, for taking a fine pencil to our manuscript and beating it into some shape, making it far better than what we had initially presented them with. Nirmal Ganguly and V. B. Tulasidhar kindly and heroically agreed to give a final, final read of the manuscript and did an excellent job of it. While we are of course most grateful to them, we also feel that perhaps they should now naturally be held responsible for all remaining shortcomings. No, of course not. Any remaining lapses of omissions and commissions in the book, despite great efforts by our editors and reviewers to prevent them, are squarely on our shoulders.

Rajat M. Nag, Harinder S. Kohli

August 11, 2023

Contents

About the Authors   xxiii
List of Figures and Tables   xxv

1. Introduction   1
   1.1   The context   1
   1.2   Structure of the book   7

PART I: THE SETTING: HERE AND DENMARK

Overview   11

2. The World We Live In   13
   2.1   Our world in 2022   13
   2.2   The Pandemic   14
   2.3   Demographics—population trends and aging   15
   2.4   Economic output and income levels   18
   2.5   Intra-country inequalities   22
   2.6   Rise of the middle classes   23
   2.7   Urbanization   24
   2.8   Human development   26
   2.9   Access to basic infrastructure   27
   2.10   Climate change   28
   2.11   People living under democracy   32
   2.12   Corruption   33
   2.13   Emergence of civic society   35
   2.14   Social media: a fast-emerging global phenomenon   35
   2.15   Access to justice   36
   2.16   Summary   38

3. Good Governance is Good Development   41
   3.1   Why governance?   41
   3.2   What is governance?   43
     3.2.1   Governance in the context of social justice: *niti* and *nyaya*   44
     3.2.2   Intrinsic and instrumental values of governance   45
     3.2.3   But what is governance?   46
   3.3   Four basic elements of good governance   48
     3.3.1   Predictability   48

3.3.2 Transparency 49

3.3.3 Participation 50

3.3.4 Accountability 51

3.4 Measures of governance 52

3.4.1 De jure and de facto measures 53

3.4.2 World Governance Indicators 56

3.5 Profiles of governance 59

3.6 Impact of governance on incomes and other development outcomes 62

3.6.1 Is good governance a luxury that only the rich countries can afford? 64

3.6.2 Does better governance also lead to better social development? 66

3.7 Governance matters 67

3.8 Demand for good governance 72

3.9 Summary 73

Annex 1 75

4. Corruption Hurts: No, It Kills 81

4.1 What is corruption? 81

4.2 Is corruption a cultural issue? An unequivocal 'No' 85

4.3 A curse for all places and all times 86

4.4 Corruption kills 88

4.5 Changing perceptions about corruption 89

4.6 Effect of corruption on economic growth, poverty, and inequality 92

4.7 Measures of corruption 95

4.7.1 Indicators based on official data 96

4.7.2 Indicators based on perception surveys 96

4.7.3 Indicators based on experiential surveys 98

4.8 Profiles of corruption 100

4.9 Summary 102

5. Institutions Matter 105

5.1 Introduction 105

5.2 What are institutions? 107

5.2.1 Institutions and organizations 110

5.3 Functions of institutions 111

5.3.1 Commitment 111

5.3.2 Cooperation 112

5.3.3 Coordination 112

5.4 Institutions matter 113

5.4.1 Influence of political power structures on institutional development 114

5.5 Contextual social settings of institutions 116
    5.5.1 Limited- and open-access orders of societies 116
    5.5.2 Practice of universal ethics and particularism in societies 118
5.6 Inclusive and extractive institutions 118
5.7 Challenges of institutional reforms in a society 121
5.8 New institutional economics meets behavioural economics 123
5.9 Summary 124
PART I: KEY MESSAGES 126

PART II: MIND AND ACTIONS

Overview 127

6. I Think—Therefore, I Am 129
    6.1 Introduction 129
    6.2 Thinking automatically and reflectively 131
    6.3 Cognitive challenges in thinking reflectively 133
    6.4 Framing and salience of information 134
    6.5 Anchoring 137
    6.6 Loss aversion, endowment effect, and the status quo bias 138
    6.7 The pressing bias of the present: the intention–action divide 141
    6.8 Choice architecture and nudges 142
    6.9 Summary 144

7. We Think—Therefore, We Are 147
    7.1 Introduction 147
    7.2 Focal points as a social coordinating device 148
        7.2.1 The meeting game 149
    7.3 Nash equilibrium 150
        7.3.1 The island game 150
        7.3.2 The crown game 151
    7.4 Challenges of collective action and social dilemmas 153
        7.4.1 Prisoner's dilemma 154
    7.5 We are humans, after all 156
        7.5.1 Reciprocity 157
            7.5.1.1 The ultimatum game 157
        7.5.2 Altruism 158
            7.5.2.1 The dictator game 158
        7.5.3 The conditional cooperators and the tit for tat strategy 158
            7.5.3.1 The public goods (trust) game version 1:
                  single trial experiments 158
            7.5.3.2 The public goods (trust) game version 2:
                  multiple trial experiments 159
            7.5.3.3 The public goods (trust) game version 3:
                  multiple trial experiments in two phases 159

7.6   Managing the commons   161

7.7   Motivations for cooperation in society   162

    7.7.1 Role of economic incentives and social preferences in inducing cooperation   163

7.8   Summary   167

8. The World of Beliefs, Norms, and Mental Models Around Us   169

  8.1   Introduction   169

  8.2   Role of beliefs in our individual and social behaviour   169

    8.2.1 Rule of law in the land of beliefs   171

      8.2.1.1 Why are some laws followed and others remain as just 'ink on paper'?   174

  8.3   Role of social norms in our individual and social behaviour   177

    8.3.1 Social norms can create good and bad equilibriums in social interactions   180

      8.3.1.1 Role of social norms in fighting corruption: why do anti-corruption measures often fail?   181

  8.4   Reckoning with social norms to influence social behaviour   184

    8.4.1 Enhancing the salience of existing social norms to shift behaviour   184

    8.4.2 Jogging latent norms to shift behaviour   185

    8.4.3 Altering social norms to shift behaviour   186

  8.5   Thinking with mental models   190

    8.5.1 Effects of the long-term staying power of mental models   191

    8.5.2 Causes of the long-term staying power of mental models   195

  8.6   Summary   196

9. Better Understanding, Better Interventions   199

  9.1   Introduction   199

  9.2   Reducing the cognitive tax on the poor   200

  9.3   Bridging the intention–action divide   202

  9.4   Better framing helps in making better choices   204

  9.5   The nudge   206

  9.6   Contending with the long staying power of mental models and norms   206

    9.6.1 Changing norms   207

  9.7   Finding ways to enhance collective cooperation   210

  9.8   Changing mental models   213

  9.9   Human agency: a critical enabler of change   215

  9.10 Summary   217

  PART II: KEY MESSAGES   220

PART III: LESSONS FROM THE PAST

Overview   221

10. How Denmark Got to Denmark and Great Britain's Journey 223
    10.1 Introduction   223
    10.2 Denmark   224
         10.2.1 Transition from a Viking to a feudal society   224
         10.2.2 Emergence of the Catholic Church   224
         10.2.3 The Kalmar Union   225
         10.2.4 Rising power of the monarchy   225
         10.2.5 The catastrophic war of 1657 and emergence of
                absolutist monarchy   227
         10.2.6 Increased state capacity, and emergence of inclusive
                economic institutions   229
         10.2.7 Continuity of reforms and professionalization of the
                judiciary and the bureaucracy   230
         10.2.8 Checks and balances: accountability of the bureaucracy 231
         10.2.9 Emergence of constitutional monarchy 1849   233
         10.2.10 Denmark to 'Denmark'   234
    10.3 Great Britain   235
         10.3.1 'To no one deny or delay right or justice':
                the Magna Carta   235
         10.3.2 England's first parliament   236
         10.3.3 The early absolutist and extractive years of the Stuarts 237
         10.3.4 The Great Rebellion of 1642 and the Restoration   239
         10.3.5 The Glorious Revolution 1688   241
         10.3.6 Transitioning to inclusive political and economic
                institutions   244
    10.4 Summary   246

11. Some Asian Journeys   249
    11.1 Introduction   249
    11.2 Japan   249
         11.2.1 The Tokugawa shogunate (1603–1868)   250
                11.2.1.1 Consolidation of power   251
                11.2.1.2 Act of Seclusion 1636: closing Japan to
                         the West   252
                11.2.1.3 Emphasis on education and improving
                         living standards   252
                11.2.1 4 Extractive institutions: feudal structure
                         of society   253
                11.2.1.5 Decline of the Tokugawas   255

11.2.2	The Meiji Restoration (1868–1912)	257
	11.2.2.1 Modernization of Japan: transformative institutional changes	257
	11.2.2.2 Education	259
	11.2.2.3 Changing social norms	260
	11.2.2.4 Changes in social structures: gradual move to open-access orders	261
11.3	South Korea	263
	11.3.1 Historical context	264
	11.3.2 Land reforms	265
	11.3.3 Education	267
	11.3.4 Bureaucracy	268
	11.3.5 State autonomy	269
	11.3.6 Transition to inclusive institutions	270
11.4	Summary	271

12. Some Other Journeys 275

12.1	Introduction	275
12.2	Botswana	275
	12.2.1 Botswana's tribal institutions	277
	12.2.2 Botswana's colonial past	278
	12.2.3 Role of traditional *Batswana* elites	279
	12.2.4 Avoiding the resource curse	280
	12.2.5 Leadership	280
12.3	Uruguay	282
	12.3.1 A contemporary transition to open-order access	282
	12.3.2 An old democracy but with clientelism	283
	12.3.3 Mounting pressure for change	285
	12.3.4 The dark years of military rule and subsequent transition to greater political plurality	286
12.4	Summary	288
PART III: KEY MESSAGES		290

PART IV: THREE FELLOW TRAVELLERS

Overview 291

13. The STATE, the Markets, and the Community 293

13.1	Introduction	293
13.2	The role of the State: at its core, to provide good governance	295
13.3	A generalized institutional framework of the State	298
	13.3.1 Political and Economic institutions	299
	13.3.2 Judicial institutions	300

13.4 Changing expectations of the role of the State in recent times 302
13.5 Limitations of State capability 306
 13.5.1 Matching the State's role to its capability 306
 13.5.2 Enhancing State capability 308
  13.5.2.1 Articulate clear rules and restraints 308
  13.5.2.2 Expose the State to greater competitive
      pressures 310
  13.5.2.3 Increase citizen voice and participation 312
13.6 Summary 313

14. The State, the MARKETS, and the Community 315
14.1 Introduction 315
14.2 The evolution of the State and the markets 315
14.3 Institutions to support and manage the markets 317
14.4 Challenges of taming the behemoth 320
14.5 State capacity to manage the behemoth 322
14.6 Summary 324

15. The State, the Markets, and the COMMUNITY 327
15.1 Introduction 327
15.2 Challenges of inadequate social capital: amoral familism 328
15.3 The need to hear the voice of the community 329
15.4 Devolving power to the community: the subsidiarity
  principle and inclusive localism 330
15.5 Empowering the community through consultation and
  information sharing 332
15.6 The need for more than consultation—need a more active
  participation 334
15.7 Challenges of governance at the local government level:
  the need for balance between the State and the community 335
15.8 Shackling the Leviathan 338
15.9 Exit, voice, and loyalty 343
15.10 Leadership 345
15.11 The Three Travellers: travelling in tandem 349
15.12 Summary 352
PART IV: KEY MESSAGES 354

16. Some Concluding Thoughts and the Way Forward 355
16.1 Introduction 355
16.2 Critical importance of good governance 356
16.3 Institutions are key 357
16.4 Human behaviour as catalyst of change 358
16.5 Importance of open societal systems and inclusive
  institutions 359

16.6 Three fellow travellers   361
16.7 Improving governance takes patience and time   362
16.8 Hopeful signs from recent examples and lessons learnt   363
16.9 Peering into the future   364
        16.9.1 Ten global megatrends   366
16.10 From Here to Denmark   374
KEY MESSAGES OF THE BOOK   376

Notes   377
Bibliography   411
Index   431

About the Authors

Rajat M. Nag is a Distinguished Fellow at the Emerging Markets Forum, Washington D.C. He is currently also a Distinguished Professor at the Emerging Markets Institute at the Beijing Normal University, Beijing and at the Advanced Study Institute Asia, Delhi. He was the Managing Director General of the Asian Development Bank during 2006–2013 and a Distinguished Fellow at the National Council of Applied Economic Research, India during 2014-2022.

Harinder S. Kohli is the Founding Director and Chief Executive of Emerging Markets Forum, a global think tank based in Washington, D.C. He is also the Founding Editor of Global Journal of Emerging Markets Economies. Having served in various senior managerial positions at the World Bank, he is the author/co-author of 15 other books and a frequent speaker on development issues at international forums and universities.

List of Figures and Tables

Figures

Figure 2.1	Total population (millions) by region (1950–2020)	16
Figure 2.2	GDP per capita (constant 2018 PPP US $) advanced and emerging economies (1950–2020)	21
Figure 2.3	Urbanization levels by region	24
Figure 2.4	Corruption—(Perceptions about corruption: country rating by region)	33
Figure 3.1	Four components of good governance working in tandem	53
Figure 3.2	Governance indicators: four income categories, 2021	63
Figure 3.3	Governance indicators by region, 2021	63
Figure 3.4	Governance indicators and income per capita (log scale), 2021	64
Figure 3.5	Governance indicators and infant mortality (log scale), 2021	67
Figure 3.6	Governance indicators and adult literacy, 2021	67
Figure 3.7	Bangladesh: governance indicators 2000 and 2021	69
Figure A1.1	Percentile rankings, by Governance indicator, for each income and regional grouping, 2021	75
Figure A1.2	Percentile rankings by Governance indicator, by country, 2021	77
Figure 4.1	Control of corruption percentile rankings by income and regional grouping, 2021	101
Figure 4.2	Control of corruption percentile rankings by selected countries, 2021	101
Figure 7.1	Prisoner's dilemma (years in jail)	155

Tables

Table 2.1   Age Profiles (Population in Millions), 2020   17

Table 2.2   Top Fifteen Economies, GDP and GDP per capita, 2020
(constant 2018 PPP US$)   20

Table 2.3   GDP by Regions, 2020, (constant 2018 PPP US$)   20

Table 2.4   GDP Per Capita by Regions, 2020 (constant 2018 PPP US$)   21

Table 2.5   Percentage of Population Classified as Middle- and
Upper-Class, 2020   24

Table 2.6   Human Development Index by Region, 2019   26

Table 2.7   Twenty Most Polluted Cities in the World, PM 2.5, 2020   31

1

Introduction

1.1 The context

Neither 'Here' nor 'Denmark' refer to any actual places themselves.

In this book, 'Here' is a hypothetical construct of a place where governance is poor, rule of law is not respected, and justice is delayed and often denied; a place where people suffer the consequences of a capricious and corrupt ruling elite; a place where people lead a life marked with fear and insecurities, deprived of basic human freedoms and dignities; a place where people fail to reach the full potential of their capabilities.

'Denmark', on the other hand, is another hypothetical construct and perhaps what Tagore dreamt of when he sang the praises of a place 'where the mind is without fear and the head is held high'. 'Denmark' is where freedom reigns, justice prevails, people live in peace and security under the rule of law, and are treated fairly and with dignity by their fellow citizens and their governments.

People in 'Denmark' mostly enjoy high social-development indicators, including incomes and quality of life. People 'Here' in general do not. (The quotes are dropped from here on indicating these two hypothetical places. If we refer to Denmark, the country, that will be clarified).

Quite obviously, Denmark is the place to be. Here is not.

Around the world, incomes have risen for people almost everywhere in recent times. In 1970, the global average per capita income was slightly less than $6,000 but by 2018 it had increased by more than two and a half times to over $15,000 (GDP per capita in constant 2011 US $). The average income of the bottom half of the population over the same period had also nearly doubled. Extreme poverty has consequently declined significantly worldwide.

At the turn of the twentieth century, almost two thirds of the world's population lived in extreme poverty (measured at $1.90 per capita daily

From Here to Denmark. Rajat M. Nag and Harinder S. Kohli, Oxford University Press.
© Rajat Mohan Nag and Harinder Singh Kohli 2023. DOI: 10.1093/oso/9780198893103.003.0001

income in constant 2011 US $). By 1970, that proportion had come down to less than half, and even more dramatically, to less than a tenth by 2021, fuelled in large part by reductions in poverty in much of Asia, particularly in China and India.

Social indicators have improved as well, often dramatically. Over the past hundred years, the global average life expectancy has more than doubled to over seventy years. All countries in the world today have a life expectancy higher than the best in 1800.

In 1960, every fifth child born around the globe that year would not live to see her fifth birthday. That rate has now come down to every twenty-fifth.

Education levels have also improved. The global adult literacy rate is now over 85 per cent, up from 56 per cent in 1950.

The world is now richer, healthier, more literate than it was just a generation back. These are all very significant, if not dramatic, achievements and there is much to celebrate.

However, the average global profile we paint above hides (as averages often do) the grim reality of significant deprivations still suffered by many around the world. It hides the fact that there are still about 648 million people (almost twice the total population of the United States) in the world who lived in extreme poverty even in 2019. Many countries suffer from the ills of high and indeed growing inequalities. Governance is poor and corruption is rife. Justice and basic freedoms are denied to many by capricious rulers. Discrimination based on faith, race, ethnicity, or gender orientation remain rampant in many parts of the world. People are not free to choose the trajectory of their own lives and many live in fear of those more powerful. In essence, there are many countries, indeed most, in the world that are still a considerable distance away from Denmark.

Why are some nations rich and others poor? Why are there such glaring differences between countries? Why does Singapore enjoy a per capita income a whopping one hundred times larger than that of the Democratic Republic of Congo ($80,000 vs $800)? Despite dramatic improvements in healthcare around the world, why do more than 500 mothers still die in childbirth (per 100,000 live births) in sub-Saharan Africa compared to only three in Finland? How did some countries make so much progress over the past hundred years or so, while others did not? These questions have occupied many. Philosophers, politicians, policymakers, academics, and private citizens have all wrestled with these issues through the ages.

Economic growth, which has long been recognised as the best poverty-reducing strategy, had a lot to do with it. But then, why do some economies grow, and others don't? Or at least, not as fast.

Geography was one of the earliest causes mentioned. The climate, particularly the heat in the tropics, made for sloth, or so the thinking went, robbing people of energy to do anything but the least to get by. And these were not the idle ruminations of some ill-informed observers. As early as 1748, Montesquieu, the French philosopher, was quite dramatic (not to mention unacceptably inappropriate in his choice of words) when he observed that 'the heat of the climate can be so excessive that the body there will be absolutely without strength. So, prostration will be passive even to the spirit; no curiosity, no noble enterprise ... laziness there will be happiness'. And he continued, lest one had missed the point, that 'the inhabitants of warm countries, are like old men, timorous; the people in cold climates are like young men, brave'.[1]

In current times, Sachs has passionately articulated the challenge of the disease burden of the tropics holding back their economic development. Noting that 'the burden of disease is considerably higher in the tropics than in the temperate climates',[2] Sachs adds that control of tropical vector-borne diseases such as malaria and helminthic infections 'remain[s] vastly more difficult to accomplish in the tropics than in the temperate zones'.[3] Malaria, for example, still affects a staggering 225 million people worldwide, more than 90 per cent of whom are in Africa. Over 400,000 people died from this illness in 2019, with almost 95 per cent of them in Africa. Children under the age of five are the most vulnerable, accounting for almost two-thirds of the global deaths caused by malaria.[4] The economic consequences of such rampant diseases are significant. While Sachs's observations are certainly correct, it would be hard to draw any general conclusions about the dominance of geography to explain the prevalence of poverty, since there are enough examples to the contrary of countries in the tropics doing well.

The concerns about many countries being in a state of serious economic and social deprivation became particularly dominant with the dismantling of colonies around the world starting in the mid-twentieth century. A global sense of urgency and keen desire to help these newly independent countries to fight poverty and underdevelopment followed. It was generally considered then that the most binding constraint in these countries was the inadequacy of capital to invest in enhancing their productive capacity, particularly physical infrastructure, roads, railways, ports, and power. If only capital from the capital-surplus countries (mostly in the West and the erstwhile colonial rulers) could be channelled to the capital-deficit regions of the world, development would follow, was the thinking. The quick and dramatic successes of the Marshall Plan in reconstructing Europe, particularly in Germany, after the ravages of the Second World War were considered robust evidence that that prescription worked. The consensus at the time was that the principal and immediate cause of the continued stark poverty in the world was lack of adequate capital.

It soon became evident, however, that while obviously important, physical capital by itself could not produce adequately sustainable economic growth. Something else was also important: human capital. A labour force which was skilled and educated enough and healthy as well was needed to leverage the available physical capital to produce and sustain growth. Policymakers recognized that an educated and healthy population is a necessary condition for contributing to and benefitting from the growth process. Hence, the additional focus on the importance of human capital.

Three decades of investments from the early 1950s by the World Bank (established in 1945), later joined by the regional development banks (the Inter-American Development Bank in 1959, the African Development Bank in 1964, and the Asian Development Bank in 1966) were thus principally devoted to enhancing the stock of physical and human capital in the developing countries. But even so, progress on the economic and social fronts in many, if not most, developing countries was not satisfactory enough even by the 1980s.

While the developing countries, be they in Asia, Africa, Latin America, or anywhere else in the world, did show more economic progress during those decades, the results were hardly stellar; they also varied greatly between regions and within the regions between countries, even when external partners pursued similar strategies. By the mid-1980s, a consensus began to emerge that while capital investments were certainly needed to produce growth, they had to be undertaken in an appropriate and supportive macroeconomic policy environment for these investments to be effective. In other words, domestic country conditions also mattered a lot.

Inappropriate and distortionary fiscal and monetary policy and foreign exchange regimes, trade barriers, and other impediments to market operations, as well as bureaucratic hurdles and controls through a 'licence raj' government mentality were all seen as equally fundamental and binding constraints to economic growth.

Getting the prices and policies right became the mantra encapsulated in what became known as the Washington Consensus. The prescription for economic development was now enlarged to include policy reform measures to address structural adjustment issues and macroeconomic distortions in the host countries.

The results of undertaking the structural adjustments were again mixed. Alleviating, if not eliminating, the binding structural constraints produced some benefits of economic growth but still fell short of expectations.

It soon became apparent that it was not only a question of devising the appropriate policies. Equally, and perhaps more, important was how such policies would in fact be implemented. Difficult as crafting the right policies might be, it was even more challenging to implement them and make them work.

The world is full of examples of technically sound projects failing because of poor project management and inadequate supervision. The much-needed policy and institutional reforms were sabotaged by vested interests. Laws were enacted with much fanfare, but simply remained on the books owing to benign (and perhaps more often not) neglect. Roadblocks were put in the way of administering justice by the more powerful. Improvements and simplification of processes to enhance efficiency and access were negated either intentionally or by piecemeal changes implemented in fits and starts. Lack of awareness among the people who were supposed to benefit from such changes did not create a constituency for needed changes. Desired improvements in public expenditure management could not materialize if the government's accounting systems remained weak.

How policies are designed and implemented has a critical impact on development outcomes, a process broadly called 'governance'. By the early 1990s, the need for 'good governance', including meeting the challenges of corruption head on, to achieve economic growth in a country began to emerge as a necessary condition for sustained development.

If all of this sounds as if we are peeling onions, that notion is not too far off the mark. Perhaps there is no clear formula for growth, after all, as Nobel prizewinners Banerjee and Duflo suggest in a mea culpa on behalf of all of us: 'Economists, ourselves included, have spent entire careers studying development and poverty, and the uncomfortable truth is that the field still doesn't have a good sense of why some economies expand and others don't.'[5] Easterly makes much the same point in his masterly book, *The Elusive Quest for Growth*,[6] in which he shows that a country's growth rates can vary dramatically from decade to decade without any particular apparent reason.

It is important to emphasize, however, that the message is not that growth does not matter. On the contrary, economic growth is the best poverty-reduction strategy. Increased incomes matter. The stellar achievements around the world in reducing poverty and improving social conditions, mentioned earlier, are a reflection of the impressive economic growth in most countries, particularly China and India, in the past several decades. Growth matters significantly, but it is a complex process involving the interplay of many factors: macroeconomic stability, appropriate allocation of scarce resources, physical and human capital, and of course, good governance.

Another important point to remember is that ultimately economic growth is only a means to an end. The ultimate goal is a better quality of life. It is about enjoying good health and basic services, including education, be assured of meeting at least the basic necessities, having one's voice heard, and living a life of dignity. Quality of life is more than just consumption.

Many of the challenges people face, particularly the poor, often do not have much to do with incomes alone but with what we loosely term governance.

Our basic proposition is that Denmark is characterized principally by good governance and the journey from Here to Denmark is thus more than only a quest for increased economic growth. It is in the ultimate analysis mainly a quest for better governance.

But how will a society deliver good governance to its citizens? Answer: through strong, sound institutions. Essentially, the basic thesis is that institutions matter in delivering good governance.

Good governance and institutions are the subjects of focus of this book.

1.2 Structure of the book

Part I: The Setting: Here and Denmark (Chapters 2–5) begins with **Chapter 2 (The World We Live In)**, which discusses the present state of the world and the many challenges it still faces.

Chapter 3 (Good Governance is Good Development) provides a broad overview of what we mean by governance. Governance is a broad, multidimensional concept meaning different things to different people. Defining good governance is thus complex. Among the many aspects of good governance people consider relevant, being treated justly, fairly, and with dignity is high on their list. In a milieu of poor governance, they widely bemoan the lack of freedom, a sense of helplessness against the more powerful in society, including the government, who dominate their daily lives. These issues are discussed in Chapter 3, including an assessment of their impacts on development, leading to a very important conclusion for policymakers: *good governance leads to good development.*

While many instinctively think of good governance as implying honest government, that is, absence of corruption, it is important to recognize that this is only one of the many aspects of governance which a society has to be concerned about. However, having said that, it is also important not to downplay in any sense how serious a scourge corruption is. It hurts the poor disproportionately and dampens the benefits of economic growth. Corruption gets in the way of enforcing policies, no matter how good their intentions or design might have been. A recalcitrant and corrupt bureaucracy has the potential to undermine policies in implementation. Efforts at enhanced tax collection to bolster government revenues cannot bear fruit if tax-collection officers can strike deals under the table with unscrupulous taxpayers. Poorly monitored procurement systems and complicity with fraudulent suppliers encourage corruption even if improved policies of procurement management are adopted.

As a matter of fact, it is perhaps no exaggeration to say that corruption kills figuratively and often literally. We discuss the effects of these seriously detrimental aspects of corruption on society in **Chapter 4: Corruption Hurts: No, It Kills.**

Achieving good governance requires strong institutions and is the focus of **Chapter 5: Institutions Matter** and indeed of this book itself.

Institutions are both the formal and the informal rules by which a society conducts itself. Formal rules, laws, and regulations are essentially aspirational. They are an expression of the standards of social conduct a society expects to uphold. However, even the world's most elegantly written constitutions and laws are nothing but 'ink on paper' if they are not implemented in both word and spirit. And that depends largely on the informal rules which govern social behaviour.

Informal rules evolve from shared beliefs, social norms, and local cultures and greatly influence how institutions function in a society. Trying to understand and analyse such functioning using standard economic models falls short for one simple reason: standard neoclassical economics heroically assumes that all actors in an economy are perfectly rational, and omniscient, and are also able to process all available information correctly and instantaneously. Such clones of Captain Spock brook no concern for anybody but themselves and act only in their own best interests. Each pursues her own self-interest but by the miracle of the Invisible Hand, it is assumed that the society she lives in reaches an optimal equilibrium and everyone in society is better off.

Such a process often works, but not always. Members of a society are 'humans' (i.e. most of us), not the robotic 'Econs' which the standard economic model assumes. Human emotions, thinking, and behaviour play a very important role in how members of society act as individuals and as members of a community. A repeated process of human interactions with other members of a society gradually produces the informal rules, and norms of mutual trust in and consideration for fellow citizens emerge (positive or otherwise). These in turn influence how institutions evolve in a particular society and how well (or not) the formal and informal rules and laws in a society work. In recent years, understanding such social preferences in driving individual and collective choices has become possible by drawing on concepts from the relatively new and rich multidisciplinary field of Behavioural Economics, (at the intersection of other social sciences and psychology beyond just economics). These are the subjects of **Part II: Mind and Actions, Chapters 6–9.**

How we think as individuals is the focus of **Chapter 6: I Think—Therefore, I Am.** But it is important to also recognize that a human is not an island unto herself. We are each unique as an individual, but we are also simultaneously part of something larger than ourselves. We are concerned about our own self-interest, but we also (usually) care about the larger good. Human sociality defines us and influences how we think, not only as individuals, but also as members of a group, a family, a society. Such a process of social thinking is studied in **Chapter 7: We Think—Therefore, We Are.**

We live in societies and communities. How we think and behave, act, and interact with others, is significantly influenced by what we think of others around us and how we expect them to act under certain circumstances. They, in turn, do the same. Over time, by a process perhaps of repeated occurrences and confirmation or otherwise of their validity, such expectations take root and become part of an individual's belief system. Over time, societies also develop norms which essentially are informal codes of conduct defining what group members are expected to do and ought to do. They are not formal, legal strictures but often serve as equally, and often even more effective self-enforcing mechanisms to ensure that a society's expectations of its members' behaviours are generally met. The beliefs and norms in turn create mental models of the world around us which instinctively guide and influence our behaviour and actions. **Chapter 8: The World of Beliefs, Norms, and Mental Models Around Us** discusses these aspects influencing human behaviour and actions.

Adding the insights from the above three chapters to the standard economic considerations expands the universe of possible institutional and policy actions available to policymakers to move 'From Here to Denmark'. That is the focus of **Chapter 9**, with the obvious title: **Better Understanding, Better Interventions.**

Time, history, culture, leadership, and yes, luck all have a role to play in the journey from 'Here to Denmark' but it would also be useful to see what lessons may be drawn from the experiences of some countries which have made this transition. By no means exhaustive, a look at some such past examples comprises **Part III: Lessons from the Past (Chapters 10–12).** Denmark's (the country's) own journey, and Great Britain's, through its Glorious Revolution in 1688 are looked at in **Chapter 10**. Almost two centuries later, the experience of Japan's transformation through the Meiji Restoration is instructive, as is Korea's (**Chapter 11**). In more recent times, the experiences of Botswana and Uruguay provide good evidence that 'history is not destiny' (**Chapter 12**).

In a broad sense, three principal institutions comprise a modern society: the state, the markets, and the community. The well-being of a society depends not only on how these three institutions work on their own but even more importantly, how well they interact and work together. Each needs to be strong on its own but also support and balance the other two. Paraphrasing Rajan,[7] too much state, the society risks turning authoritarian, too strong a market, the society risks turning inequitable, too much community, the society risks being disrupted by polarization. A balance between them is key. A symbiotic and synergistic partnership between the state, the markets, and the community is essential to make the journey to Denmark possible. We call these three players fellow travellers. **Part IV: Three Fellow Travellers** (**Chapters 13–15**) discusses these three fellow travellers individually, with special attention to their interaction and how maintaining the balance between the three moving in tandem is critical for a successful journey from Here to Denmark.

Chapter 16 concludes.

PART I

THE SETTING

Here and Denmark

Overview

Part I provides the context within which Here and 'Denmark' exist. We noted in Chapter 1 that global incomes have increased significantly over the past five decades and poverty has consequently declined dramatically around the world. Never before in human history have so many people been lifted out of poverty so quickly. Simultaneously, social conditions have also improved significantly.

Chapter 2 provides a brief account of how people the world over today are richer, healthier, more educated, and live longer than even just a generation ago. But it also identifies the significant social and economic deprivations which still haunt many around the world. Millions of people still live in dire poverty, haunted by injustice, intolerance, and lack of freedoms. Our world today is more interconnected and interdependent than ever before. The recent COVID-19 pandemic has dramatically affected all countries as the virus recognized no boundaries. While this pandemic is clearly a global challenge, many others—such as demographics, rising inequality, governance, corruption, climate change, and globalization—also cut across traditional borders. In this age of hyperconnectivity, most challenges have regional and global dimensions and often need a regional and global response. We'll also examine the interplay of these factors influencing the world we live in today in Chapter 2.

Lack of good governance is a major constraint on good development. In **Chapter 3** we look at governance, from several different perspectives, and try to answer two basic questions: what is governance and why does it matter? Good governance has both intrinsic and instrumental values.

It is good in its own right to ensure justice and fairness for all (its intrinsic value) but it is also valuable for the positive impact this has on economic and social development (its instrumental value). While accepting the value of good governance, some consider that good governance is a luxury that only rich countries can afford. This is a false dichotomy. On the contrary, we argue that bad governance is a luxury the poor countries cannot afford. If defining governance is complex, then measuring it is even more so, and we will look at some possible measures of governance in that chapter.

In **Chapter 4** we examine how corruption is a scourge of society and a major, binding constraint on development. Corruption, broadly defined as misuse of public office for private gain, is neither the exclusive domain of the poor, developing countries nor a recent phenomenon, as is often implied. It is a curse of all places and all times and has to be consistently fought. Measuring corruption is a monstrous challenge, not least because those engaging in it are understandably loath to admit or publicize such activities. The chapter discusses the seriously detrimental effects of corruption on the overall economy of a country and its pernicious effects on people, particularly the poor and the marginalized. More corrupt countries, for example, suffer from both higher infant mortality and lower adult literacy rates. For many people around the world, corruption is indeed fatal, as the subtitle of this chapter graphically states.

The case for good governance is easy to make. The real challenge, though, is how to deliver it. The short answer: through better and stronger institutions, which essentially are the formal and informal rules with which a society conducts itself. How institutions evolve in a society depends on the norms and beliefs and how the political power in that society is distributed. In other words, politics matters. Institutions are thus both context- and location-specific. Many institutional reforms fail not because the proposed measures are inappropriate prescriptions in and of themselves. They fail when they ignore the societal and political contexts within which such institutional reforms are made. Institutional designs and reforms thus cannot simply be borrowed from elsewhere and thoughtlessly transplanted. Institutions are the focus of Chapter 5.

2

The World We Live In

2.1 Our world in 2022

About eight billion human beings inhabited our planet at the end of 2022, with population growth at 1.01 per cent over 2021.[1]

Our world is more interconnected and interdependent today than ever before. The lives of these eight billion human beings intertwine through trade, urbanization, the rise of middle class, health, migration, conflicts, the Internet, and social media, and so on. Today, despite increasing material well-being for most, global populations are also increasingly showing common concerns on a variety of issues. Many of these concerns—increasing inequality, unequal distribution of the benefits of globalization, climate change—cut across traditional boundaries between advanced and emerging economies.

While there are still vast differences in the per capita incomes of people living in North America, Europe, and Oceania, and those of emerging economies, this chapter shows how the earlier sharp differences between advanced and emerging countries have started to gradually reduce as increasingly peoples in higher-income countries and large numbers in the middle-income countries in East Asia and Latin America develop many common characteristics. Many of their common (and often shared) challenges arise from newly widespread affluence and globalization; solutions to these challenges also require global and regional cooperation, as well as better governance at the national level. At the same time, much of subSaharan Africa and parts of South Asia remain starkly different. These two regions face deep-rooted problems; they remain the final frontiers of global economic and social development.

From Here to Denmark. Rajat M. Nag and Harinder S. Kohli, Oxford University Press.
© Rajat Mohan Nag and Harinder Singh Kohli 2023. DOI: 10.1093/oso/9780198893103.003.0002

2.2 The Pandemic

During 2020–2021, the pandemic—unleashed by COVID-19—played havoc with the lives and livelihoods of people in practically every country in the world. It is widely considered the worst pandemic and global health crisis in over a century.

According to the World Health Organization, over 605 million people had tested positive for COVID-19 and over 6.5 million had died by September 2022. While hardly any country has been spared, until early 2021 advanced countries in North America and Europe (with their sophisticated health-care systems) were affected the most, with Latin America the next most affected region. Asia and Africa, the most populous regions of the world, had escaped the worst until early 2021, but since the emergence of the delta variant they too have suffered much (with China as a major exception due to its draconian measures to restrict movement of people internally, but in late 2022 it too had to relax those measures that had allowed it to hold back a large-scale spread of the virus within the country where it originated). By mid 2023, the situation in China seemed to have stabilized. Indeed, most of the world appeared to have learned to live with the virus even though people were still dying from it daily though at much lower levels than in 2020–21.

Beyond the huge loss of life and massive number of people who fell ill, the pandemic has had a fundamental impact on the lives of people around the world. To contain the spread of the pandemic, country after country shut down all economic activities during 2020–21 and mandated their citizens to stay indoors. Curfews were imposed. As a result, many people had to remain confined to their homes for a year or more. Millions of businesses were closed (despite significant stimulus programmes by many countries). 2021 witnessed the biggest drop in global economic activity since the Great Depression of the 1930s. Countries closed their borders (even within the European Union). As a result, unemployment and the rate of poverty rose in most countries. Inequality—both between countries and within countries—increased. Early signs indicate that, because of the changing nature of the way work is being done now, not all the jobs lost due to the pandemic will return in the post-pandemic world. All in all, the pandemic has taken a devastating toll on human beings, mostly impacting the less well-off in both advanced and emerging economies.

One bright spot during 2020 was the success of scientists in successfully discovering testing and preparing vaccines against COVID-19 in record time. By December 2020, three vaccines (from Pfizer, Moderna, and AstraZeneca) had been approved in North America and Europe for emergency use. Soon thereafter, China, Russia, and India deployed their own vaccines. By 8 September 2021, some 4.9 billion persons, or nearly 63 per cent of the global population had been fully vaccinated. While in the abstract it is an impressive performance, these numbers hide two realities. First, until mid-2021, almost 90 per cent of vaccine orders had been placed by advanced countries in North America and Europe, in quantities far exceeding what they needed to fully vaccinate their entire populations.[2] Second, almost all major producers (the US, the EU, India), other than China and Russia, prohibited exports of vaccines to other nations. This vaccine nationalism was in direct contradiction to the long-standing expressions of global solidarity and support of the principles of free global trade by these countries themselves. As a result, while by August 2021, between 50 and 75 per cent of North Americans and Europeans had been fully vaccinated, less than 5 per cent of the populations in the least developed countries (particularly subSaharan Africa) had been vaccinated. Fortunately, in September 2021, at a global leaders' meeting convened by the UN, the US announced a new global initiative to donate one billion doses, India promised to resume exports from October 2021, and other countries agreed to pitch in as well, to vaccinate 70 per cent of the global population by the end of 2022.

2.3 Demographics—population trends and aging

Of the eight billion people in the world in 2022, the largest number lived in Asia (4.4 billion people, or some 56 per cent of total global population).

Within Asia, the East Asia and the Pacific area has by far the largest population of any subregion in the world: about 2.8 billion in 2020 (Figure 2.1). It includes two of the world's most populous countries—China

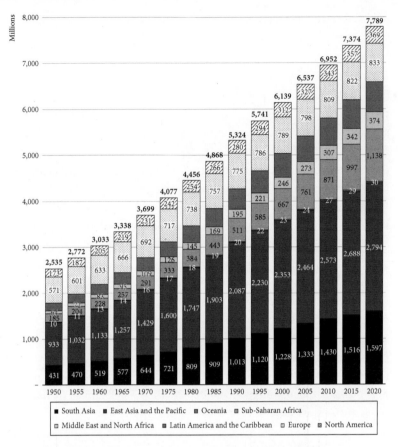

Figure 2.1 Total population (millions) by region (1950–2020)

Source: Kohli, Nag & Vilkelyte (2022); Centennial Group, In-house Growth Model, Unpublished (2021).

(1.35 billion) and Indonesia (251 million). The next three East Asian countries with the highest populations are Japan (120 million), the Philippines (ninety-nine million) and Vietnam (ninety-one million). The second most populous subregion in the world, also in Asia, is South Asia. It had about 1.6 billion people in 2020, with India accounting for about 1.26 billion. Another 200 million lived in Pakistan, and 149 million in Bangladesh. In 2023, India surpassed China as the world's most populous country (as China's population had already started to decline in 2022 while India's still continued to grow).

However, as shown in Table 2.1, there is one major difference in recent demographic trends in the two Asia regions. Over the past two

Table 2.1 Age Profiles (Population in Millions), 2020

Region	0–19	20–64	65+	Total Population	% Growth from 2000
South Asia	565	928	103	1,596	30%
East Asia and the Pacific	789	1,711	294	2,794	19%
Oceania	8	18	5	31	33%
Sub-Saharan Africa	600	504	34	1,138	71%
Middle East and North Africa	146	209	19	374	52%
Latin America and the Caribbean	210	385	59	654	25%
Europe	185	497	151	833	5%
North America	90	217	62	369	18%
Grand Total	2,593	4,468	727	7,788	27%

Source: Centennial Group, In-house Growth Model, Unpublished, (2021).

decades, the population growth in East Asia has slowed significantly (at 19 per cent, well below the global average of 27 per cent). By contrast, the population in South Asia grew by an average rate of 30 per cent, above the global average but still much lower than sub-Saharan Africa at 71 per cent and even the MeNA (Middle and North Africa) region at 52 per cent.

The world's population growth is slowing down. It had grown from just about a billion in 1,800 to around 8 billion in 2022. From an annual growth rate of around 2% per year seventy years back, the global population grew at only half that rate in 2022 over the previous year.

The three advanced regions—Europe, North America, and Oceania—have by now stable absolute population sizes, and their share of total global population has been gradually declining. While Latin America is still growing, albeit only modestly, many of its countries exhibit declining population growth rates (e.g. Brazil, Chile).

Based on recent trends, future growth in world population will essentially take place in three regions: sub-Saharan Africa, South Asia, and the Middle East. The other regions would have stable or even declining populations between now and 2050.

Within these headline counts, as would be expected, various regions have different demographic profiles. The larger regions are especially heterogeneous. For example, there are significant differences between countries within Africa and Asia. Without going into too many details, our discussion here is limited to the demographic profiles of the eight broader regions of the world, as shown in Table 2.1 above.

Advanced countries in North America, Europe, Oceania, most of Latin America, as well as large parts of East and Central Asia have *entered a period of aging societies* because of two phenomena: (i) the declining population growth rates mentioned previously, and (ii) improved health outcomes that have led to people living significantly longer than previous generations. In many countries, the total population appears to be peaking or has even started to decline. In much of Europe, the US, and advanced Asian economies (Japan, Korea, China), national birth rates have fallen below replacement rate. Japan, Germany, and many Eastern European countries are already showing declines in absolute sizes of their populations. China, the world's most populated country and still a developing economy, has already joined the growing list of countries showing a decline in absolute population. It will be the first nation in history to become old before becoming rich.

Aging of societies has far-reaching economic, social security and welfare (including health care), fiscal, and political implications for the countries concerned.

In contrast, -Sub-Saharan Africa, the Middle East (but not North Africa), and parts of South Asia (particularly Pakistan and Afghanistan) have much younger demographic profiles. As a result, they are expected to significantly increase their share of global population and work force in coming decades.

To take advantage of this potential "demographic dividend" and to ensure that the coming youth bulge is gainfully employed, these regions will need to improve their education and health systems to train their youth to participate productively in the global markets. Otherwise, large numbers of unemployed or underemployed youth could lead to serious social, political, and governance issues.

2.4 Economic output and income levels

Over the last seven decades or so, incomes have increased dramatically in both advanced and emerging economies. Global poverty levels have reduced significantly, and social indicators have also improved. As noted in Chapter 1, the world today is richer, more educated and enjoys better health conditions than ever before. The world has realized in one generation what used to take many others.

In 2020, global economic output totalled US$ 127.6 trillion in Purchasing Power Parity (PPP 2018 US$) terms.[3] Of this, US$ 56.7 trillion (PPP) was produced in the advanced economies (44.5 per cent), and US$ 70.9 trillion (55.5 per cent) in the emerging economies. The per capita income of advanced economies averaged, in PPP terms, US$50,620 and that of the emerging economies at just about a fifth of that US$10,770.

A striking feature of the past several decades has also been the steady shift of the world's centre of gravity of economic activities eastwards. Five of the fifteen largest economies in the world (in PPP terms) are in Asia (China, India, Indonesia, Korea, and Japan) and another six straddle the North Atlantic (Canada, France, Germany, Italy, the United Kingdom, and the US) Table 2.2 shows the size of these fifteen economies in GDP and GDP per capita in PPP terms (2018 US $).

The share of the emerging countries in global economic output has been steadily rising in recent decades owing to the higher levels of economic growth of countries such as China, India, Indonesia, and Vietnam. As a result, the two Asian subregions together accounted for almost half of global output in PPP terms (43per cent in 2020) (Table 2.3).

East Asia and the Pacific (which includes China, Indonesia, Japan, Singapore, and South Korea) alone accounts for more than a third (35 per cent) of global GDP South Asia (which includes three large nations: Bangladesh, India, and Pakistan) accounts for another 8 per cent of world output; thanks to its large population and despite its still much lower per capita income and productivity than those of the advanced countries and even East Asia. North America and Europe have the next two largest shares of global output; because of their high per capita income (and productivity) but also because of their significant population base. Africa, Latin America, the Middle East, and Oceania combined account for only 16 per cent share of global GDP, inspite of their large geographic sizes and natural resource bases.

It is noteworthy that while India by now is the fifth largest economy at market exchange rates (in 2023) and the third largest in PPP terms, it has by far the lowest per capita income amongst the G20 countries.

Table 2.2 Top Fifteen Economies, GDP and GDP per capita, 2020 (constant 2018 PPP US$)

Country	GDP (PPP)	Country	GDP per Capita (PPP)
China	23,435	Luxembourg	114,550
United States	20,320	Singapore	92,945
India	8,646	Ireland	92,653
Japan	5,157	Qatar	88,266
Germany	4,365	Switzerland	70,339
Russia	3,976	United Arab Emirates	63,873
Indonesia	3,205	Brunei	63,717
Brazil	3,061	Norway	63,491
France	2,912	United States	61,390
United Kingdom	2,873	Iceland	57,971
Turkey	2,472	Hong Kong, China	57,606
Italy	2,389	Denmark	57,511
Mexico	2,373	Netherlands	56,736
Korea	2,243	Sweden	54,021
Canada	1,796	Taiwan (China)	53,631

Source: Kohli, Nag & Vilkelyte (2022); Centennial Group, In-house Growth Model, Unpublished, (2021).

Table 2.3 GDP by Regions, 2020, (constant 2018 PPP US$)

Region	GDP	% of world total
East Asia and the Pacific	44,155	35%
South Asia	9,940	8%
Oceania	1,499	1%
Sub-Saharan Africa	4,184	3%
Middle East and North Africa	6,007	5%
Latin America and the Caribbean	9,304	7%
Europe	30,430	24%
North America	22,116	17%
World Total	127,634	100%

Source: Kohli, Nag & Vilkelyte (2022); Centennial Group, In-house Growth Model, Unpublished, (2021).

In 2020, there were still vast differences in per capita incomes of people in advanced economies and those living in the emerging economies, despite enormous progress made by the latter in reducing poverty during the past seventy-odd years (Table 2.4 and Figure 2.2). While, owing to higher economic growth of countries in East Asia and some in South Asia, intercountry inequalities had come down significantly before the pandemic (compared to say the 1950s), there is still a very large gap in

Table 2.4 GDP Per Capita by Regions, 2020 (constant 2018 PPP US$)

Region	GDP per capita
East Asia and the Pacific	15,804
South Asia	6,228
Oceania	48,355
Sub-Saharan Africa	3,677
Middle East and North Africa	16,061
Latin America and the Caribbean	14,226
Europe	36,531
North America	59,935
World average	16,389

Source: Centennial Group, In-house Growth Model, Unpublished, (2021).

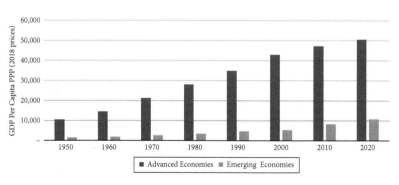

Figure 2.2 GDP per capita (constant 2018 PPP US $) advanced and emerging economies (1950–2020)

Source: Kohli, Nag & Vilkelyte (2022), Centennial Group, In-house Growth Model, Unpublished, (2021).

the per capita income (and therefore overall quality of life) of people in the advanced economies and the rest of the world. The gap is even more striking between the advanced countries (including those in Asia) and those in much of sub-Saharan Africa and South Asia. Average per capita incomes in Northern America, for example, are sixteen times those of sub-Saharan Africa.

2.5 Intra-country inequalities

Globally, income inequality has declined over the last fifty-plus years. As indicated above, this can be attributed to decreasing between-countries inequality owing to the faster growth of many large emerging economies (in the past thirty years, they have annually grown, on average, roughly 4 per cent faster than the advanced countries, according to a recently completed study by the Emerging Markets Forum).[4] However, 65 per cent of global inequality is still due to between-countries income gaps.[5] Fortunately, this between-country inequality is expected to gradually decline further in future as emerging economies grow faster than advanced economies and thus narrow their per capita income gap.

While between-countries' income inequalities have been coming down and is expected to continue, unfortunately the trend is the reverse for intra-country inequalities, in terms of both income and wealth. This is likely to be true for both advanced countries and emerging economies.

As a result, inequality has now become a global concern and a major political issue in an increasing number of countries. The global numbers in this area are heavily influenced by recent developments in several large countries such as China, India, and the US. Further, the pandemic has hit the vulnerable sections of societies worldwide disproportionately more, further aggravating the situation.

Finally, some recent studies suggest that the Covid-19 pandemic has led to a decline in per capita incomes in both advanced and emerging economies. There is also some evidence that low-income economies experienced larger declines than advanced and emerging economies as a whole did.

The bottom line is that as a result of the above three factors—large re-maining between-countries' inequalities despite major progress over the past fifty years or so; major intra-country inequalities; and the recent drop in per capita incomes, particularly in most low-income countries—we live today in a world which suffers from major disparities in per capita incomes and living standards. Intra-country inequalities are of the most concern from the domestic-policy perspective. Unless tackled head-on, and soon, they could threaten the very social, economic, and political fabric of individual countries.

2.6 Rise of the middle classes

In 2022, for the first time in known history, half of the people on earth had achieved middle-class income levels.[6]

This is an important social and economic milestone. The reason being that historically, in most societies, the middle classes have not only rep-resented stability and continuity but have also set much higher value on a greater work ethic, education, savings, and have demanded better accountability from public and political bodies. As these values spread widely in a society and take deeper hold in more countries around the world, they are likely to lead to not only better economic outcomes, but also demands for better governance. Indeed, the emergence of the middle classes, together with parallel developments in some other areas—such as social media and civic societies—discussed later in this chapter, could potentially be a powerful force for change.

The percentage of people classified as middle-class in each region is shown in Table 2.5.

Thanks to the increases in the number of people becoming middle-class in East Asia and the Pacific, Latin America, and the Middle East, we estimate that by 2025 a majority of Asians will have achieved middle-class status. This, in turn, could have a dramatic impact, not only on their econ-omies, but also on their governance. However, it would be realistic to say that within Asia, South Asia still has some distance to go before reaching the half way mark to middle income prosperity. For sub-Saharan Africa, achieving middle-class living standards is still a distant dream.

Table 2.5 Percentage of Population Classified as
Middle- and Upper-Class, 2020

Region	% of Population
East Asia and the Pacific	52%
South Asia	20%
Oceania	98%
Sub-Saharan Africa	11%
Middle East and North Africa	51%
Latin America and the Caribbean	57%
Europe	96%
North America	99%
Average (World)	47%

Source: Kohli, Nag & Vilkelyte (2022); Centennial Group, In-house
Growth Model, Unpublished, (2021), within a range of annual per capita
income of $4,595 and $41,345 in constant 2018 US $

2.7   Urbanization

A majority of the world's population (4.4 billion or 56 per cent in total)
lived in urban areas in 2020 and this trend is only growing (Figure 2.3).
Greater economic development in the emerging economies has been
accompanied by an acceleration in rural–urban migration, particularly

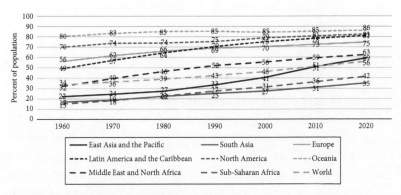

Figure 2.3 Urbanization levels by region
Source: Kohli, Nag & Vilkelyte (2022); Centennial Group, In-house Growth Model,
Unpublished, (2021).

in Asia (both East and South). This ongoing rapid urbanization has far-reaching economic, social, political, and governance ramifications.

Interestingly, in terms of urbanization, some emerging economies today exhibit characteristics that are similar to those of the advanced economies. For example, Latin America is now the most urbanized region of the world after Oceania and North America, followed by Europe, the Middle East and East Asia. Though more than half of South Asia and sub-Saharan Africa are still rural, countries like the Democratic Republic of Congo, India, and Nigeria are urbanizing rapidly; China, India, and Nigeria alone are expected to add almost 800 million additional urban dwellers in the next thirty years.

In the emerging economies, these urbanization rates have already resulted in the emergence of many megacities. Indeed, the Asia and the Pacific region already has the largest number of cities with more than ten million people (eleven out of thirty-three such cities in the world): Bangkok, Beijing, Chongqing, Guangzhou, Jakarta, Metro Manila, Osaka, Shanghai, Shenzhen, Tianjin, and Tokyo. South Asia accounts for eight more such cities: Bangalore, Chennai, Delhi, Dhaka, Karachi, Kolkata, Lahore, and Mumbai. Latin America has another six (Bogotá, Buenos Aires, Lima, Mexico City, Rio de Janeiro, and Sao Paulo), and sub-Saharan Africa already has two (Kinshasa and Lagos). Compared to these emerging countries, Europe and North America together have only three cities with more than ten million people (Los Angeles, New York, and Paris).

For the emerging economies, the challenges involved in urban management are magnified by four additional factors:

- First, owing to the inequalities and large number of poor people (particularly in sub-Saharan Africa and South Asia), cities in most emerging countries have large and crowded slum areas, with very poor, if any, public services; most are crime-ridden,
- Second, the rapid pace of urbanization, in already crowded and inadequately served cities,
- Third, the emerging economies have the most polluted large cities in the world, with unhealthy air, inadequate supply of clean water, and poor sewage systems. Climate change is likely to make living conditions even worse for people living in these cities,

- And finally, limited financial and managerial resources to cope with the urgent urban-management challenges (both in planning and enforcement) even as the public's tolerance for inaction is wearing thin.

2.8 Human development

Comparing the overall Human Development Index (HDI), produced by the United Nations Development Program, as it applies to the advanced countries and the emerging economies reveals a clear correlation between human development and income levels. However, this relationship does not always hold across all regions. Indeed, distinctions between the advanced and economies countries are not as sharp when looking at HDI as they are for per capita income, except in the case of countries in sub-Saharan Africa and South Asia.

For example, as shown in Table 2.6, most HDIs for East Asia, Latin America, and the Middle East are approaching those of North America and Europe, in sharp contrast to those of sub-Saharan Africa and South Asia. Looking at individual indicators, several East Asian countries outperform even North America and Europe in critical education tests. At the same time, South Asia and Africa suffer serious lags in crucial areas of maternal health, child mortality, and nutrition. And even Latin America

Table 2.6 Human Development Index by Region, 2019

Region	Human Development Index
East Asia and the Pacific	0.721
South Asia	0.676
Oceania	0.938
Sub-Saharan Africa	0.544
Middle East and North Africa	0.749
Latin America and the Caribbean	0.748
Europe	0.878
North America	0.928

Source: UNDP, Human Development Index, (2019): http://hdr.undp.org/en/indicators/137506, and authors' calculations

and the Caribbean, despite an otherwise high overall HDI, lags significantly behind on the education index.

As expected, even within regions there are disparities. In South Asia, Bangladesh has better HDI than India despite its slightly lower per capita income. There are similar anomalies in Africa, for example, Ethiopia does better than Nigeria, despite being much poorer.

While greater investment in human development is necessary in most emerging economies, more efficient use of the resources presently directed towards it is equally, if not more, critical. Many studies have indicated, for example, that educational outcomes in Latin America fall well short of expectation despite the region's spending fiscal resources (as percentage of GDP) similar to those spent by the OECD countries.

2.9 Access to basic infrastructure

There is clearly a major infrastructure gap between the advanced and emerging economies, except for China.

Key indicators of infrastructure stock show that advanced countries in Asia, Europe, North America, and Oceania (Japan, Singapore, South Korea) deliver much better infrastructure services to their citizens— because of both the higher amounts of their existing stock and much better management of this stock—than their emerging counterparts. China is an exception as, in many respects, it has infrastructure similar to or even better than those of many OECD countries (e.g. China's network of high-speed railways is the biggest in the world). However, it is also a fact that within the advanced countries, there are significant differences too. And some countries, like the US, which were the world leaders at one time, have had difficulties in renewing their infrastructure stock and are now trying to catch up.

But the biggest global challenges relating to infrastructure lie in the emerging economies, most of all in sub-Saharan Africa, which suffers significant deficits in almost all areas: supply of clean water, sanitation, rural roads, access to twenty-four seven power, ports, highways, telecommunications, and wideband Internet.

In terms of sheer volume, the largest investments remain to be made in Asia because of its much larger population, huge backlogs in many large countries like India, Vietnam, and Indonesia, the region's forecast higher economic growth and, of course, its larger existing stock, which requires renewal and maintenance.

To the extent that infrastructure is the backbone of development, the emerging economies cannot raise their productivity and competitiveness and thus, the economic well-being of their people, without overcoming the current infrastructure gaps.

2.10   Climate change

Climate change is an existential threat to mankind.

The Sixth Intergovernmental Panel on Climate Change (IPCC) report, put together by hundreds of top international scientists and released by the UN in August 2021, issued a 'code red alert' to the entire global community warning that our planet appears to be on a trajectory to warm by 1.5 degrees Celsius by 2040, yes, 2040, and not 2100.[7] Almost every human being is likely to be adversely affected by more frequent extreme weather events, including heavy floods, droughts, and melting glaciers.

IPCC adds credible scientific data and arguments to the already mounting evidence that climate change is already here and that it is already affecting people everywhere. The latest IPCC report also suggests that, overall, it will hurt the emerging economies much more than the advanced countries. Yet, average citizens of the advanced countries—driven by grass-roots groups—appear to be much more energized to contain global warming. Within the advanced economies, the European Union currently is in the lead in considering concrete actions to reduce carbon emissions. US has finally started taking major action under a major legislation passed in 2022 (the Inflation Reduction Act). This is appropriate in the sense that historically it is the industrialized countries whose past actions caused the problem and which have the most financial and technological resources to help tackle the problem. At the same time, carbon emissions are now rising fastest in some of the emerging economies. Climate change is a global problem and requires global solutions. Accordingly, large carbon emitters—like China, India, Indonesia, and South Africa—must also join efforts to reduce emissions as agreed at the COP26 and COP27 meetings.

Until a few years ago climate change was regarded by most as a long-term threat and its exact impact as debatable. It is now evident that climate change has already started to have negative—sometimes disastrous—impacts on all regions of the world. The major debate now is about what the global community can and will do to contain temperature rise within two degrees Celsius by the year 2100 (COP21 had set a more ambitious target of limiting the rise to only 1.5 degrees, which now seems elusive).

One concrete piece of evidence of climate change is that in the past decade the world has experienced six of the hottest ten years on record. July 2021 was the hottest month in recorded history. This global warming is leading to a much greater frequency of extreme weather conditions such as unprecedented floods, droughts, and fires. For example, in July 2021, Central Europe saw unusually heavy rains in multiple countries that led to flooding with many towns getting submerged, leading to large-scale loss of life and property. Simultaneously, in North America, while the East Coast saw heavy rains and floods, the West Coast suffered massive forest fires, mainly due to record heat and prolonged drought. Across the Pacific Ocean, China had massive floods. In the Middle East, prolonged drought caused many hydroelectric plants to curtail production, leading to major power shortages in several countries in the same month. And simultaneously there were massive fires in Russia (Siberia), Turkey, and Greece. Overall, sub-Saharan Africa has suffered more frequent droughts and parts of South America have seen numerous lakes shrink or even dry up altogether. Glaciers are melting worldwide—in the Himalayas, the Alps, the Andes, Alaska, and Antarctica. Scientists have ascribed this to ongoing climate change. These adverse weather events continued throughout 2022. And 2023 started with a relatively mild winter in many parts of the world.

The emerging economies face a diverse and challenging set of environmental issues, including extreme flooding due to rising seas, heavy rainfall, and storm surges from typhoons. During 1995–2015, storms were the deadliest weather-related disaster globally, killing 242,000 people out of the global total of about 600,000 of storm related-deaths, almost 90 per cent were in lower-income countries. Asia has more frequent weather-related disasters and related deaths than any other continent. Its populations are densely crowded into coastal regions, along multiple river basins, on flood plains, and in zones at high risk from natural hazards. Of the top ten countries ranked highest on the Global Climate Risk Index 2021,[8] three are in Asia, another five in sub-Saharan Africa, and the remaining two are in Latin America and the Caribbean.

In addition to disrupting daily lives and causing widespread damage to public property and infrastructure, these changes in weather patterns have fundamental implications for billions of people as to where and how they will live and what they will eat. For example, a rise in global temperature of two degrees Celsius is projected to lead to a rise in sea levels of fifty to 100 centimetres, directly impacting between 190 and 480 million people currently living in affected areas. In Asia alone, many cities (such as Bangkok, Colombo, Dhaka, Jakarta, Kolkata, Manila, and Mumbai) in which millions of people live will be almost entirely submerged. Similarly, millions of people in sub-Saharan Africa will have to abandon their current places of habitation as droughts choke off their supply of water. Such developments would result in perhaps hundreds of millions of environmental refugees worldwide. Additionally, the ongoing changes in climate would have a devastating impact on agriculture and food production as well as rural employment (most food production in sub-Saharan Africa and South Asia is by smallholder farmers and involves rain-fed farming). In addition to threatening food security, this could have dire consequences for the livelihoods of millions of smallholder farmers. Unfortunately, threats to agriculture are not limited to droughts alone. Rising temperatures will necessitate far-reaching changes in what is grown and where and require the introduction of new technologies (including drought resistant plants crops). It may be easier for commercial farmers in advanced countries and multinational enterprises to respond to such challenges than individual (smallholder) farmers in the emerging countries. Further, over the longer term as glaciers melt (e.g. in the Himalayas), even agriculture production on irrigated lands will suffer as river flows begin to ebb.

People in emerging economies are already suffering from other more local and immediate environmental problems. For a variety of reasons—poor urban management and lack of imposition of environmental standards on local industry—major rivers in many emerging economies are heavily polluted, even dying in many cases. Forests are receding (e.g. the

Table 2.7 Twenty Most Polluted Cities in the World, PM 2.5, 2020

Rank	City, Country	PM2.5 ($\mu g/m^3$)
1	Hotan, China	110.2
2	Ghaziabad, India	106.6
3	Bulandshahr, India	98.4
4	Bisrakh Jalalpur, India	96
5	Bhiwadi, India	95.5
6	Noida, India	94.3
7	Greater Noida, India	89.5
8	Kanpur, India	89.1
9	Lucknow, India	86.2
10	Delhi, India	84.1
11	Faridabad, India	83.3
12	Meerut, India	82.3
13	Jind, India	81.6
14	Hisar, India	81.1
15	Kashgar, China	81
16	Manikganj, Bangladesh	80.2
17	Agra, India	80.2
18	Lahore, Pakistan	79.2
19	Bahawalpur, Pakistan	78.7
20	Muzaffarnagar, India	78.6

Source: www.iqair.com/world-most-polluted-cities, 2020

Amazon forest in Brazil). The most polluted cities in the world are in the emerging economies (almost all in South Asia). Table 2.7 shows the twenty most polluted cities in the world in 2020.

While climate change is a real and present danger common to all human beings., it is also clear that it is in the self-interest of everyone—in advanced countries as well as emerging economies—to work together to mitigate and adapt to climate change by taking action at local, national, regional, and global levels. Only such actions, both individual and collective, can meet head-on this existential threat to mankind. This, in turn, will help the most vulnerable peoples in the world.

2.11 People living under democracy

The importance of human agency in traveling from Here to Denmark is a running theme in this book. A key aspect of human agency, of course, is to have a say in how one is ruled and how the affairs of the society where one lives are run. The quest to find an appropriate structure to do so is ancient. As early as the sixth century BC, *Cleisthenes* of ancient Athens had ushered in an arrangement (while by no means universal) of directly involving the citizens in political decision making.[9] Around the same time, or even earlier, ancient India (as documented in the works of *Panini* and *Kautilya*) had similar traditions of citizen involvement and holding of full and frequent public assemblies to discuss issues of common welfare.[10]

However, despite such historical antecedents, by the beginning of the twentieth century, only about 4% of the countries in the world were what could be called a combination of electoral and liberal d*emocracies*, with the remaining 96% being closed and electoral *autocracies*.[11,12]

Encouragingly, even if still not universal and not equally spread throughout the world, there has been very significant progress during the twentieth century towards empowering people to exercise voice. Today, the vast majority of people in the world—in both advanced and emerging economies —are ruled by some form of democratically elected governments.

In 2022, some 1.4 billion people lived in 'closed autocracies' without any say in the choices of their leaders but about 6.6 billion people, or 83 per cent, live under some form of electoral empowerment.[13] Comparatively, most Asians and Africans were under colonial rule as recently as 1945, and much of Latin America had either military dictatorships or were ruled by tyrants. Few citizens of today's emerging countries s had a right to vote then. By 2022, most did.

This is not to say that all democracies are equally developed or effective in reflecting the will and desires of their electorates. As a matter of fact, there is some concern about back sliding in some parts of the world. But more than six billion of the eight billion people of the world today have a right to vote, and thus, some say as to who governs them and how.

The fact that such a significant proportion of the global population have a right to vote in multiparty democracies, though many live under imperfect democracies is leading—together with various other factors discussed in this chapter—to welcome and much needed pressure for better governance and accountability of their elected political leaders.

2.12 Corruption

Corruption—both large-scale and petty—remains a major problem in many emerging countries, despite the spread of democracies in many parts of the world.

Combined with the widely held perception that the rule of law either does not fully exist or is not enforced fairly and transparently, both the average citizen and investors do not trust local institutions and political elites in most countries. This is what sets the advanced countries apart from most emerging economies, as seen in Figure 2.4.

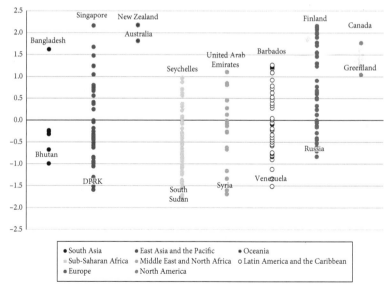

Figure 2.4 Corruption—(Perceptions about corruption: country rating by region)

Source: World Bank: World Governance Indicators, (2020): https://info.worldbank.org/governance/wgi; and authors' calculations

Three messages stand out from the above figure. First, as would be expected, the three most advanced regions—Europe, North America, and Oceania—have the highest scores (higher the score, better the control of corruption). Within the emerging countries, sub-Saharan countries as a group have the lowest scores, with the other three regions falling in between. Second, within these general regional comparisons, there is a wide dispersion in the scores of individual countries. In Europe, Finland has the best score of any country in the world, while Russia has one of the worst (the same as Nigeria's). In Africa, Seychelles did as well as Greenland in Europe, and better than most East European countries. Finally, in East Asia, Singapore was one of the three best performers in the world and North Korea one of the very worst. And third, most importantly, corruption is a major issue in most emerging economies. Most large emerging economies —Brazil, China, India, Mexico, Nigeria, Pakistan, Russia, South Africa, South Sudan—are plagued by these issues.

Large-scale corruption hurts a country's economy and people at multiple levels. Overall, corruption undermines confidence in a country's institutions and political system. Many opinion polls suggest that this is starting to become an endemic problem in many countries. Also, systemic, large-scale corruption and lack of rule of law hurt business confidence and raise risk premiums, damaging investment. They increase the cost of doing business, waste scarce resources, and reduce competition. All of this combines to slow national economic growth and hamper efforts to reduce poverty. Finally, systemic corruption diverts resources from social spending (health, education, etc.) and infrastructure development.

Petty corruption hurts individuals and undercuts the rule of law. While in terms of economic numbers, it is hard to calculate the cost of petty corruption, as it involves difficulties encountered by individuals (particularly the poor) in their day-to-day interactions with various organs of the state (e.g. police, tax inspectors, and customs officials). For the poor, the time and money involved in getting access to public services, which should be 'their right', are significant. Even more important, this undermines, if not destroys, their trust and faith in government and elected officials.

Given the far-reaching effects of corruption on societies and hence its implications for governance, this issue is discussed in much more depth in subsequent chapters.

2.13 Emergence of civic society

A major positive development of the past decades is the emergence of civic society as a major voice of ordinary citizens and an important force in public affairs in more and more countries. The interconnectedness of the Internet and the ability to amplify one's voice outside physically limited areas has allowed for the emergence of a new wave of activism and engagement around the world. This new global and interconnected civic society has taken many shapes in recent years, ranging from Western 'Slacktivism' to the revolutions of the Arab Spring, to the emergence of Q-Anon. As technology progresses, the barrier to entry to engagement with these forces—and civil society as a whole—progressively becomes lower.

This separation of location and interest, however, has resulted in a disconnect between those who care about certain issues, those who are most affected by those issues, and those who are most able to address them. For example, fighting against climate change has become a massive movement in the West, so much so that the poster child of the movement worldwide is a young Swedish woman. However, there is still limited grassroots movement in most countries which rely on heavily polluting industries to support their economies. Hopefully, over time this will change particularly with the spread of social media.

2.14 Social media: a fast-emerging global phenomenon

A major global phenomenon of the past two decades is the spread of social media. It is rapidly becoming a major force both for peer-to-peer communications and for social activism.

The explosion in the rise of social media in the past decade or so has been driven by four factors. First, wide availability of (low-cost) mobile connectivity—including in rural areas—not just in advanced countries, but also in most emerging ones as well. Second, almost universal use of mobile phones (India reportedly has 1.5 billion mobile phones for a total population of 1.3 billion). Third, the continued growing diaspora of populations in urban centres seeking to retain some connection with their home communities. And fourth, availability of multiple, easy-to-use, newer platforms like WhatsApp, WeChat, Signal, TikTok, and so on, in addition to the more mature platforms like Facebook, Twitter, and YouTube.

The result is billions of messages being exchanged daily amongst millions, if not hundreds of millions, of chat groups. While most are for sharing personal information, many are being actively used to discuss social and political issues, and how to organize to influence policies at national or even global level.

Social media's influence is likely to only increase over time, perhaps exponentially. It could potentially become a powerful force in improving governance, both domestic and global. At the same time, as we have recently witnessed in some open societies, social media can also be used to spread false information and undercut the rule of law.

2.15 Access to justice

To achieve Tagore's vision of how people should live, they should not only have a decent living standard (escape poverty and inequality) but also be able to live without fear, have access to equal justice, and feel treated as equal to other human beings in their societies. By these standards, the world still has a long way to go, not only in the emerging economies but also in many advanced countries.

While assessing people's access to justice is thus of fundamental importance, measuring this access—and even more, observing progress in it over time—is much harder than the economic and social measures discussed in this chapter above. There are multiple reasons for this, the main one being that the data on the social and economic measures presented earlier are commonly agreed by the global development community and regularly published by international agencies such as the UN agencies, the World Bank, and the IMF. On the other hand, measuring access to 'justice' is a relatively new field and hardly any, international agencies regularly publish information that covers a wide range of countries; further, there also seems to be a lack of consensus on what such appropriate measures should be. The best-known data on the subject were published in 2019 by the World Justice Project (a not-for-profit group based in Washington DC).[14] While their data do not have the rigour or the time-line to match the economic and social data published by the World Bank and IMF, the WJP survey findings summarized below are nonetheless sobering.

The WJP project takes a comprehensive view of justice in defining access to justice, or a lack to it, from the perspective of individuals around the world. It attempted to measure the gap in access to justice under three categories: 1) number of people who are unable to obtain justice due to them under their full administrative, legal, and criminal rights; 2) people who are excluded from the opportunities the law provides to them; and 3) people who live under extreme conditions of injustice (slavery).

The survey carried out by WJP came out with the following figures: as many as 1.5 billion people belonged to category one, another 4.5 billion fell into category two; and finally, 253 million people around the world still lived in slavery. Altogether, as many as over six billion people out of 7.5 billion total world population that year did not have access to one form of justice or the other. The WJP report goes on to acknowledge that obviously there is some double counting in these figures, as many people would fall into more than one category. After such adjustments, the study estimated that some 5.1 billion people in the world did not have access to justice in one or more categories as defined by it.

There are suggestions in the report that some of the individuals are resident in the so-called advanced economies, including what this book defines as 'Denmarks'. In other words, this WJP report suggests that even in countries with otherwise 'good governance' to promote economic well-being there still needs further progress to be made in terms of access to justice.

This discussion on access to justice highlights two points. First, economic and social progress run in parallel with improved access to justice; but progress in the former does not automatically lead to better justice for all. And second, improvements in movement towards equal justice for all individuals are needed in most societies, not only in emerging economies but also in many advanced economies as well.

2.16 Summary

Our world is more interconnected and intertwined today than ever before. There has been dramatic progress in both economic and social conditions all over the world during the last seven or so decades. The world is today richer, more educated and healthier than it ever was before.

A striking feature of the past several decades has also been the steady shift of the world's centre of gravity of economic activities eastwards. Five of the world's fifteen largest economies are in Asia. Even so, individual countries around the world stand differently in each of the areas discussed in this chapter. Equally importantly, they will also probably evolve differently over time. Yet, it is useful to consider how the above developments and factors could interact with each other—positively or negatively—over time through the lens of the main subject of this book: governance.

More than half the world already lives in urban areas and the emerging countries are still rapidly urbanizing. The next big wave of urbanization will occur in the poorer regions of sub-Saharan Africa and Asia. Not only are these regions are already home to some of the biggest cities in the world, they also house some of the largest slums with poor public services. They will thus face a Herculean challenge of coping with a massive influx of more people from the rural areas and their inevitable demand for urban services.

Further, Latin America and Africa also suffer the highest inequalities in the world which unfortunately are also rising in many large emerging countries. To make matters worse, while climate change is already adversely impacting the world, the worst is yet to come, and the emerging countries emerging economies would be severely impacted (especially, the poorest within them). Simultaneously, growing incomes around the world, including the emerging economies, will fuel aspirations to consume even more. Unfortunately, many around the world live in an environment ridden with corruption and poor governance. While a large majority have a right to vote, many see their politics as flawed. Many seem to be losing faith in institutions, political parties, and even democracies' ability to deliver results. Many are also beginning to doubt the benefits of globalization and the ability of multilateral institutions to solve today's problems. In short, there is a growing sense of unease with the current state of affairs in many countries.

This unease can be further exacerbated (or alleviated) by two other recent developments: (i) the emergence of social media and information technology, which allow people globally to instantly hear and see what is happening not only in their communities, but anywhere else too, and to communicate with each other on subjects of mutual interest; and (ii) in spite of several roadblocks along the way, and the growing voice and influence of thousands of local civic-society groups around the world in advocating causes in which they deeply believe.

As far as governance is concerned, these last two developments, when combined with the above-mentioned various phenomena, can lead to either of two very different outcomes, depending on country circumstances. They could lead to hopefully positive outcomes by channelling the combination of these forces into improvements in governance; or conversely cause prolonged social upheavals and political instability.

The ultimate outcomes will depend very significantly on the will and determination of the citizens of individual societies and the robustness of their institutions.

3

Good Governance is Good Development

3.1 Why governance?

In our travels over the years around the developing world, be it in Asia, Africa, or Latin America, we have spoken to many of the intended bene- ficiaries of a country's development efforts: the poor and the deprived. What has been striking about these conversations is that those we spoke with seldom talked about income poverty alone. Of course, it was a con- cern, as were the various deprivations leading from it—lack of social services, access to schools and health care, water, and sanitation facilities, and so on. But the overarching themes of their stories were fear and in- justice, and the sense of a lack of freedom. They were stories of layers of challenges they faced in the daily grind of their lives, the unfairness of which affected their very existence.

They talked about the violence and insecurities they faced in their everyday lives. They talked about the powerful village elites whose lands they tilled and who brazenly threatened them with loss of livelihood (and worse) if they didn't do their bidding. They talked about the daily humiliations they, particularly women, suffered at the hands of these powerful men (yes, almost always men). They talked about the lack of freedom to choose, to have a say in matters of grave importance to them and their lives.

They talked about the fears of losing their meagre properties because they did not have the necessary documentation to prove their ownership, and even if they did, who cared? They bemoaned being treated unjustly and not knowing who to turn to for recourse. They talked about the lack of access to justice.

They recounted attacks from strangers, and in some cases even from neighbours, based on ethnicity, caste, religion, or superstition. And they

From Here to Denmark. Rajat M. Nag and Harinder S. Kohli, Oxford University Press.
© Rajat Mohan Nag and Harinder Singh Kohli 2023. DOI: 10.1093/oso/9780198893103.003.0003

talked about gender-based domestic violence. They talked about the lack of jobs, even casual labour. They talked about the lack of money in hand to buy the basic daily necessities, their desperation and dependence on the moneylenders, and their constant nagging fear of how they will pay them back.

They talked of the feeling of disempowerment and helplessness against those more powerful than them. They talked of the indignities they faced in their interactions with the police at street corners. They recalled the high-handedness of the petty bureaucrats at the local administrative offices where they would go to collect their dues or being ignored by the medical staff (if they were present to begin with) at the primary health centre where they went to get some urgent medical care.

They talked about the unfairness of it all.

They talked of travelling for hours by bus and often on foot to collect the necessary papers and permissions to avail themselves of the government programmes due to them only to be told to be back the next day as the 'dealing officer' was away or, in this age of digital progress, 'the system was down'. They talked about their daily battles with rules and regulations and processes which they did not fully comprehend. They talked of the feeling of being supplicants and at the mercy of those more powerful than them, when in fact they were asking for no favours and nothing more than their due.

And while there often was the unstated message that perhaps the system could work faster and in their favour, if some money was offered, it was not always the case. The challenges were much deeper than corruption alone; they were essentially the 'unfreedoms' Sen has so passionately talked about, which are a combined effect of a sense of physical and emotional insecurity, violence or at least threats of it, and biases and prejudices. The challenges were compounded by processes and procedures not clearly defined and often not transparent, so that the intended beneficiaries did not know which pillars and posts they were supposed to run between. And even if they knew, poor and indiscriminate application of the rules ground them down. And worst of all, there was a constant sense of vulnerability and no accountability.

Essentially, they all talked about 'governance', or the lack of it.

And in almost every instance, our conversations ended with some variation of a resigned closing sentence: 'There is no governance here'.

We have been struck at how often we have heard this refrain all over the world.

Without necessarily defining what governance is or even actually using that word, people instinctively know and feel the effects of 'no governance' or the lack of good governance.

In a moving and powerful book, Narayan and her colleagues at the World Bank recount their conversations with over 40,000 poor women and men in fifty countries around the world to hear the voices of the poor. They note that 'from Georgia to Brazil, from Nigeria to the Philippines, similar underlying themes emerged: hunger, deprivation, powerlessness, violation of dignity, social isolation, resilience, resourcefulness, solidarity, state corruption, rudeness of service providers, and gender inequity'.[1]

Our conversations and those presented in Narayan (2000) above encapsulate a striking failure of society. Failure to deliver on a set of fundamental development objectives, which must be assumed to apply to all societies: 'freeing its members from the constant threat of violence (security), promoting prosperity (growth), and ensuring that such prosperity is shared (equity)'.[2] And the common thread running through them all: lack of governance and a plea for greater justice for all.

3.2 What is governance?

Governance is not a recent concern for society. Going back more than two millennia, Plato's *Republic (c 375 BCE)*, his disciple Aristotle's *Politics (c 350 BCE)*, Chanakya's *Arthashastra (c 300 BCE)*, Somehsvara III's *Mānasollāsa (1129 CE)* all reflect wise ruminations and advice, deeply philosophical yet practical, on how a society could best govern itself to enhance its citizens' welfare. As a matter of fact, the word 'governance', derived from the Latin *gubernare*, is itself originally derived from the Greek word *kubernaein*, meaning 'to steer'. In its most basic sense, governance is the process of how a society steers itself. It is the process of how a society manages its affairs for the overall good of its citizens. It is not hard to imagine that even the earliest human societies must have felt the need to establish some 'rules of engagement' with each other to coexist and steer their affairs. Fundamentally, these rules of engagement define governance.

But it is not just a question of articulating the rules and regulations, laws and statutes, executive orders and fiats, and policy declarations by the government to assure good governance. No doubt, the laws and regulations are important. But it is even more important to consider how a society applies them to enhance the welfare of its citizens. How they are applied, or not, is the crux of the matter!

3.2.1 Governance in the context of social justice: *niti* and *nyaya*

To be meaningful, governance needs to be looked at through the wider prism of social justice. In this context, we have found it useful to draw on two Sanskrit words, *niti* and *nyaya*, which Sen often uses in his discourses on social justice.[3]

Niti and *nyaya* both mean justice in a sense, but the nuanced difference between the two is important. *Niti* refers to the rules and regulations, organizational propriety, how you ought to behave. *Nyaya*, on the other hand, refers to realized justice. *Nyaya* recognizes the role of *niti*, the rules and the organizations, the importance of institutions, but considers the world as is.

The context in *nyaya* is the world we live in, not some idealized state of society. *Nyaya* recognizes the role of *niti* in shaping the institutional framework but focuses on implementation. It considers the context while using the rules, norms, and legal measures to ensure that justice is administered in a fair manner to govern society. *Niti* is a necessary condition to achieve *nyaya*, but ultimately, it's *nyaya* which a society aspires to achieve. Good governance must thus concern itself with both *niti* and *nyaya*.

In this context, there is another very relevant Sanskrit word, *matsyanyaya*, which means 'justice in the world of the fish'. And justice in such a world allows a big fish to devour the small fish at will. Such a situation is obviously a fundamental violation of human justice, no matter how well-laid-out the rules, regulations, and institutional structures might be. The key element of good governance is ultimately about assuring and ensuring justice, or at least the reduction of patent injustices of the *matsyanyaya*, which the 'voices of the poor' passionately articulate in our discussion above.

3.2.2 Intrinsic and instrumental values of governance

In his seminal work, *Development as Freedom*, Sen distinguishes between the 'intrinsic' and 'instrumental' values of freedom. He argues that human freedom—to choose, express views, live as one wishes—is of value by itself, to be cherished as an important, indeed inevitable, metric of development. Freedom is an intrinsic, a primary end of development in its own right. This fundamental point is distinct from the instrumental argument that these freedoms and rights may also be very effective in contributing to the economic and social progress of a society.[4]

Following this school of thought, the value of good governance arises from both its intrinsic and its instrumental values. Good governance is beneficial in its own right. It recognizes and restores—even if partially—human dignity and gives people a sense of empowerment which is of value on its own. This is its intrinsic value. But as we will see later in this chapter, good governance also leads to positive economic and social outcomes (instrumental values) as well. For both its intrinsic and instrumental values, good governance is good development.

And, just as importantly, we need to recognize that good development is not just about economic growth, not only about increases in incomes alone, important as they are. Good development, as forcefully articulated by Sen, is much broader in scope: it is about enhanced freedoms from social injustices, increased freedom to choose and reduction in the deprivations of hunger, illness, and illiteracy. Every citizen should expect and indeed deserves to enjoy three fundamental freedoms in the society she lives in: freedom from violence, freedom from want (poverty, ill health, ignorance, and other deprivations) and freedom from injustice. Governance is about the process of governing a society to provide its citizens these three freedoms. It is the process of arriving at the rules and regulations which a society wishes to live by, and then ensuring that these rules and regulations are applied in a fair and just way. If good development is seen as a broad-based attempt by society to provide its citizens a set of simultaneous freedoms, from economic and human deprivations, from violence and injustices, then good governance is a key means to that end.

As Easterly puts it most poignantly, it was no coincidence that in spite of his deep concerns about the poverty of American blacks, Dr. Martin

Luther King's 'dream was that blacks would be able to say they were ' "free at last" … not "middle class at last" '.[5]

3.2.3 But what is governance?

Interest in governance has increased dramatically in recent decades. Be it politicians, policymakers, or bureaucrats, be it academic researchers or development practitioners, or be it the ordinary citizen, people all over the world are concerned about governance, particularly the lack of it as it affects the economic and social well-being of all.

As we talk about governance, it is perhaps equally important to ask, 'governance for what?' An immediate obvious answer is, governance for economic growth. Increases in incomes and corresponding reductions in poverty are no doubt of great importance for any society. Of course, we want societies to be prosperous and free from the scourges and indignities of income poverty, but if we cast our aspirations only on economic growth, it would be too limiting. A just and fair society would want to see its people free not only from poverty but also from other deprivations such as social oppression, ill health, and illiteracy. Surely, societies would also want to be concerned with how such prosperity is shared. In earlier chapters, we had outlined the various debilitating deprivations in our societies, characterized by serious income and human development inequities. And driving this all, there is the fundamental primordial concern for societies to be safe: free from the constant threat of violence, perhaps indelibly imprinted on the human DNA to preserve itself. Incorporating Sen's concept of social justice, the World Bank neatly encapsulates the crux of the issue, 'Governance for what? Achieving the goals of security, growth, and equity'.[6] In a nutshell, governance is a society's capacity to deliver on these key outcomes, that an ordinary citizen expects and indeed deserves.

We started off by broadly describing governance as the process of how a society steers or governs itself. Easily said, but it is a complex amalgam of multidimensional and multidisciplinary considerations. Legal, political, social, anthropological, economic aspects—all have a bearing on how we understand governance and how we define it.

Not only is governance multidimensional, but it also involves multiple stakeholders, and they all must somehow come together to decide

GOOD GOVERNANCE IS GOOD DEVELOPMENT 47

and choose how they would like to steer themselves. Cárcaba et al.[7] thus define governance as being about 'the interaction between governments and other social organizations; the relationship with citizens, decision making, and accountability. Governments have a key role in this network, since good governance implies managing public affairs in a transparent, accountable, participatory, and equitable manner'.

Quibria captures the challenges of defining governance succinctly. Recognizing that governance is a complex concept with many different dimensions, he observes that 'while some have used governance expansively to refer to the entire gamut of social, political, and legal institutions that have a bearing on the functioning of the government, others have used it to refer specifically to state capacity; and still others have used it as a code word for corruption and malfeasance of the government'.[8]

Different interpretations of governance focus on different aspects of governance. Some have emphasized the political aspects of how a society chooses to govern itself and the process of arriving at that configuration. As Quibria notes, from this perspective 'political contestability and election processes; political liberties and the legitimacy of the Government democracy; and human rights, political rights, and freedom of the press are critical elements of good governance'.[9]

Another perspective emphasizes legal aspects of governance: the laws, rules, and regulations which would govern behaviour and the interactions between various members and groups in society: the citizens, businesses, and the government, essentially the principals and the agents. Under this consideration, governance is about defining the rule of law, enforcement of contracts, and securing property rights. However, this definition equally emphasizes the importance of rule *by* law and the necessary institutional arrangements (an independent judiciary, for example) to ensure that.

Yet a third grouping focuses on governance as a measure of state capacity for efficient economic management, a la Fukuyama.[10] Governance from this perspective is about the ability of the performance of agents in carrying out the wishes of the principals. In other words, it is about execution to improve the lives of its citizens: 'in improvement of the provision of public services and in efficacious management that helps avoid delays of execution, malfeasance, and corruption'.[11]

In a sense, all the aspects noted above are relevant and each incorporates a sense of social justice.

3.3 Four basic elements of good governance

Good governance essentially comprises four basic elements: predictability, transparency, participation, and accountability.[12]

Members of a society need to know in advance the laws, rules, and regulations that apply. They need to have the assurance that these will be applied **predictably** and **transparently** to all, not capriciously and unfairly with irrelevant and pernicious considerations of say, a person's station in life or access to higher-ups. An oft-repeated and sadly true story in many poorly governed states is of miscreants caught speeding, or doing worse, loudly berating the hapless policeman apprehending them. A popular saying in India captures this well: *ulta chor kotwal ko daaten* (the thief scolding the policeman).

Citizens must also have the confidence that they will be seen as agents of change and development, and not simply as supplicants or passive recipients of state largesse and that their **participation** in the efforts to expect and demand good governance will be encouraged and not ignored, or worse. Simultaneously, good governance demands accountability: people (the governed and those governing) must be held **accountable** and bear consequences for their actions. Each of these four elements of good governance is briefly discussed below.

3.3.1 Predictability

For a well-functioning society, there must be clear rules of the game set out, agreed in advance and known to all. Essentially, these are the laws, rules, regulations, and policies which would define acceptable and expected behaviour, and the consequences of not following these laws. Drivers need to know that jumping the red light is an offence. But it is not enough to know the rules of the game. It should also be known that doing so will result in specific, predictable consequences: fines being imposed, demerit points being slapped on the driver, and so on.

There must be clear predictability of this sequence of events; there should be no doubt that these consequences will follow, and nobody will be treated differently and there will be no getting away either by some money being slipped to the apprehending policeman or with threats of calling 'my father, the commissioner'.

It should be unequivocally clear in advance that the 'rule of law' will be applied equally to all, the prince or the pauper, a high-ranking official or the common man, the State and its official institutions, or private individuals and enterprises.

This predictability of a rule-based system is 'an essential component of the environment within which economic actors plan and take investment decisions'.[13] Such predictability in the legal framework and its just application provides the necessary confidence for individuals and enterprises to make business decisions, take risks, and undertake economic activities that result in growth and development. It is equally important to also note that 'in the opposite scenario, the capricious application of rules generates uncertainty and inhibits the growth of private sector initiatives'.[14]

Predictability in public policy is equally important for building the confidence of the economic actors in planning their future actions. While it is quite natural that government policies could change over time in response to changed circumstances and evolving social needs, predictability would provide an assurance that public policies will not make sudden changes based on the whims or the desires of the government or leaders in charge without a rational and justifiable basis for doing so.

The key attribute of predictability as an important element of good governance is that not only will there be 'rule of law' but equally, 'rule by law' as well.

3.3.2 Transparency

Transparency is a key enabler for good governance. The best-designed and best-intentioned rules of law will not mean much if citizens don't know about them or can't readily find out about them. If information is power, it needs to be widely disseminated and easily available to all so that this power is not cause for abuse by those in power and instead becomes empowering for all. Clarity and knowledge of government rules and regulations and awareness of citizens' rights and responsibilities are powerful tools to complement and reinforce predictability, as discussed above.

Transparency ensures that decision-makers and custodians of citizens' welfare will know that their decisions and actions, no matter how high and powerful their office might be, cannot be hidden in darkness and will indeed be exposed to light and subject to scrutiny—sooner or later—in the public domain. Transparency reduces uncertainty and makes for better decision-making by all concerned: the governor and the governed.

Transparency in the process of policymaking and implementation creates a more conducive environment for doing business in that country. No wonder then that transparency is a major consideration in all measures of the 'ease of doing business' in a country.

A major challenge in ensuring transparency is the asymmetry of knowledge, and hence, power. Those who generate and apply laws, rules, and regulations, that is, the legislators and the executive governing a society, know much more about them than those who are affected by them, that is, the ordinary citizens. This asymmetry can often be misused by the information-keepers deciding what and when they will provide to the information-seekers. But access to such information should be a matter of right, rather than being granted as a favour. It may, therefore, be necessary for societies to make legal provisions for such access through provisions like India's Right to Information Act, a very significant and powerful legislation enacted in 2014 and being reasonably well implemented, albeit patchily at times.

Concerns are often raised as to whether limits need to be placed on the principle of transparency, and whether the possibility of full disclosure of sensitive and confidential matters will inhibit full and free internal discussions of relevant issues. These are valid concerns. However, the presumption in favour of disclosure has always served society well. Establishing sensible safeguards against misuse of transparency requirements and expectations rather than blanket restrictions on disclosure seems like the wise course to pursue.

3.3.3   Participation

Nobody has a greater stake in the successful outcome of development efforts than the intended beneficiaries themselves. But the intended beneficiaries, that is, the citizens, must not be seen only as passive recipients of such a process. Instead, they need to be recognized and treated as equal agents of development. As such, they must have the right to have a meaningful say in what the best development initiatives, interventions, programmes, or projects being proposed in their name might be.

They should have the freedom to participate in the decision-making process in choosing which interventions should or should not be undertaken. They need to be an indispensable part of the discussions of what the costs and benefits (often asymmetrical) of such interventions are and how they are to be shared between citizens. In other words, citizens of the state need to be empowered to be involved in the planning, design, and implementation of development efforts which directly impinge on their welfare.

A key aspect of participation by the intended beneficiaries in any development effort is that once again, no one will be keener than they to see that policies and procedures are followed as intended. They would wish to see zero corruption in the award of contracts and no malfeasance by colluding bureaucrats, which not only is unfair but also adds to costs and causes delays. The active and constructive participation of the beneficiaries leads to better governance, improved performance, and sustainability of development efforts.

Granted that all citizens cannot obviously be directly and individually involved in all such deliberations and decision-making processes, such participation would, of necessity, be intermediated through various institutional arrangements: the chosen representatives, local chiefs, civil society organizations, for example. But the key point is that the beneficiaries must have a forum in which to make their voices heard and have a say in the process.

3.3.4   Accountability

If there is one persistent refrain which comes through loud and clear in thousands of conversations on issues of governance, it is this: 'There is no accountability'.

Accountability pins responsibility. Who is responsible for what? And what are the consequences if such responsibilities are not met? If a citizen has travelled for a day to visit the local administration office to collect her papers or her pension, but doesn't find the concerned officer at his desk and no one else can help her, who is to be held accountable?

Good governance requires public officials to be answerable for their actions. But to hold such officials accountable, there need to be clearly laid out, well-publicized criteria for their performance—predictable and transparent. A major factor which dramatically improved governance in Singapore after its establishment as a city state in 1965 was Prime Minister Lee Kuan Yew's laser focus on holding public officials to account.

Meaningful accountability also requires agreed and well-known mechanisms for people to seek redress if the expected services, at expected levels both in quantity and quality, have not been delivered. As noted by the Asian Development Bank (ADB),[15] 'the litmus test is whether private actors in the economy have procedurally simple and swift recourse for redress of unfair actions or incompetence of the executive authority'.

The accountability of public officials and the State obviously looms large in the minds of citizens when they bemoan the lack of it and because they are usually the most affected party. However, all members of a society—individual citizens, the private sector, and civil society organizations— also need to be held accountable for their own actions, and consequences must follow, imposed by legal or other means, if such actions fall short of expectations.

While the above concept of accountability is easy to articulate and accept at a philosophical level, it is a challenge to untangle a much more difficult question: Who is accountable? To whom? For what?

To summarize, the four basic elements of governance—predictability, transparency, participation, and accountability—must work in tandem to produce good governance. Figure 3.1 illustrates how they might be seen as reinforcing each other and how the absence or dilution of any one of them undermines the entire structure of governance.

3.4 Measures of governance

If defining governance is complex, measuring it is even more so. Governance is a multidimensional concept and must be measured in that context. Capturing the essence of the intrinsic and instrumental values of governance and the four principal elements comprising governance is

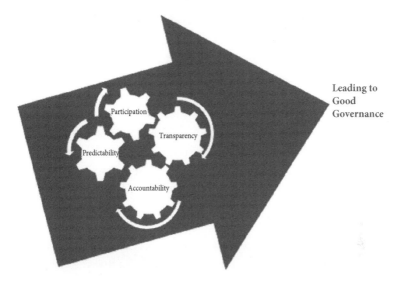

Figure 3.1 Four components of good governance working in tandem
Source: Authors

not easy, since no single measure, or even combination of measures, will be perfect or comprehensive. The best that can be hoped for are indicators, which can provide an approximate sense of what may be summed up as the core concept of governance: 'the importance of a capable state operating under the rule of law'.[16] Given the wide variation of interpretations of what governance means, it would help to consider measures of governance in two broad categories: de jure and de facto.

3.4.1 De jure and de facto measures

De jure measures may be thought of as being rules-based: is there an anti-corruption act proscribing the bribing of public officials? Does this act clearly lay out the consequences of violating this legal provision? Is there an anti-corruption agency in the country? A simple yes/no binary answer would serve as a measure of governance. If the country has an anti-corruption agency, it is assumed to be doing well on governance by this de jure measure.

But what about de facto: the reality? What is in fact happening on the ground? There might be an anti-corruption act on the books, but is it being enforced? What are the actual levels of corruption in the country? Is the anti-corruption agency effective? Is it truly independent of the government as the anti-corruption act stipulates? Can it, in fact, charge and prosecute the prime minister's son on gross corruption charges? Such de facto measures are essentially outcome-based (contrasted against the rules-based de jure measures).

For example, the most recent publication of the African Global Corruption Barometer in 2019[17] indicates that more than half (55 per cent) of the citizens surveyed in thirty-five countries in Africa feel that corruption is getting worse in their country. Fifty-nine per cent of the people think that their government is 'doing badly in tackling corruption'.[18] And yet, most of these thirty-five countries are also signatories to the African Union Convention to Prevent and Combat Corruption. If one had gone only by the metric of signatories to the convention as an indication of success in fighting corruption, the conclusion would have been different and grossly misleading.

However, it would also be wrong to conclude that de jure indicators are irrelevant and that only the de facto indicators are meaningful. Having rules and regulations enshrined in law or appropriate regulatory frameworks is a necessary but not sufficient condition for suitably measuring governance.

A very commonly used governance measure (and one over which governments around the world argued strenuously and by which they tried very hard to improve their rankings) used to be the Ease of Doing Business Indicators produced annually by the World Bank.[19] These were mostly rules-based: is there a one-stop window to get all government clearances to set up a business? How many licences are required to set up a restaurant in the neighbourhood? How long will it take to get those licences? Are these clearly specified in some rule book? Governments knew that the Ease of Doing Business Indicators were a measure of how attractive the country is perceived to be for enhanced domestic and, more importantly, foreign investments and pushed their bureaucrats to ease these rules and regulations.

But simply easing the rules and regulations on the books might not be enough to make it easier to do business. The World Bank's 2019 Doing Business Report had noted, for example, that starting a business in India (using a weighted average of the two largest cities, Mumbai and Delhi) involved ten steps which are expected to be completed in about sixteen days. While most would agree that starting a business in India has indeed become easier over the last few years, and perhaps the number of actual steps required is not too far off the mark of ten, the number of days required to complete the process varies significantly, sometimes reaching as much as ninety. Intentional bureaucratic hurdles in the approval processes, 'grease' or 'speed' money, genuine infrastructural constraints, and the 'officer concerned who has to sign off on your application is away' syndrome are all a part of the ground reality.

Thus, while the rules-based indicators are often a useful starting point, they would obviously be inadequate to assess the actual state of governance in a country or to compare governance measures across countries. At the end of the day, de facto realities are what matters.

A strong National Police Act on the books might not necessarily mean good policing at the village level. De facto realities 'are often determined by informal and unwritten conventions and practices which shape the true quality of governance in a country'.[20] If a villager is afraid to even visit the local police station, a strong National Police Act is not of much relevance to her.

De jure indicators have an advantage of clarity: either a rule exists, or it does not. Either an Act of Parliament specifying, say, the rights of peasant tenants to the land which they toil on exists or it does not. De facto indicators 'provide direct information on the de facto outcome of how de jure rules are implemented'.[21] What really matters is how the peasant tenants in this case are in fact exploited by the landowners and have no meaningful recourse to a way of having their rights recognized and enforced.

Outcome indicators capture the views of relevant stakeholders—the affected people, civil society, business participants, and experts. But of necessity, these are perceptions aggregated through surveys on the ground. One criticism often levelled against such indicators is that since they are perception- and not fact-based, they may be subject to the biases of the respondents. Understandable concerns, but perhaps overblown. As a matter of fact, since only the wearer knows where the shoe pinches, it is best to ask the affected people about how they see (and feel the effects of) the realities on the ground, and how the de jure rules and regulations are actually applied and implemented.

Over the last three decades, there has been a proliferation of governance indicators as interest and concern about governance has risen around the world. Most of them are outcome-based, as there is much greater interest and indeed relevance in actual conditions, or more accurately, perceptions of conditions on the ground. Various commercial risk-rating enterprises, international development agencies such as the World Bank, and civil society organizations such as the World Economic Forum and Transparency International, regularly publish such indicators, each looking at different aspects of governance, though understandably, corruption often takes much of the attention.

Many governments and multilateral organizations also assess the status of their governance for internal diagnostics and policymaking purposes. For almost all bilateral and multilateral development organizations, good governance is a key performance measure determining allocation of aid funds.

3.4.2 World Governance Indicators

For our purposes in this book, it would perhaps suffice if from the many governance indicators available we focused on the Worldwide Governance Indicators (WGI), produced by the World Bank.

Starting in 1996, the World Bank has produced annual updates of the WGI covering over 200 countries. Kaufmann, Kraay, and Mastuzzi (KKM), the authors of the WGI, define governance as the 'traditions and institutions by which authority in a country is exercised', and then specify six indicators—two each in three clusters—which they suggest capture the important aspects of governance.

These clusters and component indicators are:

(a) The process by which governments are selected, monitored, and replaced.
  (i) *Voice and accountability*: would measure the 'voice' people have in choosing their governments—the political rights

and civil liberties including freedom of expression, freedom of association, and a free press.

(ii) *Political stability and absence of violence/terrorism*: would capture the risks of a government being unable to carry out its mandate and being removed by violent or unconstitutional means.

(b) The capacity of the governments to effectively formulate and implement sound policies.

(i) *Government effectiveness*: essentially a measure of quality of public policy formulation and implementation, including public services, and freedom from political pressures.

(ii) *Regulatory quality*: would capture the quality of the formulation and implementation of policies, rules, and regulations that would generally govern and enhance the role of the private sector in the economy.

(c) The respect of citizens and the state for the institutions that govern economic and social interactions among them.

(i) *Rule of law*: would capture the confidence of citizens that rules (laws and regulations and perhaps even the constitution) would apply equally to all in society. These rules would be clearly defined ex ante (predictability) and enforced transparently to all (rule by law) and include protection against crime and violence, property rights, contracts, the conduct of the law enforcement agencies (the police), and the administration of law and justice (the courts); and

(ii) *Control of corruption*: would capture perceptions of citizens of how the rule of law could be circumvented by the abuse of public power for private gain, ranging from small and petty corruption to grand capture of the state by elites and private interests.

Since we will draw on the WGIs quite extensively in this chapter, it may be appropriate to discuss a bit more about how they are constructed and address some relevant concerns which are often expressed about them. (Box 3.1)

Box 3.1　World Governance Indicators (WGI)

Starting in 1996, and updated annually, Kaufmann, Kraay, and Mastuzzi (KKM) have constructed aggregate governance indicators that cover more than 200 countries and are based on over 350 variables obtained from dozens of institutions worldwide.

Undoubtedly, there are measurement challenges. Margins of error are not trivial and thus caution in interpreting the results is warranted, particularly in ranking countries. However, these margins of error have declined over time, increasing confidence in their use.

In constructing the WGI, KKM rely exclusively on perception-based governance data sources. Their sources include surveys of firms and households, as well as the subjective assessments of a variety of commercial businesses, nongovernmental organizations (NGOs), and several multilateral organizations and other public-sector bodies. Each of these sources provides a set of empirical proxies for the six broad categories of governance which are to be measured. For example, a household or firm might provide the respondents' perceptions or experiences with corruption in that country, while an NGO or a commercial data provider might provide its own assessments of corruption based on its network of contacts and clients. These different perspectives on corruption in that country are then combined into a composite indicator that summarizes their common component. A similar process is followed for the other five broad indicators.

Almost all the data sources are available annually; in a few cases, data sources are updated only once every two or three years and they are appropriately aligned with the WGI measures.

The WGI data sources reflect the perceptions of a very diverse group of respondents. And that has been the source of concern and criticism on the ground that there is a substantial difference between measuring something and measuring perceptions of it (Quibria 2014). Three principal concerns may be cited: (i) perceptions can lag in a dynamic economic context, (ii) the so-called 'halo effect' with experts drawing from the same data sources and listening to other experts, and (iii) ideological and cultural biases of foreign residents and expatriates.

KKM do not deny the possibility of all the above biases, but argue that perception data have value in the measurement of governance. Their argument, and we agree, essentially, is that in matters of governance, perceptions matter, and it runs along the following lines:

First, perceptions matter because agents base their actions on their perceptions, impressions, and views. If citizens believe that the courts are inefficient or the police are corrupt, they will hesitate to approach such institutions. Entrepreneurs, domestic or foreign, base their business decisions on their perceived view of the investment climate, government effectiveness, and the actual application of the rules of law of the land.

Second, in many areas of governance, there are few alternatives to relying on perception data. This is particularly true for corruption, which almost by definition would leave no paper trail to be captured by purely objective measures.

Third, the issue of de jure vs de facto realities. Laws against corruption might exist on the books, but they might not in fact be applied, and for an investor, that is what matters: the actual situation on the ground. Given the increased emphasis on good governance, particularly against corruption throughout the world in recent decades, most countries have formal laws, rules, and regulations protecting against bribery and corruption. In more than one hundred countries included in the Global Integrity Index, it is formally illegal for a public official to accept bribes. On a de jure index, then, each of these countries would be ranked the same, but of course, the actual situation on the ground varies widely between them. There are large differences across these countries in fact, and therefore in perceptions, which are very relevant.

Source: Abridged and adapted from Kaufmann, Kraay, and Mastruzzi (2009); Kaufman and Kraay, November (2002); Kaufmann (2003); Kaufmann (2005), and Kaufmann, Kraay, and Mastruzzi (2010).

3.5 Profiles of governance

Annex 1 presents the six governance indicators discussed above (expressed in their percentile rankings) for different income groups, for various regions across the globe, and a selected group of twenty countries.

While by no means comprehensive, the countries have been selected to broadly represent various regions of the world and some special development characteristics.

We have included Denmark, of course, being 'Denmark'. Canada is included as a consistently high-ranked country in the UNDP's Human Development Index (HDI). The world's current three largest economies—the US, China, and Japan—are in the list. India is included, as a fast-growing economy and second most populous country (soon to be first).

South Korea (hereinafter referred to as Korea unless otherwise specified) is in the list as one of the major success stories of the generation in respect of development, going from one of the poorest countries in the world in 1970 (poorer than even North Korea) and making it to the OECD club of rich nations less than twenty-five years later. Brazil and the Philippines are included, for almost the opposite reasons: from being beacons of great hope in the 1960s, they got caught in the familiar middle-income traps barely a decade later and plateaued thereafter at well below their potential.

Botswana, Chile, Georgia, and Rwanda are included as encouraging examples of countries which have shown significant spurts of improvement in governance and economic performance in the past couple of decades. Singapore has been a poster child as a small island city republic with no natural resources of its own, which moved from being a third-world country to developed-world status (with current per capita incomes among the world's highest) in one generation.

Nigeria is also in the list as an example of a large country which has squandered its huge oil wealth over the past several decades, mainly due to poor governance. On the other hand, Indonesia is another oil-rich country that recognized the need to diversify its economy away from its dependence on a single commodity (oil) export as early as the mid-1980s. It has fared reasonably well, despite the debacle it suffered during the Asian financial crisis, and is included in this list.

Bangladesh is another interesting case. Having been dismissively branded as a basket case at its birth in 1971, it has shown remarkable resilience. Not only did it prove that branding wrong, but it now almost equals India on the per capita income measure and even exceeds its much larger neighbour on several social indicators (maternal mortality, for example).

Also included are Tunisia (locus for the initial spark of the Arab Spring) and Egypt (where the spark sputtered). An emerging economy in Asia with steadily improving HDI ranking since 1990 and already in the high human-development category, Vietnam completes the list.

Several key observations follow:

By region (Figure A1.1, Annex 1):

(i) High-income countries top the percentile rankings (80 per cent plus) on all governance variables (except for Political Stability and Absence of Violence/Terrosrism, 70 per cent plus) but are significantly ahead of the upper and lower middle-income and low-income countries on each of these variables.

(ii) Low-income countries are considerably behind all other regions on all six indicators.

(iii) North America exceeds all other regions on all indicators, followed by Europe and Central Asia, and East Asia and the Pacific (excepting on Political Stability, where the latter two trade places).

(iv) Middle East and North Africa, South Asia and sub-Saharan Africa occupy the last three places, on each of the six indicators and lag behind all other regions, often by significant margins.

By country (Figure A1.2, Annex 1):

(i) Canada, Denmark, and Japan are all in the top eightieth percentile on all six indicators.

(ii) Singapore, is in the top eightieth percentile on five of the six indicators (excepting Voice and Accountability for Singapore, where it falls to the fortieth percentile)

(iii) US makes the top eightieth percentile only for four (Government Effectiveness, Regulatory Quality, Rule of Law and Control of Corruption) of the six indicators and drops to the seventieth percentile for Voice, and Stability and the fiftieth percentile for Political Stability.

(iv) China and India are in similar deciles for three of the six indicators (Rule of Law, Regulatory Quality, and Political Stability). India is significantly ahead on Voice and Accountability, where India is in the fiftieth percentile and China in the fifth. China is ahead on Control of Corruption and Government Effectiveness.

(v)   Botswana, Georgia, and Rwanda are all ahead of China and India (and some others, too) on four indicators (Political Stability, Regulatory Quality, Rule of Law, and Control of Corruption), and almost at par with India, but behind China, on Government Effectiveness. Botswana is also ahead of both China and India on Voice and Accountability, though Georgia and Rwanda are ahead only of China on this score.

(vi) Bangladesh is a paradox, as it scores poorly on all indicators, being no higher than the third decile on any of them. And yet, as alluded to earlier, Bangladesh has done reasonably well on the economic front, and even better on social issues. This will be discussed later in this chapter.

While the six governance indicators all focus on different but important aspects of governance, it would be helpful to see if a composite picture could emerge from the six considered collectively. An elegant way would be to present these indicators in the form of a web diagram where the value of each indicator (not its percentile ranking) is shown on each of the spokes of the web. The area under the irregular hexagon could then be interpreted as a proxy of overall governance, at least as defined by the six indicators.

Figure 3.2 plots the web diagram for high, upper and lower middle-income, and low-income countries. Similar conclusions emerge as before, that is, the composite governance scores for these four income categories of countries are strictly in the order of their per capita incomes. Figure 3.3 plots by regions of the world, and again, the more economically advanced economies score higher than the poorer ones.

3.6 Impact of governance on incomes and other development outcomes

One conclusion clearly follows from the above: richer economies do better than the poorer ones on each of the dimensions of governance.

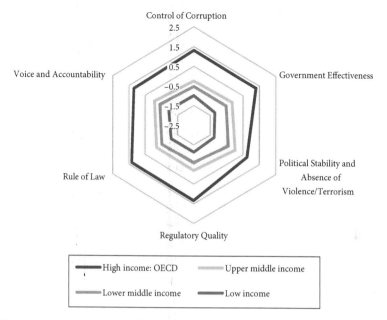

Figure 3.2 Governance indicators: four income categories, 2021

Source: World Bank: World Governance Indicators (2021): https://info.worldbank.org/governance/wgi; and authors' calculations

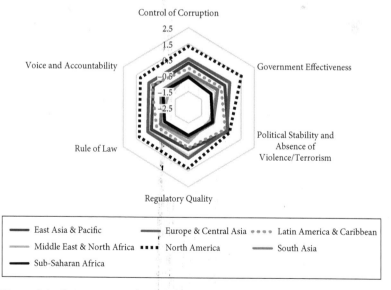

Figure 3.3 Governance indicators by region, 2021

Source: World Bank: World Governance Indicators (2021): https://info.worldbank.org/governance/wgi; and authors' calculations

3.6.1 Is good governance a luxury that only the rich countries can afford?

Figure 3.4 presents the relationship between the six governance indicators and per capita incomes for our twenty selected countries, aggregated by income levels into three (low, medium, and high) groupings. Like the global picture, it reveals a clear link between per capita income and the level of a governance indicator. And in each case, the relationship is clearly positive: the higher the level of governance, as measured by any of the six indicators, the higher the per capita incomes.

However, while the strong correlation between income growth and governance is interesting, what about the causality? Does better governance lead to higher incomes? Or is it the other way around? Do richer countries have better governance because they can afford to put more resources into ensuring better governance (paying civil servants higher salaries, for example)? Is good governance a luxury that only the rich countries can afford?[22]

The answers to these questions have important implications for policymakers. Should a country first focus on economic growth, get rich,

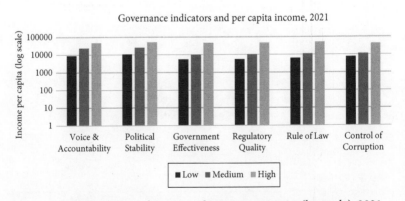

Figure 3.4 Governance indicators and income per capita (log scale), 2021

Source: World Bank: World Governance Indicators (2021): https://info.worldbank.org/gov ernance/wgi; World Development Indicators (2021): https://databank.worldbank.org/source/ world-development-indicators; and authors' calculations

and then worry about improving governance? Or is it more important to improve governance first, which would then enhance economic growth and thus, incomes?

Studies by Kaufmann et al. provide some clear-cut answers to these questions:[23,24] 'the causality is from good governance to higher per capita incomes and not the other way around.' Using statistical analyses to separate out the effects of per capita income on governance, they note that 'although there is a rapidly growing literature that identifies the causation from better governance to higher per capita income, that is not the case for identifying causation in the opposite direction, from per capita income to governance.'[25] This is quite a straightforward, unequivocal statement. Higher incomes do not automatically lead to better governance and conscious and deliberate actions by both the governor (the State, the government) and the governed (the citizens) would always be needed to ensure good (better) governance.

This is also a very powerful conclusion, with an important policy implication. One cannot get rich first and then become honest. Countries cannot focus on economic growth first to get richer, and then on improving governance. Many resource-rich countries (Nigeria comes to mind) squandered their newly found wealth on unproductive expenditures which fuelled corruption and high inflation, as they focused on economic growth without simultaneously building the necessary institutional structures to foster good governance. This implies that countries must proactively undertake positive and sustainable governance reform measures as part of the initial starting points of a development process. A country can only expect a virtuous process of improving governance leading to higher incomes rather than the other way around. This, then, is a direct rebuttal of sometimes-held views that poor countries cannot afford the luxury of good governance. Quite the contrary: it is the poor countries who cannot afford the luxury of bad governance.

In a seminal study using cross-sectional data drawn from 150 countries, undertaken almost two decades back, Kaufmann et al. concluded that a one-standard-deviation improvement in governance causes 'between a 2.5 fold (in the case of voice and accountability) and a 4-fold increase in per capita income.'[26]

3.6.2   Does better governance also lead to better social development?

While it is certainly an encouraging finding that good governance leads to higher incomes, it would be an insufficient achievement if it helps only in raising a country's GDP, important as that is. Surely, the ultimate goal of a society must be to improve the overall quality of life of an average person, rather than only her income. Raising a country's per capita GDP is a means of achieving this larger goal rather than an end in itself. An important means, no doubt, but not enough. As Sen and many others have noted, the well-being of a country's citizens derives from many factors: their health, education, sense of agency, freedom from violence, freedom to choose, a sense of worth and self-respect, the quality of the physical environment they live in, and having their voices heard. In fact, as Banerjee and Duflo have noted, 'a higher GDP may be one way in which this [*quality of life and a sense of empowerment*] can be given to the poor; but it is only one of the ways, and there is no presumption that it is always the best one.'[27]

Thus, to make a stronger case for the benefits of good governance, it would help if we could argue that good governance not only results in higher incomes but also leads to improvements in socially desirable outcomes as well. Fortunately, such is the case. Figures 3.5 and 3.6 show the relationship between the six governance indicators (for the population comprised by our twenty selected countries), and infant mortality and adult literacy, respectively. In each case, countries with better governance fare better on these social indicators as well, and often dramatically so.

For example, infant mortality for countries in the top third (shown as High in Figure 3.5) of, say, Rule of Law, stands at eight per 1,000 live births compared to thirty-nine (almost five times as high) for countries in the bottom third (Low) on the same indicator. Similarly, Figure 3.6 shows that countries in the top third of the Rule of Law index enjoy almost universal (93 per cent) adult literacy, while those in the bottom third are much lower, at 77 per cent.

The study by Kaufmann et al. referred to earlier showed similarly impressive results. They note that 'improved governance has a strong negative impact on infant mortality of proportionally the same magnitude as

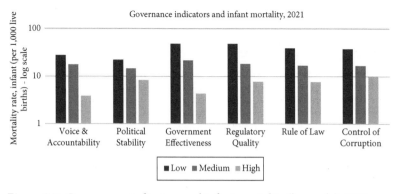

Figure 3.5 Governance indicators and infant mortality (log scale), 2021

Source: World Bank: World Governance Indicators (2021): https://info.worldbank.org/gov
ernance/wgi; World Development Indicators (2021): https://databank.worldbank.org/source/
world-development-indicators; and authors' calculations

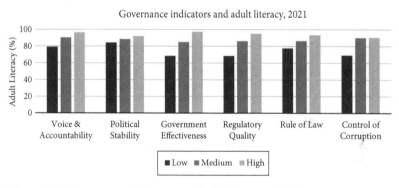

Figure 3.6 Governance indicators and adult literacy, 2021

Source: World Bank: World Governance Indicators (2021): https://info.worldbank.org/gov
ernance/wgi; World Development Indicators (2021): https://databank.worldbank.org/source/
world-development-indicators; and authors' calculations

for per capita incomes, and between a 15- and a 25-percentage-point improvement in (adult) literacy'.[28]

3.7 Governance matters

It is fair to conclude, then, that good governance matters. Good governance results in more efficient and effective use of scarce national resources

(natural, physical, and, perhaps most importantly, human), providing a greater impetus to growth, increased incomes, and better development outcomes. More importantly, bad governance has a disproportionately greater negative impact on the poor. The poor have less ability to deal with corruption or to work their way through an opaque system or a maze of bureaucracy.

However, it is also quite possible to see economic growth in a country even without good governance, at least for a while. For example, Nigeria in the oil boom period, or Indonesia, despite well-recognized governance deficits, in the Suharto era; but we believe that such growth is not sustainable. Such episodes of growth happen as spurts, which then fade away and do not last over a sustainable period, as evidenced not only for the two examples just noted, but throughout economic history across various regions around the world.[29]

Consider the Soviet Union: its economy (GNP) grew by an impressive average annual growth rate of 4.2 per cent over the period 1928–1985 and even higher (4.7 per cent) if the World War II period is excluded. With a population growth of about 1.3 per cent over that period, its GNP per capita grew at an impressive 3 per cent annually over that long stretch of fifty-seven years.

Breaking down by shorter periods tells an even more impressive story during the decades of the 1950s and 1960s, when the economy grew at an average of 5.7 per cent and 5.2 per cent respectively. As a matter of fact, until the late 1960s, 'the era of rapid Soviet growth and of Sputnik, the main question among Western scholars was not *if* but when would the Soviet Union catch up and overtake the United States?'[30]

The mood of that period can be gauged simply by the fact that as the colonial powers rapidly unwound their presence in Asia and Africa during the fifties and sixties, many newly independent countries seriously considered the Soviet model, with the State as the prime (often the only) mover of the economy as a viable development alternative to pursue.

However, the Soviet economy had started to sputter by the early 1970s and its growth rate had declined to only 2 per cent by the early 1980s. And the rest, as they say, is history. It would be too simplistic to explain this decline away by ascribing it to the 'Soviet model' alone. At heart, the issue was much deeper and essentially boiled down to lack of appropriate in-clusive institutions (an issue which we will look at in much greater depth in the later chapters of this book) in the country resulting from the lack of good governance rather than just the political system itself.

China does not score too well on several of the Worldwide Governance Indicators, and yet its economic growth over the last three decades has been stellar, though it has hit some roadblocks recently. The Philippines and Vietnam also provide interesting contrasts, again challenging the conventional wisdom on governance. Vietnam has more closely followed Chinese-style reforms, while the Philippines has adhered more closely to conventional expectations of good governance (as summarized in the six components above). And yet Vietnam is growing at a much healthier clip than the Philippines, which seems to show many of the tell-tale signs of getting caught in a middle-income trap.

Bangladesh is another striking example of such a paradox. Figure 3.7 plots the governance web for the country for the years 2000 and 2021.

Over that period, the area under the irregular hexagon (a composite measure of governance) has reduced. However, the country's per capita GDP (in PPP terms in constant 2017 international $) has more than doubled (from $1,937 to $4,444); adult literacy has increased by over

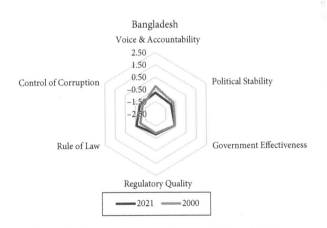

Figure 3.7 Bangladesh: governance indicators 2000 and 2021

Source: World Bank: World Governance Indicators (2021, 2000): https://info.worldbank.org/governance/wgi

50 per cent (from 47.5 per cent to 73.9 per cent); infant mortality has dropped by about 65 per cent (from 63.9 per thousand live births to 23.5); and its ranking on the HDI has moved up by five notches. Quite an impressive performance, governance challenges notwithstanding.

Would it then follow from the examples of China and Vietnam or Bangladesh that governance does not matter for economic and social development? A very different conclusion from what we had argued earlier: that governance matters. Not quite. Quibria provides a valuable insight. He argues that measures of governance such as the WGI are 'too coarse to capture the nuances of governance-growth interactions' and suggests that each of these indicators are not equally important for growth at each stage of development and in each society.[31]

Bangladesh's successes, despite weakened governance over the last two decades deserve further reflection. Its per capita GDP is now almost at par with India's and it equals or outperforms its richer and larger neighbour on several social and human development indicators. Life expectancy at birth seventy-three against seventy, infant mortality twenty-four against twenty-seven, and adult literacy in the two at just about the same level, at around 74 per cent.[32]

Building on Devarajan,[33] Quibria cites three important factors to explain:

(i)   a symbiotic relationship between the government and the civil society born out of necessity when the country was born out of a civil war, and there was hardly a government in place. International and national non-governmental organizations (NGOs) filled the vacuum by delivering basic services, such as health, family planning, and education, and by creating microcredit schemes. As these efforts proved effective, the government made space for these NGOs, and the private sector, in some cases contributing to their financing.

(ii) the presence of a vibrant, active, and effective civil society that not only delivers services, but also provides some accountability to government; and

(iii) Bangladesh is a densely populated, homogeneous society in which innovations spread like wildfire. Soon after one village discovers something that works, neighbouring villages find out about it and adopt it. As a result, family planning, microfinance, and other programmes took off in Bangladesh more easily than they might have elsewhere. By the time the government grew strong enough to control the NGOs and others, it was too late, as microfinance, family planning, and private schooling, for example, had already become prevalent.[34]

The miracle economies of East Asia, for example, initially put much greater emphasis on economic aspects of governance, such as government effectiveness and regulatory quality, rather than on the political aspects of governance, such as voice and accountability. In addition, they consistently emphasized human capital formation (education and health) and had above-average-quality institutions (and resultant implementation capacity) given their stage of development. That allowed them to concentrate on economic growth (including foreign investment and knowhow), for example, ahead of other countries with weaker institutions and poorer implementation capacity.

These examples of countries showing impressive performance on economic and social development even when their governance indicators do not show much lustre is not an argument that governance does not matter. Rather, it should be interpreted as indicating that growth is a complex process, and a combination of factors—governance among them—is at play. And further, different aspects of governance become more relevant at different stages of development of the country. However, equally important is the fact that no country with poor governance scores is in the high-income group or among those with high values of UNDP's Human Development Indicators, that capture a composite profile of incomes, health, and education. And historically there is also no evidence that those countries with poor governance have been able to sustain economic growth over a consistently long period of time.

It would be fair then to unequivocally assert that good governance is a catalyst for a country's holistic growth. However, it would also be misleading to assert that governance is the only factor that matters. Other factors do too, such as physical and human capital, sound macroeconomic management, and so on. They all work in a mutually reinforcing process. The narrative of good development must not be cast as binary. Arguing for the primacy of one set of factors (say, macroeconomic stabilization) while excluding others (say, governance) is a false dichotomy.

3.8 Demand for good governance

It would be naïve to think that just because good governance matters, it would happen from the goodness of the heart of the governors. There has to be demand for it (good governance) from the governed (the citizens) and it would thus be relevant to reflect on what factors might be driving such demands.

Mohamed Bouazizi's self-immolation on a street in Tunisia in 2010 which triggered the Jasmine Revolution and subsequently the Arab Spring, or the nuns facing down tanks on the streets in Manila as part of the People's Revolution in the Philippines in 1986, or the various hues of Revolutions in the former Soviet Union in the early 2000s were all essentially desperate cries but also powerful demands of ordinary citizens for good governance. Even if expressed in less dramatic and extreme forms, we saw and heard similar cries in our work and travels around the world and we have enumerated some of them in this chapter. While oppression, denial of justice and loss of dignity are obvious drivers for the demand for good governance, several other drivers, individually and collectively, also play an important role in creating such demand. While we will discuss such drivers in some more detail later in the book (Chapter 16), we note a few below.

Increased incomes lead to increased aspirations, and greater demand from citizens for better services and better governance. Demographics is another important driver as is urbanization. The young the world over are less tolerant of the status quo and less accepting of the patient, and sometimes even resigned, credo of their elders that 'that's how things have always been here' and instead demand greater accountability. Traditional hierarchies and informal power structures hold less sway on the urban population, particularly the youth, who are thus more demanding of the authorities. Increasing literacy has similar effects on demand for better governance. As the quality of human capital improves, education, aided by the explosion in social media and communications technology, opens up the world to the youngsters. This increased awareness essentially holds a mirror to them to recognize the ill effects of poor governance around them and the need to improve. Increased demand for better governance follows.

An important consequence of greater human agency (better education and health) is the realization that the governed (i.e., the citizens) should not simply be seen as passive recipients of State (the government) largesse. Rather, the citizens should rightly be considered as active participants in the decision-making process of development and the fast-growing influence and voice of the civic society and non-governmental organization in most parts of the world makes such participation possible.

None of the above factors work in isolation. All or many of them may simultaneously be at play, mutually reinforcing each other resulting in greater demand for good governance.

3.9 Summary

Good governance is good development. It is not only conducive to economic growth and higher incomes (its instrumental value) but even more importantly, it leads to greater freedoms from violence, from want (poverty, ill health, ignorance, and other deprivations), and from injustice (its intrinsic value). Governance is the process of governing a society to provide its citizens such freedoms. Good governance essentially consists of four basic elements: predictability, transparency, participation, and accountability.

If good development is seen as a broad-based attempt by society to provide its citizens a set of such simultaneous freedoms, then good governance is a means to that end. Essentially, good governance enhances the social welfare of the citizens and gives them a sense of well-being, of living in a fairer, just society.

Measuring governance and its impact is a complex process. Given the wide range of interpretations of what governance means, it is helpful to consider measures of governance in two broad categories: de jure or rules-based and de facto or outcomes-based. While the de jure indicators are a useful starting point, de facto realities are what matters.

Looking at several governance indicators for different income groups, in various regions across the globe, and for a selected group of twenty countries, some interesting conclusions follow:

High-income countries top the percentile rankings (80 per cent plus) on all governance variables and are significantly ahead of the upper-middle-income and low-income countries, both globally and regionally.

But does it follow that good governance is a luxury that only the rich countries can afford? Do higher incomes lead to better governance? Studies show quite convincingly that the causality is the other way around, that is, better governance leads to higher per capita incomes. This has an important policy implication: countries cannot attempt to get rich first and then focus on improving governance. That will not be a sustainable development strategy. On the contrary, countries must undertake positive and proactive governance reform measures as part of the initial starting points on their journey to Denmark.

Economic growth is undoubtedly a key means of reducing economic and human deprivations by raising incomes and reducing poverty. Good governance encourages growth because it encourages investments. Investors are encouraged if they can reasonably predict the consequences of their actions in an environment of good governance. More importantly, bad governance has a disproportionately greater negative impact on the poor, who have less ability to deal with corruption or to confront the powerful elite or to work their way through an opaque system, a maze of bureaucracy.

There is evidence around the world of countries doing well economically even when they do not score well on governance measures. But this should not be interpreted as showing governance does not matter. On the contrary, they perhaps reflect the fact that all variables used in constructing the indicators such as the WGI are not equally important for growth at each stage of development in a society. The importance of governance for growth is further buttressed by the evidence that growth in poorly governed states is usually unsustainable in the long run.

In discussing governance, it is also important to consider what factors might be at play in creating demands for better governance. A younger and more urbanized population, blessed with greater human capability (higher literacy and better health conditions) are identified as among the more important drivers, working to mutually reinforce each other in creating societal pressures for better governance.

Annex 1

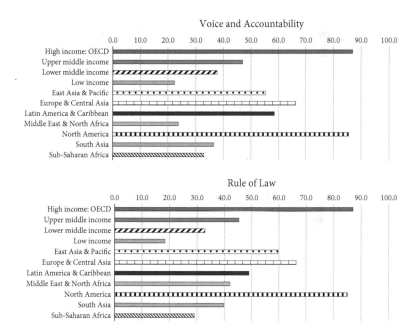

Figure A1.1 Percentile rankings, by Governance indicator, for each income and regional grouping, 2021

Source: World Bank: World Governance Indicators (2021): https://info.worldbank.org/governance/wgi

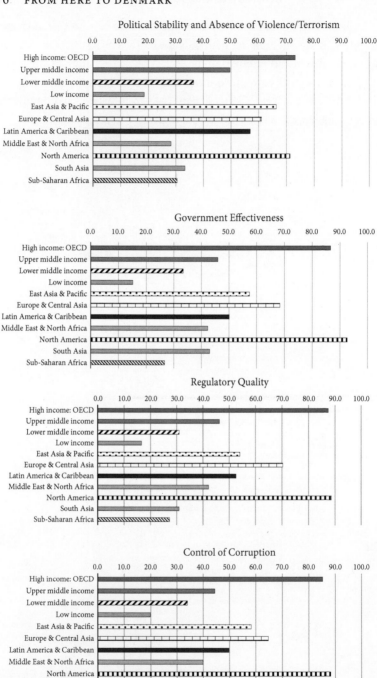

Figure A1.1 Continued

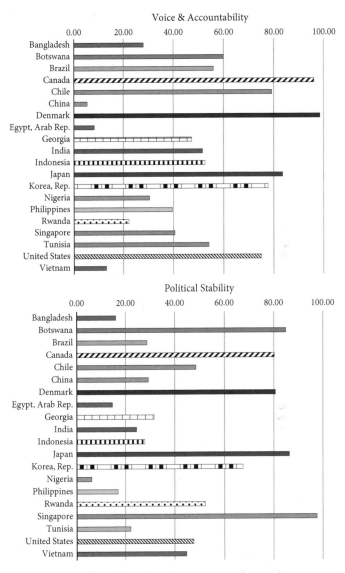

Figure A1.2 Percentile rankings by Governance indicator, by country, 2021

Source: World Bank: World Governance Indicators (2021): https://info.worldbank.org/governance/wgi

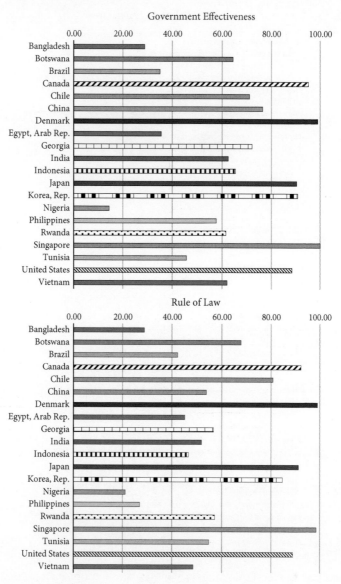

Figure A1.2 Continued

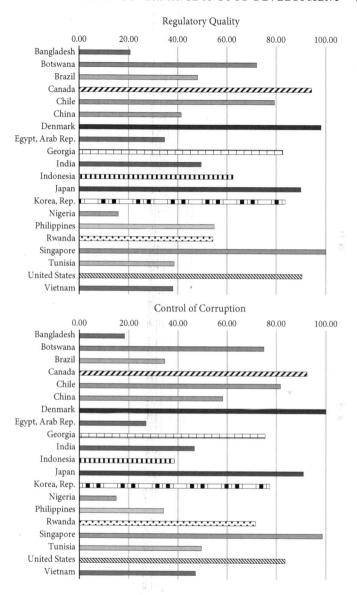

Figure A1.2 Continued

4

Corruption Hurts: No, It Kills

4.1 What is corruption?

Most of our dinner conversations in Delhi veer at some point in the evening towards the ubiquitous issue of corruption. It was almost a confirmation of a survey the BBC had reported on UN International Anti-Corruption Day as far back as in December 2010, which had been based on polling more than 13,000 people across twenty-six countries. It had concluded that 'Corruption is the World's most frequently discussed global problem'.[1] This finding is not surprising. Corruption, big and small, affects the daily lives of millions of people throughout the world, particularly in the poorer countries. But what is corruption? Everyone 'knows' what corruption is, or at least they know it when they see it, and certainly when they are the victims of it. Everyone has an opinion on what it is or how much of a bane it is, but defining it is another matter.

Let us begin by clarifying that while addressing corruption is a very important element of good governance, the concept of good governance (as discussed in the previous chapter) is broader than just dealing with corruption alone. But since corruption (rightly) occupies significant attention whenever one talks about governance, we think it is important enough to merit a chapter on its own.

The word 'corruption' derives from the Latin root *corrumpere*, meaning 'to pervert or deprave, to rot or contaminate, to spoil'. Note that all these attributes are expressed in moral terms, as indeed corruption has been seen to be immoral since ancient times. The Ancient Greeks and Romans certainly recognized the problems of bribery, including in influencing judicial decisions. Cicero, as a gifted prosecutor, witnessed this in plenty and framed his arguments about these problems by his concerns about moral corruption.[2,3]

From Here to Denmark. Rajat M. Nag and Harinder S. Kohli, Oxford University Press.
© Rajat Mohan Nag and Harinder Singh Kohli 2023. DOI: 10.1093/oso/9780198893103.003.0004

As far back as 1756, Dr. Samuel Johnson, in compiling his seminal work *A Dictionary of the English Language*, defined corruption as 'wickedness; perversion of principles; loss of integrity'.[4] Interestingly, a similarly classic dictionary of the English language compiled about 250 years later[5] also includes 'evil or morally depraved' as one of the definitions of corruption.

When we asked people, 'What is corruption?', we were struck with the raw emotion with which they often expressed their moral outrage on the subject. Corruption, for those who suffer the daily indignities of being subjected to it at the hands of the policeman who won't let them pass a checkpoint, or the petty official who won't sign off on a form to release the funds without some 'baksheesh', is the total lack of integrity or decency in those who perpetrate it. There is a deep sense of injustice and often despair that the 'agent' (the official) acting on behalf of the 'principal' (the Government) is in fact betraying the public interest.

In line with Cicero, and other classical authors, and even more contemporary ones, Rotberg argues that corruption 'is a question of fidelity, of agents being faithful to the public interest—the key regard of principles. Corruption occurs when an agent betrays the public interest'.[6] Brasz describes corruption as the 'treacherous venom of deceit',[7] a phrase which poignantly captures the feeling of the grieving Cambodian father who we will meet later in this chapter.

A similar moralistic view also pervaded the thinking about collective corruption where an entire society could be considered corrupt. In 416 BCE, Athens attacked the much smaller and neutral island of Melos to force them to join the Athenians against Sparta in the Peloponnesian War. In his scathing critique of the decision by the Athenians to do so, the Greek historian, Thucydides, 'cast all Athens and not just its leaders into a state of lost virtue and moral disrepute; and indeed, the morality of an entire political order was called into question'.[8] Thucydides considered the state of Athens to have lost its moral compass and thus to be corrupt.

Dobel builds upon the work of several classical philosophers—Thucydides, Plato, Aristotle, Machiavelli, and Rousseau—to describe the corruption of a state essentially as rendering it one where the citizens do not have the moral capacity to 'make reasonably disinterested commitments to actions, symbols, and institutions, which benefit the substantive common welfare'.[9] In other words, the body politic is subsumed to be a hostage of individual interests rather than the other way round. The entire body politic is corrupt.

Mulgan sums up this moralistic view: 'Corruption is a term of unqualified ethical condemnation … It combines the moralism of words such as "sin", "evil", or "wickedness", with added psychological implications of personal depravity and debased character.'[10] While the motivation for taking a moralistic view of corruption is understandable, the challenge then is how to make it operational? Whose moral standards will be used to judge what is corrupt behaviour? Whose ethical judgements shall prevail? Whose morals, whose ethics will be the benchmark?

Implicit in all the 'moral' definitions presented above is the concept of breach of trust by those on whom trust has been reposed, that is, by the agents who are expected to act in the best interests of the principal. Thus, corruption must somehow be linked to the standards of service expected from the office-holder and the extent of deviation from such expectations. Presumably such deviations would occur because the agent pursues his personal interests at the cost of the service he is expected, or in fact, required to provide on behalf of the principal.

Building on this concept, Nye has defined corruption as 'behaviour which deviates from the formal duties of a public role because of private-regarding (personal, close family, private clique), pecuniary or status gains; or violates rules against the exercise of certain types of private-regarding influence.'[11] This definition is broad enough to include the commonly perceived attributes of corruption: '*bribery* (use of a reward to pervert the judgment of a person in a position of trust); *nepotism* (bestowal of patronage by reason of a relationship rather than merit); and *misappropriation* (illegal appropriation of public resources for private-regarding uses)'.[12]

To be corrupt, according to Nye, a rule/law has to be violated. If it's not illegal, it's not corrupt. If there is no law against campaign financing in a country, how can it be considered corrupt even if it is quite clear that the donor will expect returns in some form or another (attractive tax breaks, favourable regulatory treatment, or an ambassadorial appointment perhaps)?

Let's look at a less dramatic example. In many countries, getting public services (passports in India, for example) on a priority basis on payment of fees is common and legal and thus not considered to be corrupt.

However, even some years back, such a system was not in place in India, and people would regularly pay touts who would bribe their way to a faster turnaround, which would thus be considered a corrupt activity.

Implicit in Nye's formulation is the inherent tension in the principal–agent relationship. Corruption arises as the divergence between the principal's (say, the State, on behalf of the citizen) interest and the agent's (civil servant) private interests. According to Klitgaard, 'corruption occurs when an agent betrays the principal's interests in pursuit of her own'.[13]

In a similar vein, Bardhan says that 'in a majority of cases, corruption ordinarily refers to the use of public office for private gains, where an official (the agent) entrusted with carrying out a task by the public (the principal) engages in some sort of malfeasance for private enrichment which is difficult to monitor for the principal'.[14]

Nye's comprehensive statement has since been rephrased by many to simply define corruption as the 'use of public office for private gain through violation of a rule'. Simple and elegant.

The words 'private gain' encompass all the three aspects Nye had identified as possible components of corruption. 'Private gain' does not necessarily have to involve pecuniary gain alone. Missing medical personnel at government dispensaries during working hours or public-school teachers insisting that their students come to them for paid private after-school lessons are no less guilty of corrupt practices than those who might take cash bribes instead. In this definition, rules define what is corrupt. If no rules are broken, there has been no corruption, even if the action might have been morally questionable.

But Bardhan urges that a distinction be made between 'immoral' and 'corrupt' transactions. He suggests, for example, that paying off a blackmailer (who can be considered immoral) to 'stop him from revealing some information which may be unpleasant' may be neither illegal nor corrupt. On the other hand, say 'paying off a policeman not to torture a suspect' would be illegal and corrupt, but may not be considered immoral (given what the bribe was for: to prevent the policeman from doing what he is not supposed to do).[15]

No definition of corruption will be perfect and comprehensive, nor will it be acceptable to everyone and in all circumstances. But the simple definition above: 'use of public office for private gain through violation of a rule' comes close to capturing the key essence, and we will use it so in this book.

4.2 Is corruption a cultural issue? An unequivocal 'No'

This is a good place to pause for a while and reflect on a major issue which often bedevils any in-depth discussion of corruption, not so much in defining it, but rather in attempts to explain it as a culture-specific phenomenon. Evidence: the prevalence of gift-giving in some cultures (in Asia and Africa, for example). Notwithstanding the history of bribes spanning four millennia, in all cultures and countries across the globe, there is a perception that such cultures might be more tolerant of corruption and ill-gotten gains.

Noonan rejects such a hypothesis, as do we: 'Bribery is universally condemned. Not a country in the world that does not treat bribery as criminal on its lawbooks. In no country do bribetakers speak publicly of their bribes, or bribegivers announce the bribes they pay; an innate fear of being considered disgusting restrains briber and bribed from parading their exchange'.[16]

In the course of our work and our travels, we have never met a person who does not clearly understand the difference between a gift and a bribe. Klitgaard notes that 'anthropological studies in Bangladesh, Ghana, and the Philippines show that peasants understand well the difference between a gift and a bribe, and they loathe the latter'.[17]

In his deeply insightful book, *The Problem of Corruption*, Alatas holds a ruthlessly honest mirror to the state of corruption in Asia and how deep its tentacles spread. However, he also strongly repudiates the perception that 'Asians have a different sense of public morality. What was missed is the fact that the prevalence of corruption and maladministration in Asian societies was a violation of the norms rather than an expression of them'. He bemoans that 'when it comes to Western societies as early as those of ancient Greece, the prevalence of corruption was considered a violation of the norms'.[18] Alatas also refers to efforts by the great Chinese reformer, Wang An Shih (1021–1086 CE) and the Islamic scholar and judge, Abdul Rahman Ibn Khaldun (1332–1406 CE) to fight corruption as evidence of concerns about such practices in Muslim and Chinese cultural traditions.[19]

The point here is that cultural relativism, that is, the notion that some cultures are more prone to be corrupt than others, is not borne out by facts. Thus, it would not be a very productive lens through which to understand the phenomenon of corruption and how to deal with it. This is also another reason why the definition we have adopted, 'use of public office for private gain through violation of a rule', is helpful. Banerjee argues in support of this definition for both pragmatic and conceptual reasons. Pragmatic because 'the emphasis on breaking formal rules (as opposed to moral or ethical ones) sidesteps the need to make ethical judgements and thereby avoids the need to have a deeper discussion of cultural differences'.[20] Conceptually sound because 'the emphasis on all kinds of gain rather than just monetary sidesteps a measurement problem: bribes by their very nature are hard to measure, whereas rule breaking is easier to measure'.[21]

4.3　A curse for all places and all times

In any discussion of the reasons for poverty around the world, the word 'corruption' springs up almost immediately. It's almost too easy to believe that corruption is the root cause holding poor countries back in their journey from Here to Denmark, and if only this scourge of corruption were somehow removed, then all would be well. No doubt corruption is a grave challenge for most poor countries; 'an insidious cancer of a national body politic, invasive and unforgiving (as) it spreads relentlessly'.[22] But it would also be wrong to consider corruption as exclusively a poor-country phenomenon. Another implicit strain in these conversations is that corruption is a recent malady afflicting the poor states (many of which were colonies) in their post-independence period in the second half of the last century. Again, not true.

Considered to be one of the ten Attic orators (the greatest orators of the classical Graeco-Roman era, in the 5th–4th centuries BCE), Hypereides (c.390–322 BCE) was a leader of the Athenian resistance to King Philip II of Macedon and Alexander the Great. His career was marked by his prosecution of several highly influential and powerful Athenians: Autocles for treason, Aristophon for malpractice and abuse of high office, and Philocrates for accepting bribes and favours from the Macedonian king. But it was his prosecution of his erstwhile political ally and colleague Demosthenes which drew our attention.

The case: the Harpalus affair. Harpalus was a Macedonian noble and treasurer of Alexander the Great's huge finances and had returned to Athens from Babylon with a considerably large army and a fleet of ships, not to mention wealth, under rather suspicious circumstances. Demosthenes was a political heavyweight but was accused of being bribed by Harpalus for protection of both his person and his wealth. His defence was that he had done so for totally political reasons and not received any monetary compensation whatsoever. Sounds familiar?

Hyperides' prosecution was fiery: 'But of all these things, Demosthenes. It was you who decreed that a guard should be posted over the person of Harpalus. Yet when it relaxed its vigilance, you did not try to restore it and after it was disbanded, you did not prosecute those responsible. I suppose you went unpaid for your shrewd handling of the crisis. If Harpalus distributed his gold among the lesser orators who had nothing to give but noise and shouting, what of you who control our whole policy? Did he pass you over? That is incredible'.[23] In pleading for a tough sentence, Hyperides urged the Assembly (the jury) to: 'Remember the tombs of your ancestors and punish the offenders in the interests of the whole city.'[24] Demosthenes was found guilty and imprisoned.

Around the third century BCE, Chanakya (350–275 BCE) served as philosopher, teacher, adviser, and prime minister to King Chandragupta Maurya, helping him establish the Mauryan Empire (322–185 BCE), which at its peak extended from parts of modern Iran and included most of the Indian subcontinent. During this period, Chanakya penned an extraordinary treatise in Sanskrit, the Arthashastra: a comprehensive guide to statecraft, an all-encompassing treatise on politics, economics, military strategy, justice, ethics, law, and, of particular interest to us, corruption.

Ever the clear-eyed realist, Chanakya (also known as Kautilya) harboured no illusions that 'just as it is impossible not to taste honey or poison that one may find at the tip of one's tongue, so it is impossible for one dealing with government funds not to taste, a little bit, of the King's wealth'.[25] Not only did he clearly recognize the possibility of corruption in public life, but he proceeds to discuss in rather exquisite detail forty ways in which dishonest officials could enrich themselves at the expense of the state, and then suggests appropriate punishment for each such misbehaviour.[26]

At the Temple of Hibis, in the Kharga Oasis (about 600 km south of Cairo) is an edict inscribed in Greek, issued in 48 CE by Vergilius Capito, then Prefect (Governor) of the province of Egypt during the reign of Emperor Claudius. It's a fascinating admonition of errant officials who might be tempted to extort necessary food and other supplies, including accommodation, from the local population without fair compensation. It also warns such errant officials against 'padding their expense accounts' and clearly lays out the penalties that the Governor would impose on them. While there is debate among scholars whether Capito's edict was referring to 'extortion', which 'was common and widespread in the Roman provinces',[27] it is quite clear that it recognized the problems of abuse of power and corruption which the Governor was keen to address.

This is a rather long-winded way to say that no country or period has a monopoly on corruption. This point is well made by Noonan, who in his brilliant book *Bribes*, traces in fascinating detail a 4,000-year-old history of bribes and corruption from ancient Mesopotamia and Egypt to modern America; from the Code of Hammurabi (a Babylonian legal code enacted by King Hammurabi around 1754 BCE) to the Lockheed Affair (a series of bribery scandals from the late 1950s to the 1970s involving the US aerospace company and high-level government officials and political leaders in Germany, Italy, and Japan in what was then described as the biggest post-war bribery case).[28]

4.4　Corruption kills

At first glance, this section appears almost redundant. Do we really need to go through the well-known and deeply felt litany of ways that corruption hurts our society?

Its pernicious effects are discussed by all but are suffered disproportionately by the poor. The ills of corruption and the economic costs (by some estimates exceeding $6 trillion 'in poor countries between 2001 and

2010 with devastating impacts on the livelihoods of ordinary people') have been extensively documented in the literature.[29] Yet, it is important to recognize that we are not just speaking about the effects of corruption in an academic sense. Corruption hurts deeply at the individual, community, national, and indeed global levels and thus deserves some recounting.

Corruption can sometime seem to be a nebulous phenomenon, its cause and effect less obvious than those of some other crimes. But don't be fooled by the (mostly) slow burn of this affliction. Recall the deep anguish and the helplessness of a father in Cambodia, who had tried to get medical attention for his desperately sick son but kept getting shunted from one clinic to another; there were no doctors at one, no medicines at another, no help to be found until it was too late. His son died. Relating this horrific story to us, he was a jumble of grief, resignation, sorrow, and anger, with which he almost spit out the words: Corruption kills.

When we were thinking of an appropriate heading for this section, the first thought which came to mind was what the grieving Cambodian father had said, 'Corruption kills'. We were struck that the same words were the title of a paper written on the first anniversary of the devastating earthquake in Haiti (7.0 on the Richter scale) on 12 July 2010.[30] About a quarter of million people had died in that disaster, with another 300,000 injured. However, another very severe earthquake (6.3 on the Richter scale) a year later in New Zealand killed fewer than 250 people and fewer than 2,000 were injured. The authors estimated that a staggering '83 percent of all deaths from building collapses in earthquakes over the past 30 years occurred in countries that are anomalously corrupt'.[31] Indeed, Corruption kills.

4.5 Changing perceptions about corruption

Corruption, in its many forms, has been getting extensive attention from the news media, literature, and even cinema, and thanks to greater public awareness, attitudes towards corruption have changed significantly in the last three decades. It is almost incomprehensible that barely half a century or so back, corruption was not necessarily viewed as negatively as it is now.

In an excellent tour d'horizon, Mungiu-Pippidi and Hartmann note that in the 1960s and 1970s, many scholars in fact considered corruption as an enabler of development, as a 'natural feature of every state at an early stage of modernization and development'.[32] Shils observes (mistakenly in our view) that low-level corruption would not be detrimental to the development of states that gained independence in the 1950s and 1960s in Africa and Asia 'since it introduces a certain amount of flexibility ... (and) "humanizes" government'.[33]

Leff (1964) believed that bribing bureaucrats who are responsible for economic policies and regulations could benefit economic growth in underdeveloped countries, stating quite clearly that 'if the government has erred in its decision, the course made possible by corruption may well be the better one'.[34] An immediate corollary of this is that Leff would view corruption as a necessary evil, perhaps, but necessary to 'grease' the wheels of an unresponsive government.

Prominent scholars of the time subscribed to this view. Leys argued that incentivizing bureaucrats to cut red tape would help in speeding up the process of establishing new enterprises.[35] Agreeing with these perceived benefits of corruption, Nye added that corruption may be an important source of capital in the formation of governments.[36]

Adding his voice to this line of reasoning, the iconic political scientist, Huntington, famously wrote, 'In terms of economic growth, the only thing worse than a society with a rigid, over-centralized, dishonest bureaucracy is one with a rigid, over-centralized, honest bureaucracy'.[37]

To be fair to that generation of thoughtful and serious scholars, it must be noted that they were formulating their views at a time when the instances of corruption were not as egregious. Remember Mrs. Marcos' infamous 3,000 pairs of shoes and her $7 million shopping sprees;[38] or Mr. Mobutu's $5,000 per haircut (his hairdresser was apparently flown in first class every two weeks from New York to Kinshasa)?[39] But as grand, earth-shattering cases of corruption started coming to light and academics looked more deeply into this phenomenon, the narrative began to change.

One sure sign was that the 'C' word started getting mentioned in reports and policy statements of international organizations and uttered in the polite company of international diplomacy. The Asian Development Bank published its policy on Good Governance in August 1995, explicitly recognizing corruption as a development challenge.[40] At the World Bank's Annual Meeting on October 1, 1996, in Washington DC, the Bank's president James Wolfensohn declared in no uncertain terms: 'We need to deal with the cancer of corruption', and went on to say, 'Corruption is a problem that all countries have to confront. We will support international efforts to fight corruption. The Bank Group will not tolerate corruption in the programs that we support, and we are taking steps to ensure that our own activities continue to meet the highest standards of probity'.[41]

Another significant development around this time was the founding of Transparency International (TI), a global coalition against corruption. Established in 1993 by some remarkably courageous and committed champions who had seen the ravages of corruption—petty and grand, at first hand—TI adopted a vision nothing short of 'a world free of corruption' and is now a global movement working in over 100 countries 'to end the injustice of corruption by promoting transparency, accountability and integrity'.[42]

The basic rationale underlying the views of corruption as being an enabler of development essentially considered corruption as a pricing mechanism to correct some of the market failures plaguing the developing countries and facing the challenges of 'an inefficient and rigid bureaucracy'. Arguments that corruption (grease money, for example) can mitigate or circumvent such distortions assumed that such distortions were exogenous, that is, external to the system. In fact, as Bardhan notes in his survey paper on corruption, it is quite possible that 'these distortions are not exogenous to the system and are instead often part of the built-in corrupt practices of a patron–client political system'.[43] If this were so, the purported grease money could well throw sand in the wheels of the very process it is supposed to speed up. Myrdal (1968) and Banerjee (1997) had also raised this possibility.[44,45]

As a matter of fact, based on some fairly detailed econometric work, Kaufmann and Wei (2000) conclude that 'there is no evidence to support the "grease" argument'.[46] They further assert, though somewhat more tentatively, that indeed, the contrary may be true. That is, corrupt officials may slow things up to extract more bribes, and also because corruption contracts are not enforceable in courts, for obvious reasons. Shliefer and Vishny make a similar point that the illegality of corruption and the need for secrecy make it distortionary and costly.[47]

In a fascinating and powerful book *Citizens Against Corruption: Report from the Front Line*, Landell-Mills refused to waste any time or words 'to debunk the often-quoted canard that corruption helps to oil the wheels of incompetent government bureaucracies. This is dangerous nonsense and leads to the perpetuation of crimes that impinge most on the poor and the vulnerable'.[48] We concur with this view.

4.6 Effect of corruption on economic growth, poverty, and inequality

But if there is confirmation from the above observations that corruption does not help, there is now also a wide range of studies and academic research showing just how much corruption hurts. In one of the first studies of its kind based on cross-country analyses, Mauro concluded that 'corruption lowers private investment, thereby reducing economic growth'. Mauro gives an example that 'if Bangladesh were to improve the integrity and efficiency of its bureaucracy to the level of that of Uruguay (this corresponds to a one standard deviation increase in the bureaucratic efficiency index), its investment rate would increase by almost five percentage points, and its yearly GDP growth rate would rise by over half a percentage point'.[49] These are striking effects indeed.

The rationale for the detrimental effects of corruption on growth deserves some elaboration. If corruption is seen as a tax on profits from the productive sector, an increase in corruption would amount to a tax hike which would encourage a shift in activities from the productive to the rent-seeking sector. And rent-seeking activities (as argued by Murphy et al.) retard growth principally through two channels.[50]

First, rent-seeking activities enjoy natural increasing returns, that is, 'an increase in rent seeking activity may make rent seeking more (rather than less) attractive relative to productive activity ... rent seekers have a "strength" in numbers. If only a few people steal or loot, they will get caught; but if many do, the probability of any one of them getting caught is much lower, and hence the returns to looting are higher'.[51]

Second, even if corruption might be perceived as a tax hike, its effects are more distortionary since efforts have to be made to keep such corrupt transactions secret. Corrupt government officials may distort investments towards those (say defence and large infrastructure projects) 'on which bribes can be more easily collected without detection'.[52] Such substitutions are more likely to be at the cost of more innovative or socially desirable (and necessary) activities, such as health and education. It follows that since 'innovation drives economic growth, public rent seeking hampers growth more severely than production'.[53]

Li, Xu, and Zou also confirm that corruption indeed retards economic growth rates. Looking at several regions of the world, they estimate that 'the direct effects of a one standard deviation increase of corruption on the growth rate is a reduction of a 0.83 percentage point'.[54] And since economic growth is indeed the best poverty-reduction strategy, any factor which reduces growth (corruption in this case) negatively affects poverty-reduction efforts. Equally importantly, they also conclude that corruption affects inequality but 'in an inverted U- shaped way. Inequality in countries with an intermediate level of corruption is higher than in countries with little or rampant corruption'.[55] The phenomenon of low inequality in non-corrupt societies is understandable, though a similar phenomenon in high-corruption situations appears to be bit of a paradox. Perhaps, when everyone is on the take, there is 'brotherhood among thieves'.

Gupta et al. provide robust evidence that high and rising corruption increases income inequality and poverty. They show that 'an increase of one standard deviation in corruption increases the Gini coefficient of income inequality by about 11 points and reduces income growth of the poor by about 4.7 percentage points per year'.[56] In a very insightful study, ADB had compared the actual poverty headcount rates with the poverty headcount rates simulated keeping inequality unchanged from the 1990s to the 2000s for several countries in Asia and concluded that had inequality not increased, the poverty levels in each case studied would have fallen significantly.[57] This is a significant finding: 'inequality matters not only because of ethical or moral issues (intrinsic value) but also because inequality dampens the effect of growth on poverty reduction'.[58]

In addition to hurting growth and exacerbating inequality, corruption affects a society in a myriad of ways. A rich body of academic research over the past three decades has added significantly to this enquiry. Corruption tends to increase the size of public expenditure, particularly in large infrastructure projects (airports, roads, and railways), and more so in their construction (where the scope of corruption is higher because of the big-ticket items) rather than in their regular operation and maintenance. Similar motivations of corruption result in poor quality of infrastructure (recall the example of the Haiti earthquake). For similar reasons, many governments also tend to underinvest in health and education, which are generally less easy to extract rents from.[59]

Corruption also dampens a government's ability to mobilize revenues, constraining its ability to carry out its functions and provide public services. The IMF (2015) notes that, 'Corruption within the revenue administration remains a significant concern in many countries. This may involve bribery by the taxpayer to understate liability or avoid registration, or extortion from them by the threat of over-assessment. The damage to revenue, compliance, and respect for the wider tax system can be chronic, and the effects in shaping its real incidence profound.'[60]

Most of the urban low-income settlements around the world are not recognized by the state, and its residents thus do not enjoy legal access to even basic utilities such as electricity and water. Enter the 'water mafia' or 'water lords' and their minions. For a price, illegal water connections or periodic access to municipal water are provided. For a price, indeed!

In a study undertaken in 2013 by a local non-governmental organization of Kaula Bandar, an unauthorized Mumbai low-income settlement, it was estimated that depending on the season, households in this area 'spend an average of 52 to 206 times more than the standard municipal charge of Indian rupees 2.25 (US dollars 0.04) per 1,000 liters for water. During the monsoon season, 50 percent of point-of-source water samples were contaminated. Stored drinking water was contaminated in all seasons, with rates as high as 43 percent for E. coli, and 76 percent for coliform bacteria.'[61]

This is not an isolated example. Millions of people around the world face such effects of corruption in basic public-service delivery by the State, be it in health care, education, water and sanitation, or a myriad of services a citizen may reasonably expect from her government, especially when they are available for those who can 'afford' it.

According to TI's 2017 Global Corruption Barometer, a quarter of respondents worldwide claimed that they had 'paid a bribe for public services in the 12 months prior to when the survey took place.'[62] And what makes it worse is that low-income households are more likely to have paid bribes to access basic services than their wealthier compatriots. Just ask a resident of Kaula Bandar!

Drawing on several underlying surveys and background research papers, a TI study on this subject states unequivocally that 'Corruption in service delivery has been shown to have negative effects on poverty rates, human development indicators, mortality rates, school drop-out rates, trust in governments, and civil unrest'.[63]

Our discussion so far has focused on the instrumental values of absence of corruption: it enhances economic growth, reduces inequality, and improves the management of government revenues and expenditures.

But as a society, we should also value the absence of corruption as a desirable state of affairs in its own right: that is its intrinsic value. Basu, who straddles the academic and policy world with equal ease and depth in each, says, 'One reason I refuse to partake in the debate about whether corruption enhances, or thwarts growth is my view that corruption should be considered unacceptable in a civilized society no matter what it does to growth. In my life as an economic adviser, nothing distresses me more than the news breaks on corruption that we get every so often. Our citizens deserve better'.[64]

4.7 Measures of corruption

Established in 2011, *I Paid a Bribe* is a unique web-based platform in India where people can self-report details of bribes paid with details of the bribe amount, who the bribe was paid to, and services rendered. They can also compliment exemplary behaviour where a public servant provided service honestly and efficiently without asking for a bribe, or in some cases refusing a bribe. Even though those reporting have the option to remain anonymous, this still remains an uncommon initiative, since there hasn't been a mad rush to replicate it elsewhere in the world. Of course, this hesitation is understandable since neither party in such transactions is seeking publicity for a 'laudable deed' that they would be proud of. An act such as paying or demanding bribes is better done in the dark, at least from the point of view of the perpetrators. Hard data on corruption are thus hard to come by.

If defining corruption is challenging, measuring it is even more so. And yet measuring corruption, imperfect as such measures might be, is imperative to get a sense of the current extent of corruption and to track changes over time.

4.7.1 Indicators based on official data

Trying to use official statistics to measure an illegal activity like corruption will not be very helpful. Official statistics, by definition, cannot measure what essentially is an unofficial (illegal) activity, and so are neither comprehensive nor insightful. Data on corruption cases reported, prosecuted, and convicted, which might be collected from, say, a national anti-corruption agency or the legal authorities, would be more of an indicator of numbers of corruption cases unearthed in public, than of the actual extent of corruption in a country. High or low levels of prosecution of corruption cases in a country are no reflection of what is really going on in that country.

4.7.2 Indicators based on perception surveys

Corrupt activities are deliberately hidden and come to light only through scandals, investigations, or prosecutions. We thus have to accept that 'no accurate way exists as yet to assess absolute levels of corruption in countries or territories on the basis of hard empirical data', and thus, proxy data will have to do.[65] A commonly used source of such proxy data is the use of perception surveys. As the name implies, such surveys seek the views or perceptions of selected respondents (experts, residents, and external observers) on various aspects of a particular issue in a country. In this case, extent of corruption, how serious is the government in fighting it, people's attitudes to corruption, corruption trends in the country, and so on.

Since 1995, TI has published its annual Corruption Perception Index (CPI), now widely accepted worldwide as the global standard. In constructing this index, TI does not conduct a survey of its own. Rather, it aggregates several other polls/surveys and is thus essentially a poll of polls. The CPI 'scores and ranks countries/territories based on how corrupt a country's public sector is perceived to be by experts and business executives. It is a composite index, a combination of 13 surveys and assessments of corruption collected by a variety of reputable institutions'.[66] The CPI is a 'freedom from corruption' index, thus the higher the score the less corrupt the country; and also, the CPI captures only public-sector corruption.

Another well-recognized index of elicited perceptions about corruption is the World Justice Project Rule of Law Index, first published in 2008. Covering 128 countries and jurisdictions, this Index 'relies on national surveys of more than 130,000 households and 4,000 legal practitioners and experts to measure how the rule of law is experienced and perceived worldwide'.[67]

The WJP Rule of Law Index is disaggregated into eight components, each with an index of its own. They are Constraints on Government Powers, Open Government, Fundamental Rights, Order and Security, Absence of Corruption, Regulatory Enforcement, Civil Justice, and Criminal Justice. Of these, the Absence of Corruption index is of interest to us here. Its objective is to assess how far public officials in the executive, the judiciary, the legislature, and the military and police eschew abusing their public office for private gain. Three forms of corruption are considered: bribery, improper influence by public or private interests, and misappropriation of public funds or other resources.

Recall another widely used global perception index on corruption. In place since 1996, this is the World Governance Indicator (WGI), which we discussed in the last chapter. We noted there that the WGI has six components, one of which is Control of Corruption and has an index of its own (WGICC). This component is focused on 'capturing perceptions of the extent to which public power is exercised for private gain, including both petty and grand forms of corruption, as well as "capture" of the state by elites and private interests'.[68]

In the context of statistical robustness, it would be useful to refer to the cautionary note of the architects of the WGI themselves. They observe that '[d]ue to the inherently unobservable nature of the true level of governance in a country, any observed empirical measure of governance will only be an imperfect proxy for the broader dimension of governance that it reflects, and the data informing the WGI are no exception. The practical consequence of this is that our estimates of governance are subject to nontrivial margins of error ... (however), using the WGI, we find that even after taking margins of error into account, it is possible to make many meaningful cross-country and over time comparisons.'[69]

All the indicators mentioned above are statistically robust in assessing perceived levels of corruption. They are aggregate indicators attempting to present a broad profile of corruption in a country in one overall measure. They do so by aggregating the individual underlying indicators capturing various aspects of corruption (bribery, embezzlement, state capture, for example). However, each specific individual indicator will be, by definition, an 'imperfect measure of the broader concepts to which it pertains, no matter how accurate or reliable it is.'[70] All indicators of governance would be subject to measurement errors, and as long as they are explicitly recognized, each of the above aggregate indicators can be considered statistically sound. They can be 'a useful way of combining, organizing, and summarizing information from different sources, thereby reducing the influence of measurement errors in any individual indicator.'[71]

Since all these three indicators are based on perceptions which take time to change, short-term comparisons between and within countries may not be very meaningful. In using any of them to assess, for example, how well a country is doing in fighting corruption, it would be best to consider the trend line rather than year-to-year differences.

4.7.3 Indicators based on experiential surveys

Despite statistical confirmation of the robustness of the use of the above indices, there is often the criticism that perception surveys do not reflect reality. Somewhat true as that might be, still, perceptions matter. If people (citizens, experts, and potential investors) perceive high levels of corruption in a country, there must be a basis for that perception, and almost everyone will respond accordingly, say, in making investment decisions.

However, this reservation about perception-based corruption indicators led to the suggestion of using 'experiential' indicators instead. To construct such indicators, respondents are asked not about their perceptions of corruption, but about their actual experiences with corruption.

A well-known feature of any statistical survey is the gap between what people say when they are asked about their perceptions on an issue and their responses based on their own personal experiences. As Klitgaard notes, 'this is particularly so when the behaviour in question is associated by some people with shame, stigma, or possible punishment'.[72] He cites some interesting examples: roughly a quarter of non-voters in the United States report having voted immediately after an election; only about half of those who test positive for marijuana, cocaine, and opiates report having used the drugs. As noted earlier, objections to perception-based indicators (such as the CPI) are based exactly on this characteristic.

In response to such concerns about perception-based indicators and to make as widespread an effort to measure corruption as possible, TI introduced an experiential indicator, the Global Corruption Barometer in 2003. Periodically, TI conducts a survey (in contrast with the CPI, where TI does not conduct any surveys on its own) of citizens around the world, asking them about their direct personal experience of corruption in their daily lives.

The latest such survey was conducted between March 2014 and January 2017. Interviewing more than 160,000 adults covering 119 countries, the survey found, for example, that almost 57 per cent of respondents felt that their government was doing poorly in fighting corruption in their country. Nearly a quarter said that they had paid a bribe when accessing public services in the last twelve months. Key public-sector institutions were seen to be corrupt. More than a third said that the police and elected representatives were the most corrupt, followed by government officials and business executives. It was encouraging, however, that more than half the respondents felt that ordinary people like themselves could make a difference in the fight against corruption.[73]

Of course, there are many heartening stories of people selflessly fighting the good fight. Sometimes these individual stances vortex into movements and big changes happen. For example, the passing of the Jan Lokpal Bill, also referred to as the Citizen's Ombudsman Bill, was instigated by civil society activists in India and the bill was passed in 2014 by the national Parliament. Jan Lokpal is an independent body to investigate and curb corruption, compensate citizen grievances, and protect whistle-blowers. Even though it has its flaws, the countrywide civil society movement to lobby for it just goes to show how affected and invested common people are in respect of this infraction called corruption.

Several experiential indicators of corruption have been proposed and developed over the past few years. Rothstein and Teorell developed a measure of 'impartiality' in government.[74] Escresa and Picci (2015) constructed a Public Administration Corruption Index.[75] Mungiu-Pippidi and Dadasov devised a new Index of Public Integrity.[76]

Interestingly, in all cases referred to above, the correlation between perception-based and experiential indicators is significantly high. TI notes, for example, that 'the CPI contains informed views of relevant stakeholders, which generally correlate highly with objective indicators such as citizen experiences with bribery as captured by the Global Corruption Barometer'.[77] The other three indicators noted in the previous paragraph all reported very strong correlation coefficients, over 0.85.

Since the experiential indicators are strongly correlated with the perception-based indicators, one could reliably use either. Since we have already presented the WGICC in an earlier chapter as a component of the World Governance Indicator (WGI), we will continue to use it in our further discussions on profiles of corruption.

4.8   Profiles of corruption

Figures 4.1 and 4.2 are a plot of the profiles of corruption of the same groupings (by income classifications, regions, and individual countries) that we looked at in discussing profiles of governance in Chapter 3.

Some broad observations from these figures are as follows:

i)   Control of corruption is correlated with income levels. High-income countries (both by income groupings and by regions) do a much better job of controlling corruption than middle- or low-income countries. Thus, North America performs best on this score, followed by Europe and Central Asia, while South Asia and sub-Saharan Africa occupy the last two positions.

ii) The same conclusion broadly applies at individual country levels as well. Poorer countries fare worse than richer ones in controlling corruption. Singapore, Canada, and Denmark occupy the top three

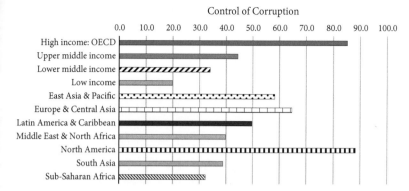

Figure 4.1 Control of corruption percentile rankings by income and regional grouping, 2021

Source: World Bank: World Governance Indicators (2021): https://info.worldbank.org/governance/wgi

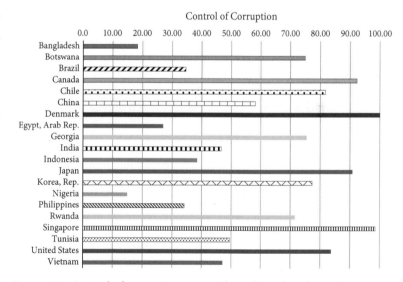

Figure 4.2 Control of corruption percentile rankings by selected countries, 2021

Source: World Bank: World Governance Indicators (2021): https://info.worldbank.org/governance/wgi

positions while Bangladesh, Egypt, and Nigeria share the dubious honour of being at the bottom of the list in our group of twenty countries.

However, it would be misleading to impute a one-to-one correlation between income levels and control of corruption. Thus, even though in 2021, Bangladesh had a per capita income of only about 70 per cent of Nigeria's, it did slightly better than Nigeria on the control of corruption. Obviously, factors other than income affect the extent of corruption in a society, but the general point here is that no country which does not manage to control corruption can expect to get rich.

4.9 Summary

A strong sense of moral indignation and outrage at egregious acts of corruption in many countries around the world adds an emotional context to the word 'corruption'. Given the broad spectrum of activities which may be considered corrupt, there are many valid definitions of the concept. But we find defining corruption as 'use of public office for private gain through violation of a rule' helpful for conceptual and pragmatic reasons.

Conceptually sound because emphasizing all kinds of gain captures the fact that the many forms of non-pecuniary transaction may be just as insidious or even worse than money changing hands. Defining it in terms of gains neatly sidesteps a measurement problem: bribes by their very nature are difficult to measure, while the breaking of a rule is easier to establish. It's pragmatic because defining corruption in terms of 'violation of a rule' makes the decision binary: one has either violated a rule or not.

Corruption is sometimes presented in terms of 'cultural relativism', that is to say, some cultures are more prone to being corrupt than others. We reject such a hypothesis. Corruption is a curse for all places and all times: from ancient Mesopotamia to modern-day, advanced economies, from the time of King Hammurabi of Babylon in 1754 BCE to present times. However, this is not to minimize the scourge of corruption for most poor countries: an insidious cancer in their national body politic, invasive, and unforgiving, as it thwarts their efforts to achieve economic and social progress.

Surprisingly, though, the general attitude towards this cancer on society was more accepting, even in academic circles, as recently as the late 1980s. Some argued that corruption is a necessary evil, necessary to grease the wheels of an unresponsive government. Corruption was seen as a pricing mechanism to correct some of the market failures facing a country because of its inefficient and rigid bureaucracy. Fortunately, attitudes against corruption gradually began to harden, and its tolerance started diminishing, at least in theory. Corruption began to be recognized by governments, international organizations, and academe as a treacherous and serious obstacle to growth.

Various studies have confirmed that corruption retards economic growth, reduces incomes, exacerbates inequality, and hampers delivery of public services. Countries with high corruption also suffer from poor social development indicators, such as higher infant mortality and lower literacy rates.

All the effects we talk about above are what would essentially be instrumental effects. But as a society the absence of corruption should also be valued as being desirable in its own right, and corruption considered as unacceptable no matter what it does to economic growth.

5

Institutions Matter

5.1 Introduction

The insidious effects of poor governance, including the scourge of corruption, on society are well recognized and have been the subject of our study in the previous two chapters. But how is good governance to be delivered? Answer: through strong institutions, and to that topic we now turn.

Economists have long recognized that institutions play an important role in influencing economic performance. As early as 1920, Alfred Marshall wrote about the effects of institutional structures on economic and social behaviour.[1] But interestingly, institutions played a very minimal role in mainstream neoclassical economics till about the mid-1980s. The subject of academic attention till then was how best an economy could efficiently use its available resources and 'different institutional arrangements were seen merely as "allocative means" for meeting the conditions required for Pareto optimality'.[2] In this discourse, the emphasis on allocative efficiency essentially made the discussion of development institution neutral. We had earlier highlighted the emphasis on physical infrastructure, human capital, macroeconomic policies, social and environmental issues placed by national governments and international development agencies in their development assistance programmes. Concerns about governance and institutions are only a relatively recent phenomenon (of the last five decades or so) in discussions about development.

No doubt the neoclassical approach successfully established the theoretical basis of economic efficiency and the critical role of prices in allocating resources. But it did so under ideal conditions of perfect information, costless transactions, and perfect individual rationality and foresight. While this approach has long dominated mainstream economic thinking, it is fair to note that the stringent assumptions of the frictionless

From Here to Denmark. Rajat M. Nag and Harinder S. Kohli, Oxford University Press.
© Rajat Mohan Nag and Harinder Singh Kohli 2023. DOI: 10.1093/oso/9780198893103.003.0005

models of perfect competition and perfect information had not gone unchallenged.

Coase had raised the issue of transaction costs in determining economic decisions and outcomes in the real world as far back as 1937. His classic paper led to further enquiry by him and others into how property rights affect economic decisions and outcomes and ultimately the critical role that institutions play in shaping economic behaviour.[3] In fact, it would be no exaggeration to say that Coase's work spawned an entire new field of study of institutional economics, generally referred to as the New Institutional Economics (NIE). Among others, Alchian,[4,5] North,[6,7,8] Williamson,[9,10] Libecap,[11] Eggertsson,[12,13] Furubotn and Richter,[14] along with, of course, Coase[15] himself, were among the early pioneers of the NIE.

Among these scholars, North is generally recognized as the principal protagonist of the NIE. As an economic historian, he was keen to study the economic past, not so much for academic historical interest but to draw lessons from the past and suggest possible policy options for future economic development. He looked for new tools to do so, since he had concluded that neoclassical economics is 'simply an inappropriate tool to analyse and prescribe policies that will induce development ... it is concerned with the operation of markets, not how markets develop ... how can one prescribe policies when one doesn't understand how economies develop?'[16]

And this was because, as we have mentioned earlier and North emphasized, neoclassical economics was modelled as a frictionless and static world and thus 'contained two erroneous assumptions: (i) that institutions do not matter and (ii) that time does not matter'.[17] NIE did not, of course, discard neoclassical economics: it rightly retained the fundamental assumption of scarcity and hence the critical role of prices in determining resource allocation. However, it modified the rationality assumption, which in turn is based on the instantaneous availability of perfect information which the economic actor can process, and added the dimension of time.

Notwithstanding that transaction costs are an obvious fact of life and that institutions naturally shape and influence economic behaviour, it took quite a while for these thoughts to seep through. Coase was awarded the Nobel Prize in Economics only as late as 1991, more than half a century after his pioneering paper recognizing these phenomena. Interestingly, North and Williamson, among the principal and early proponents of NIE, were accorded the same honour in relatively quick succession (in 1993 and 2009, respectively). Several other scholars have since been similarly honoured with the Nobel in related fields of study and the critical role of institutions has now become part of the mainstream study of economic and social development.

In a widely acclaimed work almost half a century back, North and Thomas posited the issue thus: 'The affluence of Western man is a new and unique phenomenon. In the past several centuries he has broken loose from the shackles of a world bound by poverty and recurring famine and has realized a quality of life, which is made possible only by relative abundance.' How did this happen? Their straightforward answer: 'efficient economic organization.'[18] They argued that such organizations are key to economic growth as they 'entail the establishment of institutional arrangements and property rights that create an incentive to channel individual economic effort into activities that bring the private rate of return close to the social rate of return.'[19]

But perhaps we are getting ahead of ourselves. Let us first define institutions and how they matter in fostering economic and social development.

5.2 What are institutions?

As is often the case, commonly used terms have several, imprecise definitions. 'Institutions' is one such term. And, while a precise definition for as basic a concept as institutions would indeed be welcome, perhaps one should also pay heed to Arrow's advice that 'since research in this area is still in its early stages, undue exactness must be avoided.'[20]

In a fundamental sense, institutions are rules—formal and informal— guiding social interactions, including their enforcement arrangements. They evolve over time, reflecting the history, culture, and politics of a society. They sometimes become formalized and sometimes not, but they essentially become the rules of engagement in a society.

According to North, institutions are 'the rules of the game in a society, or more formally, the humanly devised constraints that shape human interaction.'[21] North expands this concept by observing that institutions reduce uncertainty by providing a structure to everyday life. They are 'a guide to human interaction, so that when we wish to greet friends on the street, drive an automobile, buy oranges, borrow money, form a business, bury our dead, or whatever, we know (or can learn easily) how to perform these tasks.'[22]

Two key features of any definition of institutions are: i) constraints and ii) enforcement. Members of a society, the governors and the governed alike, all have constraints placed on their behaviour for the overall welfare of others. These constraints can be formal and codified in a country's constitution, laws, rules, and regulations. But they can also be informal. They can be generally accepted norms and conventions of behaviour, and self-imposed codes of conduct, even if they are not formally articulated in any legal provisions. Institutions can thus also be formal or informal.

But, simply defining the constraints, formally or informally, is not enough. They will also need to be enforced and arrangements to do so must therefore be included in the definition of institutions.

Individual rights, for example, embedded in legal provisions would constrain the state from expropriating private property or violating rules of law. Adam Smith articulated this as such (even if he did not use the word 'institution') more than two centuries back in his seminal work *The Wealth of Nations*, written as long ago as 1776:

'Commerce and manufactures can seldom flourish long in any state which does not enjoy a regular administration of justice, in which the people do not feel themselves secure in the possession of their property, in which the faith of contracts is not supported by law, and in which the authority of the state is not supposed to be regularly employed in enforcing the payment of debts from all those who are able to pay. Commerce and manufactures, in short, can seldom flourish in any state in which there is not a certain degree of confidence in the justice of government.'[23]

Institutions, in effect, define the incentive structure of a society. Building on this general concept, Ostrom, another Nobel laureate recognized for her groundbreaking work on institutions, particularly on the collective use of shared resources (the commons), offered a rather comprehensive definition of institutions and it is probably helpful to quote her at length. According to her, institutions can be defined as

> 'the sets of working rules that are used to determine who is eligible to make decisions in some arena, what actions are allowed or constrained, what aggregation rules will be used, what procedures must be followed ... what payoffs will be assigned to individuals dependent on their actions ... All rules contain prescriptions that forbid, permit, or require some action or outcome. Working rules are those used, monitored, and enforced when individuals make choices about the actions they will take.'[24]

Working rules must be common knowledge and monitored and enforced. Notice the emphasis on rules and enforcement in Ostrom's definition above. Again, working rules may be formal (expressed in laws, rules, and regulations) or informal (through social norms and conventions). An interesting and important implication of common knowledge is that 'every participant knows the rules, and knows that others know the rules, and knows that they also know that the participant knows the rules.'[25] This provides a critical motivation to follow the rules: if a participant expects others to follow the rules, she had better do so herself.

The important point is that the set of rules (i.e. institutions) provides structure to everyday life, reduces uncertainty, and simplifies decision-making. Institutions provide the framework within which human interaction can take place in a society. A key corollary of this is that living within this framework motivates participants to cooperate in their day-to-day interactions so that the costs of coordinating economic and other activities (i.e. transaction costs) can be reduced.

North's telegraphic description of institutions as 'rules of the game' is analogous to the rules of the game in say, football, or any other sport. All such games are played within a structure of formal rules (some incomprehensible, of course, such as in cricket—but that is another matter). But there are also typically unwritten codes of conduct (helping an opposing player to his feet whom you might have tripped, hopefully unintentionally) emphasizing fair play and a sporting spirit, which everyone is expected to follow.

However, these rules will not by themselves ensure that the game is played fairly. That would depend not only on setting out the rules which everyone knows and assumes others to know (i.e. are common knowledge), but also on how well the rules are enforced and monitored. Thus 'an essential part of the functioning of institutions is the costliness of ascertaining violations and the severity of punishment ... the formal and informal rules taken together with the type and effectiveness of enforcement shape the whole character of the game.'[26]

5.2.1 Institutions and organizations

In common parlance, 'institution' and 'organization' are often used synonymously. Institutional strengthening is a high-priority activity of governments and development agencies, and a term very commonly used. But what this often means is 'organizational strengthening': types of technical assistance to enhance human capacity, introducing better processes, newer and more elaborate management information systems, and so on. Going back to our sporting analogy, if institutions are the rules of the game, organizations are the players. Organizations, be they economic entities (firms, trade unions, family enterprises), political bodies (parties, Parliament, a city council), social (clubs, churches), or educational (schools, colleges) consist of individuals who come together with some common purpose to achieve certain objectives. Institutions would be, for example, the Articles of Agreement of a firm, the Charter of a club, the Code of Conduct of the city council members, or the rules of football.

Organizations give life and shape to social interactions guided by the framework of the institutions. The workings of an organization are obviously thus influenced by the institutional setting within which it exists. Organizations evolve or change reflecting the opportunities provided by the existing institutional settings. North makes an interesting observation in this regard and suggests that 'if the institutional framework rewards piracy, then piratical organizations will come into existence. And, if the institutional framework rewards productive activities, then firms will come into existence to engage in productive activities.'[27] But, to complete the story, one needs to recognize that this influence is not only a one-way street. Organizations, too, influence institutions to adjust to changing circumstances in a society: 'it is the interaction between institutions and organizations that shapes the institutional evolution of an economy.'[28]

5.3 Functions of institutions

For a society aspiring to ensure security, prosperity, and justice for all its citizens, its institutions would have to provide the three following functions, broadly encapsulated as the Three Cs: Commitment, Cooperation, and Coordination.[29]

5.3.1 Commitment

Be it a word given, a handshake, a signature, a law, or an edict etched on a stone tablet, a token of commitment is worth something only if honoured in the future. For any of these to be meaningful in guiding future actions, it must be credible.

But how much does the spoken word really mean? Words are just utterances made by an individual. What is a law? Mere ink on paper. What value do Hammurabi's edicts have? They are mere words carved on a stone tablet. The worth of these words lies in the belief by others that they will be honoured, that commitments will be fulfilled.

For the recipient of such commitments, be it the Maghrebi trader being assured of getting paid at the other end by the final buyer, or a citizen buying property seeking assurances against forcible expropriation by the state or taxation which would not be retroactively imposed, it is critically important to have confidence that these 'commitments' are credible.

For citizens, physical security is perhaps the most important commitment of the state. They must feel assured that the state will keep them physically safe from violence while they go about their daily lives. A fundamental defining characteristic of a modern state is thus the monopoly over violence, which the citizens have accorded to it in return for the assurances of protection against any violence by any domestic or foreign actor. Any breach, real or perceived, of this trust unravels the credibility of the state's commitments and reduces them to mere utterances, or ink on paper. Ensuring the credibility of commitments is thus a key function of institutions.

5.3.2 Cooperation

No number of laws and edicts can replace the basic glue of trust to hold a society together. Mutual trust is critical, not just between the state and citizens, but between people themselves as well. Citizens' willingness to contribute to collective efforts, that is, to cooperate, depends on mutual trust, and belief in others' willingness to also do the right things. An oft-observed phenomenon is that more people will be willing to pay taxes if they believe others will do the same. They don't wish to be the 'only suckers around'. People must believe that others will stop at a red traffic light for them to do so as well.

Societies face fragmentation of their social contracts without cooperation. The recent steady rise of populism (often degenerating into an unfortunate sense of narrow nationalism and even xenophobia) in many developed and developing countries reflects this breakdown of mutual trust. A second critical function of institutions is thus to build an enabling environment in a society for mutual trust and cooperation not only between its members and the state, but also amongst the members themselves.

5.3.3 Coordination

Institutions also need to facilitate coordination between different units and forces in a society. Many well-conceived programmes in many countries falter because of lack of coordination between various public and private agencies involved, directly and indirectly. Precious resources are wasted because of lack of communication or channels to coordinate efforts. Even for something as basic, but critical, as deciding which side of the road to drive on, a society needs to coordinate. Essentially, a society needs to have mechanisms in place which help its members to converge on a common position. Institutions—formal (laws, rules, and regulations) or informal (beliefs, norms, and conventions)—help societies do that, that is, coordinate.

5.4 Institutions matter

Over the last several decades renewed attention has been paid to the question of why some nations remain poor while others prosper. Among the many possible reasons offered, the importance of institutions in enhancing the economic and social development of a nation has increasingly been emphasized. Among them is a widely referenced work by Dani Rodrik and his colleagues (2002), which telegraphs its conclusions in a precise soundbite title, 'Institutions Rule'. Considering geography, international trade, and institutions (particularly regarding the role of property rights and the rule of law) as possible determinants of income levels around the world, they conclude that 'the quality of institutions trumps everything else'.[30] While this conclusion might be a bit too sweeping, the larger and important point is that institutions matter.

In their seminal, widely acclaimed 2012 book *Why Nations Fail*, Acemoğlu and Robinson compellingly boil down their answer to the title question to 'institutions, or more correctly, the lack of them'.[31] Taking several striking examples of countries all over the world (including next-door neighbours such as the Koreas and neighbouring towns across the US–Mexico border who share the same geography and culture), of which some have prospered and others have not, they conclude that it is the institutions, not geography or culture, which determine whether a country enjoys sustained prosperity or not.

It would be an incomplete conclusion, however, if we just stopped at saying that institutions matter. Yes, institutions matter, but which ones is also an important query.

Bardhan observes that most of the literature focuses primarily on security of property rights, whereas 'in general, economies at early stages of development are beset with coordination failures of various kinds ... and in dealing with (such) failures ... there are all kinds of collective action problems'.[32] Asymmetry of political power between citizens makes resolving distributive conflicts difficult and 'may be at the root of a great deal of institutional failures that are so common in poor countries'.[33]

In a similar vein, Acemoğlu and Robinson argue that while differences in prosperity across countries are driven by differences in economic institutions, they in turn 'depend on the nature of political institutions and the distribution of political power in society'.[34] As a matter of fact, it would perhaps not be much of an exaggeration to say, adapting a US Presidential campaign slogan from the 1990s, 'it's the politics, stupid'.

The ease of changing (improving) economic institutions thus depend on how easy it would be to change political institutions. But, it is often not in the interest of the political elite to redistribute power or transform the political institutions. The situation is further exacerbated by the fact that some in society may in fact enjoy de facto political power (say, by access to arms, mercenaries, and political agents), which the political institutions might not have granted them de jure. It is obviously not in the interest of such power groups to allow, let alone seek, any changes in the existing political institutions. It follows then that reforming political institutions is not easy, and thus not the economic institutions either.

5.4.1 Influence of political power structures on institutional development

Just as in football, in society too, people need to know the rules of the game in advance. More importantly, they need to know how these rules will be enforced and the consequences of not playing by the rules. These rules can be articulated formally as laws or rights, even enshrined in the country's constitution, government policies, or they could be part of a set of informal rules guiding social behaviour embedded in a society's beliefs, conventions, and norms. As a matter of fact, the formal and informal rules together comprise the 'rule book' by which a society exists and functions.

A major temptation for policy advisers and development practitioners (and to which we, the authors, have also often succumbed) to 'correct' a malpractice in a society, has often been to immediately think of another new law that can be adopted or a new policy to be announced. But the sad truth is that almost all countries, including most developing ones, already have enough (perhaps too many) laws on the books, covering almost all aspects of life. The problem is not that they do not have enough laws on the books, the challenge is that the laws are not implemented, or at least not effectively. Many existing laws simply languish on the books. India, for example, by some estimates has over 30,000 laws between the federal and state governments,[35] and 'a disproportionate number (of them) gathering dust and worse, occasionally invoked to harass and use strategically'.[36]

Why is this so? More often than not, the immediate answer is lack of political leadership. However, while not totally incorrect, there are two problems with this line of reasoning: one, if indeed there were such an omnipotent and omniscient leader at the top, then the laws which the leader does not like would be ignored, amended, or scrapped willy-nilly; and second, and more fundamentally, deciding on a particular law and implementing it is a matter of interaction and political bargaining between the various actors in a society, and not just the job of the leader.

A key aspect of this bargaining process is the unequal distribution of power in society. How well institutions function in a society thus crucially depends on how successfully the decision-makers, elites, and other groups bargain, which in turn is 'determined by the relative power of actors, by their ability to influence others through control over resources, threat of violence or ideational persuasion (de facto power), as well as by and through the existing rules themselves (de jure power)'.[37] Another important determinant of the relative power of actors is the stock of their human capital (health and education) and not only their physical capital (financial or other resources). Understanding the power asymmetry in a society is thus critical in suggesting appropriate institutional arrangements in that society. Such power dynamics obviously varies from society to society.

Development practitioners have sought to learn lessons from successes to come up with 'best practices' that can perhaps be transplanted in other geographies. But an immediate constraint in many countries appeared to be their limited institutional capacities and thus, a logical conclusion followed: strengthen the institutions, build capacity.

Undoubtedly, institutional capacities are important. But building capacity is not a matter of just training staff and sending them for development courses at home or abroad. No doubt, such training programmes are often much needed and do help, but they are not enough. It is also not just a matter of designing smart and clever organograms and revised job descriptions. Fukuyama argues quite correctly that even 'within the limited domain of organizations, there is no optimal form of organization, both in the private sector and for public sector agencies ... Most good solutions to public administration problems, while having certain common features of institutional design, will not be clear cut "best practices" because they will have to incorporate a great deal of context specific information.[38]

As we have noted above, a greater and more fundamental binding constraint in institutional strengthening is the asymmetry of power between various actors of society. Those with greater power prevail in pursuing or stalling reforms in their interest. Institutional arrangements and structures cannot thus be simply transplanted from elsewhere, no matter how successful they may have been in the erstwhile host country. As Rajan observes, 'The United States Constitution, when adopted by Liberia, turned out to be just a piece of paper with none of the effective checks and balances that fill the Federalist Papers and characterize how the United States work.[39]

5.5 Contextual social settings of institutions

However, while institutions are context-specific, some broad groupings of these contextual settings would help to understand the dynamics of how institutions could support a society in achieving its aspirations of security, prosperity, and equity. To some such possible groupings we now turn.

5.5.1 Limited- and open-access orders of societies

In some fundamental and far-reaching ways, North et al. have proposed a new conceptual framework of interpreting recorded human history to better understand 'how developing societies structure their economic policies and polities in order to solve the universal problem of violence and disorder.[40] North starts from the premise that reducing the dangers of violence and disorder is an essential starting point for good development.

According to this framework, human society, in the history of its evolution over the millennia, has devised only two significant orders of organizing itself. A third, the primitive order, consists of hunter-gatherer societies and is not very relevant here. First, a limited-access order (LAO): a society where powerful individuals or the elite possess privileges and means to create limits on access to resources and economic functions to generate rents. These elites have 'privileged access to social tools enabling them and only them to form powerful organizations' and they manage to keep others (bulk of the society) out.[41] 'Here' is a perfect example of a LAO, also sometimes referred to as the 'natural state', since most of the world still lives in this state, almost as if that were the natural state for the world to be in. Second, by contrast, a much smaller proportion of the world lives in open-access order societies (OAO), which 'rely on competition, open access to organizations, and the rule of law to hold the society together'.[42] Denmark (both our aspirational construct and the country) is an OAO.

In the natural state or LAO, elites hold the political power (often backed by physical power) to actively manipulate the social order to regulate access and economic competition, thereby creating economic rents which only they enjoy. The elites also use these rents to create social order, control violence, and establish social cooperation for their own, rather than the larger polity's, advantage and welfare.

By contrast, in the open-access order or OAO all citizens are empowered to form economic, political, and social organizations to pursue any activity (except violence). Once again, the importance of human capital in such empowerment cannot be emphasised enough. Such empowered citizens can pursue their own interests, and open entry induces competition, which in turn dissipates rents. By their very construction, political and economic transactions are impersonal in the open-access order and based on transparent and predictable criteria, as, for example, a driving licence is issued based on the results of a test and some clearly laid-out criteria. In a limited-access order, by contrast, transactions are personal. A trite but unfortunately very symptomatic example would be the same driving licence being issued based on who you know or, more to the point, how much you are willing to offer as a bribe.

As North and his colleagues note: 'the logic of the LAO creates incentives such that the delivery of government services always depends on whom the recipient is connected to ... (and) the administration of welfare programmes, business licences, and judicial services all require personal exchange—and often bribes—in limited access orders'.[43] What is important to note is that it is not that the formal organizations of the bureaucracy or the judiciary don't exist in the LAO, but that the game is played differently: the rules of the game, that is, the institutions, are different. And not surprisingly the rules are often written by the political elite in their own favour.

5.5.2   Practice of universal ethics and particularism in societies

Much akin to North's open and limited-access orders of societies, noted social scientist Mungiu-Pippidi articulated the concepts of ethical universalism and particularism in societies. In the former, a society is assumed to be fair and just, operating under ethical norms of universalism. In such a society, all citizens are treated equally and fairly, which may occasionally be infringed, but more as an exception than a rule. Such societies are characterized as adherents of universal ethics. Unfortunately, the reality is that most societies practise particularism, where people are treated differently depending on their particular social status and economic power. Unequal treatment is the norm in particularistic societies: 'a culture of privilege reigns in societies based on particularism'.[44]

5.6   Inclusive and extractive institutions

Institutions matter, but which are the desirable ones?

Acemoğlu and Robinson distinguish between inclusive and extractive institutions in determining the economic fate of a nation. They argue that rich countries are rich because they have inclusive political and economic institutions, while poor countries are not because their institutions, by contrast, are extractive.

Inclusive economic institutions create the incentives and opportunities for a large majority of the people in a society to innovate, adopt new technology, and aspire to achieve prosperity because they believe they can. This would include the standard neoclassical requirements of secure property rights, rule of law, and the uninhibited entry and exit of new entrepreneurs in any enterprise. The critical requirement for inclusivity is that these incentives and rights must be available to a large majority of the people.

Inclusive economic institutions 'require secure rights and economic opportunities not just for the elite but for a broad cross section of society'.[45] It is important to note that even if the institutions of secure property rights, protected by courts instruments of law, and public services are indeed available for minority elites such as the white settlers in South Africa during the apartheid times, or the sugar-plantation owners in colonial Barbados or the slave owners in the US South, these institutions weren't inclusive for society as a whole and hence did not create widespread and sustainable prosperity for all. On the contrary, such institutions were extractive: a small group of elites captured (extracted) the benefits of growth to their advantage. Inclusive institutions include the population at large in the process of governing in a predictable, transparent, and accountable manner, thereby reducing—if not eliminating—the process of exploitation by a few. Extractive institutions do the opposite: they extract incomes and wealth from many to benefit a few.

We had earlier noted that political and economic rules determine how a society functions. But who writes the rules? Obviously, the politically powerful. Those who hold political power would most likely decide what is in their own interest. The distribution of political power has a significant influence on the political process and the ultimate outcome of writing and enforcing those rules. Unless there are enough checks and balances from other groups holding adequate political power to counterbalance, extractive political institutions would emerge, as would extractive economic institutions. By contrast, if the political power is broadly shared among a plurality of members in a society, inclusive political and economic institutions would most likely result. It is essentially then a tussle between the different groups in the society to decide whose interests would prevail.

Interestingly, pluralism is a necessary but not sufficient condition for the existence of inclusive political institutions. Drawing on instances around the world to make their point, Acemoğlu and Robinson emphasize that unchecked pluralism could lead to chaos, as they graphically describe the state of affairs in Somalia, where 'the society is deeply divided into deeply antagonistic clans … and the power of one clan is only constrained by the guns of the other'.[46]

Late nineteenth/early twentieth-century German sociologist and political scientist Weber had defined the essence of a functioning state by identifying the state with the 'monopoly of violence' in society.[47] Without such a monopoly of violence, the state cannot play an effective role as enforcer of law and order, assure security of life and property, provide public services, and regulate and support economic activity. And, when the state fails to 'achieve almost any political centralization, society sooner or later descends into chaos, as did Somalia'.[48] So, to be truly inclusive, political institutions need to be both sufficiently centralized and yet pluralistic (broad-based). Otherwise, they would degenerate to become extractive.

Political and economic institutions are mutually reinforcing and induce a process of a strong synergistic feedback loop. Extractive political institutions vest the political power in the hands of a few elites, who then use it to devise extractive economic institutions to suit their interests. These extractive institutions in turn enrich the same elites, enabling them to further consolidate and even enhance their political power. Colonial powers in the Indian subcontinent, or plantation owners in the Caribbean islands, survived and indeed thrived economically with their extractive economic institutions only because their supporting political institutions were equally extractive.

An opposite feedback loop would operate with inclusive institutions. A broad-based distribution of political power, that is, inclusive political institutions, would induce economic rules which would favour the larger interests of society and result in inclusive economic institutions. They in turn 'create a more equitable distribution of resources, facilitating the persistence of inclusive political institutions'.[49]

The above raises an interesting question: can inclusive political and extractive economic institutions coexist, or vice versa? Unlikely, given the synergies between the two. Their coexistence, even if it were to happen for a while, would be unstable. Consider the feedback dynamics discussed above: if the political institutions was inclusive, it would mean the political power structure would be widely diffused and no elite group would enjoy an unfair advantage, let alone a monopoly, in political power. It follows, then, that the various groups in the society would not let any one group dominate in the share of the economic returns either, that is, the economic institutions could not survive for long if they tended to be extractive.

Similarly, if the economic institutions were inclusive but the political institutions were not, then the economic institutions would dilute the economic returns the elites enjoyed under the benefits of the extractive political institutions. Quite naturally, the elites would fight back and if they were strong enough, the inclusive economic institutions would gradually turn extractive. But, if the elites were unable to turn the tide, they would gradually lose political power to the larger society and fold into inclusive political institutions themselves. Either way, the simultaneous existence of inclusive and extractive institutions is unstable.

5.7 Challenges of institutional reforms in a society

It would be useful to pause here, to ask how the inclusive and extractive institutional constructs proposed by Acemoğlu and Robinson relate to North's open or limited access systems or Mungiu-Pippidi's universalistic or particularistic societies. In a way, these constructs are answering different, though related, questions. Acemoğlu and Robinson are asking what type of institutions will lead to good governance and good development. Their answer: inclusive rather than extractive institutions. North and Mungiu-Pippidi are asking, how will such inclusive institutions evolve in a society? Their answer: when the society moves to an open-access or universalistic state. The logical question to ask then is, how can this transition from limited- (particularistic) to open-access (universalistic) orders be engineered? North and his colleagues don't pull any punches: 'There is no easy answer to this question, no magic bullet'.[50]

Seen through the lens of North's open- and limited-access orders, or Mungiu-Pippidi's universal and particularistic societies, it becomes clear why many proposed institutional reforms do not work. Not because the proposed institutional forms (such as property rights, rule of law, legal and judiciary structures) are inappropriate prescriptions in and of themselves, but because they are grafted onto limited-access orders or particularistic societies when in fact, they would work only in open-access or universalistic societies. As North et al. note, 'it is one thing to create courts and justices and another to ensure that they can sustain the independence necessary to produce the impartial delivery of justice'.[51]

Similar advice on paying attention to the context also comes from several other scholars and practitioners. Rodrik observes that 'what works will depend on local constraints and opportunities' and adds that 'designing appropriate institutional arrangements requires local knowledge and creativity ... in a second best (that is, real) world, the nature of the binding constraints and their interactions with other distortions will influence the desirable arrangements'.[52]

Acemoğlu also cautions that 'there is no general recipe for improving institutions', adding that 'institutional reforms must have internal driving forces and what types of reforms can be successful will vary from country to country'.[53]

The above observations are sobering, even depressing. Does this suggest that institutions cannot be reformed? If that is so, are we pursuing a fool's errand and is it the case that societies might as well accept that history is destiny?

Fortunately, history shows that difficult as it is, institutional reforms making them more inclusive can and do happen as societies transition from limited- to open-access orders. Political elites would be willing to compromise and agree to share their monopoly on power, particularly the use of violence, when the alternatives are worse. They do it not out of their magnanimity but in their own long-term interest. They might recognize that other emerging forces in society or other alliances might jeopardize not only their present state but also their future welfare, when they might lose even more, and not just wealth and privileges but their physical well-being as well. Experiences in various parts of the world through history bear this out.

Consider Denmark in the 1600s: its institutions and governance were extractive. Many things were indeed 'rotten in the state of Denmark'. But they changed with changes in the political fortunes of the landed elites and the empowerment of the ordinary citizens. The Glorious Revolution in Great Britain and the Meiji Restoration in Japan are among other examples of countries moving from limited- to open-access order and subsequently prospering. In more recent times, the experiences of South

Korea, Botswana and Uruguay would be good evidence that history is not destiny. In each case, the political elites compromised and made concessions to avoid a worse outcome. There may thus be value in studying the trajectories of some of these countries which have made such successful transitions and seeing if some relevant lessons may be learnt, and we do so later, in Part III of this book.

And, of course, a country might fortuitously find a transformational leader, who can bring about deeper and more fundamental changes in society by influencing societal preferences and beliefs. Almost single-handedly, Nelson Mandela, for example, deeply influenced his fellow citizens' beliefs about racial harmony, tolerance, and forgiveness, and steered South Africa away from its long-standing apartheid policies. In their lifetimes, Mahatma Gandhi and Martin Luther King, Jr, catalysed similar transformations in their societies, 'bending the arc of the moral universe towards justice'. But while we may draw justifiable inspiration from them, history also cautions us that such people will occur rather infrequently. We cannot thus depend on the providential emergence of such leaders. Instead, as we will discuss later in the book, the transition to more inclusive institutions will have to be driven from below. Under such a situation, citizens will need to be empowered with enough human capital (education and health) and allowed to participate more meaningfully in the political process of governing their societies.

5.8 New institutional economics meets behavioural economics

We began this chapter by noting how about half a century ago Coase, North, and others expanded the thinking about the relevance of institutions in the development process: from a view that 'institutions do not matter' to recognizing that they do, and often significantly so. This new field of economics, dubbed the 'New Institutional Economics', essentially recognized that the neoclassical assumption of perfect rationality is rather onerous and unrealistic. Humans are not always coherent, forward-looking, and consistent in their behaviours. Real people can be selfish, pursuing their self-interest, but they can be incredibly and unexpectedly generous, as well. Based on such a realistic perspective of human nature, institutions are best considered to be the rules—formal and informal—which define the framework within which human interaction takes place in a society. This implies that how people think and behave individually and collectively would influence how institutions would evolve and function in each social context.

Over the past three decades or so, such a study of human behaviour on an individual level and on the level of membership of a society has become possible through significant advances in a new branch of economics—behavioural economics—which incorporates valuable insights from psychology, sociology, political science, and anthropology. This enables the study of human interactions through a wider lens than economic considerations alone. Such an approach thus meaningfully recognizes the interplay of economics, politics, and society in influencing human behaviour and the evolution of institutions in a society. Going into these human behavioural issues is the subject of the next part of our book.

5.9 Summary

Institutions are the rules—formal and informal—which define the framework within which human interaction takes place in a society. These rules place constraints on the behaviour of members in a society, the governors and the governed alike, for the overall welfare of the community. Simultaneously, institutions also set out how society will enforce these rules. Such constraints and enforcement mechanisms can be formally codified through laws, rules, and regulations, or they can evolve informally as generally accepted norms and conventions of behaviour and self-imposed codes of conduct.

Institutions are context-specific and thus institutional arrangements also must be tailored to the specific circumstances of that context. Designing appropriate institutional arrangements thus requires local knowledge, particularly of the local political power dynamics in that society. Broadly, societies may be categorized as either limited- or open-access orders, also referred to as particularistic or universalistic societies. In the former, access to economic and political opportunities is limited to the elites rather than being open to all.

How strong or weak the institutions are in a society has a decisive influence on the state of its governance and economic performance. But it is not economic institutions alone which matter. As a matter of fact, how the economic institutions evolve and perform in a society also depends on the distribution of political power and thus the nature of political institutions in that society. Institutions are inclusive if all members of that society have equal or open access to the rights and privileges of citizenship. Such institutions create equal opportunities and incentives for all without undue and unfair intrusion by the state or other citizens. Extractive institutions do not.

Inclusive institutions are thus broad-based and pluralistic while extractive institutions are captured by elites who can dictate the rules of the game, that is, bend the institutions to their advantage. Further, inclusive institutions can exist only in societies which ensure the security of life and property. This, in turn, requires a degree of centralization of power to be vested in the state with its presumed 'monopoly on violence'. Otherwise, chaos would reign.

Nations fail when they are dominated by extractive political and economic institutions. The obvious challenge for societies is how to build and nurture an inclusive set of institutions. Since institutions are context- and location-specific, there are no general, universally valid recipes for doing so. Institutional reforms cannot be readily imported and unbridled faith in transplanting best practices from elsewhere would be unproductive.

However, drawing conclusions of helplessness and the immutability of history would also be equally wrong. There are relevant lessons to be learnt from the experiences of countries around the world which have indeed made the transition from extractive to inclusive institutions and prospered as a result. Denmark itself is a sterling example. We will consider this and other such experiences next in Part III of this book.

Part I: Key messages

1. *To achieve economic and social progress, good governance matters.*
2. *To deliver good governance, inclusive economic and political institutions matter.*
3. *Institutions are inclusive when all members in a society have equal access to rights and opportunities.*
4. *Institutions are context and location specific and there are thus no silver bullets for institutional development.*
5. *Institutional reforms have to be home grown and so-called best practices cannot be transplanted from elsewhere.*

PART II
MIND AND ACTIONS

Overview

Till the early 1970s, institutions did not play a significant role in mainstream economics which, dominated by neoclassical economic theory, was essentially institution-neutral. Its emphasis was on 'frictionless' models of the economy based on assumptions of costless transactions, perfect information available to all and complete individual rationality. Individuals were assumed to be robotic, homo economicus (Econs), always rational and consistent, rather than homo sapiens (Humans), that is, most of us.

However, as we saw in Part I, institutions matter. They are the rules—formal and informal—of the game. But, how well the game is played ultimately depends on the individuals comprising that society. And that in turn depends on answers to several questions: how do a wide variety of actors think and act individually and collectively? How do they process the beliefs, norms, and conventions of the society they live in? How do people perceive the laws of the land, how and to what extent do they cooperate with each other in the provision of collective goods? How do the formal rules (the constitution and the laws), and more importantly the informal rules (the norms, conventions, beliefs) emerge in a society?

Surely it would be misleading to brush these questions away as inscrutable elements of human behaviour, too complex and random to consider, or assuming that they cancel each other out following the law of large numbers when members of a society interact. There are overarching psychological, social, and cultural influences on these processes, which ultimately determine how institutions evolve and function in a society.

Since all human actions and reactions begin with a process of thinking, this Part of the book discusses how humans think and how such thinking affects human choices and behaviour.

In **Chapter 6** we look at the fascinating ways in which the human mind works. Thinkers, psychologists, philosophers, scientists, and social scientists have long been trying to figure out how humans think and behave, and we will review some of their theories and ideas. Human beings live in groups, be it the family, the community, or the society as a whole which form our social networks. And what we think as an individual is deeply influenced by what we believe others are thinking, which in turn is influenced by what they believe about what we believe, in a circular process of reinforcement. Thus, it is not only what one thinks as an individual which matters but also what we think collectively. In **Chapter 7**, looking through the prism of game theory, we study how social networks and social norms influence individual decision-making and simultaneously how we think collectively. Social norms, beliefs, and our mental models formed over time also significantly inform that process, and influence our thinking, and these are discussed in **Chapter 8**.

Our attention to issues of human thinking and behaviour is not only out of curiosity and academic interest. Meaningful insights into human behaviour can vastly improve the design and implementation of institutional arrangements and development policies. Indeed, they are crucial in determining how a society might move from Here to 'Denmark'. Better understanding of behavioural aspects can enable policymakers to design better policy and institutional interventions and greatly reduce chances of failure. That is the focus of our study in **Chapter 9**.

6

I Think—Therefore, I Am

6.1 Introduction

Adam Smith's insight, in the latter half of the eighteenth century, that 'It is not from the benevolence of the butcher, the brewer, or the baker that we expect our dinner, but from their regard to their own interest'[1] was as brilliant as it was stunning. It boldly stated that society did not need any central coordinator to make the economy work; the pursuit of self-interest by individual citizens would also benefit society as a whole, as if guided by an 'invisible hand'. However, it took another century and a half before modern economists Arrow, Debreu, and others formally proved that under some assumptions that 'competitive equilibrium exists, all individuals pursuing their self-interest lead society to an optimal state'[2].

One of their key underlying assumptions was that an individual is consistently rational and omniscient, can instantaneously process all information available to her and reach a final decision. She has complete self-control and is driven only by self-interest. In a light-hearted dig at you-know-who, Thaler and Sunstein call her a 'homo economicus', or the Econ. Thaler is an economist himself, a Nobel Prize winner at that. In effect, then, an Econ 'can think like Albert Einstein, store as much memory as IBM's Big Blue, and exercise the will power of Mahatma Gandhi'[3]. Somewhat like Captain Spock in the popular TV series *Star Trek*.

Let us distinguish the Econ from homo sapiens, or humans, that is, most of us, who are not blessed with these extraordinary qualities. Instead, humans display 'bounded rationality, bounded will power, and bounded self-interest'[4,5] Humans are not always rational. They don't have all the information at their fingertips and, in any case, can't process it all immediately and optimally. They also certainly give in to temptation (recall your last diet which was broken at the sight of a chocolate

From Here to Denmark. Rajat M. Nag and Harinder S. Kohli, Oxford University Press.
© Rajat Mohan Nag and Harinder Singh Kohli 2023. DOI: 10.1093/oso/9780198893103.003.0006

cake), and are also not always selfish and thus do not always act in their self-interest alone. Humans have emotions and morals, reciprocate with love and kindness, and can be altruistic. Sometimes they feel a certain way but inexplicably act in exactly the opposite way. Humans are also not only individuals unto themselves but members of a family, a society, and they are concerned about the welfare of others, and not themselves alone. And thus, their behaviour is also affected by social norms, culture, and collective beliefs. They use mental images (models) to make quick links from the present to the past.

Neoclassical economics does not deny such issues of human cognition and motivation. But they are treated as superficial and thus, considered to be a part of a 'black box' simplifying the 'messy and mysterious internal workings of actors'.[6] Free market stalwarts like Friedman gave the necessary intellectual cover for such a view. He boldly asserted that social and psychological factors need not be issues of concern in considering market outcomes,[7] and that 'there is only one social responsibility of business: to use its resources to engage in activities designed to increase its profits so long as it stays within the rules of the game, which is to say, engages in open and free competition without deception or fraud'.[8]

Following this logic, a key assumption often made by development economists and practitioners in the past (including us, the authors) has been that human behaviour is too complex to be incorporated in any formal economic policy decision-making, and that in any case the effects of these behavioural issues would probably cancel each other out when large numbers of people interact, as they do in markets. No doubt, such simplification in ignoring psychological and social influences on human behaviour helps in dealing with complex, macro policy issues. But it is also then incomplete and often leads to misleading policy prescriptions and inappropriate institutional designs.

Human thinking and thus behaviour is a complex interplay of emotions, 'contextual cues, local social networks and social norms, and shared mental models. All of these play a role in determining what individuals perceive as desirable, possible, or even "thinkable" for their lives'. Ignoring them is a serious lapse in the policymaking process. Rather difficult and incomplete as it might be, analysing behavioural drivers (like understanding how individuals think and how collective behaviours—such as widespread trust or widespread corruption—could develop in a society) would positively improve the processes of designing and implementing better policy and institutional architectures.[9]

To be fair, the caricature of the Econ is just that, 'a caricature', though not a wild exaggeration. It is not our intention to offer a detailed critique of Homo Economicus, but it serves our purpose to make the point that we will arrive at a better understanding of how we act and react if we describe our model of human behaviour more completely, that is, as humans rather than as Econs. That is the purpose of this and the next two chapters.

6.2 Thinking automatically and reflectively

In his 2002 Nobel Prize lecture, Kahneman posed a simple question: 'A bat and a ball cost $1.10 in total. The bat costs $1.00 more than the ball. How much does the ball cost?' Politely, Kahneman did not wait for an answer from his august audience. If you answered ten cents, you would be in good company. It appears to be *intuitively* logical. About 50 per cent of Princeton students and 56 per cent of students at the University of Michigan had given the same answer, but unfortunately it is wrong. The correct answer is five cents.[10]

What causes this frequent (and obvious when pointed out) error? The answer to this lies in our thinking process. Contrary to what we might wish to believe, we are not deliberative or reflective thinkers (carefully working out the pros and cons of our actions). In fact, most of our thinking is instinctive and automatic. But sometimes (as in answering the question above), our automatic thinking fails us when taking recourse to the reflective thinking would serve us better.

Psychologists and philosophers have long recognized these two systems of thinking: one that is automatic, unconscious, and fast; and the other, reflective, controlled, conscious, and slow. In the psychology literature they are respectively called System 1 and System 2.[11] System 1 operates almost instinctively; it is effortless and associative. On the other hand, System 2 is reflective, deliberative, and requires time and effort to process. It consciously considers options and is based on reasoning that requires concentration.[12,13]

Kahneman makes a further observation that 'although System 2 believes itself to be where the action is, System 1 is the hero. It effortlessly originates impressions and feelings that are the main sources of the explicit beliefs and deliberate choices of System 2'.[14] Though the terms Systems 1 and 2 are widely used in the literature, we will henceforth call them by a more common usage: automatic and reflective.

The automatic and reflective systems always interact, though the former runs automatically, constantly generating impressions, intuitions, intentions, and feelings to feed into the latter. Consider, for example, that instead of the bat and ball question, when our automatic system kicked in instinctively with our answer, we are asked, what's 17 x 24. Our automatic thinking realizes that answering this question needs more than a gut reaction and takes a back seat while the reflective thinking process takes over. Most of the time, the reflective system need not and does not react and is not called into action. It 'normally stays in a comfortable low-effort mode, in which only a fraction of its capacity is engaged'.[15]

The division of labour between the automatic and reflective system is incredibly efficient: the gut reactions of the former and its swift reactions to challenges are usually appropriate. Through an evolutionary process that is associative, parallel, and fast, it has learned what is needed for survival and this has served humans well. But for precisely this reason, it also has biases which can introduce systematic errors. Automatic thinking, for example, has little understanding of logic or statistics and tends to answer easier questions than originally asked (e.g. the bat and ball question). Thus, when things get more difficult and complex (multiply 17 x 24), the reflective system (rules-based, conscious, serial, and slow) takes over and makes the deciding call (even though there are several situations when people say 'this is a difficult call, I will go with my gut reaction').

Automatic thinking is key for our survival and has, as we just noted, an evolutionary heritage. Perhaps based on many unfortunate incidents, our ancestors learnt that it was safer to run as fast as one could upon seeing a yellow and black striped animal (later called a tiger) rather than stand there to reflect on whether it was just a large cat, or whether it really was hungry, looking for its next meal, and whether it would prefer to take home a human or another animal. That's probably how the human instinct to run for one's life developed and that's why automatic thinking has been hardwired into us for our survival. At the same time, automatic thinking can also lead us to make serious errors in choices for which a more reflective thinking mode would be desirable. The challenge then is to see if there are ways to 'nudge' the automatic thinking to pause and seek help from its reflective partner as and when appropriate.

6.3 Cognitive challenges in thinking reflectively

The above observations about the two systems of thinking have far-reaching policy and institutional implications. Public policies, rules, and regulations designed from assumptions of complete unbounded rationality (which Econs possess, but not humans) will automatically assume that people will use and analyse information in an unbiased and rational way. Further, it will be assumed that people will draw on their reflective systems, consciously pause to assess the options, weigh the pros and cons of their decisions, and take their time to decide what's best for them. But evidence shows that people under cognitive strain (be it due to poverty, time pressure or financial stress) often find it difficult to activate their reflective thinking, which leads them to make less-than-optimal life choices and decisions.

Consider the following:
A case study of sugar cane farmers in India revealed that they fared worse on a series of cognitive tests they took just before harvest (when their funds are low, they are worried about finding enough labourers to harvest their crop) than on similar tests taken after the harvest with these stress points removed. The study reported a striking finding: 'the difference in scores is roughly equivalent to three quarters of the cognitive deficit associated with losing an entire night's sleep'.[16]

Faced with a sudden need for funds for a medical emergency, the pre-harvest farmer would most likely go to the nearest moneylender to borrow at high rates rather than pause and systematically think through other possible more favourable alternatives. Similarly, if the school fees for her daughter fall due during this period, it is quite likely that the farmer will withdraw her from school rather than considering other possibilities, including going to the school principal and requesting more time to pay.

Treatment for many diseases, such as HIV/AIDS, around the world fails not necessarily because of unavailability of medicines but because of incomplete adherence to the treatment regimes. More often than not, it is not that the patient is not aware of the importance of strictly following the daily regime, but after a long and hard day, she is just too preoccupied and exhausted, and simply doesn't get around to taking her daily cocktail of pills.

Both are examples of the effects of the cognitive stress under which people cannot consciously draw on their reflective thinking to deliberate on the consequences of their actions and end up take the seemingly easy way out: borrow from the neighbourhood moneylender, withdraw the child from school, or skip the medicine at bedtime.

It follows that designing policy and institutional interventions assuming that individuals think reflectively and not automatically can easily go wrong. Many health campaigns are mounted on such a belief, with mass scale testing to detect a disease, say tuberculosis, made a priority. But, even when people are well aware of the risk of being infected, and the severe consequences of the illness, they might still not get the tests done. Reason: the immediate costs, inconvenience, or often the impossibility of taking time off from work to take the tests, and the burden of lost earnings. Thus, people will often forego the preventive measures in the face of these immediate obstacles, ignoring the possibility of long-term severe consequences.[17] This is a classic illustration of people thinking automatically and not reflectively, contrary to the implicit assumption made by policymakers in designing the programme to begin with.

6.4 Framing and salience of information

To be effective, the automatic thinking system has to be 'fast and frugal (using) simple rules in the mind's adaptive toolbox for making decisions with realistic mental resources', that is, bounded rationality.[18] The automatic system relies on a framework of understanding, partially based on one's own personal experiences in the past and partly perhaps imprinted on one's DNA as part of human evolution. Such a framework enables the automatic system to quickly and almost instinctively sift through a myriad of items of information to decide what is relevant for the issue at hand and what is not.

Consider a doctor in an emergency room having to make almost instantaneous life-and-death decisions on the immediate course of action she needs to take on a patient who has just been brought in in the throes of a heart attack. Using only three simple questions (systolic blood pressure less than 91, age greater than 62.5, and evidence of sinus tachycardia), a fast and frugal heuristics (framework or frames) was developed by Breiman and colleagues in the early 1990s which has performed remarkably well in most cases.[19]

Framing an issue thus defines a quick boundary (context) within which the automatic thinking system considers an issue. Without such a frame, the automatic system could not have functioned at all. However, in one's instinctive desire to be 'fast and frugal', frames may be drawn too narrowly, and an individual could thus ignore some relevant or key information in reaching a decision. Consider the example in the previous section of people forgoing tuberculosis testing in the face of some immediate obstacles, surely small relative to the possible serious consequences of delaying treatment, if the person's infection goes undetected for a while. Individuals frame the problem too narrowly, with serious negative consequences later. The same is true for the sugar cane farmer or the sick, young mother.

In drawing an appropriate frame (neither too narrow, so missing out on relevant information nor too broad, so as to hinder automatic thinking), the way the information is presented influences whether the mind perceives it as salient: 'a piece of information is salient when it stands out against other pieces of information'.[20] It follows that if the salience of an available piece of information is modified (either by downplaying or enhancing it) by the way it is presented, then it can influence the choice that the automatic thinking system makes. This has significant implications for policy and institutional designs.

Consider the following example from a field trial in the United States:[21] it is common in many countries for the poor to borrow money through what are called 'payday loans'. These are small, short-term, unsecured loans that are readily available but have very high interest rates. Usually, the borrowers are told only that the next instalment is due on the next payday at a fixed dollar amount. For example, for borrowing $100, they would pay $10 if repaid in two weeks, $20 if repaid in a month, and so on. The dollar amount to be repaid is thus the only salient information for the borrower, but she has no reference point to compare the alternatives. Automatic thinking would judge: well, I need the money, and

I am paying only $10 for it since I will pay it back on my next payday in two weeks' time. There is nothing for the reflective thinking to help with, since there is no other information, and the borrower applies too narrow a decision frame.

Now, suppose that, through a new law or regulation, lenders are required to tell the borrower not only how much she would have to pay back in two weeks, but also how much it would cost her if she borrowed on her credit card instead. Much to her surprise, she would find that she would have to pay much less: $1.50 (instead of $10) at say, a thirty-six-per-cent annual interest rate (usually) charged by the credit card company. This new information, which becomes more salient for the borrower, now enables her reflective thinking to kick in with a flashing message saying: 'Think! See if you can get the money from another source instead, like your credit card.' This small intervention of requiring that additional information on alternatives be provided, would also be much cheaper than other policy options to help the poor, say by offering subsidies on loans. As the study observes, 'seemingly minor and low-cost policy changes may have a large impact on the achievement of development goals and the reduction of poverty'.[22]

In the above example, the framing of the issue was changed by introducing a new piece of information. But the salience of an item of information can also be changed without making any demands for additional information, which might not always be available or might be difficult to meet (think of the political pressures that payday lenders could exert to block the proposed measure). This can be done by simply restating the available information differently. How an issue is framed matters.[23]

Consider this: during pre-surgery discussions, a surgeon, wishing to be very truthful, says, 'Out of one hundred people who have this operation, ten are dead after five years'. This sounds quite alarming, and so the automatic system quickly concludes that this is a rather risky proposition and the patient quickly takes his leave. Alternatively, suppose the surgeon says 'Well, 90 per cent of people are still alive after five years', the automatic system now hears the information quite differently and positively, even though the content of the message is the same. But the framing and the salience of the information regarding the surgery's risk has changed, and that makes all the difference for the automatic-thinking system.[24]

6.5 Anchoring

In his fascinating book *Thinking, Fast and Slow*, Kahneman describes an experiment he and his colleague Tversky undertook. They rigged a wheel of fortune so that it would stop only at 10 or 65. They then spun it in front of a group of students at the University of Oregon taken as their subjects and asked the students to write down the number at which the wheel stopped, which of course was one of the two numbers. They then asked them two questions: 'Is the percentage of African nations among UN members larger or smaller than the number you just wrote?' 'What is your best guess of the percentage of African nations in the UN?' Rationally, the spin of the wheel is totally irrelevant to answering the two questions. But it wasn't. The average estimates of those who saw 10 or 65 were 25 per cent and 45 per cent, respectively.[25]

Strange as it sounds, these results are not uncommon at all. As a matter of fact, many variations of this experiment have been conducted around the world with different audiences and they all yield similar results. Seemingly irrelevant information has a disproportionate influence on judgements. This is the phenomenon of the anchoring effect, an extreme form of automatic thinking. As Kahneman observes: 'what happens is one of the most reliable and robust results of experimental psychology: the estimates stay close to the' (*supposedly irrelevant*) 'number that people considered—hence the image of an anchor'.[26] Notice that the anchoring effect is similar in a way to the narrow framing phenomenon discussed in the previous section: unwittingly, our automatic thinking system lets the anchor define a range for the frame and thus narrows it, often leading to less-than-optimal decisions.

The anchoring effect is just as strongly felt in the real world. Anchors play an important role in how people decide on money matters, say when they decide how much to contribute to a cause. In a study assessing the environmental damage caused by oil spills in the Pacific, participants were asked about their willingness to contribute to save 50,000 offshore seabirds from such spills. Some were asked that question with a lead-in anchor sentence suggesting contributions of $5 or more. The control group was simply asked the question without an anchor. The results were striking. With the anchor group, the contributions averaged $20, while in the control group, contributions were over three times as high on average

($64). When the anchor was raised to $400, the offered contributions rose correspondingly, to $143.[27]

Similar anchoring effects were obtained in several other studies. In the heavily polluted region of Marseilles in France, for example, residents were asked what increases in the cost of living they would be willing to accept for living in a healthier, cleaner region. Results of the survey showed anchoring effects of over 50 per cent.[28]

Policymakers can effectively use the principles of the anchoring effect to help people under cognitive stress make better decisions. Such help becomes particularly important in helping the poor make better financial decisions, as in the case of the payday loans. Requiring the lenders to clearly display the significantly lower costs of alternative borrowing not only makes this new information more salient, but it also provides a new anchor for the poor borrower. She can now more rationally assess the very high cost of the payday loan and consider other possible options.

Consider another area of public policy: the awards for personal injury cases, which are often large. Medical and legal associations whose members—the doctors and the lawyers who are often the targets of malpractice suits—have often lobbied for legal caps on such awards. One could argue that such a cap would be beneficial for doctors. But the cap (say at $1 million) would now serve as an anchor, and while the larger awards would be ruled out, the smaller awards (which are perhaps also much more frequent) could now become much higher. Serious offenders would benefit, while the many less serious ones would suffer.[29]

6.6 Loss aversion, endowment effect, and the status quo bias

When Rajat arrived in Canada in the early seventies, credit cards had just been introduced and there was a major controversy around their usage. Many merchants were charging a surcharge for the use of the cards, since they had to pay a service fee to the issuing banks. Customers baulked at paying the surcharges (usually 3 per cent), and the issuing banks were unhappy too, since the use of their cards was then not 'free', as they had led people to believe. The banks ultimately agreed to let the merchants charge a higher price, provided this higher price ($103) was shown as the regular price and those paying cash would be seen as getting a discount of $3. Frankly, Rajat couldn't see what the fuss was about and concluded that it was just a ploy of the big banks to squeeze money out of unsuspecting people. But he hadn't heard of Kahneman or Tversky or Thaler. They were then working on some basic aspects of human behaviour, and one of these aspects was that people think of surcharges as out-of-pocket expenses, while discounts are simply the opportunity costs of foregone benefits. Of course, rationally the results are the same (that's what reflective thinking would say). But automatic thinking says 'No, paying the premium is giving up something I have (money in pocket); that's a loss, and I don't like it.'

Consider the famous mugs story: in hundreds of classes and real-life experiments, Thaler undertook his first (now famous) classroom experiment with twenty-two of his students at Cornell in 1985. He bought eleven coffee mugs with the Cornell insignia at the campus bookstore and placed them in front of alternate students in his classroom. They were gifts from him, thus, nobody had to pay anything for them. He asked students who had not been given a mug to closely inspect their neighbours' newfound wealth and then make an offer to buy it. Mug owners were asked to respond with their counteroffers. The results were striking: those who got the mugs (free) were reluctant to sell them at prices only slightly lower than the price of the mugs at the university bookstore, which they all were presumably well aware of,[30] whereas rationally one could argue that they should be willing to sell for any amount greater than zero.

Various versions of this experiment have been performed worldwide with strikingly similar conclusions: losses are roughly twice as painful as gains are pleasurable.

This is the phenomenon of loss aversion, and once again an illustration that framing matters, as it changes the salience of the relevant information which serves as the reference point. In assessing the change in value, the automatic system immediately asks: with respect to what? People look at changes from a reference point rather than absolute values. A loss hurts more than an equivalent gain (loss aversion) as we saw in our two examples above. No wonder, then, that we all love the perennial 'Grand Sale' where things marked down by 20 per cent are more appealing than the same product at the same (lower) price, but not on sale.[31]

Loss aversion arises from what is called the *endowment effect*: what you own is part of your endowment, and 'people valued things that were already part of their endowment more highly than things that could be part of their endowment that were available but not yet owned.'[32] People consider the money in their pocket as their endowment, and thus paying the $3 premium on credit card use as an out-of-pocket expense (an outflow) is not appealing. A regular price of $103 will be seen as just that, the price of the product being bought.

Another interesting feature of Thaler's mugs experiment was that not only were the mug-holders reluctant to sell, but the potential buyers were equally reluctant to buy and offered prices no more than half those at the university bookstore. While part of the reason for the low offers might have been a sense of envy at the windfall-gainers, they were also displaying what psychologists call *the status quo bias*. Having the mug in hand is now the new reference point for the new gainer. Equally, not having it is a reference point for those who didn't get one, and both are now reluctant to move from their present state, a bias in favour of the status quo. 'To do nothing is within the power of all men', quipped Samuel Johnson. Through a series of decision-making experiments, Samuelson and Zeckhauser found that individuals disproportionately stick with the status quo. Various studies around the world confirm that in making crucial life decisions, say on selection of health-care plans, retirement programmes, and various insurance schemes, status quo bias is substantial and often the default option for many, even if unintended.[33]

Again, concepts of loss aversion and status quo bias have very significant implications for public policy and institutional designs since they often work together as forces to inhibit change.

Loss aversion can also be an effective tool in motivating performance. Fryer et al. report an interesting experiment at nine schools in Chicago during the school year 2010–11.[34] At the beginning of the school year, teachers were randomly selected to participate in a 'pay for performance' programme. One set of teachers received a traditional bonus at the end of the year, linked to student achievement. Another group were given a lump sum payment at the beginning of the year with the proviso that they would have to return all or some of it at the end of the year if their students did not achieve predetermined performance targets. The results of this experiment were quite striking, very much in line with the expectation of the loss-aversion principle. Framing the incentive programme in terms of losses rather than gains leads to improved student outcomes. Teachers in the second group perceived the refund of a bonus as a loss of income and felt more motivated to ensure their students met performance standards. Fryer et al. found that the impacts are significant, increasing average teacher quality roughly by more than one standard deviation.

6.7 The pressing bias of the present: the intention–action divide

We began this chapter with a fundamental point: that humans have bounded willpower. Individuals thus consistently make inconsistent choices over time. The present is always more salient, even when the future benefits foregone are higher than the costs incurred now. Recall the avoidance of the tuberculosis test, discussed earlier. This is the bias of the present, which we know only too well; the tendency increases the farther we are from the deadline. It's more fun watching that tennis match right now, than finishing the assignment which is not due until next week anyway. Of course, the deliberative system can recognize the cost of succumbing to the present bias, but has limited capacity and often does not kick in.

Recall the new year resolutions we make, be it to shed those extra pounds or to quit smoking. And then the present bias kicks in: enjoy this piece of cake now and I will cut back even more tomorrow; have this smoke now (the dinner was so good) and promise I will go without any tomorrow. The deliberative system could have controlled these impulses of the automatic, but by the time it kicks in, the cake or the smoke has already been enjoyed. Damage done.

The pressing present bias wins, resulting in what is referred to as the intention-action divide, with potential negative consequences in the future. Recognizing this phenomenon of present bias, conscious policy interventions are enacted that 'create reminders, or remove small impediments in such areas as savings, adherence to health regimens, and voting in elections have had successes in narrowing intention-action divides'.[35]

6.8 Choice architecture and nudges

While it is reassuring to know that once it kicks in, our reflective thinking deliberates on the possible options and consequences of an action, bear in mind that it 'works on data that is retrieved from memory, in an automatic and involuntary operation of the automatic thinking'.[36] The reflective thinking does not have access to any independent data source or information other than what the automatic thinking process feeds it. It stands to reason then that the simpler the presentation of options, or use of anchors to make one option more salient than another, the easier it will be for the automatic thinking process to feed better information to the reflective thinking system when it takes over. This is the essence of choice architecture.[37]

Note that the reflective system, by its very nature, is lazy. It prefers to stay in the background, saving its energy for later when the automatic system, unable to come to some quick conclusions or decisions, calls upon it. A good choice architecture is a simple architecture. By simplifying the options, a good choice architecture encourages the automatic thinking system to co-opt the reflective thinking sooner than it might otherwise have done, leading to better decisions.

For example, with a better choice architecture highlighting that the payday loan is substantially more expensive than other alternatives, the stressed young American mother can make a more informed and better choice for her borrowing, as can the sugar cane farmer about keeping her child in school or not.

But even with a better choice architecture which makes it easier for an individual to judge which would be a better option for her to choose, it does not necessarily follow that she will follow through with action. Recall the intention-action divide we had discussed in the previous section. This is where a 'nudge' comes in handy.

Consider long distance driving, particularly at night. Drivers may doze off and wander into oncoming traffic. The occasional speed bumps on an otherwise not too busy highway would rattle the car and wake up the dozing driver who would then hopefully take a coffee break. Putting in the speed bumps on a smooth road is a nudge and can save lives.[38]

A nudge, according to its originators Thaler and Sunstein, is 'any aspect of the choice architecture that alters people's behaviour in a predictable way without forbidding any options or significantly changing their economic incentives.'[39] Notice what a nudge is not: it is not a mandate for people to do this or that. It does not force, forbid, penalize, nor does it reward any particular choices. However, it 'influences choices in a way which will make choosers better off, as judged by themselves'[40] and it works by suggesting a particular choice by changing the default option, the salience of a particular information, the anchor, or the reference point.

Nudges help humans do what they have always wished for, but somehow never did. It follows then that to be effective, a nudge must also be easy to do, but since it is not a mandate, must also be easy to avoid. Thus, 'putting the fruit at eye level counts as a nudge. Banning junk food does not.'[41]

Consider human organ donations. Many would like to do this, but registering for it is not always a pleasant task and more often than not, not easy. Most countries adopt an opt-in policy, where donors have to explicitly sign in. In other words, fill in forms to register in the donor registry. Easier said than done. Recognizing this human inertia (the intention–action divide), several countries in Europe (Spain, Portugal, and France among them) provide opt-out features: you are presumed to have given consent unless you explicitly opt out. In a comparison of deceased organ donor rates worldwide, countries with opt-out legislation tended to have much higher rates (about twenty-three people per million population) than those with opt-in legislation (about fourteen).[42] But even this presumed consent process isn't as simple as it sounds. Medical staff still often double-check with family members who may have other preferences and often might not even know the wishes of the donor: whether they had really wanted to donate or had simply done nothing (which is what most people do). Thus, even though more effective than the opt-in provision, the opt-out option is not an effective nudge, as it is not quite so easy and straightforward in implementation.

A more effective nudge is a variation of the opt-in policy tried in some states (Illinois, Alaska, Montana among them) in the USA: at the time of renewing their driving licence, people are asked whether they wish to be an organ donor. If they do, their wish is recorded on the driving licence itself. Simple and easy: hence, a nudge.[43]

6.9 Summary

Standard neoclassical models of economic behaviour are based on a fundamental assumption of perfect and unbounded rationality of individual consumers and producers, labelled 'homo economicus', or Econs. But, in reality, homo sapiens, or humans, (i.e. most of us) are not blessed with these extraordinary qualities. On the contrary, humans display bounded rationality, bounded willpower, and bounded self-interest. Since all human actions and behaviour are influenced by the process of thinking, it is important to model this process based on this reality of boundedness. Assuming humans to be Econs can lead to misleading and erroneous policy prescriptions and institutional designs.

Psychologists have long recognized that human thinking is a function of two simultaneous processes: one that is automatic, instinctive, unconscious, and fast; and the other reflective. controlled, conscious, and slow. These two processes always interact, the former constantly generating impressions and intuitions which feed into the latter. The automatic system intuitively draws on an evolutionary pool of data hardwired into our minds and using default options and mental shortcuts produces adequately well-adapted decisions with minimal effort. The reflective system, on the other hand, is more deliberative: it consciously weighs the nuances of various options before deciding on one.

Evidence shows that under cognitive strain, people often find it difficult to think reflectively, leading them to make less-than-optimal life choices and decisions. Under such stress, people frame their choices too narrowly, not consciously considering other, better options.

Irrational as it might seem to the Econ, humans often act irrationally. Incorporating this reality into public-policy decisions, some seemingly minor and low-cost policy changes can have large impacts in achieving better development outcomes. Consider, for example, the trait of status quo bias, a built-in reluctance to not move away from the present. Crucial life decisions are deeply influenced by such phenomena.

'Now' is always more salient even when the future benefits foregone are higher than the costs incurred now. This bias also leads to the intention–action divide, where the intention to do something now doesn't always get translated into action.

Most humans find these realities of their thinking and subsequent action (or the lack of it) as fairly serious impediments in making the right choices. While the automatic system serves humans well, they could also veer towards the less-than-optimal choices without having recourse to the reflective system, particularly in complex decisions with longer-term consequences. In such situations, a nudge may help. Simple but suitable public policy and institutional changes, many of which can be seemingly minor and low-cost, can help a society do better. By better framing, a nudge can influence how the automatic-thinking system might recognize different salient points and seek more readily the help of its reflective partner to make more reasoned and better choices.

7

We Think—Therefore, We Are

7.1 Introduction

Anthropologists have long recognized that we are shaped by the society around us. We are group-minded individuals, and we act and behave as members of a group. Our individual set of beliefs, behaviours, and actions is significantly influenced by others in our group, for example, our family, community, and society. These human predispositions, human sociality, define us. While we each have our own traits and preferences and natural dispositions, we also see the world from a social perspective.

As discussed in previous chapters, much of neoclassical economics is based on the fundamental assumption that people are both rational and selfish. And the working of the 'invisible hand' assured us that we need not feel any pangs of conscience for such behaviour either, as our individual pursuit of self-interest will also be to the benefit of society. Robinson, a passionate critic of neoclassical economics (and often labelled the Rational Rebel), summarized it succinctly and with some sarcasm: 'By this means, the moral problem is abolished. The moral problem is concerned with the conflict between the individual interest and the interest of society. And this doctrine tells us that there is no conflict; we can all pursue our self-interest with a good conscience.'[1]

But we know from our own actions and behaviours that we are not always rational, nor are we concerned only about maximizing our own welfare with never a care for others. We value our social relationships, and more often than not cooperate with our neighbours, treat them fairly, and expect the same in return. We are not islands unto ourselves, and thus recognize the value of collective actions, knowing that our lives are better because of the collective efforts of others in our society and that we could not have done it all on our own. We value group identity and take pride in our own social status and place in the social hierarchy. We tend to respect

From Here to Denmark. Rajat M. Nag and Harinder S. Kohli, Oxford University Press.
© Rajat Mohan Nag and Harinder Singh Kohli 2023. DOI: 10.1093/oso/9780198893103.003.0007

and live by common rules of behaviour and social norms, sometimes even at some personal cost. Essentially, what others think, expect, and do influences our own preferences and decisions. Human sociality is 'like a river running through society, it is a current that is constantly, if often imperceptibly, shaping individuals'[2] and thus has significant bearing on how social norms and behaviours emerge which in turn influence the nature of institutions which take shape in that society.

The analysis of interactive rationality and social behaviour is governed by such interactions with others in society and our reactions to each other's 'rational' actions. To be effective, policymakers thus need to recognize these aspects of human sociality, value the need for social coordination, and build them into appropriate policy designs and institutional interventions. Some basic elements of game theory will be useful for understanding how individuals coordinate their behaviours and actions in various social settings and we will bring them in as needed.

7.2   Focal points as a social coordinating device

In 1960, Schelling authored his classic *The Strategy of Conflict*,[3] which laid out some insightful applications of game theory to the issue of nuclear war.[4] But, of course, the influence of his work extended well beyond that limited area of national security, critically important as it was. Myerson, who won the Nobel Prize in Economics in 2007 (two years after Schelling), went so far as to say that 'Schelling's focal-point effect needs to be understood as one of the great foundational ideas of social philosophy.'[5]

A key element of Schelling's enquiry was how people might be able to coordinate their behaviour. And such coordination is necessary for a society to generate social changes for the greater welfare of its members, even when they are unable to directly communicate with each other.

He posits a scenario where a couple lose each other in a department store. What would they do? (And this was in the pre-cell phone days, so no marks for the easy answer: call). Schelling argues that the relevant question is not 'what would I do if I were she', but 'what would I do if I were she, wondering what she would do if she were I, wondering what I would do if I were she?'[6] His insight is the need to 'coordinate predictions, read the same message in the common situation, and identify the one course of action that their expectations of each other can converge on.[7] Perhaps, the last time they had been to this store they had enjoyed an ice cream at the fifth-floor parlour, and both had commented what a special treat it was and that would be what the other partner would think too and thus that would be the place to look first. Schelling continues that 'we cannot be sure they will meet, nor would all couples read the same signal; but the chances are certainly a great deal better than if they pursued a random course of search.'[8]

The ice cream parlour in this example is the 'focal point',[9] providing a clue for the couple to coordinate their behaviour by. This may sound like wishful thinking, and Schelling himself admits that finding a focal point 'may depend more on imagination than on logic, more on poetry or humour than on mathematics'.[10] But the fact is that more often than not, it works and serves as a useful and efficient social coordinating device.

Schelling had proposed several experiments to test his proposition, and many of them have been repeated around the world with similar conclusions.[11] An oft-quoted example is Schelling's own experiment, which runs as follows: you and your friend have agreed to meet tomorrow (in New York City), but before you could discuss where and when, the phone line goes dead, and you can't reach her any more. Where and when will you meet?

7.2.1 The meeting game

Schelling found that his experiment 'showed an absolute majority managing to get together at Grand Central Station (information booth), and virtually all of them succeeded in meeting at 12 noon'.[12] We ran some very informal experiments on our own and the results were very similar. Of course, depending on the city, age, and preferences, the choice of meeting place and time varied, but similar groups generally converged. Our friends usually chose quieter places and reasonably early hours in the day, as distinct from our much younger nephews and nieces, who chose to meet late in the evening and at some popular (and rather noisy) disco.

People were able to think of some clue which enabled them to coordinate their behaviour. The memory of a happy visit to the ice cream parlour, all our trains bring us to Grand Central and that's where we usually meet, and so on. In each case, such triggers were the focal points. Just to repeat, the issue of concern is not what a person would pick as her own preference or first instinct, but her expectation of what others would pick who, in turn, would think what she would be expecting others to do, and so on.

7.3 Nash equilibrium

It would be interesting to ask ourselves why we are so keen on focal points. What do focal points help us achieve? Put simply, focal points help us to get to a state of equilibrium (referred to in game theory as the Nash equilibrium) 'where nobody can profit by deviating (unilaterally) unless somebody else deviates first. At such a state, each player will be using a strategy that is a best reply to the strategies of the other players.'[13] Society as a whole is better off in such a state, where each member is as well off as possible without harm to anybody else. This is thus a desirable state for a society to aspire to in the journey from Here to Denmark where collectively the members of that society are better off than not.

Note that an equilibrium need not be unique. Multiple equilibrium points are possible. The couple who got lost in the department store could choose any number of places to look for each other. Each such place (the Lost and Found section in the basement, the Perfumery on the ground floor, or the ice cream parlour on the fifth floor) could be an equilibrium, provided both partners chose the same one. Otherwise, they would make several, fruitless rounds of the various floors. In the Meeting Game, any number of places and any reasonable (or unreasonable) hour would be an equilibrium so long as both friends chose the same. And this is where Schelling's insight of a 'focal point' is relevant: to help people coordinate their actions, guide them to a choice which they all converge on, where each is better off individually and collectively.

7.3.1 The island game

Let us illustrate this with another simple but very relevant example called the Island Game.[14] Consider an island. Two people (strangers to each other and each with a car among their belongings) arrive on this

uninhabited island with good roads and hospitable surroundings—
with plans to settle there.[15] One of the first issues they will have to resolve: which side of the road will they drive on? It doesn't matter which
side they choose as long as it is the same. This game thus has two equilibria: both choose left, or both choose right. A right/left combination will
be disastrous. This is where a focal point can be helpful in converging to
an agreement (a unique equilibrium). If both are, say, from Thailand, it is
natural that they will agree to drive on the left. Similarly, if both are from
the USA, they will instinctively drive on the right. In either case, they will
arrive at a safe, unique equilibrium. But if one is from Thailand and the
other from the US, their individual reference frameworks might not be of
much use and they will either have to find other means of coordination or
they will be stuck in a bad equilibrium, with frequent accidents.

7.3.2 The crown game

Consider another interesting game: The Crown Game.[16] You are seated in
a circle with a group of strangers, each with a prominent name tag. Each
player is asked to write down the name of any one person in the group.
If everyone chooses the same name, everyone gets $100. You can even
write your own name if you believe that others will choose you too. But
if people write different names, then nobody gets anything. But just before the game starts, someone walks in and places a big, shiny crown on
one player's head and walks away. Who do you think you and the others
would choose? To win, the players need to coordinate. And with nothing
else to go by, they might as well coordinate by naming the person with the
crown. A focal point has been created.

As Myerson notes, the crown by itself has no intrinsic effect on the pay-
off structure of the game, 'but it may affect each player's rational decision
by affecting his expectations about what others will do'.[17] However, some
very relevant questions on legitimacy and fairness about the choice of the
person who was crowned may be raised, which we ignore for now.[18]

The large and prominent Meeting Point signs at airports and many
shopping malls serve the same purpose: they create a focal point. Of
all the places you may think you could find your partner who you have
lost in the crowd (café, bookshop, florist ... all are valid choices and thus

possible equilibrium points, provided you both choose the same), the Meeting Point sign serves as a lighthouse beacon. It is more than likely that it is where you will find yourself going to meet your partner, expecting her to do the same. In each of the examples above and generally in life too, multiple equilibria are possible, and focal points essentially help in steering the participants to one of them as a possible and unique equilibrium.[19]

However, it also needs to be recognized that a focal point might not always be unique. Schelling's work shows 'that the process by which we convert cues from the environment into a choice of a coordination strategy is largely unconscious'.[20] Essentially, the focal point reflects human psychological capacity to guess how others might react to a given situation, particularly people from similar cultural backgrounds following similar conventions. There is also a growing body of thought that this concept might be evolutionary in nature.[21,22,23] Thus, even though multiple focal points may be possible (in which case they won't be so useful in choosing a unique equilibrium point), it is likely that people of similar backgrounds might choose the same focal point after their mental deliberations. The point here is that Schelling's focal point will not necessarily work all the time, a fact that Schelling himself recognized. 'It is not being asserted that they will always find an obvious answer to the question; but the chances of their doing so are ever so much greater than the bare logic of abstract random probabilities would ever suggest.'[24]

Just as an equilibrium need not be unique, it also might not always be a socially desirable outcome. In the next chapter, we cite the example of the traffic chaos that Rajat frequently faces near his home in Gurgaon. Each driver gets into the intersection believing that's the only way to make his way through, which inevitably results in a logjam. The focal-point approach in this case brings them all to enter the intersection simultaneously, leading to chaos: obviously a situation of bad equilibrium.

Just like the group of drivers in this example, entire societies can get stuck in collective patterns of behaviour, leading them to bad equilibria. The challenge for a society then is to see if there are possible interventions to nudge them out of such situations. While not easy, since such shifts need a change in the beliefs and norms in a group or society, these situations are not always impervious to change, either. Some interventions can shift a pattern of behaviour, say corruption, or racial segregation, which is obviously detrimental to the welfare of the society, to another, better equilibrium.

7.4 Challenges of collective action and social dilemmas

Societies often face collective-action problems. Consider what is generally referred to as the tragedy of the commons, illustrating the well-known free-rider problem implicit in the collective actions of a society. In a classic paper published in 1968, American ecologist Hardin suggested the following: picture a pasture open to all. As a rational individual, each herdsman seeks to maximize his gain. By adding one more animal to his herd, he gains the direct benefit of feeding it for free, but does not individually bear the cost of that overgrazing. So, he adds another and then another. But, of course, every other herdsman sharing the commons makes the same calculation too, and as Hardin says: 'Therein is the tragedy. Each man is locked into a system that compels him to increase his herd without a limit—in a world that is limited. Ruin is the destination toward which all men rush, each acting in his own best interest.'[25]

Consider the global emission challenge: another classic example of the tragedy of the commons. Though here it is not a question of extracting something from the commons but putting in something undesirable— noxious fumes into the air, or sewage and toxic chemicals into the water. The challenge of the free-rider problem is the same. The polluter (be it an individual or a country) finds that 'his share of the cost of the wastes he discharges into the commons is less than the cost of purifying his wastes before releasing them. Since this is true for everyone, we are locked into a system of "fouling our own mess", so long as we behave only as independent, rational free enterprisers.'[26] Each person individually (the herdsman, the polluter) is a free rider: taking in the benefits and avoiding the costs, but ultimately everyone is worse off.

These are challenges we often face as a community but fail to resolve satisfactorily with each actor acting in her self-interest, rational as it might be, where collectively we are all worse off.[27] To put this in an analytical framework, let us again start with a bit of game theory, the analysis of interactive rationality and social behaviour.

7.4.1 Prisoner's dilemma

Social dilemma essentially arises as the clash between 'individual rationality' (to maximize one's own welfare) and 'collective rationality' (to maximize the collective welfare). First conceptualized in 1950, by two scientists, Flood and Dresher, of the RAND Corporation, in the context of some studies of Cold-War strategic interactions, this dilemma was illustrated by Tucker, a Canadian mathematician, in a game, the prisoner's dilemma. The dilemma was an appropriate metaphor for the Cold War, where two blocks (east and west) are in conflict (each exerting their political influence), while sharing a common interest (preserving global peace). Over time, this game has become a classic in social dilemma research and an anchor in game-theoretic literature.[28]

Consider the game: the police have arrested two individuals (Players 1 and 2) suspected of a serious crime, but the proof they have is only enough to convict them of a lesser charge. The only way that the police can convict them of the serious charge is by getting a confession. The game runs as follows: the players are put in separate rooms with no means of communicating with each other and are told that if Player 1 confesses and Player 2 does not, then the former will get off lightly (and thus get, say, one year in prison), but the latter will be convicted based on his mate's confession and thrown in jail for five years. Of course, the same applies the other way around too. If both confess, each will be convicted based on the other's confession; but as a reward for their cooperation, their sentence will be reduced to four years in prison. However, if neither confesses, they will be convicted of a minor theft, and each will spend two years in jail.

Let's put the above pay-offs in a simple 2×2 matrix; see Figure 7.1.

In game-theory parlance, the two actions of the players are generally termed 'cooperate' and 'defect'. In this game, the two players 'cooperate' with each other when they deny; they 'defect' from each other when they confess.

What should the players do, given that the pay-off for the action of each depends on the action of the other? Each knows what the other knows, and it is assumed that each will act rationally to maximize his individual pay-off. For each player individually, the best option would be to confess (only one year in jail), but this would hold only if the other

		Player 2	
		Deny	Confess
	Deny	2, 2	5, 1
Player 1			
	Confess	1, 5	4, 4

Figure 7.1 Prisoner's dilemma (years in jail)

doesn't. His worst option would be to deny while his partner confesses (five years in jail). He knows, of course, that the best option for both collectively would be for neither to confess, as they would both then get only two years in jail.

However, neither can confidently assume that the other won't confess, and hence the dilemma. What if he denies but his accomplice confesses? He is then worse off. Safer then that he confesses. However, the accomplice is going through the same thought process, and both end up confessing and each gets sentenced to four years in jail. Thus, a rational strategy for each individually turns out to be detrimental for them collectively. They would both have been better off if neither confessed.

The situation (Confess, Confess) is a Nash equilibrium which results when no single player can do better by unilaterally shifting to a different strategy. In the prisoner's dilemma example, if Player 1 unilaterally deviates to Deny, while Player 2 remains at Confess, Player 1 is worse off with a pay-off of five years in jail. Player 2 would face a similar fate if he unilaterally deviated. Thus, it is in their individual interest to stay in this Nash equilibrium state, that is, both confess; but obviously, it is a 'bad equilibrium' for both, since collectively the players are each worse off than if they had both denied.

This is the social dilemma: doing what appears to be best for the individual would not be so for the society as a whole and ultimately, neither would it be for the individuals. This is also in essence the argument in Sen's insightful analysis of what he called the 'Rational Fools':[29] people in a group, each acting 'rationally' in their supposed self-interest, are in fact being foolish, because they are then collectively and thus also individually worse off.

Another important insight from the prisoner's dilemma game is that you should 'in deciding your own strategy, be aware of other people's rationality'.[30] One reason why many well-intentioned, public pro-grammes fail to perform as hoped (e.g. massive leakages in India's public food-distribution system) is precisely this: failure to anticipate the reactions of the intended beneficiaries and the agents who will be responsible for implementing the programmes.

7.5 We are humans, after all

As discussed earlier, much of neoclassical economics is based on the fundamental assumption that people are rational, selfish, and consistent over time. In game theory parlance, this implies that we are programmed to do what we rationally consider is best for us individually, not care for others, and that our tastes do not change. Defection, rather than cooperation, is thus the dominant strategy in the prisoner's dilemma game—as is free riding in the case of public goods. As Dawes and Thaler note, 'People are assumed to be clever enough to figure out that defection or free riding is the dominant strategy and are assumed to care nothing for outcomes to other players; moreover, people are also assumed to have no qualms about their failure to do "the right thing" '.[31]

But does the above really describe us? Do the above scenarios always hold true in practice? Most of us would say NO. Yes, we can be and often are selfish, but we are also altruistic at times: we reciprocate kindness; we cooperate. People give to charity, families support each other, a complete stranger jumps into the lake to save a drowning child, people donate blood, and the list goes on. And these are not just wishful thinking. Bicchieri observes that 'almost 50 years of experiments on social dilemmas show cooperation rates ranging from 40 percent to 60 percent, and everyday experience shows people making voluntary contributions to public goods, giving to charities, volunteering, and refraining from wasting resources'.[32]

Almost all of us have experienced this generosity during the Covid 19 pandemic. Selfless volunteers and innumerable good Samaritans showed up for humanity. Hirshleifer sums it up well: 'From the most primitive to the most advanced societies, a higher degree of cooperation takes place than can be explained as a merely pragmatic strategy for the egoistic man.'[33]

Game theorists have devised some experimental games to explore and test some of these features of human social behaviour. Let's consider some.

7.5.1   Reciprocity

Since, by their very nature, use of public and collective goods cannot be restricted (common grazing ground, for example), it is a key axiom that in a world of Econs, people will not cooperate to arrive at an optimal use pattern; instead, working in their self-interest, they will try to take advantage of others (be free riders). But as Bicchieri and Hirshleifer have noted, experiments on social dilemmas display a fair bit of cooperation. Interestingly, experiments also show that people are not willing to play suckers; they will tend to reward those who cooperate but punish those who do not, even if doing so hurts them as well. This is the essence of reciprocity, and the Ultimatum Game below is designed to test this phenomenon.

7.5.1.1 The ultimatum game
In this experimental game, two parties play anonymously– Player 1 is the proposer and Player 2 is the respondent. Player 1 is given an endowment and then asked to give some of it to the second player. Player 2 has a binary choice: accept or reject the offer. If she accepts the offer, both players walk away with their share of the endowment. But if she rejects the offer, neither player gets anything, and the endowment is returned to the experimenter.

The self-interest hypothesis would suggest that Player 1 should offer a bare minimum and maximize her share of the endowment, and Player 2 should accept any amount offered: it's a windfall, anyway.

Interestingly, results of this experiment conducted all over the world show a different and reasonably consistent result. Under varying conditions and with varying amounts of money, proposers routinely offer to give away substantial amounts (50 per cent being the most frequent offer), and respondents frequently reject offers below 30 per cent.[34]

An interesting insight on this Ultimatum Game follows if the game is tweaked a bit: if the low offers are made by a computer instead of a human proposer, they are rarely rejected. It follows then that the low offers from human players must have been perceived to be unfair and selfish, and thus rejected by the respondents. The actual amount offered is not the reason. It is the uncooperative attitude of the proposer which the responder, finds unacceptable, and is willing to punish her (the proposer) even if it means that she (the respondent) herself loses as well.[35]

7.5.2   Altruism

7.5.2.1 The dictator game

As in the Ultimatum Game, Player 1 (the dictator) is given an endowment and she has to unilaterally decide how much she wishes to share with the second player. The second player must accept whatever she is offered.

If the Econ model applies, one would expect the dictator to offer a minimal amount. However, results of many rounds of this game played all over the world again offer a different conclusion: the dictators do not always choose the most selfish outcome. As a matter of fact, literature suggests the amounts are 'nontrivial; roughly 20 percent of the endowment'.[36] There are a few challenges and caveats to this experiment but largely it goes on to show that people are altruistic and behave in non-rational ways.

7.5.3   The conditional cooperators and the tit for tat strategy

Let us revisit the tragedy of the commons. To do so, we look at a slightly different game, the Public Goods Game, to test the hypothesis that people always freeride and see how others confront the free riders. We will look at three versions of this game and find some very interesting conclusions emerging from each.

7.5.3.1 The public goods (trust) game version 1: single trial experiments

A group of players, usually between four and ten in number, are each given an initial endowment. Players can keep the money and go home, or they can invest some or all of it in a common pool for a public good. The experimenter doubles whatever has been put in the common pool and distributes it equally among all participants. Thus, in an experiment with four people with an initial endowment of, say, $10 each, the best outcome would be if everyone contributes their entire endowment, creating a common pool of $40, which the experimenter doubles to $80, and each player then goes home with $20. However, if one of the players decides to freeride and puts in only half her endowment, then each player will end up with $17.50. The free rider of course also gets the same share and takes home $22.50 in total, while the other three take home only $17.50. Obviously, the worst outcome for all is that no one puts any money into the common pool.

To remove any unforeseen biases, this single-trial experiment has been conducted with several variations: in terms of size of group (four to eighty), subjects playing for the first time, repeat players, and varying amounts as financial stakes. Results from each variation have been similar.

The logic of tragedy of commons would predict that acting in her self-interest, the dominant strategy for each player would be to defect, that is, not contribute anything to the common pool. However, the results of these experiments were strikingly different. Typically, there are substantial contributions to the common, public good pool: about 40–60 per cent of the initial endowment.[37] Marwell and Ames report similar results with one interesting (shall we say, revealing) exception: in an experiment conducted with economics graduate students at the University of Wisconsin, the contribution rate fell to 20 per cent (cheekily reported in their article titled 'Economists Free Ride: Does Anyone else?'[38]

7.5.3.2 The public goods (trust) game version 2: multiple trial experiments
This is the same as version 1, excepting that the experiment is repeated several times, usually ten.

7.5.3.3 The public goods (trust) game version 3: multiple trial experiments in two phases
This is the same as version 2, except that after the first ten rounds, players are told that they will repeat the same experiment for another ten rounds.

Very interesting results emerge. In version 2, the contribution rate remains high for the first few rounds (around 53 per cent, well within the 40 per cent to 60 per cent range), but then drops off sharply to less than

20 per cent.[39] However, in version 3, the levels of contribution went up again, almost to the earlier levels.[40]

A key conclusion of these three games is that contrary to the expectation of the tragedy of the commons, people do not always freeride: they also cooperate and reciprocate. Thus, in version 1, the level of cooperation is high. Cooperation is the dominant strategy, with everyone expecting others to do the same. But in version 2, after a few rounds, when the cooperators realize that not everyone is playing fairly, they punish the non-cooperators by reducing their own cooperation, even if they also lose in the process, since everyone's collective outcome now gets worse. They now reciprocate hostility with hostility, defection with defection. Free riding is now the dominant strategy, but as we saw in the tragedy of the commons, ultimately everyone is worse off. In version 3, playing the next round of the same games, the free riders have realized that their non-cooperation has been noticed and is resulting in a less favourable outcome for them, and thus decide to switch back to play the game in a more cooperative spirit. The collective contributions to the common pool thus go up again.

Based on the above (and the results of a computer-based global competition to find the best strategy to solve an iterated prisoner's dilemma game which is essentially version 3 of the Public Goods Game), Axelrod drew out a very powerful and effective strategy for mutual cooperation, *Tit for tat*: start with a cooperative move and thereafter do what the other player did on the previous move.[41] Three important features of this strategy are clear: be nice to begin with, but don't get taken to be weak; however, also be forgiving (respond only to the other player's last move, not what she did on earlier ones). Essentially, people are 'conditional cooperators': they cooperate if others do but are not willing to play suckers. They are willing to hit back at free riders, even at the cost of their own loss of welfare.

Interestingly, this phenomenon holds true across all societies. In an experiment conducted in Colombia and Vietnam in 2013, and compared with results from six developed countries, researchers found that while the proportion of free riders varied (from under 5 per cent in Colombia to about 35 per cent in Japan), in no country do free riders dominate.[42] The idea of conditional cooperation has particular relevance for dealing with major dilemmas societies often face, like managing the commons, as discussed next.

7.6 Managing the commons

Managing the commons at global, national, or community level presents pressing social dilemmas. An American political economist, Ostrom (1933–2012), devoted her long and distinguished academic life to this enquiry: can societies arrive at self-governing models of governing the commons without an overpowering, overwhelming sovereign (the Leviathan)? Her short answer: yes, and her conclusions were based on groundbreaking fieldwork conducted all over the world on the management of common pooled resources (CPR), for which she was awarded the Nobel Prize in Economic Sciences in 2009.

Among the many instances of managing the commons that Ostrom looked at, we draw on four: forests in the mountains of Switzerland and Japan, and irrigation systems in Spain and the Philippines. What makes these examples particularly interesting is how long these commons have existed—between 300 and 800 years, and thus, findings from their performances cannot be ignored on count of temporary, special factors. Significant opportunities existed in each of these cases for people to violate the rules and reap significant benefits, and yet 'given the temptations involved, the high levels of conformance to the rules in all these cases have been remarkable'.[43]

While the cases differ significantly from each other in their physical settings, economic and social backgrounds, and thus their operational rules, they share four striking similarities: i) local collective management; ii) operational rules are decided by the beneficiaries and implemented and closely monitored by them directly (or by staff hired by them); iii) graduated sanctions; and iv) the rights of the locals to devise their own institutions to manage the commons, which are not challenged by external governmental authorities. Similar successes from locally managed CPR systems are also seen in more contemporary studies.[44,45] An interesting finding from all these studies is that conditional cooperators were more successful in managing the commons. Voluntary cooperation is a key element of sustainable commons management but with the assurance that others will cooperate as well, and the participants were willing to invest in costly behaviour monitoring to ensure cooperation.

7.7 Motivations for cooperation in society

Under what conditions will cooperation emerge in society? This is a fundamental question with significant implications for human progress, indeed, for survival and development of effective institutions. Scholars and philosophers have reflected on this issue for centuries. Writing more than three centuries back in 1651, Hobbes had a rather pessimistic view. He believed that cooperation is not a natural instinct for selfish individuals; and without a strong, central power, people would compete on such ruthless terms that life ultimately would be 'solitary, poor, nasty, brutish, and short'.[46]

Hume, one of the greatest humanists of all time, had a much kinder view of human nature and rejected the view that selfishness is our basic human condition and wrote almost a century after Hobbes in 1740, 'I feel pleasure in doing good to my friend because I love him, but do not love him for the sake of that pleasure'.[47]

Smith's view of human nature, widely misunderstood as being rather bleak à la Hobbes, was actually more akin to Hume's, expressing very similar views as the latter: 'How selfish soever man may be supposed, there are evidently some principles in his nature, which interest him in the fortune of others, and render their happiness necessary to him, though he derives nothing from it except the pleasure of seeing it'.[48]

Results of the experiments we reported earlier, and Axelrod's tit for tat strategy, are essentially consistent with Hume's and Smith's view. Most people are conditional co-operators, willing to cooperate with those who cooperate themselves but punish those who don't. This is an encouraging conclusion and seems to hold across cultures, as seen in Ostrom's research.

However, lest we have given the impression of unbridled optimism and naïve faith in virtuous human nature, it is instructive to remember one of the opening sentences of Axelrod's book, referred to above: 'We all know that people are not angels'.[49] A similar note of caution is expressed by

Ostrom et al. (1992) in discussing the results of the various experiments on reciprocity and cooperation (some of which are included above): 'We cannot replace the determinate prediction of *no cooperation* with a determinate prediction of *always cooperate*' (italics in original).[50] It would be fair to assert, however, that all observations, in experiments and in real life, successfully refute the rather extreme and bleak Hobbesian conclusion that order is possible only with the presence of a sovereign who would impose strict rules and impose sanctions on those who would not comply because 'covenants without the sword are but words and of no strength to secure a man at all'.[51]

The idea of conditional cooperation has important implications for what we had earlier called social dilemmas, be they issues of momentous consequence such as international conflicts involving the use of nuclear weapons, or of keeping personal promises.

Essentially, human nature is not binary. People are not always selfish, but they are not angels either. They are conditional cooperators, and this insight is quite powerful for policymakers. In designing institutional interventions, policymakers need to recognize that while people will consider their own selfish interests, they are also willing to cooperate, but will not accept freeriding by others. Greater transparency, public disclosures, and greater accountability of public officials are thus important tools for enhancing the spirit of conditional cooperation in society. We will come back to some of these issues in Part IV, where we discuss the role of the state, the markets, and community as important institutions in achieving social harmony and enhancing social welfare, that is to say, delivering good governance.

7.7.1 Role of economic incentives and social preferences in inducing cooperation

A major tool in a policymaker's toolkit to induce cooperation in a society and get people to contribute to collective goods (that is, to exhibit pro-social behaviour) is the use of economic incentives. These would include taxes, subsidies, penalties, fines, and rewards. Drawing on the fundamental assumptions of a rational, selfish individual in each of us, it is believed that people will respond appropriately to such economic inducements or costs. For example, pollution tax will increase the cost of a polluting activity and thus reduce its frequency, while a subsidy on say, mid day meal at schools will have the opposite effect. While the value of economic incentives is not to be minimized, we also know that people have innate feelings of altruism and reciprocity, ethical commitments, and intrinsic motives to help others, and these make us feel good about ourselves when we act on them. Given this, how do explicit economic incentives interact with social preferences to produce pro-social behaviour?

Almost half a century back, Titmuss wrote his pathbreaking book, *The Gift Relationship: From Blood Donations to Social Policy*. It described the British system of blood donations where, working within the framework of the country's socialized medicine, donors voluntarily give blood to strangers without any material reward. It is essentially a gift of 'life' for 'love', the 'values we accord to people for what they give to strangers; not for what they get out of society'.[52] Titmuss contrasted the British situation with the American system, where blood is often sold to commercial blood banks, and often by those who are in dire need of money, arguing that turning blood into a commodity erodes people's sense of obligation to donate blood and diminishes the spirit of altruism. Predictably, Titmuss's book unleashed quite a passionate debate on both sides of the Atlantic on the merits or otherwise of a state or market-oriented provision of health services. But our principal concern here is not that, but the other debate which ensued: that perhaps 'policies based on explicit economic incentives may be counterproductive when they induce people to adopt what Titmuss called a "market mentality" or in some other ways compromise pre-existing values to act in socially valuable ways'.[53]

Economic incentives convey information from the principal (one offering the incentive) to an agent (one to whom the incentive is offered). How such information is perceived by the agent provokes her reaction. Consider the award of an incentive for higher output on the factory floor, or better academic performance. That may signal to the agent that the task is not attractive, or is too hard, or at least the principal thinks it is beyond her usual capability and thus needs the additional incentive of a reward. It could also be interpreted as a signal that the principal does not trust the agent's intrinsic motivation for the task. All these signals (whether correctly interpreted or not is beside the point) are negative for the agent and crowd out her social preferences to perform well for its own sake and 'feel good' about it.

In deciding the level of effort to put into a task, individuals instinctively frame the situation as either monetary or social. The former is sensitive to economic incentives, the latter is not. As a matter of fact, offering compensation for the latter (social) may be counterproductive. An experiment conducted with several hundred American university students indicated much lower willingness to help a stranger load a sofa into a van with a small monetary incentive than with none.[54] In an experiment conducted in Israel, high school students collected more money on a fundraising campaign for a local charity when it was purely a voluntary effort than when they were offered a small compensation.

Monetary incentives often dilute the softer human aspects of an interaction, reducing it to a near-market transaction which an individual does not feel any social obligation to fulfil. It may also change individuals' beliefs about the behaviour of others: people may believe that monetary incentives are in place because the social norm is that people do not contribute without compensation. Interestingly, in the above examples, higher compensation increased the willingness to help with the move and also showed a slight improvement in the collection performance of the high school students. This shows that economic incentives might work if they are adequate to overcome the negative dampener of the payment on social preferences. Thus, 'pay enough or don't pay at all'.[55]

Trust is a major motivator in encouraging pro-social behaviour and as noted earlier, explicit economic incentives can damage social norms of trust.

Consider a variation of the Trust Game we discussed earlier: Player 1 chooses how much of an initial endowment she will share with Player 2. The experimenter tops up this amount by a factor greater than 1 which is given to Player 2, who then decides how much to give back to Player 1.[56] If the players are purely selfish, Player 1 can choose not to share any of her endowment to begin with, or Player 2 can choose not to give anything back once she has received the additional top-up money. However, that's not what happened in the experiment. In most cases, Player 1 did share as evidence of her trust and Player 2 did give back, often more than the original amount Player 1 had shared, in reciprocity to her trust.

A modified version of this game to test the effect of incentives on be-haviour was undertaken in Costa Rica with a group of senior executives and students. Under this modification, Player 1 can impose a fine on Player 2 if a high enough amount is not returned by Player 2. The results showed that the fine reduced the voluntary returns. One could argue that Player 2 need not necessarily perceive the fine as a sign of distrust but as an effort by Player 1 to exercise explicit control or monitoring, which are equally unwelcome and detrimental to cooperation.[57]

As we saw in Titmuss's explanation of people shying away from blood donation when it was paid for, economic incentives may also suggest per-missible behaviour and trigger what psychologists term the 'moral dis-engagement effect', a process that occurs because 'people can switch their ethicality off'.[58] Consider the experiment at a day-care centre in Israel, where to deter parents coming in late to pick up their children, a fine was levied, with the expectation that this would reduce tardiness. In fact, the opposite happened: the number of tardy parents doubled. The parents in-terpreted the fine as a price to 'buy' the extra time their children stayed at the centre. What had previously been a moral issue, not to keep the teachers waiting, became an economic transaction. Morality was disen-gaged and replaced by a market transaction, at least from the point of view of some parents.[59]

In each of these cases, economic incentives could have signalled to the agents some form of bad news: it could be about the nature of the task (not worth doing), or the principal's views (too difficult for the agent to do, lack of trust) and hence the incentive is being offered since the agent must need some additional motivation to do the task. But more insidi-ously, this effect can continue even after the incentive (positive or nega-tive) is removed, when the agent does not return to the pre-incentive mode, as if a residual memory of the bad news lingers on. Indeed, in the day-care centre experiment, even after the fine was removed, the tardy parents who had been fined were still more likely to be late in picking up their children than those in the control group, who had not been fined. A likely explanation is that once the fine had conveyed the message that it is acceptable behaviour to pay a price for being late, it is difficult to re-verse the 'moral disengagement', even when the fine is removed (simply seen as the price being reduced to zero, but the issue still being about a market transaction).

The above are all examples of 'crowding out', where economic incentives and social preferences are at odds, thus becoming substitutes for each other. Interestingly, this is not always the case. 'Crowding in' can also happen, making the incentives and social preferences complement each other, say 'as in the case of pricing garbage collection as a way to encourage recycling and reduced waste'.[60]

Recall the Public Goods Game (version 3) discussed earlier in the chapter. In that game, players who were freeriding had been caught out and were penalized by those who were conforming to the norms and cooperating. Results show that the free riders increased their levels of cooperation in subsequent rounds of play, evidence of the previous recalcitrant players now being crowded in.

It is important to emphasize that the above discussion is not to argue that economic incentives do not matter. They obviously do. But, to get a more complete picture of how incentives work (or sometimes don't), it is important to recognize that, such economic incentives interact with social preferences, as complements or substitutes. This interaction has significant implications for institutional and policy designs; this is a subject we will explore further in the following two chapters.

7.8 Summary

Humans think not only as individuals but also as members of a social group influenced by those around them: their family, community, and society at large. Their decision-making and actions are influenced as much by their individual thinking as by their circumstances, contexts, social networks, and norms. Their collective behaviours for the better (such as creating widespread trust) or for worse (such as the existence of widespread corruption) develop and evolve as an interaction between their individual and social thinking.

To survive in society, people need to coordinate their actions and cooperate with others. Such social coordination is necessary to generate social changes for the greater welfare of society, particularly when people are unable to communicate with each other directly. Insightful application of some key concepts of game theory, such as Schelling's focal point, serves as a possible useful and efficient social coordinating device to get society to a state of equilibrium where nobody can profit by deviating unilaterally. However, an equilibrium need not be unique. Multiple equilibria are possible, some good, some not. Societies will obviously wish to be in a good equilibrium situation where good governance prevails, and this is where challenges of collective actions (tragedy of the commons, climate change) and social dilemmas arise.

A classic illustration of this challenge is provided through the well-known game of prisoner's dilemma: doing what appears to be in the best interest of an individual would not be so for society as a whole and ultimately not for the individual either. This leads to Sen's well-known theory of Rational Fools, where people in a group 'rationally' pursue their own self-interest but in the process hurt the overall group welfare and ultimately themselves as well.

To induce cooperation in society, policy makers often undertake economic measures such as imposing taxes, penalties and fines or offer subsidies and rewards. However, while the value of such economic incentives is not to be minimised, their design needs to recognise people's intrinsic social preferences as well.

Policies and institutional practices designed on the premise that people are always self-interested and fully rational in their decision-making can be incomplete and misplaced if cognitive, psychological and social influences on human behaviour are ignored.

Thankfully, thankfully humans are not always 'rational'. While not always angels, they are not always selfish either. They can also be altruistic, help others in need, cooperate for the greater good, and trust each other.

Humans are conditional co-operators in the sense that while people will consider their own selfish interests, they are also willing to cooperate but will not accept freeriding by others. This is an important insight for policymakers in designing institutional responses. Greater transparency, public disclosures, and greater accountability of public officials are thus important tools to enhance the spirit of conditional cooperation in society by assuring citizens that others are also pitching in.

8

The World of Beliefs, Norms, and Mental Models Around Us

8.1 Introduction

As we discussed in the previous chapter, humans do not exist in isolation as islands unto themselves. Humans are also social animals. Human sociality, 'the tendency among humans to associate and behave as members of the group affects decision making and has important consequences for development'.[1] Three concepts which significantly influence how humans think, behave, and act individually and socially are 'beliefs', 'norms', and 'mental models' we form over time. What people believe about others influences their own decisions and actions. Norms, on the other hand, may be thought of as informal self-enforcement mechanisms which develop in a society over time. These unwritten rules guide group members on what they are expected to do and ought to do. Our unique life experiences, understanding, and opinions help us frame and process the world around us. These personal, internal representations of external realities are our own mental models. And these are the broad concepts we are going to look at in some depth in this chapter to further our understanding of the multilayered, unpredictable, and ever-enigmatic human thought and behaviour which in turn significantly influence how institutions evolve and function in societies.

8.2 Role of beliefs in our individual and social behaviour

Rajat lives in Delhi. There is a T-junction near his house where traffic chaos reigns every day, particularly during rush hours. Cars from all

From Here to Denmark. Rajat M. Nag and Harinder S. Kohli, Oxford University Press.
© Rajat Mohan Nag and Harinder Singh Kohli 2023. DOI: 10.1093/oso/9780198893103.003.0008

directions drive into the junction, block each other off and then pain-fully inch their way through the intersection with much yelling and some choice words being hurled around. You'd think that a 3-Way Stop sign system would solve the problem immediately. There is one. Alas, it's pointless because no one stops. As someone quipped: 'What's the point of stopping to let somebody else pass? I would be there all day.' Obviously, this view is much more prevalent than Rajat's, when he in-sisted on stopping and awaiting his turn, which mostly never came. Not only did he get some strange glances from others at his odd behaviour, but he was also honked at for 'holding up' the traffic. Defeated, he then meekly joined the crowd, realizing that otherwise, he would indeed be there all day.

Harinder lives in Washington and at the main 4-way crossing near his house, he faces a similar traffic rush every morning. His passage through the crossing is much less eventful.

Why the traffic chaos in Delhi? It's not because people can't see the STOP sign displayed quite prominently, or that they don't know what that octagonal red sign means. The chaos arises because Driver A believes that no one will stop and of course, the others believe the same about him and each other. So the difference is not in the presence or absence of the rule but in the belief about what others will or will not do, which determines the outcome. Beliefs are salient drivers of human behaviour. Before someone shrugs and says, using a typical Delhi expression, that 'Delhi drivers are like that only ', let us hasten to add that drivers from Delhi are very law-abiding in Washington.

In a very powerful essay, *The Power of the Powerless*, penned in 1978, Vaclav Havel, the Czech dissident who became the country's presi-dent in 1989, makes this point most eloquently. He talks of the then Communist system

pulling everyone into its power structure, making everyone an instru-ment of a mutual totality, the auto totality of society. Everyone is in fact, involved and enslaved, not only the greengrocers, but also the prime ministers. Differing positions in the hierarchy merely establish differing degrees of involvement... Both, however, are unfree: each merely in a somewhat different way. The real accomplice in this involvement, there-fore, is not another person, but the system itself.[2]

Hume had made a similar point much earlier about the centrality of beliefs: our beliefs—our beliefs about what others believe—and in turn, what they believe about our beliefs, and so on. Writing almost two and a half centuries before Havel, Hume says 'No man would have any reason to *fear* the fury of a tyrant if he had no authority over any but from fear; since as a single man, his bodily force can reach but a small way, and all the farther power he possesses must be founded either on our own opinion, or on the presumed opinion of others'.[3]

Basu sums it up elegantly in a simple sentence: 'We are all citizens of the republic of beliefs'.[4] Binmore is equally emphatic, though a bit more poetic: 'We are bound only by a thousand gossamer threads woven from our own beliefs and opinions'.[5]

8.2.1 Rule of law in the land of beliefs

In most of the developing countries we visited in the course of our work, the phrase 'not following the rule of law' came up quite frequently in our conversations with people. Not following the rule of law was correctly identified as one of the root causes of the lack of good governance, lack of economic progress, and the sense of 'unfreedoms' in the minds of many in those countries. Unfortunately, the immediate—almost reflexive— reactions of many governments and policy-makers is to come up with more laws rather than asking why people don't follow the existing laws in the first place, and perhaps equally interesting: when they do, why do they do so?

There is a problem of squatting on public land, let's specify a law against it with stiff penalties (fines and even jail terms to boot). Burning coal is bad for the environment. Let's ban it.

In our work globally, we have been struck (and truth be told, we have ourselves often been party to such decisions) with how readily governments have passed new laws and regulations to control some activities. But how well have the laws worked? Are the laws merely on the books? If they are not enforced well or not at all, why not?

As a matter of fact, most countries around the world—including emerging countries—have, if anything, a surfeit of laws and regulations. The challenge is in their adequate implementation and effectiveness.

For example, between the central and state governments, India has over 30,000 laws on its books, some almost two centuries old, dating back to 1830, many antiquated, or even yet to be implemented.[6] However, it would be incomplete and unfair, not to acknowledge that many laws are indeed enforced effectively and followed by the citizens. So why do some laws work while many others do not?

One could argue—as Basu does—that 'after all, the law is nothing but some ink on paper, rules written down on paper by a parliament or an inscription on a stone ordered by a king, or some digital document in today's world'.[7] If that is all, then why would mere 'ink on paper' change behaviour?

As discussed Chapter 4, there is no dearth of anti-corruption legislation and anti-corruption commissions around the world. Why are most of them ineffective? And why do people think that another effort along similar lines will make a difference?

Let us begin with a neoclassical model of applying the law to see how it might affect an individual's behaviour on any particular action. Becker's work in this context on crime and punishment is seminal. In his celebrated paper [8] with the same title, Becker laid out an amoral view of crime including corruption, drawing on some basic ideas of mainstream economics, which could be broadly summarized thus:[9]

Consider an entrepreneur planning to invest in a project, a new resort within a lovely, wooded forest area, whose expected net benefits (all benefits net of all costs) is B. Conventional economics would give a clear decision: she should invest if $B>0$.

But now consider that the government, having been made aware of the dangers of allowing a resort to be built within the forest area, thereby greatly endangering the environment, declares the forest a reserve area and bans any construction within the forest. with a fine F for non-compliance. Take F as the pecuniary cost of the penalty, including the economic cost of a prison sentence. Further, assume that given her past experiences, and knowing how the government machinery works, the entrepreneur assesses that the probability of being caught and punished is p.

So, now her investment criterion changes to: invest if $B>pF$.

To prevent the project from going ahead, the government's decision rule should be the obverse, that is, choose p and F such that $B<pF$.

The equilibrium point in this example will then depend on the values of p and F that the Government will be able to bring to bear, and the entrepreneur's trade-off between B and pF.

The government can try to raise F to be a high enough deterrent, knowing of course that there are practical limits to how high the fines can be in any society. Similarly, the government can raise p, but in doing so, the government would have to expend greater resources—by hiring a larger number of monitoring staff and police, equipping them with more resources, more prosecutors, more magistrates, and so on. There are thus practical limits to how high p can be as well.

But the general point of this neoclassical Becker model[10] is this: introduction of a new law (banning construction in the forest area) changes the pay-off matrix of the entrepreneur and hence, her behaviour. However, as we had noted, the Becker model is based on an 'amoral view of crime, including corruption'. That means that the fine F can simply be thought of by our entrepreneur as a price (an additional cost C) in her decision whether to undertake the investment or not.

Of course, this is not how it would play out in reality. The imposition of the fine immediately opens up the possibility of the entrepreneur trying to bribe the inspector by offering b to avoid the penalty altogether, and her investment decision function changes again: she will invest if $B > b$. This can induce further iterations if, despite paying the bribe, she is not sure that the erring inspector will not renege on his deal though presumably, both p and F would now be lower (after all, there must be some honour among thieves). We can (but let's not) complicate this even further by hypothesizing that since presumably giving and taking bribes are both crimes, these would also be built into successive iterations of the investment decision by the entrepreneur.

Instead, let us turn our attention to the inspector. The neoclassical model[11] sees the laws as 'commands' to the agents of the state to implement the laws and impose punishments as stipulated. But the agents of the state are not just robotic agents without preferences of their own. How would the inspector in our example react to the offer of a bribe by the entrepreneur? He could quite possibly be an honest man, who does not even consider the offer of a bribe and might even be so offended that he imposes an extra penalty on the errant investor. Or he could refuse the bribe 'because he has his boss (the chief) who is watching over him'.[12]

Why would the chief herself not be tempted? Well, because she has her boss (the minister) to worry about, and so on up the hierarchy.

So, in a way, the motivation for each person to follow the new law is not that it exists, but that what each 'believes' the others will do. The entrepreneur will follow the law if she believes that the inspector would charge her with more serious violations, if she tried to bribe him. The inspector will follow the law because he believes the chief will do so and so on up the chain. The outcome would be exactly the opposite, of course, that is, the new law would not be followed if the actors in our example believed the opposite—that they would be open to the bribe.

8.2.1.1 Why are some laws followed and others remain as just 'ink on paper'?

Laws, no matter how well-crafted, will remain unimplemented and be nothing more than mere ink on paper if we believe others will not follow them. Let's now weave the concepts of equilibrium and focal points to answer a fundamental question we had raised earlier: why are some laws followed and others not? On its own, a law does not change the game of life (when all actors of society are considered: individual citizens and agents of the state alike) nor does it change the pay-off matrix. The only thing a law can do is change an individual's beliefs about what somebody else will do. And how will that happen? It will happen if the new law creates a new focal point, which would shift society to a new equilibrium.

Recall the example of Myerson's crown game: a group of strangers were asked to name a person among them, and if they all choose the same person, everybody wins $100 each. With a crown being placed on one person's head, nothing really changes. The game remains the same, and the pay-offs are the same. But the new focal point (created by the crown, equivalent, say, to the introduction of a new law) can affect the outcome. How? By changing expectations that others will name the person with the crown.

Let us go back to our three-way stop example. Given people's belief that others won't stop to give way, 'thus, I won't stop either'. The focal point is obviously 'nobody gives way' and the outcome is a bad equilibrium: traffic slows to a crawl as cars block the intersection. Now, suppose a new law is brought in: drivers not stopping at the three-way stop signs will be fined $30. Will this change the situation to a good equilibrium with an outcome of smooth traffic flow? No. The errant driver could have stopped at the stop sign even before the new law was imposed. He didn't because he did not believe other drivers would stop. Why should the driver now assume that other drivers will change their behaviour? Fear of the fine? Who will impose the fine? The policeman? But the policeman didn't pull anyone up earlier for not stopping at the stop sign. Why should he now become more committed because a new fine has been imposed?

Note that the new law cannot create a new equilibrium; all that it can do is direct society to another (but pre-existing) equilibrium. Whether that shift will in fact happen (smooth traffic flow in this example) will depend on beliefs: what each driver believes others will do in response to the threat of the fine being imposed, not the new law itself. Creating a new law does not necessarily achieve a different outcome by itself. As Basu has pointed out, 'any outcome that is made possible by creating a law could have happened without the law'.[13]

At first glance, this seems rather counter-intuitive. But let's reflect on this for a moment: in the three-way stop sign example, we saw that the desired outcome of the new law could have been achieved if people respected the stop signs which already existed, leading people to believe in each other. The desired outcomes of an anti-dowry law or anti-female mutilation law could just as well be achieved without them if people's beliefs were different. Similarly with laws against discrimination based on race, creed, caste, colour, or gender identity.

A large body of literature has evolved in the past few decades on informal but effective self-enforcing group behaviour without the presence of formal laws and the evolution of spontaneous order, or order without law. Greif[14,15] talks about the Maghribi traders conducting their business across the lands and seas based on family and intra-community links. Basu[16] makes the point that a society could achieve freedom of speech through informal social sanctions and threat of ostracism. Ellickson[17] describes how neighbours in Shasta County, US, apply informal norms rather than formal legal rules to resolve their disputes. Sugden[18] notes an unwritten rule in a fishing village on the Yorkshire coast regarding the gathering of driftwood after a storm was implemented without ever appealing to the courts or the police to enforce.

By itself, a new law cannot create a new equilibrium. All possible equilibrium points already exist with or without the law. What a new law can do, however, is suggest a possible shift to a new, better outcome. A law cannot command this shift to happen; it can only suggest. A new law can create a new focal point using the law's suggestive or expressive power.[19] But even a new focal point cannot ensure such a shift of equilibrium; after all, the focal-point approach is only a coordinating device to help society achieve a better outcome. A better outcome will be achieved only if the actors believe that others will believe, who in turn will believe that others will believe that the shift will be in their long-term interest (be it to stop at the stop sign, or not to pay a dowry).

We can also use the focal-point approach to answer another question we raised earlier: why do many laws remain unimplemented and un-enforced? Why do they just remain as 'ink on paper'? And why does it happen more frequently in the developing world? There could be a couple of reasons.

First, there are perhaps too many laws. In almost all the developing countries we have worked in, there seemed to be an excess of them. Not only are there too many laws, but they often overlap and sometimes even contradict each other. We can thus well empathize with Hadfield's la-ment: 'law, law everywhere, and no legal order in sight ... such that no one could possibly comply with them all'.[20] With so many laws and re-gulations, it is very challenging for many developing and resource-poor countries 'to identify and resolve conflicts in sets of overlapping rules'; and 'promote coherence, simplicity, and efficiency in their legal frame-works'.[21] An inevitable consequence of the overlapping and contradictory messages from this muddled web of laws and regulations is the difficulty of creating focal points. Without such focal points, the laws cannot per-form their suggestive roles, and are thus not effective.

To explain the second reason, let's begin with a parable.

One day, a vain king decided that the lake in his palace was not spe-cial enough. All other kings have lakes too, so his should be a lake of milk instead of water. Grandly, he decided to call it the Dudhsagar, or 'sea of milk' (kings can always bestow grandiose names). The court-iers were ordered to drain all the water from the lake; the palace priest was summoned and asked to propose the most propitious night for the lake to be filled with milk. But rather than using his treasury cof-fers, the king decreed that each subject of the land would pour a jug of milk into the lake and voila, Dudhsagar would be in place. And so, on the announced night, the subjects all duly filed in and did what they were told.

At the crack of dawn, accompanied by a roll of drums and blowing of conch shells, the king and his entourage arrived for the grand occasion of taking the first bath in the new lake but alas, it wasn't a sea of milk as he had commanded, but just a lake of water. Each subject had poured in water, possibly thinking, what difference would his one jar make? And of course, everyone else had done the same. Not a single jug of milk was poured in, and the king had his lake of water back.

We're not sure how the story ended for the courtiers and the subjects, but that is not our principal concern here. What is of interest to us is how this could be used to explain why laws are not followed.

This parable perfectly illustrates what Sen has called the 'isolation paradox'.[22] His proposition may be summarized thus: consider a community of N people, each of whom must do one of two things—A: pour water or B: pour milk. Each is individually better off doing A while expecting others to do B. However, the outcome, in the absence of collusion between all, is A, a Pareto inferior collective outcome (a lake of water rather than of milk). As can be seen, this N-person game is only an extension of the two-person, non-zero-sum game of the prisoner's dilemma.

In the above parable, the king's edict was directing his society to a non-equilibrium point, where if everyone pours in milk, and one person does not, then she is better off, and no one is worse off. Such an equilibrium cannot be sustained without compulsory enforcement and that is not a viable option.

Thus, if a law directs society to a non-equilibrium point, there will be no focal point either, and the law will remain unimplemented. And it is an unfortunate fact that many laws do therefore indeed remain mere ink on paper.

8.3 Role of social norms in our individual and social behaviour

Rajat picked his bread roll and caused a minor (well, it did not appear so minor at that time) chaos at the dinner table. Apparently Rajat had taken his neighbour's bread roll. And then, of course, the neighbour had to take *his* neighbour's, and the merry-go-round continued. The hostess tried to lighten the moment by raising a toast, but that didn't help much; the damage was done. Unbeknownst to him, Rajat had violated a rule of dining etiquette at that American dinner table—that the bread on the left and the drink on the right belonged to him. To this day, Rajat does not even touch his bread till his neighbour has.

We wait in a queue to board a bus or buy a train ticket, expecting others to do the same and knowing that they expect the same of us. And if somebody cuts in, there are often protests from others, or at least mutterings and dirty looks.

Both examples above illustrate social norms at play, with a subtle but important difference.

In both cases, there is an expectation of socially enforced behaviour: we are expected to take the dinner roll on our left, we are expected to wait in a queue. In the second case, however, there is an additional dimension of 'ought to'. We ought to wait in the queue, and if we don't, there will be consequences (even a slight glare, or worse). Bicchieri and Mercier [23] have termed the former an 'empirical expectation' (all take the bread on the left; all wait in a queue) and the latter a 'normative expectation' (all those who wait in the queue believe that I ought to do so as well).

Empirical and normative expectations together define social norms. The important distinction is that in normative expectations, there are consequences to not conforming. And norms, as informal self-enforcement mechanisms, exert a powerful influence on individual decision-making and behaviour, and are thus often considered to be the 'glue' or 'cement' of society.[24]

Around the world, norms vary widely. They can be exciting to see at work, but it is also challenging to navigate around the nuances and meanings of foreign norms. Bicchieri captures it well, calling it the 'grammar of society'. She describes norms as the language a society speaks, 'the embodiment of its values and collective desires, the secure guide in the uncertain lands we all traverse, the common practices that holds humans together'.[25]

There are obvious efficiency arguments in favour of norms (it helps everybody if people wait in line rather than rush for the bus door), and many norms thus evolve to encourage socially desirable behaviours: punctuality, not littering, talking softly (particularly on the ubiquitous cell phones on crowded trains), and so on. We discussed in the previous chapter how norms such as reciprocity and cooperation help in successfully undertaking collective action. We also saw that in the classic prisoner's dilemma game, a Pareto improving—Nash equilibrium—situation could follow from a strategy of cooperation (neither prisoner confessing) rather than not. If the prisoners were from a community where such a cooperation strategy was the norm, which they followed, both would have been better off.

Trust was the essential basis of the Maghribi traders, a group of Jewish traders in the Mediterranean in the eleventh century. Rather than travel over long distances with his merchandise, the Maghribi trader would send the goods to his agent, another Maghribi, and the sole basis of the transaction was the norm of mutual trust between the two as members of the same community. Not only was the agent expected to act in good faith (empirical expectation), but the norm was clear that he ought to represent his principal in good faith to the ultimate buyer (normative expectation). The consequence of not doing so was also clearly understood by all agents. Every Maghribi merchant (the principal) was expected to hire only member agents in good standing, and to never hire anyone who had cheated another member of the community. It is fascinating to think that the entire institution of the extensive Maghribi trade was built on this norm of social trust. But this is not just an isolated instance from the distant past. Such a system of trade based solely on trust is still widely practised among Gujarati diamond merchants in western India to transport very high value diamonds and gold through 'angadias' (trusted couriers).

However, there are other norms that might not have any obvious efficiency arguments. For example, driving on the right; the norms serve just as well if people drive on the left, but there would be chaos if some drove on the left and others on the right. The key point here is that analogous to grammar, to use Bicchieri's phrase, a system of norms evolves but some of those might not be the product of conscious human design and planning.[26] During human evolution, it's almost as if developing and adhering to norms got hardwired into people's DNA.

As a matter of fact, it would be no exaggeration to claim, as Sunstein does, that 'social life is not feasible—not even imaginable without them. In fact, there are norms about nearly every aspect of human behaviour. There are norms about littering, dating, smoking, singing, when to stand, when to sit, when to show anger; when, how, and with whom to express affection; when to talk, when to listen, when to discuss personal matters'.[27] Essentially then, norms are shared patterns of behaviour, beliefs, and practices that are acquired via social learning. No wonder, then, that norms vary between societies.

Some go even further. Eric Posner, an American legal luminary, makes the point that even if a society can exist without laws, it cannot survive without norms. 'In a world with no law and rudimentary government, order of some sort would exist. The order would appear as routine compliance with social norms and the collective infliction of sanctions on those who violate them, including stigmatization of the deviant and the ostracism of the incorrigible.'[28]

8.3.1 Social norms can create good and bad equilibriums in social interactions

Social interactions don't necessarily have only one possible outcome or equilibrium. Multiple equilibria are possible. In our traffic chaos case, for example, two distinct outcomes can emerge, one desirable and the other not. People could choose to stop at the STOP sign, proceed on a 'first come' basis; traffic would then flow smoothly, resulting in a good equilibrium. Alternatively, people could ignore the STOP sign, make it a free-for-all, and in no time create a gridlock. Chaos would ensue, leading to a bad equilibrium.

Social norms could play a crucial role in guiding the drivers to the good rather than bad equilibrium. If the norms were to favour people being law-abiding in general, a focal point would be created prompting people to follow the traffic rules, resulting in a good equilibrium. Once a norm is established, everybody knows which equilibrium is chosen by society, and it is then in everyone's own interest to adhere to it and in the process, norms become self-reinforcing, in this case, for the better.

Consider another interesting example: norms of punctuality. In many parts of the world, if you arrive at a dinner party on time, you might not necessarily win any brownie points for being punctual. On the contrary, you might embarrass the hosts who are not yet ready to receive you, and none of the other guests would have arrived anyway. In fact, many guests would breeze in almost an hour late with no apology but rather an air of feigned exasperation: 'what to do? So many commitments'. Of course, you would learn your lesson fast and expecting everyone else to be late, so would you the next time. The opposite would happen in some other parts of the world (Japan comes to mind), where you would feel sheepish if you arrived even a few minutes late, with everyone else well settled into the evening by then. Next time, you would probably arrive a few minutes early and circle around the block to ring the doorbell at your host's home on the dot. Once again, two very different equilibrium points are possible: one of tardiness and the other of punctuality, and both are operating norms in their respective settings.

Recall the point made earlier: the same rash driver in Rajat's neighbourhood in Delhi strictly follows all the rules when he drives in Harinder's neighbourhood in Washington and is punctual too. There is thus nothing innate about the culture or individuals in a society which causes them to be bad drivers or tardy in their daily actions. The same individual can behave quite differently in different cultures and these behaviours of bad driving or tardiness 'may be simply an equilibrium response of individuals to what they expect others to do (and they expect others to expect from them)'.[29] In other words, our own behaviours are just 'best responses' to how we expect others to behave. Each person is behaving rationally from her individual perspective, but collectively the community of drivers or dinner party guests are worse off—the classic prisoner's dilemma situation.

Societies can and do get stuck in bad equilibrium, as easily as they might in good equilibrium. They indulge in practices which are damaging and harmful to individuals and their society as a whole. Corruption, open defecation, female genital cutting (FGC), violence against women and children, discrimination and intolerance based on gender, race, caste, sexual orientation, or religious beliefs are just some of the most obvious ones.

8.3.1.1 Role of social norms in fighting corruption: why do anti-corruption measures often fail?

In our earlier chapter on corruption, we broadly defined it as the use of public office for private gains and noted its serious ill effects on society. In thinking of corruption and ways of fighting it, the usual approach is to consider it as an act by an errant individual (the bureaucrat, the police, the politician) which society must collectively deter and punish as appropriate. But what if a society sees corruption differently? What if a sense of reciprocal kinship and community in that society leads people in public office to feel a sense of obligation to take care of their own kith and kin? What if there is a strong expectation by the extended family and relatives of a high-ranking office-holder to provide them with money and favours? What if there is a shared belief that such behaviour is widespread, expected, and tolerated by that society? In fact, there appears to be sufficient evidence in many societies around the world to answer all these 'what if' questions in the affirmative. In other words, corruption can be a social norm, and not an aberration. In such societies, it can be argued that 'it has been the default social norm throughout much of history'.[30,31]

What is striking in many cases is that individuals might not even personally subscribe to some of the values underlying these negative practices, but their collective behaviour (as shown through their actions) might be different, reflecting the existing social norms. Social norms are a function of collective beliefs. They are not necessarily what an individual believes herself, but what she believes others expect her to do and what she ought to do to avoid facing unpleasant consequences. In this example of corruption, there could well be many who privately find the practice abhorrent and in conflict with their personal values, but they still go along with it simply to avoid the costs of standing out and bearing the consequences. A study in India in the mid-1980s found that the norm of corruption was so entrenched, that any official who demanded no more than the going rate as a bribe was considered to be honest.[32]

Results from a study of the pattern of diplomats paying fines for parking violations in New York City were revealing. Note that legally they cannot be forced to pay the fines owing to the diplomatic privileges that they enjoy. Nevertheless, diplomats from countries where corruption is low generally paid the fines, while those from countries with high levels of corruption did not, suggesting that social norms influence one's perceptions of corruption.[33]

The point here is not to suggest in the least that corruption is an acceptable practice. But simply having laws against corruption or organizations tasked with fighting it in place will not be enough. Concepts of beliefs and social norms provide a useful insight into ways to better combat corruption and achieve better governance, a recurring theme in this book. It would be fair to say that sometimes due to pressures from their own people, though more often than not to keep donors placated, political leaders of all stripes around the world decry the ills of corruption with full-throated vigour, if not sincerity. Strong (at least on paper) anti-corruption strategies, regulations, and even legislations are promulgated, and anti-corruption commissions and boards are established. Unfortunately, as observed by Transparency International, 'evidence showing that anti-corruption reforms in general and legal reforms in particular have a direct impact on reducing corruption is thin.'[34]

Case in point: Venezuela has a specific Anti-Corruption Law and a National Anti-Corruption Body mandated to enforce it. Libya has in place a National Anti-Corruption Commission, while Nigeria's anti-corruption efforts are led by its Economic and Financial Crimes Commission. In early 2020, Lebanon adopted a National Anti-Corruption Strategy covering the five-year period 2020–2025, the first of its kind in the history of the country. A detailed, well-written document, it proclaims that 'it expresses an unprecedented political will and supports efforts aiming at devising sustainable solutions.'[35] However, based on its Corruption Perception Index, Transparency International ranked all these countries towards the very bottom of the 180 countries they reported worldwide in 2020 thus: Venezuela 176, Libya 173, Nigeria 149, Lebanon 149.[36]

A principal reason for this situation is that most of the conventional measures tend to treat corruption as a typical 'principal-agent' problem. In such a situation, it is the principal who has to be protected from the agent's possible nefarious activities, since the agent has the informational asymmetry in his favour. But the truth may be just the reverse. The principal, as an elite actor who holds the levers of power, benefits from the rent-seeking activities he indulges in and has all the incentives not to let anti-corruption measures work.

Perhaps, then, corruption can instead be better understood as a 'collective action' problem rather than a 'principal-agent' relationship. ([37,38,39,40]) In a collective action problem, person 1 will pursue a suboptimal option A even when she knows that she would be better off pursuing option B, but only if everyone else also pursued option B. But she also knows that she would be worse off if she chose option B while others chose A. Thus, since she has no confidence that her fellow citizens will do the right thing (choose option B), she and all others end up choosing option A, and everyone is worse off as a result.

In thinking of corruption, a similar phenomenon exists. Members of a society may all agree that corruption is bad. They also may know that, as a group, they are worse off with existing corruption, and it is therefore in their interest to support anti-corruption measures. Paradoxically, however, they will still slip the policeman a bribe to avoid being charged with jumping the red light. As Anna Persson et al. note: 'the short-term costs of being honest are comparatively very high since this will not change the game. Hence: why should I be the sucker?'[41]

This phenomenon of collective action has a very corrosive influence on society's attitude towards corruption. It dilutes trust within a society and 'without norms of trust, the tragedy of the commons is unavoidable'.[42] Rothstein accurately captures the social dilemma that follows when trust is in short supply, and which can be paraphrased thus : I would pay taxes if I knew others were paying too, and the tax authorities were not corrupt; but since I cannot assume either of these two conditions to hold, I evade taxes, as do others, and all suffer: a classic result of collective action pushing the system to a suboptimal equilibrium.[43] Once the system gets there, it stays there (stable but suboptimal), caught in what is often referred to as a 'Corruption Trap'. The challenge for any society is therefore how to nudge themselves out of the corruption trap and that in turn is a function of how political power is distributed in that society.

8.4 Reckoning with social norms to influence social behaviour

Social norms can lead a society to a socially desirable or undesirable equilibrium. A major challenge for policymakers, then, is how to reckon with and hopefully change social norms which cause, at least in part, undesirable social outcomes. Easier said than done, of course, but there is some encouraging evidence of its being possible to do so.

8.4.1 Enhancing the salience of existing social norms to shift behaviour

We have noted that empirical expectations (what we expect others to do) have significant influence on our own behaviour and actions. But what if our perception of others is wrong, shrouded in 'pluralistic ignorance'? Consider the well-researched issue of binge drinking on many US college campuses.[44] The general conclusion of such studies is striking—not only did students drink because of their beliefs about what is expected of them, but they were also mostly mistaken about how much everyone else wanted to drink (pluralistic ignorance). Interventions to make this information public proved successful 'because once this widespread disconnect was revealed, everyone could reduce their drinking without fear of social sanction.'[45]

In their book, *Nudge*, Thaler and Sunstein make similar observations from an example in Montana to address the issues of binge drinking and smoking. They refer to a large-scale educational campaign which put out messages such as 'Most (81 percent) of Montana college students have four or fewer alcoholic drinks each week. Most (70 percent) of Montana teens are tobacco free'. Their conclusion: the strategy produced 'big improvements in the accuracy of social perceptions and also statistically significant decreases in smoking.'[46]

Humans usually reciprocate, but as we saw in the previous chapter, as conditional co-operators. This insight can be put to good use to enhance the salience of existing norms to influence social behaviour in desirable ways. Consider the perennial problem governments, particularly in the developing countries, face in collecting taxes. Past experiences have shown that threats of punishment, audit crackdowns, and other punitive measures have not usually worked and instead, can make the situation worse. The cues people pick up from such campaigns are often counterproductive. People feel that tax evasion is widespread, and might even be tempted to join the crowd. On the contrary, the UK Government found that compliance increased more when citizens were informed that most of their neighbours had already paid their taxes, triggering a reciprocal behaviour.[47]

8.4.2 Jogging latent norms to shift behaviour

Another possible way to shift behaviour to a better equilibrium would be to jog certain norms, which are probably latent, and thus do not immediately come to mind. For example, even if people might not know the staggering statistics of road traffic deaths (globally about 1.25 million annually, more than twice the number of victims of war and violence combined),[48] people know from their personal observations and the local media how serious the problem is. Yet, on a day-to-day basis, people do not change either their expectations or their behaviour, though everyone frets about the terribly dangerous drivers on the road.

Ninety per cent of road deaths occur in low- and middle-income countries, Kenya among them. Habariyama and Jack report on an experiment in Kenya to test whether a behavioural intervention urging passengers to 'heckle and chide' could reduce accidents. Several minibuses (among the main culprits in causing accidents in the country) were randomly selected to display prominently placed stickers saying 'Don't just sit there as he drives dangerously! STAND UP. SPEAK UP NOW!' The results were dramatic: insurance claims fell by a half to two-thirds, from an annual rate of 10 per cent without interventions; and claims involving injury or death fell by at least half. Drivers themselves confirmed that the heckling by the passengers played a significant role in their driving more safely.[49]

8.4.3 Altering social norms to shift behaviour

While reducing pluralistic ignorance of what others think and do and jogging of existing social norms no doubt influence change of behaviour, changing social norms in the true sense of the word is much more challenging. Since social norms are supported by shared normative beliefs, the process of change itself must be a collective one. And the complexity of this process becomes apparent when we recognize that not only must the empirical expectations change, but the normative expectations must change as well.

Let us consider the example of female genital cutting (FGC). It is practised in many societies in Africa and is certainly not an isolated cultural norm, reflecting a rich network of beliefs (its religious justifications, effect on health, or lack thereof).[50] This in spite of the fact that while an individual parent might not necessarily be convinced of these beliefs and may in fact have serious doubts about them, they nevertheless still follow the practice. They do so not only because they expect others to do the same (empirical expectations), but also because of their fear of social ostracization (normative expectations) if they don't.

The practice of open defecation is another striking example. In recent years, the Government of India has mounted a campaign of Clean India (Swachh Bharat) under which, among other things, toilet ownership has grown significantly. However, the practice of open defecation persists, though it has decreased, even when the rural households own latrines.[51] The reasons for its continued practice are very similar to those in the case of FGC. People's normative expectations tend to be closely linked with the perceived expectations of their reference group. In a survey carried out by Gauri et al., more women than men tended to associate latrines in a house with dirtiness ('gandagi') and again, feared their neighbours' reactions to the use of latrines at home.[52]

Norms determine what social behaviours and actions are 'right or wrong in the eyes of the others ... shunned or discouraged and when individuals and families will be ostracized and cut off from the support of others'.[53] Thus, while norms help to coordinate social actions and responses, and are a robust means for societies to resolve conflicts and generate a shared set of understandings, they can also create a rigid set of expectations and reinforce unequal social-power relations. The norms can thus create 'a cage, imposing a different but no less disempowering sort of dominance on people'.[54]

Thus, to bring in changes in social norms not only must there be changes in people's expectation of what others will do, but also in their confidence that they indeed will. Credibility of commitments is therefore important. Empty promises are nothing but cheap talk, and the norms will remain in place. Yet, norms can and do change, and sometimes fairly rapidly after a long period of resistance.

Laws change not only incentives but also the social meaning of actions and can thus be an effective tool for changing social norms. Essentially, more than the sanctions and disincentives that these legal measures provide, an even more important role of law is what may be called its expressive powers to coordinate people's behaviour and inform their beliefs, in effect, to change the focal points. As McAdams observes, 'Because the law is full of requirements, we can easily miss its *suggestive* influence. If individuals share an interest in coordinating their behaviour, they tend to engage in the behaviour they find mutually salient—the focal point. In these circumstances, I claim that law facilitates coordination by making a particular outcome salient'.[55]

For example, for a long time, ice hockey players in North America were reluctant to wear helmets. It turned out that the principal social meaning of wearing helmets was that despite all the projections of machismo, the wearer was in fact a wimp. In 1979, the National Hockey League adopted a rule making it compulsory for the players to wear helmets. Wearing the helmet then became only a matter of following the rules, which was the overriding norm for all players. Over time, the social meaning of wearing helmets on ice changed, and so did the norm.[56]

Changes in the public attitude towards smoking provide another useful illustration of how laws can be used to affect social norms. In 1964, the US Surgeon General issued a report confirming for the first time that smoking was dangerous to health. It is now difficult to imagine that till then, 'while some intuitive feeling that smoking was harmful existed among a number of Americans, there was no widely accepted authority that settled the factual question of the healthfulness of smoking.'[57]

Several legal moves followed: higher taxes, restrictions on advertising, gradual bans on smoking in theatres, airplanes, and public transport. These sanctioning and expressive powers of law, combined with greater awareness and rising concerns about the effects of second-hand smoke, turned the tide (reached a tipping point). From a situation where the non-smokers used to be relegated to the back of the restaurant, 'the smoker (became) on the defensive as the act of smoking (was) increasingly banished from many social circles, and the smoker so frequently admonished not to smoke.'[58] Non-smoking is now the default option for public places; if there is no sign explicitly permitting smoking, assume it is not allowed. The combination of the sanctioning and expressive powers of law and the campaigns to convince people that smoking even second-hand was dangerous to health led to the 'denormalization' of smoking and the transformation of social norms surrounding it.[59]

What we see in these examples is the rather important effect of laws derived from their sanctioning and expressive powers. Since people can come to value the things they experience, 'legal changes that shift the short-term costs and benefits of action can contribute to longer-term and self-sustaining behaviour changes.'[60]

Consider the example of recycling. Initially, the trigger for people to recycle came from the sanctioning powers of law: local laws required recycling, and fines had to be paid for non-compliance. But with the increasing convenience of recycling, social consciousness and awareness of environmental issues, and the suggestive powers of law to legitimize it even further, acts of recycling gradually transformed into favourable social norms. Indeed, they became internalized as personal norms. People's thinking shifted to—I recycle not because others do, or I expect others to do it, or I will face their disapproval if I don't. I recycle because that's the right thing to do.[61]

While laws (through their role in creating new focal points) and their consistent enforcement are an important tool in changing social norms, it is also important not to exaggerate the point. Stuntz[62] and several other scholars (Platteau[63] and Aldashev et al.[64] have observed that laws must not appear so distant from existing social norms as to lose credibility. As Stuntz says, 'If the law strays too far from the norms, the public will not respect the norms, and hence will not stigmatize those who violate it. Loss of stigma means loss of the most important deterrent the criminal justice system has.'[65]

This is the reason why giving in to the immediate temptation of changing some of the norms in society through legal measures doesn't often produce results. Consider again the practice of FGC. Imagine the adoption of a law which abolishes it. It is highly unlikely that such an injunction would work if individuals, even those who might personally feel that the practice is wrong, are not sure that others would follow the new law, or indeed if the government would be able to enforce it. To be the first one to depart from the practice risks social ostracization. The new law could be so out of sync with the existing norms that it could just remain as ink on paper. To move away from a shared norm, individuals will have to be assured that the commitment implied by the new law is credible.

Changing norms essentially requires finding solutions to a collective-action problem: an assurance that being the first one to comply (to abandon the practice of FGC, for example) would not expose them to a first-mover disadvantage, facing the wrath of normative expectations of others in society. Laws by themselves would not be able to ensure that this will happen. At best, 'it would appear, *prima facie*, that external interventions such as new laws may *facilitate* behavioural changes.'[66] Notice that laws can only *facilitate*, not cause, the behavioural changes.

Since such changes must be collective, Sunstein (1996) suggested the idea of 'norm entrepreneurs' in a society to initiate the process of change.

These entrepreneurs could be community leaders, opinion makers, or well-connected individuals with high credibility who can play a key role in effecting changes in social norms.[67]

8.5 Thinking with mental models

Being bounded humans, we are bound by our human limitations (we are human after all) in processing all available information, inputs, and stimuli simultaneously and instantaneously. To do so takes time and energy. Therefore, without even being aware of it, humans use mental models (short cuts, heuristics, or rules of thumb) to filter, categorize, and process all these pieces of information almost automatically. Some short cuts are innate to human nature, resulting in our thinking automatically. Others emerge from our shared social experiences, families, communities, and from our collective beliefs and social conventions passed down over generations.[68] Human thinking is influenced heavily by learned mental models, which evolve over time in an individual's mind as a synthesis of all these forces and processes, but are not the same as say, social norms. Mental models are ultimately an individual construct of one's own understanding, interpretation, and perception of the larger world around and one's place in it.

While it might well be impossible for individuals to make most decisions in their daily lives without the use of mental models, shared mental models are equally important for a society's meaningful existence. Without such shared mental models 'it would be impossible in many cases for people to develop institutions, solve collective action problems, feel a sense of solidarity, or even understand one another'.[69]

Norms tend to focus on specific behaviours and are socially enforced. By contrast, mental models are personal and self-enforcing. Consider caste discrimination in India. After centuries of abominable discrimination, people of lower castes have created mental models leading them to believe that their station of life is lower, and they behave accordingly. We have been struck by how even in this day and age some people bow, pay obeisance to people of higher castes by not even meeting their eyes and addressing them as 'my lord and keeper'. In a way then, the effects of negative mental models can be even more insidious and long-lasting than negative social norms. In the latter, people may not necessarily subscribe to the view underlying a norm, but still practise it for fear of social stigma or even ostracization. Mental models, on the other hand, are internalized values and people use them instinctively to interpret the world around them and act accordingly.

8.5.1 Effects of the long-term staying power of mental models

Mental models are environment- and society-specific. They arise from collective experiences over time in that environment and within that society, but not in others. This also implies that historical experiences exert a powerful influence on mental models that are often passed down from generation to generation through a process of social learning. Past experiences affect current perceptions as well and while some intergenerational transfers can be beneficial and enable present thoughts and actions to draw on the wisdom of past knowledge and practices, they can be harmful as well, and hold back progress and development.

Take for example a community's instinctive sense of trust, a key motivator of cooperation and mutually supportive behaviour in a society, as we saw in the previous chapter. In a fascinating study, Nunn and Wantchekon[70] showed that current differences in trust levels within Africa can be traced back to the transatlantic and Indian Ocean slave trades, which lasted for almost 500 years (from about 1400 to 1900). A pernicious feature of the slave trade (among many others) was a breakdown of social trust among local communities. Some of them were the middlemen for the white slave traders, 'turning brothers against each other, chiefs against subjects, and judges against defendants'.[71] Under these circumstances, trusting one's neighbours, one's friends, or even one's own family would be a poor survival strategy. Thus, 'in areas heavily exposed to the slave trade, norms of mistrust towards others were likely more beneficial than norms of trust, and therefore, they would have become more prevalent over time'.[72] The collective experiences of those periods have passed on down through the generations, and the built-up mistrust of strangers is evident even today, well over a century after the slave trade ended.

Consider the effect of mental models on levels of social capital in a society. During 1954 and 1955, the Banfield family—Edward Banfield, an American political scientist, his wife, Laura, and two children, then eight and ten—spent nine months living among the local villagers of Chiaromonte, a community of about 3,400 people, most of them poor farmers and labourers, in the southern Italian region of Basilicata. Based on his experiences of that stay, Banfield wrote what was to become a classic anthropological study, *The Moral Basis of a Backward Society*.[73] Interestingly, in this book, Banfield used a fictitious name for the village, Montegrano rather than Chiaromonte (perhaps to protect the identity of the villagers he had lived with).

He observed a self-interested, family-centric society whose members refused to help others in the community, unless there was something in it for them. He coined the now famous term 'amoral familism'—concern only for their immediate, not even extended, family—to describe a phenomenon of the inhabitants' striking lack of social capital: the habits, norms, and networks to motivate people to work for the common good. Banfield found a community which was poor, and where life was hard and often lonely, with rather limited socializing among the residents. He attributed the backwardness of the place essentially to a lack of civic trust and feelings of envy and suspicion of each other, seeing life around them as a zero-sum game: someone else's welfare would be at their cost.

While the situation that Banfield described above might be an extreme, sociologists and anthropologists studying the social and economic development of Italy have long commented on the significant disparities between the southern part of the country, which is more like Montegrano and the northern part, which is more open and community-minded, with considerably more social capital and greater economic development (Jones,[74] Putnam et al.,[75] and Guiso et al.[76]).

Could distant historical experiences explain this difference, even if only partially? To find out, a quick thumbnail sketch of Italy's medieval history might help.

By the turn of the last millennium, the existing system of imperial government in Italy (German in the North, Byzantine in the South) had started to disintegrate, with control ceded to local forces. Soon thereafter, a powerful Norman presence emerged in the South, and the new Norman kingdom began to flourish economically. And 'by the end of the 12th Century, Sicily—with its control of the Mediterranean Sea routes—was the richest, most advanced, and highly organized State of Europe'.[77] However, the regime was strictly autocratic, with rigorous social and political controls on the region's population. Even after the royal powers started to diminish about a century later and the southern barons gained power and autonomy, the southern towns and cities did not. As a matter of fact, 'as the centuries passed, the steep social hierarchy came to be even more dominated by a landed aristocracy endowed with feudal powers, while at the bottom, masses of peasants struggled wretchedly close to the limits of physical survival'.[78] While the barons are long since gone and the economic situation is overall much better, what is striking is that even several centuries later, Banfield (1958) observed the same sense of social apathy, amoral familism, lack of contribution to collective efforts, and consequent lack of social capital in Montegrano, in southern Italy.

In contrast, efforts to establish any centralized power faltered in the North, leading to the emergence of several independent city states, with their principal common interest being to avoid any re-emergence of the imperial powers. While they differed in their internal governance organizations, a striking feature common to all of them was a sense of collective welfare. At the risk of ostracism (threat of exclusion from trade, a very costly punishment) if it was violated, the residents of the city states established a 'sworn pact' (patto giurato) in which 'a town's inhabitants agreed to provide mutual help and collaborate to solve problems of common interest'.[79]

Based on her lifelong work, Nobel Prize winner Ostrom had concluded that direct participation by residents in community life contributing to collective goods (such as jointly managed irrigations systems) gives them a sense of empowerment and enhances their social capital, a trait which is then transmitted to succeeding generations through socialization. In reporting the results of their detailed econometric work, Guiso et al. confirmed this and explained Banfield's field observations. Scoring what they call self-efficacy beliefs—beliefs in one's own ability to complete tasks and reach goals—they found that fifth-graders today in the former northern free city states consistently score higher than their southern counterparts. They concluded that 'Italian towns during the Middle Ages that were free city-states exhibit higher levels of civic capital today. The duration and degree of independence of the historical free city-states also affect today's civic capital positively'.[80]

Using data from the plague era (Black Death) pogroms in Germany during the late 1340s, Voigtlander and Voth traced a strong correlation between anti-Semitism then and its subsequent horrifying levels in Nazi Germany.[81]

Alesina et al.[82] identified the use of the plough in agriculture as influencing the status of women in subsequent periods: using ploughs required greater upper-body strength and thus gave men a comparative advantage. Looking at societies across countries and various ethnicities where ploughs were not used, they found that female participation even several generations later in the workplace, politics, and entrepreneurial activities is higher. Gender role attitudes in such societies were also more positive.

All the above examples suggest the influence of past collective experiences on subsequent beliefs and behaviour even centuries later, as if those distant memories are etched into one's persona, creating mental models which people draw on instinctively as part of their thinking process.

Mental models may also limit or enhance an individual's abilities to adapt to new opportunities. Consider the issue of self-perception of identity, which can significantly influence behaviour and performance. A much-referred-to study in Uttar Pradesh in India assessed the influence of caste identity on children's intellectual performance in classrooms.[83] Fifth- and sixth-grade boys were given a maze test in two groups, both including students from low and high castes. In the control group, the caste of the students was not identified, and students from the low-caste group performed just as well as those from the higher castes. In the other group, the name and caste of each student was revealed, and there was a dramatic drop of over 20 per cent in the performance of the low-caste students. Because they were reminded of their caste, the low-caste identity had become salient in the minds of the children, and perhaps centuries of discrimination have created these unfortunate mental models in the young minds.

Over time, mental models often may well outlive their relevance and become counterproductive. Take the issue of mistrust in many African countries, born out of the horrors of the slave trade, discussed earlier in this chapter. Even more than a hundred years after the slave trade ceased, the existence of that mistrust is now a serious detriment to economic development in those societies. People in such societies have less confidence in their governments, in the laws of the land and their enforcement. They are also more averse to using financial intermediaries and less willing to contribute to collective goods. Nunn found 'a robust negative relationship between the number of slaves exported from each country and subsequent economic performance. The African countries that are the poorest today are the ones from which the most slaves were taken'.[84] Lack of mutual trust, a wise survival strategy at one time, is now holding back entire countries from rightful social and economic growth.

An important observation follows from the above. Evolution of institutions and successful efforts in changing social norms, practices, and behaviour in a community are influenced by their past experiences and will thus vary from place to place. No one society will respond to just the same incentives as others.

8.5.2 Causes of the long-term staying power of mental models

If people were perfectly rational, as assumed in standard economic models, they would recognize when their beliefs are inconsistent with outcomes and change their beliefs accordingly. But people are not Econs, they are humans: a psychological, social, and cultural actor and 'what he sees and the inferences he draws from it are themselves affected by his mental models'.[85] Consequently, humans can live in a world of 'equilibrium fiction', giving mental models their long staying powers. Of several complex factors which might be at play, two are perhaps more relevant in explaining why.

One, belief traps. If people believe that their neighbours are not to be trusted, then they will reflect that in their daily life, socially and in transactions as well (recall the example of Montegrano). They will pass on these beliefs to their children, and the cycle will continue. Breaking out of belief traps is costlier for an individual when the consequences of doing so are higher, for example, the practice of FGC in some societies. Breaking out of the belief can prove costly for the family and the girl, if others in the society don't follow suit. The driving force in continuing with this practice is thus not necessarily that the family believes in the practice, but they are caught in the belief trap that others believe it is good and they will be socially censured if they break out of that practice. There is safety in the status quo, no matter how detrimental the practice might be.

Two, confirmation bias. We tend to find reasons to confirm what we already believe and ignore or question what we don't. When confronted with evidence to the contrary, we are sceptical and more likely to demand to check if it is true, and more likely to discard it as spurious. And we use these beliefs not only to confirm how we look at or think of others, but often more damaging and misleading is how we see ourselves.

8.6 Summary

We are all 'citizens of the republic of beliefs'. This has immediate implications for the state of good governance and for evolutions of institutions in a society.

Studies around the world confirm that poor governance in most countries is not due to insufficient laws and regulations on the books but rather their ineffective implementation. So, why are some laws followed in some societies but not in others? A simple answer: 'beliefs'. People follow the law if they believe others will follow it too. Otherwise, they just remain as 'ink on paper or edicts on a stone tablet'.

Contrary to beliefs which are individualistic though shaped by social influences, norms are a social construct and are also important for their contribution to social order. Essentially, they are the language a society speaks as an embodiment of its collective values and social desires.

Norms make social interactions more predictable but can also lead to good or bad outcomes. When people follow norms which are damaging to the society and individuals, societies can get stuck in bad equilibrium. Systemic corruption, practices of female genital cutting, violence against women or intolerance of minorities are just some of the most egregious examples.

Social norms influence collective behaviour, for better or for worse. Evidence shows that while humans can be altruistic and kind, they are conditional cooperators: 'I will cooperate if you do'. This is a valuable insight which can be used to enhance the relevance of existing social norms and nudge them to better social outcomes. Another possible way to shift behaviour to a better equilibrium would be to activate latent norms.

In its most basic sense, changing norms requires finding solutions to collective-action problems. It requires an assurance to the first movers against the existing norms, that they will not suffer the wrath or ostracization of others in society. Such assurances will need the combined efforts of the state and 'norm entrepreneurs' in society.

Over the course of evolution, humans have learned to use mental models to simultaneously process available information and respond to the situations at hand, often instantaneously. Mental models evolve over time in an individual's mind as a synthesis of all their shared social experiences, passed down over generations, but are not the same as social norms. Social norms are socially enforced, while mental models are self-enforcing.

The effects of mental models can be insidious, and even more so than negative social norms. At least in the case of social norms, there is the possibility that they might be adhered to only in the fear of stigmatization or ostracization. There is thus the possibility of change. Mental models, on the other hand, are internalized values and thus much more resistant to change.

Beliefs, norms, and mental models all play a critical role in how informal rules of actions and behaviour evolve in a society, and hence also how the institutions take root and evolve in that society, for better or for worse.

9

Better Understanding, Better Interventions

9.1 Introduction

Policies and institutional practices designed on the premise that people are only self-interested and always fully rational in their decision-making can be deficient and flawed. As we have seen in the previous chapters in this part of the book, humans often think and behave in unpredictable, emotional, and irrational ways. Cognition, as well as psychological and social influences, affect human behaviour. Collective human behaviours for the better (following traffic rules) or worse (systemic corruption) develop through an interaction of individual and social thinking, which is dynamic and context-specific. As such, policy and institutional interventions need to take these parameters into account and cannot be universally applied as some standard prescriptions of 'best practice'.

The three previous chapters have discussed how humans think individually and socially, and how their beliefs, social norms, and mental models of the world around them influence their thinking and actions. It follows from those discussions that in addition to the standard economic considerations, incorporating findings from the relatively new field of behavioural economics (based on insights from a wide variety of disciplines such as psychology, sociology, anthropology, and political science) expands the universe of underlying assumptions that discussions on institutional development should draw upon. Better understanding of these aspects of human behaviour and actions should allow policymakers to propose better institutional and policy interventions on the path From Here to Denmark. Evidence around the world shows that 'seemingly minor and low-cost policy changes may have a large impact on the achievement of development goals and the reduction of poverty'.[1]

From Here to Denmark. Rajat M. Nag and Harinder S. Kohli, Oxford University Press.
© Rajat Mohan Nag and Harinder Singh Kohli 2023. DOI: 10.1093/oso/9780198893103.003.0009

9.2   Reducing the cognitive tax on the poor

Thinking of poverty only as shortage of money is taking a rather narrow view of the lives of hundreds of millions of people in our world today. Poverty manifests in pervasive issues like injustice, social discrimination, limited access to basic services like safe water, affordable housing, health care, education, and jobs, as well as vulnerability to hunger and malnutrition, and restricted opportunities for social mobility and growth. And above all, it manifests in the emotional and mental toll it takes to keep one's mind, body, and soul together day after hard day, in a world that is utterly skewed in favour of the rich and powerful. Poverty is powerlessness in the face of the harsh realities of life. It forces the poor to focus on the immediate present at the cost of the future. If a mother has to worry about the next meal for her children, or how to stave off tomorrow the moneylender who has been hounding her to pay her past dues, she has less bandwidth to think of cognitively more demanding issues. Thinking of investing in her child's education or that stomach ache which has been bothering her for some time is farthest from her mind. The constant, daily stress of poverty essentially imposes a 'cognitive tax' on her mental resources.

Recall the example of the sugar-cane farmers in India who typically receive their incomes in a rather lumpy fashion at the time of their harvest. Pre-harvest, they are considerably cash-strapped, feel poor, more indebted, and in considerable financial distress. Indeed, right before the harvest 'they are much more likely to be holding loans (99 versus 13 per cent) and to have pawned some of their belongings (78 versus 4 per cent)'.[2] Their cognitive powers are thus compromised during such periods of duress, and quite understandably during this period they are much more concerned about the present than able to think coherently about the future.

Now consider this family having to decide about their child's education at that time. Fees for the next academic term need to be paid now or else the child will be struck off the rolls at school. The family is well aware of the benefits of education, but the pressures to meet the immediate expenses of living till the next harvest trump their concerns for the future of the child. The choices are stark. Most likely the farmer will withdraw his child from school.

In Chapter 3, we recounted our conversations with the poor where a recurring theme was the onerous burden of dealing with bureaucracy and accessing government services and programmes for which they are eligible. In other words, they were all speaking of the cognitive taxes which poor governance imposes on the poor. Simplifying procedures, easing access to government offices, providing information in a clear and easy-to-understand manner would all be of obvious help. Easier said than done, of course, but they do make a substantial difference.

Devoto et al. report a programme introduced in Morocco to provide piped water to low-income households in Tangiers.[3] But the bureaucratic process was so tied up in knots (the usual load of forms and documents, authorization from local authorities, down payments in person) that six months into the programme, a very small proportion (only a tenth) of the households had signed up. By contrast, among the control group which received all the necessary information at their doorstep, and assistance in filing the necessary papers for the credit and water connection, the up-take was significantly higher: 69 per cent.

Poverty also creates 'poor frames through which people see opportunities ... it blunts their capacity to aspire'.[4] The various injustices and accompanying indignities they suffer at the hands of officials and society in general makes many poor people feel incompetent and hopeless. And often rather than aspire, they give up so as to avoid the shame of the humiliations ('when they assist you, they treat you like beggars').[5] Data from a World Values Survey,[6] for example, confirm that the poor have a higher tendency to report that life is meaningless, and that it is better to live day to day because of the uncertainty of the future. They consequently reject uncertainty and risk, a very understandable sentiment since their risk-bearing capacity is rather limited. However, the more serious and insidious point is that they would often not even want to aspire for what could easily be within their reach if their mental resources were not so taxed by the grind of their daily living.

Let us go back to the case of the sugar-cane farmers in India. Knowing that farmers are cash rich after the harvest, if the school authorities were to synchronize the demand for the payment of school fees accordingly, outcomes could be significantly different. The farmers would be under considerably less cognitive stress at that time and thus be able to make more rational decisions about continuing their child's education.

Similarly, as will be discussed in the next section, Kenyan farmers increased their fertilizer application significantly when they were given an option of pre-purchasing fertilizers at the time of their harvests, rather than months later when they actually need the fertilizers but when they would be strapped for cash.

Broadly, if poverty is seen through a wider lens of what it does to people's thinking and behaviour, it could result in far more effective and wholesome policy and institutional responses. Relatively minor but innovative changes taking into account the behavioural and cognitive aspects of individual thinking can make a big difference to the outcomes of the decisions made.

9.3 Bridging the intention–action divide

Consider another interesting case: limited use of fertilizer in many parts of the world. Standard neoclassical economics would offer several reasonable and plausible explanations: prices are too high, or fertilizers are not readily available, or that the farmers are not fully aware of the benefits of using fertilizers. The policy responses from such diagnoses would then logically focus on subsidies, devising means to increase supply and access, and increasing agricultural extension outreach to the farmers.

Duflo and her colleagues looked at these issues in Kenya, but from the perspectives of the farmers' thinking and subsequent actions. Their conclusions and resulting policy prescriptions were strikingly different. Based on extensive fieldwork, they found that fertilizer is sold in small amounts and is thus reasonably affordable; so price is not a binding constraint. Nor is availability, as the nearby market centres (albeit a thirty-minute walk away) are usually well stocked. Duflo et al. estimate that 'the annualized rate of return to fertilizer turns out to be between 52 percent and 85 percent depending on whether we use data on farmers using only top-dressing fertilizer (the high estimate) or data on farmers using any kind of fertilizer (the low estimate)' but either way it is substantial, and farmers are well aware of these potentially significant benefits of applying fertilizer.[7] Asked why then they do not use fertilizer, 'farmers rarely say fertilizer is unprofitable, unsuitable for their soil, or too risky: instead, they overwhelmingly reply that they want to use fertilizer but do not have the money to purchase it'.[8] Essentially, the age-old cash-flow problem: a very different diagnosis from what would be arrived at if behavioural issues were not considered.

Like the sugar-cane farmers in India, the farmers in Kenya have sufficient resources available at harvest time, but that is not when they need the fertilizers. They need it much later, when they are low on funds, and even though they might have intended to save money for later to buy fertilizer, they have failed to follow through on those intentions. This is a classic intersection of two behavioural phenomena: poverty consumes cognitive resources, and humans have bounded willpower. The former forces attention on to the immediate, bringing forth the automatic rather than the deliberative system of thinking and the latter causes the intention–action divide.

There's nothing unusual about either of these phenomena. Studies have shown that the cognitive depletion resulting from financial stress is neither geography- nor culture based. It is poverty-induced, be it in India, Kenya, or the United States. Similarly, succumbing to immediate temptations or procrastinating is an all-too-familiar human trait. Kenyan farmers are no exception. A farmer rich in cash after the harvest finds there are many other demands on her money she must meet rather than saving to buy fertilizer for use several months later.

Consciously building in these behavioural realities can lead to very different and more effective solutions. If walking to the market is a binding constraint, perhaps home delivery would help. If insufficient funds to buy fertilizer was the constraint, perhaps a forced savings plan might be the answer. Duflo et al. tested these options through a pilot Savings and Fertilizer Initiative (SAFI). Under this programme 'a field officer visited farmers immediately after harvest and offered them an opportunity to buy a voucher for fertilizer, at the regular price, but with free delivery' of the fertilizer later in the year when needed.[9] The results were dramatic. Providing home delivery increased fertilizer use by a very substantial 70 per cent, as much as a 50-per-cent subsidy would have. These are very significant findings: the reason behind limited fertilizer use wasn't prices, availability, or ignorance on the part of the farmers of the benefits of fertilizer use. Offering a financial product (vouchers for later redemption with fertilizers delivered when needed) reduced the intention–action divide. The benefit of home delivery reduced the procrastination. Thus, altering the timing of purchases and building the costs of home delivery into the final price were found to be as effective as a significant subsidy in improving the rate of application of fertilizer, with positive fiscal implications for the government and farmers alike.

A major cause of the intention–action divide is the present bias. The present is more salient than the future: the pressures of 'now' dilute the thoughts of benefits 'later'. Now (requiring scarce cash outlays) becomes more salient and even significant benefits in the future are sacrificed. This often results in inconsistent and poor choices over time.

Some of such compromises can in fact be life-threatening. Consider the case of HIV/AIDS. The medication for its treatment is now easily and affordably available around the world. However, a major challenge in its treatment is the irregular adherence to the strict regime of taking the pills twice daily. But even patients fully aware of the importance of following the regime fall short: the daily pressures of life come in the way of sticking to the daily routine, with serious future consequences. However, some minor behavioural interventions can make a difference. An experiment in Kenya provided some significant results. Weekly reminders to the patients by SMS increased adherence to the regime by 13 per cent and the 'findings suggest that despite SMS outages, accidental phone loss, and a dispersed rural population, the weekly intervention was effective at a very low marginal cost'.[10]

9.4 Better framing helps in making better choices

We have earlier discussed the case of the payday loans in the US. Just informing a borrower how much she would have to pay back in two weeks does not give her any reference point to compare against alternatives. And being financially distressed and thus under cognitive stress, she automatically applies a rather narrow decision frame. As a matter of fact, her automatic thinking probably says: I need the money now and I have to pay ONLY $10 at the end of the two-week period, which is 'peanuts'. But a broader framing of the same situation in which she is told what the equivalent cost would be, say, if she borrows on her credit card, changes her reference point. It is no longer just the absolute amount ($10) that she has to pay, but the higher cost of the payday loan. As it turns out, they are significant: not just peanuts. Of course, she still might have to take the payday loan if her credit card limit is already breached, or if she doesn't have a credit card at all, but giving her this additional information triggers her reflective thinking to make a more informed and better decision.

In their insightful book *Poor Economics*, Banerjee and Duflo[11] cite the example of fruit sellers in Chennai, India. A typical fruit seller buys fruit on daily credit, paying back Rs 1,046.90 at night for every Rs 1,000-worth of fruits she got in the morning from the wholesaler. She might see it as only Rs 46.90 a day, but it amounts to a staggering interest rate of 4.69 per cent daily, well over 1,700 per cent (yes, one thousand seven hundred per cent) annually, and that too at simple interest. Certainly not peanuts. Shocking as this is, the point of greater interest is Banerjee and Duflo's brilliant finding that if our fruit seller drank two fewer cups of tea for only three days (thereby saving Rs 5 a day), she would have saved enough money in ninety days to be completely debt-free. Trust the maths of these two Nobel Laureates; or you can use your reflective thinking to check it out. The fruit seller would increase her income by Rs 40 a day, equivalent to about half a day's wages. Just imagine! all by giving up only six cups of tea. One would expect the fruit seller to grab this opportunity as 'these vendors are sitting under what appears to be as close to a money tree as we are likely to find anywhere. Why don't they shake it a bit more?'[12]

Good question: why don't they? The answer is in the framing of the issue and the peanuts effect. Under the cognitive stress of cash-flow constraints, the fruit seller does not go through a deliberative process of adding up the costs and doing a lengthy cash-flow analysis, but instead relies on her automatic thinking to sell her fruit, drink her tea, pay the 'peanuts' to the creditor, and go home.

As a matter of fact, this insight led Professor Muhammad Yunus to the revolutionary idea of microfinance. Yunus is widely regarded as the father of this global movement, first initiated in Bangladesh in the 1970s, and has been recognized for his work by the award of the Nobel Prize (for peace) in 2006. While no panacea, microfinance institutions have played a significant role in reducing rural poverty, not only in Bangladesh, but also around the world, empowering women, and significantly promoting good governance in many sectors of rural economies.

9.5 The nudge

As individuals, we are constantly making big and small decisions, making choices from a bewildering, complex, and sometimes even contradictory array of options. We do so by drawing on our automatic and deliberative thinking, which makes one option more salient than the others. A 'nudge' may further help in this process and may even change our behaviour. Notice that a nudge is not a mandate: it does not force, forbid, penalize, or even reward any particular choice. It merely suggests, but it could be a necessary and very useful trigger for us to choose better.[13]

Drawing on these insights of how individuals think, and with the assistance of cleverly chosen nudges, policy and institutional interventions can be much better designed. By consciously employing mechanisms such as better framing, anchoring, simplification, and reminders, policymakers can help people make better choices, which in turn can result in reduced poverty and other benefits of improved social outcomes. Note, too, that those interventions using such mechanisms are also relatively low-cost alternatives to other policy alternatives, such as subsidies or targeted loans for the poor.

9.6 Contending with the long staying power of mental models and norms

As we saw in the previous chapter, mental models emerge in a society through shared experiences, and can be passed down generations. They have long staying powers, almost as if they are etched on to one's DNA. While they can have positive effects, say, in bequeathing high social capital to the folks living in Northern Italy or jointly beneficial collection on the ancient irrigation networks in Bali, they can also outlive their relevance and be counterproductive, for example seen in the enduring absence of mutual trust in several African societies long after the slave trade had ended.

But some mental models may never have been useful to begin with. Recall the case study from India where publicly revealing the caste identity of students in a mixed-caste group negatively influenced the performance of the so-called low-caste students. When the caste identities were not made salient, the low-caste boys performed just as well as the high-caste boys. However, when the castes were revealed, the performance levels of the low-caste boys plummeted. Thus, highlighting the caste identity triggers an automatic response in them to alter their behaviour to fit the expectations of their unfortunate mental models. The bright and capable low-caste student probably starts thinking: 'I can't, or dare not, excel . . . I must know my place'.

The power and persistence of mental models are striking. Changing them is difficult and cannot be done overnight, but they are not immutable either. Conscious policy interventions 'may be able to expose people to alternative experiences, ways of thinking . . . that expand mental models'.[14] This may enable society to contend with the long staying powers of mental models and change them, or even eliminate them over time. Though norms and mental models are not the same concepts, they have similar characteristics, and as we saw earlier in this chapter, changing norms is difficult as well. Norms develop over time, based on shared experiences, and are socially enforced. And, like mental models, they can also become irrelevant or even counterproductive for the host society over time.

9.6.1 Changing norms

Consider the issue of female genital cutting, discussed earlier. According to available UNICEF estimates, at least 200 million girls and women alive today have been cut in thirty-one countries,[15] even though the practice is globally recognized (including by countries who, ironically, still practise it) as a violation of the women's human rights and has many harmful consequences. However, though still widely practised in some countries, with a frequency as high as 90 per cent in some countries such as Somalia, Guinea, and Djibouti, there has been an overall decline in the prevalence of this practice over the last three decades. In the 31 countries with nationally representative data, the prevalence has declined from about half of girls so cut in the 1980s to about a third now. What is of interest to us is: how did such a change happen to a centuries-old practice over a relatively short period of time? It is interesting to note a parallel with another sordid ancient practice: foot binding of women extensively practised in China even as late as the beginning of the twentieth century. But within one generation, this thousand-year-old practice had ended. How? Reformers first drew attention to the fact that foot binding was exclusively a Chinese practice, not practised anywhere else in the world. Foot binding was an exception, not the rule. They explained the advantages of natural feet and perhaps most significantly, they formed 'natural foot societies' as a direct effort to change the social norms encouraging foot binding. Members of such societies 'pledged not to allow their sons to marry women with bound feet, as well as not to bind their daughters' feet'.[16]

Norms often persist not because people believe in them themselves, but because they believe that others do and fear sanctions if they deviate from that behaviour—a classic collective-action problem. This was as true for the practice of foot binding as it is for FGC. In other words, even if the practice of cutting is not part of an individual's mental model, it could well be part of his norms. Many families still practise cutting out of concerns that their daughter may never be able to marry and fear of sanctions and ostracization by others, who in turn probably do the same for similar reasons. Breaking this norm required a tipping point, as in China with the natural foot societies. But researchers found that the girls' families also needed to be offered a 'counter norm' to anchor the change: in this case, it was the basic norm of the importance of health of their daughters and the hope that others in the community would do the same, that is, abandon the harmful practice and adopt the counter norm.

In Ethiopia, this was done by holding public weddings for couples who chose to break with tradition. During the ceremony, the bride and bridesmaids wore signs that read, 'I will not be circumcised. Learn from me!' The groom wore his own placard saying, 'I am happy to marry an uncircumcised woman'.[17] Slowly at first, but then as the campaign caught on, supported by government action, the tide turned. Attitudes began to change. From a 60-per-cent level of support for the practice even as late as 2000, a mere five years later the reported support had dropped by half to 31 per cent. Further, 'younger mothers (15 percent) are nearly five times less likely to have a daughter cut than older mothers (67 percent), indicating that the practice is becoming less common among the youngest age group'.[18] This is of great significance as it implies that not only is the practice of FGC declining and the norm changing, but the mental model of the younger generation, particularly girls and young women, is shifting away from the practice as well.

In Senegal, it was one small group at a time. The first small group of families who resolved to discontinue the practice in 1997 recruited some more, who in turn convinced others, till a tipping point was reached. Twelve years later, in 2009 more than four thousand Senegalese villages were FGC-free.

In Egypt, the approach to confronting the issue of FGC was based on the positive deviance process: 'focus on the successful exceptions (i.e., positive deviants), not the failing norm'.[19] Thus, the campaigners focused on the 3 per cent of the women who had not been subject to FGC and got them to speak on camera to tell their stories and what could be learnt from them.

These are all very encouraging findings, not only portending continued declines in the practice of FGC but more broadly presenting the argument that norms and mental models need not be considered immutable. True, changes of long-held beliefs are neither easy nor quick, but such changes can and do happen. While mental models are often more durable, 'social states are often more fragile than might be supposed because they depend on social norms to which people may not have much allegiance'.[20]

In each of the cases cited above, and more generally, the first movers or the norm entrepreneurs exploit this fact and gradually create the tipping points (the new norm bandwagons) when the existing norms begin to give way. What is striking is that after a long period of an existing norm which appears totally entrenched and unyielding, societies may experience 'norm cascades' when there are sudden rapid shifts towards new norms. 'The attack on apartheid in South Africa, the fall of Communism, the use of the term "liberal" as one of opprobrium, the rise of the feminist movement' would be examples of such cascades.[21]

Changing norms needs collective actions. Participatory deliberations, public commitment, a slow but steady push to raise awareness by a group of norm entrepreneurs, empowering the affected people, their families and friends, the value of positive deviance, or offering a counter norm to anchor the change, are forms of such actions. Another important means of shifting norms is the collective efforts of the government and the use of law. We discussed these at some length in the last chapter but let it suffice to remind ourselves here that laws and regulations can change not only the incentives for actions but also the social meaning of those actions. Thus, the social meaning of the wearing of helmets or giving up smoking or recycling can be altered through legal means to brand them as virtuous desirable behaviours.[22]

9.7   Finding ways to enhance collective cooperation

We know that while individuals can be selfish, they can also be cooperative, but do not wish to be taken for a ride by others: 'Voluntary cooperation is fragile because individual willingness to cooperate depends on expectations about the co-operation of others'.[23] An experiment at Hokkaido University revealed this phenomenon well: subjects cooperated more fully when assured that others who did not cooperate would be punished.[24] Introduction of punishment increased cooperation. In other words, humans are conditional cooperators and research shows that people would thus more readily enter into institutions with like-minded cooperators. This is an important insight for policymakers when considering interventions and societal institutions. Institutions to enforce the rule of law in a society may thus be more effective if they 'enhance the salience of social preferences by assuring people that those who conform to moral norms will not be exploited by their self-interested fellow citizens'.[25] The assurance of a third party (the state, for example) that they will penalize free riders allows citizens to act pro-socially and contribute to the collective good without the fear of being exploited by their less co-operative compatriots.

Another institutional insight follows from the above: a case for greater transparency. Making transactions more public, particularly of those in positions of authority, greater disclosures, and building in opportunities for ordinary citizens to observe their conduct may be helpful in assuring a fair sharing of social obligations by all.

We have seen earlier that in his pathbreaking study of voluntary blood donation in Britain, Titmuss had observed that economic incentives can sometimes be counterproductive: they could overwhelm and crowd out social preferences. However, it would be wrong to conclude that economic incentives by themselves are the cause of this crowding out and thus should have 'a reduced role in the governance of economic interactions.'[26] Economic incentives and social preferences could sometimes be complements (reinforcing), and sometimes be substitutes (distracting) for each other. This is so because incentives do not just provide economic signals by changing relative prices, but they also convey social meanings of trust, reputational image, and norms in the context of that society's cultural framework. Thus, what causes the crowding out or crowding in is not the incentives per se, but how they are perceived by the target audience, and this 'depends on the social relationships among the actors, the information the incentives provide, and the pre-existing normative frameworks of the actors.'[27] In designing appropriate incentives to motivate greater social cooperation and contributions to public goods, policymakers thus need to be sensitive to the effect of the cultural and social contexts on the incentives. Since societies display varying degrees of altruism, reciprocity, and mutual trust in different situations, the optimal policy responses have to be accordingly tailored.[28]

Recall the doubling in the number of tardy parents at the Israeli day-care centre when a fine was imposed on them for coming late to pick up their children. By contrast, a small tax on grocery bags enacted in Ireland resulted in a dramatic 94-per-cent reduction in their use in only two weeks.[29] Identical (dis)incentives in both cases: totally opposite results. Social preferences were crowded out in one case and crowded in in the other. It is not thus the incentives per se which matter, but the context in which they are carried out.

In the case of the day-care centre, no justification was provided for the introduction of the fine—how rampant the lateness was, how it was inconveniencing the teachers. Parents thus saw the fines as a market solution and felt 'morally disengaged', since they were now buying the extra time during which the children stayed at the centre. Hence, there was no need to feel guilty or embarrassed for being late. By contrast, a substantial publicity campaign preceded the introduction of the Irish plastic-bag tax, which was presented as a social obligation of a good citizen to reduce the use of plastic in the country. Paying the minimal tax was not the issue. People responded positively to the greater cause for a collective good.

The information content of economic incentives is an important factor in determining how such incentives are perceived. In the Public Goods games, it is often seen that fines imposed by peers on free riders, or on low contributors, has positive effects and hence the emergence of the tit for tat strategy is an appropriate strategy to motivate cooperation. By contrast, fines imposed by principals on agents are seen as authoritarian imposi-tions and thus instinctively resisted.

The key challenge for policymakers is thus to see how incentives can be designed which are 'more likely to be complements rather than sub-stitutes for social preferences, crowding them in rather than crowd them out'.[30] To do this, policymakers would need to activate people's pro-social instincts 'such as the desire to be treated fairly, seen as reputable members of the community and recognise their feelings of shame when others re-gard them as having failed in this'.[31]

Easier said than done, but it would help policymakers to understand the nature of sociality to begin with. In societies with low social cap-ital, as in the example of Montegrano discussed in the previous chapter, the diluting effect of incentives will be minimal. Economic incentives will probably work quite well here. By contrast, not only might eco-nomic incentives be less effective in societies where social preferences are stronger, as in the North Italian communities, they might also be less needed.

Cultural context also matters, and identical interventions are likely to be perceived differently in different societies. Consider two variations of a trust game played in different cultural settings: Saudi Arabia and the US. In the first version, Player 1 (the investor) can offer a part of her en-dowment to the investee, Player 2, which will also be supplemented by the experimenter. Player 2 can pay back whatever she wishes to Player 1, who must accept and has no option of recourse. In version 2, Player 1 has the option of imposing a fine if she feels that Player 2 has betrayed her trust. Compared to version 1, a substantially larger fraction of the Saudi investors trusted their partners under version 2, while a substantially smaller fraction of American investors did.[32] Again, the same incentives but opposite results in the two cultures.

Obviously, both economic incentives and social preferences are im-portant in designing appropriate and effective policy and institutional interventions. The challenge for policymakers is to know ex ante (or at least be able to make a reasonable judgement) the effects of the incen-tives before implementing them. How might the proposed incentives interact with the social preferences of her target group: will one crowd out or crowd in?

The cases and experiments cited above are all ex post and even then, the findings and conclusions have not always been clear-cut. However, literature points to a possible guiding principle: present the incentives as an effort to motivate individual behaviour changes, for example, not to use plastic bags, to achieve a socially desirable outcome, that is, less pollution, rather than 'being offended by it as either unjust or a threat to her autonomy or in some other way reflecting badly on her intentions'.[33]

9.8 Changing mental models

Ultimately, societies must find ways to change mental models which might have emerged in the distant past, but unfortunately still persist even though they are no longer valid or relevant and in fact, may even be counterproductive. New mental models more suited to the present circumstances are obviously needed.

Mental models play a significant role when people make big life decisions—whether or not to educate their daughters, to save and invest, to actively participate in civic matters. Consequently, mental models affect development policymaking as well. In designing appropriate economic and social laws, regulations, and policies, and assessing the viability of implementing them, policymakers need to recognize and understand the mental models that people may be using to react to those initiatives.

Mental models and institutions such as caste and gender roles are closely related, and sometimes policies to change institutions may be adopted which may hopefully influence and thus change the mental models as well. Consider a significant institutional change in India: a 1993 constitutional amendment (the Panchayati Raj Amendment Act) which mandated that one third of leader positions in the village councils would be reserved for women. Contrary to some early fears, the gender quotas 'do not seem to create a backlash among citizens—rather evidence suggests that voters use new information about how female leaders perform to update their beliefs about women'.[34] A study by the Poverty Action Lab co-founded by Banerjee and Duflo concluded that 'quotas improved men's perceptions of women as leaders, ... (and) increased the aspiration of girls'.[35] Interestingly, another study found that women were more likely to get elected in constituencies which previously were designated as reserved for women only.[36] Changes in the institution of political affirmative action for women contributed, at least somewhat, to changes in the attitudes of men towards women.

Catching them young could be a possible avenue for changing mental models. Since primary school and early education comprise a formative experience for children, what they learn and are exposed to at home and in school helps shape their mental models. In the US, bussing children to schools outside their immediate neighbourhood was an effort in such 'horizontal teaching systems', in which children from different racial and economic backgrounds would interact both inside and outside the classrooms. Hopefully, this helped change the mental models of the youngsters regarding racial prejudices and discrimination at an early age before their inherited mental models had taken deep roots in their psyche.

The suggestive powers of powerful role models or exposure to different cultural and social practices through, say, the media, can also have significant influences on people's mental models. First Lady Betty Ford was the first prominent public figure to utter the words 'breast cancer' following her diagnosis of the disease and radical mastectomy in September 1974. It is widely believed in the oncology community that Mrs Ford's open declaration was the beginning of National Breast Cancer Awareness campaigns in the US and a surge of women getting tested, diagnosed, and treated at much earlier stages of this disease followed.[37]

In several studies around the world, greater exposure to the outside world through television has been found to affect mental models. In a groundbreaking anthropological study, significant changes in perceptions about the outside world were noticed after the introduction of television in an isolated area of the Amazon, in Brazil. This happened particularly in two ways: 'i) an increase in the knowledge of facts about the world at large and ii) change in the community's perception of its own collective life quality'.[38] In India, a three-year-long study in five states of the country concluded that the introduction of cable television in rural areas affected gender attitudes with significant increases in women's autonomy, decreases in the reported acceptability of domestic violence and son preference, greater use of contraception and spacing of childbearing and increased school enrolment for younger children.[39] A radio soap opera, *Twende na Wakati* (Let's Go with the Times), in Tanzania on the adoption of family-planning methods, aired in the early 1990s, was linked to subsequent increased interspousal communication about family planning, increased approval of contraceptive use, and increased current practice of family planning.[40]

Stating the obvious, perhaps, but it is important to emphasize that all such measures, as noted in this chapter, should be seen as small but important steps in the complex and long (often multigenerational) process of changing mental models, but which in turn have significant effects on institutional changes in a society.

9.9 Human agency: a critical enabler of change

The previous sections above and the chapters in this part of the book have discussed how individuals as humans (rather than robotic Econs) can be inconsistent in their behavior, selfish at times looking out only for their interests but also simultaneously generous and altruistic, often to total strangers. We have also discussed how people behaving rationally from their individual point of view may end up collectively in a 'bad equilibrium' suffering the consequences of Sen's 'rational fools' syndrome.

Given these realities of human nature (which cannot just be assumed away as is done in neo-classical economics), how would a society shift from bad to good equilibrium (high to low, preferably zero, corruption)? How could society shift to a more desirable 'focal point' (rule by law rather than a free for all)? How would a society break out of the 'cage of norms' (FGC or the dowry system)?

We have discussed at some length how challenging these shifts can be since they depend critically on beliefs, norms, and mental models. Many of these, if not immutable, have almost been hard wired into our individual and collective DNAs. But history also tells us that societal changes can and do happen, even if very slowly, as we will see in the next part of this book. Sometimes the changes happen due to exogenous shocks (such as a war) or fortuitous events (such as the emergence of a transformational leader). But sometimes changes also occur endogenously due to internally generated pressures in a society, and it would be useful to see what such enabling factors for the changes might be.

Underlying all social changes- be it in individual beliefs, or social norms or mental models-is a principal actor: the individual. As an individual, she has to be the first mover; ultimately, it is her agency -often defined as her control over the life she wishes to pursue- that will make the difference. Education and health are the two basic constituents of a person's agency and thus in its journey from Here to Denmark, a society cannot but consider providing these two public goods as a critical starting point or building blocks.

In the language of Sen's pathbreaking capability approach, education and health both increase an individual's assets ('beings' and 'doings') and her 'capabilities' to transform them into well-being, both for her and the society she lives in.[41,42]

Education and health are basic human rights and are to be cherished on that basis alone-their intrinsic values. But their instrumental values to unlock an individual's capabilities and enhance their stock of human capital are no less important.

Evidence around the world convincingly show that education enhances the civic engagement of their population and creates greater social cohesion and higher levels of social capital. As a recent World Bank study succinctly concludes, 'education increases awareness and understanding of political issues, fosters the socialization needed for effective political activity, and increases civic skills.'[43] Similarly, studies in Benin and Nigeria show that increased education substantially expanded the civic and political engagement of their population, even decades later.[44,45]

Difficult as changing beliefs and social norms are (and mental models even more so), education is a major force to accelerate that process for reasons mentioned above. Evidence from advanced and emerging economies alike show that education increase trust, tolerance, and civic agency. These are key ingredients that enable 'norm entrepreneurs' to shift norms and move society to a more favorable focal point or a better equilibrium (of course, often at a very slow pace).[46,47] Strikingly,

education has multigenerational effects as well-education begets educa-
tion- and countries that 'had achieved mass education by 1870 had less
corruption in 2010'.[48]

We had previously noted how our individual behavior depends to a
large extent on what we believe others will do and of course, they in turn
do the same. Thus, greater the opportunity of interacting and communicating with others in a society, greater would be the potential civic engagement in that society. As noted above, education would facilitate such
an engagement. Participation in the conduct of affairs of the society is
critical for open access orders in that society to emerge where people can
expect and indeed demand justice and equal access to opportunities, irrespective of gender, caste, creed, or religion. In other words, such participation would facilitate the emergence of inclusive institutions in that
society.

Health is the other crucial element of human agency. It is also a basic
freedom that all individuals and indeed all societies aspire to. Like
education, good health is valuable in its own right (its intrinsic value)
but has significant instrumental value as well. In fact, health is a crucial enabler of all other well-beings, such as education. We have noted
above several key attributes of education in enhancing individual and
collective welfare. Education also plays a crucial role in moving society to a better equilibrium. However, on closer examination, it is not
hard to see that none of education's values would be realized if an individual were also not healthy. Thus, as Sen observes, 'in any discussion
of social equity and justice, illness and health must figure as a major
concern'.[49]

To draw a broad conclusion, it follows that health and education are
the essential building blocks for inclusive institutions which in turn are
necessary for a successful travel from Here to Denmark.

9.10 Summary

Basing public policy choices and institutional designs on neoclassical
assumptions of unbounded rationality can be misleading. A better
understanding of how humans actually think and act will lead to better

interventions. One immediate conclusion of such an understanding is that social contexts matter. What would work in Denmark would not work Here. Thus, policy and institutional prescriptions need to be context-specific and cannot be some imported models of 'best practice'.

The relentless grind of poverty imposes a disproportionately unfair cognitive tax on the poor. It narrows the frame of choices they believe are open to them, and so they often choose options which are costlier, thus exacerbating their income deprivation and compromising their future.

Humans are also not blessed with unbounded willpower and hence suffer from the intention–action divide: our good intentions do not always translate into action. While succumbing to the temptation of procrastination is an all-too-familiar human tendency, it is exacerbated by the cognitive depletion resulting from the financial stress of income poverty. And again, consciously building these behavioural realities into institutional designs can produce some effective solutions.

Research in psychological and behavioural sciences show that 'bounded' humans could sometimes use some help in their complex decision-making process, a nudge. A nudge is not an externally imposed 'thou shalt' mandate. It just draws one's attention to some salient information or practice, but that gentle suggestion could trigger a better response from the human automatic and reflective thinking processes, to choose a better option. Evidence shows that drawing on these insights of the human thinking processes, and with the assistance of some nudges, policy and institutional interventions can be better designed, leading to reduced poverty and better social outcomes.

By the very nature of their evolution, norms and mental models have long staying power. They can have positive effects of the collective knowledge and wisdom of the ancestors bequeathed to successive generations. But they can also outlive their relevance and be counterproductive. Changing the negative norms and mental models is not easy, but they are not immutable either.

Changing norms needs collective action. Participatory deliberations, empowering the affected people, raising social awareness, or offering a counter norm to anchor the change, are some such possible actions. Actions by the government and the use of a law can also help. Laws change incentives, and thus the motivation for action.

Changes in mental models can follow a similar process but are usually more difficult to bring about, since they are self-enforced. Such a model leads to a mental image of the larger world around oneself, and one's place in it, which is difficult to shake off once it takes root; but with better understanding of these behavioural aspects, societies can devise better institutional interventions.

Due to the long staying powers of human beliefs, social norms and mental models, societies often get stuck in situations of bad equilibrium, becoming captives in a cage of norms. Moving to a better equilibrium is not easy. But changes do happen, though often at a very slow pace. Human agency is a key enabler of that process. Education and health are crucial constituents of human agency and are essential building blocks for building inclusive institutions in a society. To move from Here to Denmark, public policy will thus need to focus on these areas as matters of greatest urgency.

Part II: Key messages

1. *Humans are not always fully rational. A better understanding of how humans think and act will lead to better design of institutions.*
2. *Social contexts matter.*
3. *Due to the long staying powers of human beliefs, social norms and mental models, societies often get stuck in situations of bad equilibrium.*
4. *Moving to a better equilibrium is not easy but changes do happen, though often at a very slow pace.*
5. *Human agency is a key enabler of that process.*

PART III
LESSONS FROM THE PAST

Overview

Open any newspaper, on any given day, anywhere in the world, and it is highly likely that you will be looking at some lurid details of yet another example of 'bad governance', be it a gross violation of the rule of law, egregious corruption in high places, or injustices visited upon the poor and the weak. Libraries full of books and journals are replete with instances of bad governance around the world. We would hardly be adding much value if we added some more examples to the litany of such cases.

What we want to do instead is to look at some examples of 'good governance': countries which started from Here and have managed to chart a path to Denmark, even if all might not have quite reached there as yet. They have significantly improved their governance over time, confronted injustices—big and small—in the lives of their people, reduced the incidence of corruption, built credibility, and fostered faith in the system and institutions which have withstood assaults on their integrity and performed well.

History teaches us that societal changes from limited-access orders to open-access orders take time—often centuries and generations; best practices cannot be arbitrarily transplanted; dynamics of local politics, culture, and social norms drive behaviour and are hard to change, and when they do, they take time and do so in response to internal driving forces and not to external demands.

But experiences in various parts of the world and at various times in the last millennium also offer hope that things can change for the better. Denmark, the country, is itself an eminent example of changing the course of history to become a leading light of good governance, freedom, and well-being such that it has become a metaphor for itself.

Its institutions and governance at one time (in the 1600s) were in very poor shape; many things were indeed 'rotten in the state of Denmark'. But with concrete, sustained steps, things improved, slowly but steadily. Great Britain and Japan are other examples of countries which moved from limited- to open-access order and prospered. But again, these processes were set in motion centuries ago. In more recent times, the experiences of Botswana, South Korea, and Uruguay provide some evidence that 'history is not destiny'.

In Part III of this book, we look at the real-life transformational journeys of these countries from Here to Denmark. The intention is to see if some common themes may be gleaned, and lessons drawn from their experiences.

10

How Denmark Got to Denmark and Great Britain's Journey

10.1 Introduction

We start with the usual suspect: Denmark, the country, as the proxy of Denmark, the metaphor. From a state of 'something is rotten in the state of Denmark' as Prince Hamlet lamented, Denmark has, over time, become a beacon of good governance, and 'getting to Denmark' is the professed objective of many a country.[1]

More recently, Francis Fukuyama has extolled the virtues of 'Denmark' as 'a mythical place that is known to have good and political institutions ... is stable, democratic, peaceful, prosperous, inclusive. Everyone would like to figure out how to transform Afghanistan, Haiti, Iraq, Nigeria, or Somalia into *Denmark*'.[2]

But even if 'Denmark' were to be a mythical, hypothetical construct, it would be instructive to see how Denmark, the country itself got to 'Denmark', and is our first case study in this chapter.

We had discussed the concepts of limited- and open-access orders in a society in a previous chapter and noted that institutions in the former tend to be extractive, while they are inclusive in the latter. We had also noted that good governance ultimately thrives only in open-access-order societies which enable inclusive institutions to take root. Prior to the seventeenth century, extractive institutions were the norm throughout history. Britain was no exception, and yet it was here that the 'first truly inclusive society ... and the Industrial Revolution emerged'.[3] We also look at how that happened as another instructive case study in the evolution of an open-access-order (inclusive) society.

From Here to Denmark. Rajat M. Nag and Harinder S. Kohli, Oxford University Press.
© Rajat Mohan Nag and Harinder Singh Kohli 2023. DOI: 10.1093/oso/9780198893103.003.0010

10.2 Denmark

10.2.1 Transition from a Viking to a feudal society

At the turn of the second millennium, as Denmark was transitioning from a Viking to a feudal society, the country was still reasonably pluralistic. Though a king (Sweyn II Estridsson r: 1047–1074) ruled, the *things*, or local assemblies of freemen, governed. Usually headed by the local chieftain, the *things* were a unique medieval Scandinavian institution consisting of the most influential members of the local communities (the male heads of households) who decided on royal succession, legislated on all relevant issues, and also served as the court, settling all legal issues of contention.

However, as feudalism gradually took hold in the Scandinavian countries, including Denmark, the political power of the landed aristocracy increased at the cost of the common subjects and the king as well. As a matter of fact, in 1282, the nobility moved to formally limit the power of the then reigning monarch, Erik V, by presenting him a charter very much along the lines of the Magna Carta in England. That charter (the *haandfaestning*) was essentially Denmark's first constitution, which established a Danish parliament (the *hof*) and extracted some far-reaching concessions for the Danish nobility in return for their support of the king. Among the concessions were the provisions that the *hof* would function as the land's highest court, nobles could not be imprisoned simply on suspicion, and that the *hof* would be called to meet at least once a year. The local *things* gradually lost influence, pluralism suffered, and the aristocrats governed with a newly constrained monarch on the throne.

10.2.2 Emergence of the Catholic Church

The trend towards diminished pluralism in Denmark was exacerbated by the gradual emergence of another power centre in the country: the Catholic Church, which had started establishing its presence in the Danish territory as early as the tenth century. By the end of the thirteenth century, the Church had amassed significant wealth and power, and the monarch now had to contend with not only the landed aristocrats and the nobility but also the Church, which had to be accommodated in the power structure of the country. This was done in 1360, when the then reigning monarch, Valdemar IV, reached a 'great national peace' accord, under which the *hof* was replaced by the Rigsråd (Council of the Realm)—consisting of the nobility and the high prelates of the Church and the king's Retterting (Court of Law), which became the Supreme Court. In essence, then, the country's political institutions still remained extractive, as 'Danes were in reality not represented in a national assembly, and thus had no say in political matters'.[4]

10.2.3   The Kalmar Union

The 'great national peace' accord gave Valdemar IV and his heirs time and space to consolidate Denmark's political and military powers. Through strategic alliances and marriages, the then Danish King Erik III managed to get himself crowned as the monarch of Sweden and Norway as well, in 1397 in Kalmar, Sweden, establishing the so-called Kalmar Union of the three Scandinavian states. The Union, never smooth in any case, still managed to survive for more than a century, but disintegrated in 1523 when Sweden declared its independence, bringing the Kalmar Union to an end.

10.2.4   Rising power of the monarchy

Throughout this entire period, Danish institutions continued to remain extractive, and society became more restrictive (limited access à la North, particularistic à la Mungiu-Pippidi), with the monarch assuming even more powers of exclusion at the cost of both the nobles and the Church. Prior to the fifteenth century, wealth was the principal determinant of nobility: any Dane who could assure the King of providing a certain number of able-bodied men for military service, at his expense, could become a noble, enjoying tax exemption status and other social privileges. The King gradually changed the entry requirement to now prove that his father and grandfather, at least, had enjoyed similar privileges. But more importantly, even then the title of a noble was not assured, and could only be granted by the King at his pleasure, and which he now accorded more sparingly. The number of nobles gradually declined, with fewer people now left to challenge the monarch in the Rigsråd, but the ones who remained as nobles became more powerful, with important ramifications for the monarch later.

The changes in the Danish Church were much more dramatic. Reformation of the Catholic Church, which ultimately led to the establishment of Protestantism, had begun to influence all of Western Europe in the early sixteenth century. Denmark was no exception. In the midst of political turmoil and a civil war, the Danish Lutheran Church was established in 1536, with the reigning sovereign as its supreme secular authority. The newly crowned and empowered monarch, King Christian III (r: 1537–1559) arrested the Catholic bishops, virtually eliminating their political influence in the country, and confiscated all church property, vastly adding to the Crown wealth. This permanently eliminated the influence of the Catholic Church in Denmark, but also minimized the potential influence of the Lutheran Church, since the monarch was now also its head.

Simultaneously with the above developments, the peasants also suffered further losses in their political power, which was minimal in any case to begin with. A devastating outbreak of the plague in the mid-fourteenth century, expropriation of their lands when they could not pay off their debts, steady migration of labour from the rural areas to the towns as the country urbanized, all caused significant shortage of labour for agriculture, which was still the principal source of economic activities and livelihood in the kingdom. However, rather than seeing a rise in their bargaining power and wages reflecting the shortage of agricultural labour, the peasants lost power instead. The landed aristocracy used their economic and political power to cartelize the labour market and established the institution of *vornedskab*, akin to serfdom, through which the peasants were 'bonded to their place of birth, and men between the ages of 14–36 could not leave their current estates without the permission of the landowner'.[5]

An immediate outcome of these developments was greater concentration of power in the state: that is, the monarchy. New central administrative offices were set up, among them the Rentekammeret (precursor to the modern-day Ministry of Finance and Treasury), in charge of the collection and auditing of state revenues, and the chancery, in charge of maintaining all public records. Administrative capacities were gradually built up; improved processes of levying and collecting taxes and duties led to more efficient financial administration.

A strong central state marked the reign of the next two monarchs but their preoccupation, perhaps even obsession, with trying to reinstate the Kalmar Union and win back Sweden almost proved to be their undoing. Even after Denmark's involvement in two long and inconclusive wars, the Northern Seven Years' War (1563–1570) and the Thirty Years' War (1618–1648), Sweden was still independent, and Denmark's financial situation continued to be precarious.

10.2.5 The catastrophic war of 1657 and emergence of absolutist monarchy

The next event turned out to be a major turning point in Denmark's history. During the reign of Frederick III (r. 1648–1670), hostilities broke out again with Sweden in 1657 as part of the First Northern War. Denmark suffered a catastrophic defeat, leading to the humiliating surrender of almost a third of the then joint Danish-Norwegian kingdom to Sweden. As a matter of fact, it would perhaps be no exaggeration to say that 'Denmark was only saved by its geographic position. Other states (The Netherlands) intervened in favour of Denmark because they feared total Swedish dominance in the Baltic Sea.'[6]

Several far-reaching consequences followed, with serious implications for how economic and political institutions ultimately developed in Denmark:

The immediate impact was a huge loss in state revenues collected from the lost provinces, and this, coupled with the crippling costs of waging the war in the first place, resulted in a severe economic downturn 'in which the state came close to bankruptcy'.[7]

As head of the state and the Church, the monarch was in a double bind. Not only was he entrusted with looking after the welfare of his subjects (for which he was increasingly short of funds), but also his military ambitions and wars with Sweden had created what has been termed a 'fiscal-military state'.[8] And the financial needs of the fiscal-military state were indeed very pressing, particularly with the loss of a third of the state.

Interestingly, the subjects judged the monarch, King Frederik III (r.1648–1670), somewhat more kindly than they viewed the nobles. This might have been partly due to the monarch's being accorded a special halo as the temporal head of the Church, and the physical proximity of the aristocracy to the subjects, leading them to be seen as the greater cause of their misery, rather than the monarch in distant Copenhagen. There was also a general perception that, while the King had made heroic efforts during the siege of Copenhagen through the hard winter of 1659 to fight the Swedes, the nobility had not risen to the occasion, and had seemed more intent on preserving their narrow interests rather than the country's defence. The special privileges they enjoyed, particularly their exemption from paying any taxes, had always been galling to the common subjects, and it now boiled over in the wake of the catastrophic defeat in the war with Sweden.

With strong support from the common subjects, the bourgeoisie, the ecclesiastical estates, and at least some sections of the military, King Frederik III rose to this extraordinary situation and was acclaimed as the hereditary sovereign of the country. This was a very significant move. Thus far, Denmark had had an elective monarchy, and though the eldest son of the monarch had usually been elected as his successor, the aristocracy had held considerable power and influence in the rule of the country. The adoption of the hereditary monarchy gave King Frederik III the assurance of unchallenged continuity beyond him, and he moved fast to consolidate his power. In 1665, he compelled the nobility to accept a new constitution—Lex Regia, or the Royal Law of 1665—which gave the monarch 'unrestricted and absolute power, his main task being to keep the Kingdom undivided and enforce the Lutheran religion'.[9] The new Constitution (also dubbed the King's Law), the only written absolutist constitution in Europe, eliminated the Rigsråd and diluted the special privileges the nobility had so far enjoyed. Political power was now vested very personally in the King himself and his newly established Privy Council. Thus began a long and durable period of 'absolutism' in Denmark, which was to last till 1849, when it gave way to a constitutional monarchy governed under a parliamentary system.

10.2.6 Increased state capacity, and emergence of inclusive economic institutions

The newly empowered monarch needed a centralized administration to mobilize resources, and among the first steps he took was to reform the bureaucracy, which till now had been more under the control of the aristocracy. As a matter of fact, many of the high offices in the civil administration were held by the nobles themselves.

The purpose of rationalizing the bureaucracy was essentially threefold. First, the monarch wanted an efficient civil service which, among other functions, would aggressively collect taxes for the rather depleted central treasury. Second, in return for paying the higher taxes, subjects demanded that they be treated fairly and receive service and security from the Crown, which the monarch wisely acceded to. But to do so, having an impartial and a competent bureaucracy in the Weberian framework was critical. And third, the monarch wished to reduce the powers and influence of the aristocracy.

Astutely, the monarch also abolished many of the distinctions of rank and class, which had crept into the Danish social hierarchy; and all citizens were now considered equal. Gradually, the prominence of the nobility in the country's civil service was diluted, and a new group of bourgeois bureaucrats emerged to take their place. Given their non-noble origins, it was expected that they would be more loyal to the monarch, and more likely to have no political agenda of their own. And in fact, that's what happened. The new corps of carefully chosen civil servants knew that they had been appointed because of their competencies, not because of their wealth or noble origins. But a clear message was also conveyed to the bureaucracy: they had all been appointed by the monarch at whose pleasure they served, no government job was now a sinecure for life, and performance was key.

Lest one gets too carried away and believes that all ills of the past had been cleared in one fell swoop, it would be fair to recall that the past practice of 'selling of public offices' did not disappear immediately.[10] But even so, an immediate change had been achieved: even when these offices were sold, the needed qualifications and competencies for appointment to the job were not ignored.

Simultaneous with the centralization of the State (through stronger state administration institutions) another critically important consequence followed: emergence of inclusive economic institutions. With the diminution of the nobility, the peasants now enjoyed greater mobility of movement to where the demand for workers was, rather than being 'bound' to a particular noble to till his land in serfdom. Recognition of property rights also began to be recognized by law and the strengthened bureaucracy and judiciary could assure the common subjects of the sanctity of their person and property.

10.2.7   Continuity of reforms and professionalization of the judiciary and the bureaucracy

A striking feature of the Danish reform process was its continuity, with successive monarchs reinforcing and building on their predecessors' commitment and implementation of the reforms to fight poor governance. The reforms were also gradually but firmly entrenched in law. For example, while Frederick III made fighting bureaucratic corruption a high priority for his rule under the new absolutist constitution, it was his son and successor, Christian V (r. 1670–1699) who gave much heft to these measures by legally banning the taking and giving of bribes in 1676. Under the Danish Law of 1683, forgery and embezzlement by civil servants was explicitly declared as a crime, with accompanying strict penalties specified. These laws were subsequently toughened further in 1690, including even hard labour and life imprisonment for such crimes.

Further anti-corruption measures were introduced, with greater penalties, by the next monarch, Frederick IV (r. 1699–1730) in 1700, by explicitly bringing the military within the ambit of such measures.

In recognition of the need not only to have strict legal proscriptions against corruption, but also to enforce them well, the monarchy also emphasized the importance of an effective and efficient judiciary. Even in the early years of the absolutist reforms, Danish Law specified strict codes of behaviour expected from the judges and court officials. It is instructive that throughout the eighteenthth century, successive monarchs found it necessary to constantly emphasize and reinforce their commitment and determination to fight poor governance: 'the ban on bribery was renewed over and over and separate groups of officials, such as customs officers, were specifically addressed'.[11]

The start of legal studies at the University of Copenhagen in 1736 led Christian VI (r. 1730–1746) to demand that judges in the crown courts needed to have formal law degrees.

A fundamental political fallout of the emergence of absolutist monarchy in 1660 was the systematic dilution of the influence and power of the aristocracy and the landed nobility. But a corollary of this was the increased direct responsibility and accountability the monarch now bore to ensure his subjects' welfare, peace, and stability in the kingdom. No longer would the monarch have the buffer of the aristocracy between him and his subjects. He would now need a direct line of communication with them, and the Danish Law of 1683 specifically provided for the citizens of the state to be able to directly petition the monarch. A system of petitions (*suppliker*) was established through which an ordinary citizen could bring any matter of concern to the attention of the monarch. This was no idle 'feel-good' sop to the citizens; as Jensen notes in her strikingly detailed paper, 'over the eighteenth century, the use of petitions increased dramatically. If in 1706, the Danish chancellery had received 1,539 petitions, by 1799, it was dealing with 11,298 petitions'.[12]

By the end of the eighteenth century, recruitment to the Danish civil service had become essentially meritocratic, the bureaucracy professionalized with clear rules for entry, performance and behaviour standards laid out, and several provisions for strict penalty for malfeasance embedded in law.

10.2.8 Checks and balances: accountability of the bureaucracy

Certain regulations instituted by the reigning monarchs in the early nineteenth century for close ground-level monitoring made sure that the bureaucracy didn't become as privileged and influential as the aristocracy of preceding generations.

An oversight process started in 1803 and, strengthened over time, kept the bureaucracy in check. Such teams had a wide-ranging authority to inspect the books and accounts of the regional and local governments, ensure compliance with the existing laws, particularly on graft and expected service delivery standards, listen, and scrutinize complaints (*suppliks*) from the general population, and report back their findings and conclusions to the Chancellery and sometimes directly to the monarch himself. An important systemic finding of these field-level inspections in various parts of the kingdom was that the local and regional administrators were not keeping their books satisfactorily. It was not necessarily always intentional, but 'the standard procedures for checking audits and accounting in general were out-of-date, badly organized, and inefficient',[13] and made misuse of state funds, even embezzlement possible.

In 1841, a law was finally adopted which 'introduced a more detailed keeping of accounts, separate account books for separate offices, and a considerable intensification of audits'.[14] The law also abolished civil servants' right to borrow from public funds, a feature which had allowed them this privilege so long as they returned these funds when the accounts were checked. A larger outcome of the 1841 legal reforms was the adoption of new penal codes for corruption in office, wherein the old rules and regulations about official conduct were clearly and comprehensively enshrined in law. There was also equal emphasis on implementation.

Most of these governance reforms in Denmark may be described as proscriptions, following a 'stick' approach. But the monarchs realized that 'carrots' would also be necessary to induce good behaviour. In addition to granting status and honour to those in the service of the Crown, the financial emoluments of civil servants throughout the country were increased under a fixed-salary regime (abolishing the erstwhile part fixed–part variable fee-payment structure). By the latter decades of the nineteenth century, the civil servants were sufficiently reasonably well-off to 'become part of the well-to-do middle class'.[15]

Another important feature of the Danish constitutional reforms was that pensions were recognized as a matter of right rather than an act of royal kindness extended by the monarch at his discretion. The new laws in 1849 under the first constitutional monarch of Denmark, Frederick VII (r. 1848–1863), gave all civil servants the right to receive a pension at age seventy. Interestingly, a couple of years later (in 1851), the law was amended to specify that the pension benefits could also be withdrawn if misconduct in office was later to be found. A strong inducement indeed for a civil servant to practise good governance!

10.2.9   Emergence of constitutional monarchy 1849

Recall our discussion on limited- and open-access order in societies, and the critical importance of the political power structure and contextual social settings in the evolution of institutions. Placing Denmark within that framework, it would follow that the absolute power held by the monarch under the King's Law of 1665 did not allow for the political institutions in the country to be inclusive. During the absolutist period, the monarchy had focused almost exclusively on the greater, and indeed much-needed then, centralization of state power in the person of the monarch. To be fair, successive Danish monarchs practised what has been called 'enlightened despotism', operating within the rule of law and with an increasingly professionalized and competent Weberian bureaucracy and judiciary. However, there was very limited pluralism in the society and institutions were still not inclusive.

Inspired by the French Revolution in the 1790s, demands for political reforms grew around Europe. Further motivated by the example of Norway's adopting its constitution in 1814, which strengthened the legislative powers of the *Storting* (the national Parliament), and the July Revolution in Paris of 1830 (the second French Revolution), a national liberal movement also took root in Denmark, starting with the middle classes of Copenhagen. Its principal demands centred around greater political say through a representative government guaranteed by a formal constitution.

The reigning monarch (Frederik VI) made some concessions and consultative assemblies were established in 1834, but with the representatives to be chosen by the landowning aristocrats, propertied townsfolk, and farmers holding property above a certain size. With only 3 per cent of the population thus having the right to vote, the representation was obviously meaningless, and, in any case, the representatives could only debate and propose laws, and were essentially advisory bodies.

The demands for a greater citizen voice in the country's politics received a major boost as the farmers joined the national liberal movement, which reached a tipping point in 1848 on the heels of revolutions that same year in France and Germany. The reigning monarch, Frederick VII, who had succeeded to the throne earlier that year, agreed to summon a constituent assembly. This led to the end of absolute monarchy in Denmark, to be replaced by a system of constitutional monarchy within the framework of a new constitution, the so-called June constitution, adopted on 5 June 1849. The new constitution now provided for two chambers (the *Folketing*, the lower house, and the *Landsting*, the upper house) sharing legislative powers with the King and his cabinet of ministers, while the courts exercised independent judicial power. The constitution also guaranteed freedom of religions, assembly, and the press.

The transition to constitutional monarchy in 1849 initiated the process of increased plurality and the emergence of inclusive institutions in the country. Even though it took another long sixty-six years to extend voting rights to all adult citizens, irrespective of gender, property holdings, or literacy requirements, Denmark was now well on its way to becoming 'Denmark'. Slowly but surely Denmark transitioned from a limited-access-order state, à la North (a personalized state where who you knew mattered) to an open-access state (an impersonalized, competitive state where what you know matters), states akin to Mungiu-Pippidi's transition from particularistic societies to an ethically universal one.

10.2.10 Denmark to 'Denmark'

In broad brushstrokes, it may be said that the trajectory of Denmark's (the country) journey to 'Denmark' began as early as the mid-1500s with gradually increasing centralization of state powers, with the monarch simultaneously assuming the role of the Head of the Government and of the Danish Lutheran Church. While this reduced pluralism in running the affairs of the state, it enabled the monarch to address issues of ground-level corruption, nepotism, and exploitation of the common folk by the nobles and aristocrats. It was Denmark's remarkably good fortune that successive monarchs persisted in building and expanding on the reforms initiated by their predecessors and the professionalization of the state bureaucracy and the judiciary continued apace for the next three centuries. Economic institutions gradually became more inclusive by increasing labour mobility, recognition of property rights, and emphasis on educational qualifications and competence in recruitment to the civil service and the judiciary. However, the political institutions were still not inclusive, with the monarch holding absolute authority, though exercised in what has been called "enlightened despotism". It was not until 1849 that the country's political institutions started becoming more inclusive, when Denmark moved to a system of constitutional monarchy with political power held by elected bodies of a Parliament. The governance process in the country gradually became more participatory and the country continued to expand the political space for genuine participation by all in a system of robust parliamentary democracy since then.

10.3 Great Britain

10.3.1 'To no one deny or delay right or justice': the Magna Carta

Barely thirty kilometres west of Central London lies a bucolic meadow alongside the river Thames which witnessed one of the most significant events in the course of British history. The meadow was Runnymede, and the event was the signing of the Magna Carta (the Great Charter) by King John on 15 June, 1215. It was not an event the King particularly cherished. He had lost the Angevin-Plantagenet lands in France which had so crippled England financially that the barons, the elite on whom the King depended, had rebelled. They forced him to sign the charter of liberties which emphasized the primacy of the law over all, including the monarchy itself, enshrined in the clause: 'To no one will we sell, to no one deny or delay right or justice'. The first tenuous steps to transition from limited access to an ultimately open order of society, à la North, had been taken in England some 800 years back.

Among other restrictions on his unbridled authority, the King agreed that he would consult with the barons to raise taxes. Of course, the King was most unhappy to have his hands thus tied and had hoped to disregard the charter as 'mere ink on paper' as soon as the barons left Runnymede. But the barons knew their wily King well enough. They did not disarm, as the King had hoped, nor did they go back home. Soon King John lost patience and got the Pope to annul the charter he had just put his royal seal on. But the die was cast, the unquestioned authority of the monarch had been challenged, and England had 'taken its first hesitant step toward pluralism'.[16]

But by no stretch of imagination did this mean that the extractive institutions then existing in England were soon to give way to inclusive ones. As a matter of fact, it would take almost another five centuries before that happened, with the Glorious Revolution in 1688 and the subsequent Industrial Revolution from the mid-1700s, but the process had begun.

Coming back to King John, he did not live long enough to see if his gambit of annulling the Magna Carta would pay off. He died of a short illness (a victim of poisoning, some suspect) barely a year later, in October 1216, and was succeeded by his nine-year-old son, Henry III.

Meanwhile, the Charter had already been widely circulated to bishops and churches around the kingdom and had struck a deep chord in the minds of the elites and ordinary subjects of the realm. And the advisers and governors of the young boy king wisely reinstated the Magna Carta in November 1216—an event probably even more significant for the political evolution of England than the original signing of the Magna Carta itself.

10.3.2 England's first parliament

The political forces unleashed by the Magna Carta resulted in England's first elected parliament in 1265. A remarkable feature of this development was that not only was Parliament now a formal institution challenging the powers of the monarch which had so far gone unconstrained, but a broader section of the society was also now politically empowered. Of course, the fledgling parliament represented only the interests of the elites, the minor aristocrats, the landed gentry, and those in commerce and industry. The common folk were still left out but the process of inclusion had begun.

While these were no doubt significant developments in the move to greater pluralism in England, unsettled political conflicts still continued. We noted earlier (Chapter 5) that evolution of inclusive institutions in a society requires the simultaneous existence of pluralism and centralization of power in the State with a 'monopoly on the means of violence'. The armed power of the aristocrats had prevented this from happening so far in England. However, this began to change with a significant move by the monarch to rapidly disarm the aristocrats, thereby increasing the central power of the State.

Several actions by King Henry VIII (r. 1509–1547) also had significant long-term institutional implications for the country. First, around the 1530s, he established the basic elements of the country's first civil service, leading ultimately to the formation of the executive branch of the State, which till then had essentially been an extension of the royal household. Next and more dramatic was Henry VIII's breakaway from Rome in 1534 on the grounds of the Catholic Church's not accommodating his wish to dissolve his marriage with Queen Catherine, and his subsequent 'Dissolution of the Monasteries' Act, by which all Church lands now belonged to the monarch. Both these moves dramatically reduced the power of the Church and simultaneously, further strengthened and centralized state power.

10.3.3 The early absolutist and extractive years of the Stuarts

With pluralism and centralization both now under way in England, the conditions for inclusive institutions to take root in the country had begun to emerge, but the process was slow and far from complete. By and large, the political and economic institutions still remained primarily extractive during the Tudor period. The last Tudor monarch of England and Ireland, Queen Elizabeth I, died in 1603 without an heir. James VI of Scotland succeeded her as James I, the first Stuart monarch of Great Britain (r. 1603–1625). An immediate problem besetting the new Stuart monarch was the usual one: money. Parliament provided the Crown with limited state funds collected from taxes and customs, typically for purposes such as fighting wars, but otherwise, the monarch was on his own. He was free to raise his own funds and spend as he wished, but was always short of funds. To make up for these shortfalls, James I (and then his son and successor, Charles I, r. 1625–1649) regularly sold portions of the Crown lands, which then progressively reduced future assets available to raise further revenue.

The Stuarts devised two further means to raise new revenues: First, rather honestly called 'impositions', which were essentially additional customs duties imposed on external trade. A particularly despised one was the so-called 'ship money' imposed in 1634. It involved taxing the coastal counties and later extended inland as well to support the Royal Navy. Second, not so honestly called 'loans', often extracted under threats, whose repayments, both in time and amount, were rather uncertain. The Crown would often arbitrarily delay repayments, reduce the interest rates, or not pay the principal at all. The unwilling and unwitting creditors, of course, did not have much recourse against the monarch. At the same time, since neither of these two measures were technically taxes, the Crown did not need parliamentary assent and in fact, could survive even without calling Parliament to session, at least for a while.

These two monarchs (James I and Charles I) extracted more funds by other subtle and not-so-subtle revenue-enhancing measures. They offered monopoly rights to existing or potentially new businesses and sold peerages and hereditary titles. Particularly insidious was the 'dispensation' offered to individuals for a price, and to essentially flout a specific law or regulation, and at times, the Crown simply seized private property. In 1640, for example, in a particularly brazen display of abuse of power, the Crown 'seized £130,000 of bullion, which private merchants had placed in the Tower for safety, causing numerous bankruptcies'.[17]

Despite all this, the Stuarts were always short of funds. Tensions between the King and Parliament and an increasingly large number of the subjects mounted. The situation was further exacerbated by Charles I who, more so than his father, was also more aggressive in wishing to strengthen the monarchy at the cost of a diminished Parliament. Charles demanded that Parliament provide him with more funds, when Parliament, of course, was in no mood to grant him anything without exacting significant concessions from the monarch, limiting his powers and assuring respect for traditional property rights and institutions.

Three institutional issues dominated the stand-off:[18]

First, the monarch could issue royal ordinances by proclamation, and thus could essentially bypass Parliament on most matters (excepting taxation and waging war, since he would need funds for doing so, if nothing else). Though these ordinances did not have the full power of law (i.e. were not passed by Parliament), that was a small detail for the monarchs, who often flouted the rules with impunity.

Second, abuse of the Star Chamber (established by Henry VII in 1497 and composed of Privy Law Counsellors and judges of common-law courts as a higher court of appeal). Under Charles I, the Star Chamber was increasingly used to reverse unfavourable judgments against the Crown by the common law courts.

And third, the control by the Crown of the Government's purse strings, particularly the judiciary. Judges were directly paid by the Crown, and hence their independence often compromised.

Over time, through these three institutional arrangements, the monarchy increasingly became more absolutist and the institutions more extractive, and the Crown continued to acquire the executive, legislative, and judicial powers of the state without much oversight of Parliament.

10.3.4 The Great Rebellion of 1642 and the Restoration

The tensions only worsened over time, and the country slid into a civil war (also called the 'Great Rebellion') in 1642. Before it was over in 1651, King Charles I had been beheaded (in 1649) on charges of 'high treason'; his son and heir, Charles II, had fled to Europe; the monarchy and the House of Lords were abolished; and Oliver Cromwell, an army general and statesman, took the reins of the 'new republic' as Lord Protector and head of state and the Government in 1653. Cromwell immediately took to correcting the monarchy's egregious excesses. The Star Chamber was abolished, restrictions against monopolies enforced, and property rights restored, with an act requiring that all property disputes would now be under the final jurisdiction of the common-law courts. Land tenure arrangements, hitherto grossly in favour of the feudal lords, were dramatically altered and feudal tenures abolished by an act of Parliament in 1660, paving the way for more inclusive political and economic institutions to emerge in the country.[19]

However, Cromwell soon fell out with his political allies, particularly in Parliament, and though he did bring in some much-needed institutional changes, described above, there was growing resentment of him and particularly his son Richard, who succeeded him upon his death in 1658. The increasing antagonism towards the Cromwells and a general state of political impasse and chaos in the country led to mounting pressures to invite the King back.

Charles II returned from his exile in France on 29 May 1660, ending a rather short-lived new republic (also called the Interregnum 1649–1660) and restored Stuart rule for the next twenty-eight years, a period generally known as the 'Restoration'. King Charles II began his reign by trying to make up for his father's and grandfather's excesses. He reached out to his subjects, offering a general pardon to all for any previous offences against him or his father, emphasizing his keen desire for religious tolerance and reiterating security for private property.

All this was easier said than done, particularly on religious issues. The Parliament was in no mood to be seen as losing any influence and sought to establish a rigid Anglican orthodoxy. What complicated matters greatly was that anti-Catholicism was virulent in the kingdom by now with strong suspicions of the monarch's sympathies for the Catholic faith, confirmed by several of his own actions. His warm relationship with King Louis XIV of France, who was also a generous financial benefactor, was obviously looked at with great suspicion. Things got progressively worse, particularly when in 1672, the King's brother, James, Duke of York and presumptive heir to the throne (Charles II had no legal children of his own), openly confessed to his conversion to the Catholic faith, and fears of papal interference, aided by King Louis XIV, to convert the kingdom to Catholicism reached fever pitch.

Simultaneously, the King continued to be beset with financial woes and mounting debts, leading to the Stop of the Exchequer, that is, the monarch's declaring that he is suspending payment of his bills. To stem some of the growing tide of resentments and frustrations of his subjects, the King even arranged for his niece, James's eldest daughter, Mary (later to be Mary II) to marry William of Orange (later to be William III), the Protestant Prince of Orange and Chief Magistrate of the Netherlands, in 1677. However, this did not do much to assuage concerns about James's Catholicism for long and in 1679, a group of parliamentarians (known as the Whigs)[20] introduced a bill (the Exclusion Bill) to exclude James, the heir presumptive, from the throne. Though the Bill was passed by the Commons, support was by no means unanimous, as another group, the Tories, while seriously concerned about James's Catholic beliefs, were still unwilling to confront the monarch so directly. Support in the House of

Lords was even less, and the Exclusion Bill did not become law, but the gauntlet had been thrown.

Fortunately for the King, various military wars in Europe had started coming to an end by then, North American trade was flourishing, and colonization of the Caribbean islands had begun, and the monarch's financial situation started to improve.

Emboldened by the political support he could still muster, but even more so by his now improved financial situation's making him less dependent on Parliament, the King decided to take on the Whigs, a faction of rebel parliamentarians. He did so by a process of rechartering of local governments, starting with London. This allowed the Crown to withdraw the charters of many urban centres and disenfranchise much of the opposition. It was no coincidence then that 'of the 104 members of Parliament returned in the mid-1680s by the boroughs receiving new charters, only one Whig was elected'.[21] Charles II died in 1685 at the peak of his power and was succeeded by his brother James (now James II).

Though the new monarch offered strong assurances to preserve the primacy of the Anglican Church, his actions over the next three years suggested otherwise. He continued to appoint Catholics to senior positions in his court, removed many of the serving judges and justices of peace, and essentially set out to systematically create a Catholic state. The King was now on a collision course even with his natural supporters, the Tories. The concerns of Tories and Whigs alike boiled over with the birth of a male heir to James II in June 1688, clearly raising the prospect that there would be a Catholic successor to the throne. Writing on behalf of many others in Parliament, seven leading Protestants invited William and Mary of Orange to take the British throne; they readily agreed and landed with a large sea and land force at Torbay on the English coast on 5 November 1688, ushering in the Glorious Revolution. James II fled to exile in France and William (now William III) and Mary (now Mary II) were proclaimed joint monarchs of Britain in early 1689.[22,23]

10.3.5 The Glorious Revolution 1688

The significance of the Glorious Revolution (1688–1689) for Britain was not just the change of the head (heads in this case) that wears the Crown, but the fundamental institutional changes that it (the Revolution) brought about in the country. It laid the ground for the first Industrial Revolution some seven decades later and the country's subsequent economic growth.[24]

While William and Mary had been offered 'the Crown on a platter', so to speak, it was not a carte blanche to rule as they pleased. The new monarchs were also presented with a Revolution Settlement, by which Parliament sought to restructure society's political institutions and the balance of power between the monarch and Parliament.

Throughout the Stuarts' reign thus far, the principal issue of conflict between them and Parliament was what the latter saw as the monarch's arbitrary and steady encroachment of political power. Not only the Parliamentarians, but subjects in general, wealthy landed gentry and the common folk alike, —always felt vulnerable to the monarch's arbitrary attempts to appropriate their liberty and their wealth—a classic symptom of extractive institutions. The Revolution Settlement, and later the Declaration of Rights (which ultimately was enshrined as the Bill of Rights in 1689), limited the Sovereign's power, reaffirmed Parliament's claim to control taxation and legislation, and provided guarantees against the flagrant abuses of power which James II and the other Stuart kings had committed. However, the solution could not be to simply impose conditions of good behaviour on monarchs, but to also devise mechanisms to make such commitments credible and self-enforcing. Of course, memories of the fates of Charles I and James II would no doubt serve as credible threats to encourage compliance, but the Bill of Rights also laid out the conditions, which would trigger responses by the Parliament.

Three distinct and significant institutional changes were ushered in by the Glorious Revolution. First, the Crown would no longer be above the law. All royal powers were now subordinated to common law, and prerogative courts such as the Star Chamber, which enabled the monarch to enforce his or her proclamations, were abolished, and 'the supremacy of common law courts, so important to protect private rights, was thereby assured'.[25] Judges would no longer serve at the monarch's pleasure and could only be removed by both houses of Parliament, thereby ensuring the independence of the judiciary from the Crown.

Second, the sovereign would no longer be the sole ruler of the land. Instead, it would now be the 'King in Parliament', with a clearly defined and accepted role of Parliament in the ongoing management of the government.[26] The monarch could no longer be allowed to call or suspend Parliament at his or her discretion. A Triennial Act (1694) re-established the principle of regular parliamentary sessions, and the Mutiny Act (1689) restrained the monarch's control over military forces by restricting the use of martial law. And even more restrictive, the monarch was forbidden to maintain a standing army in time of peace without Parliament's consent.

Third, Parliament would now play a significant role and exercise authority in financial matters of the realm, and have the sole authority to impose new taxes and to approve and audit government expenditures. But Parliament was also pragmatic enough to accept that simply putting these controls on the monarch's behaviour would not work without resolving the Crown's genuine financial constraints and needs. Parliament, therefore, committed that adequate funds would be provided to the Crown for its legitimate needs, but with the provisions of checks and balances, as noted. The borrowings of the government would thus be in the name of the state and not to the personal account of the Crown. In a sense, The Glorious Revolution was thus a fiscal revolution as well.[27]

The most consequential effect of these changes was that they reduced the monarch's arbitrary powers. These then not only provided greater security of economic liberties and property rights to the citizens of the realm but assured them of their political liberties and personal rights as well. For example, even though the Habeas Corpus Act (forbidding arbitrary arrests of citizens) was passed in 1679 (under the rule of Charles II), it was regularly ignored, but was now strictly enforced by the empowered magistrates. As a direct consequence of these changes, private rights became fundamentally more secure.[28]

The monarch was now acutely aware that in ignoring the commitments made to Parliament he or she ran the credible risk of losing the Crown (or worse, the head wearing it). And now that the Crown had been assured of adequate tax revenues, there was no major motivation for the monarch to violate personal property rights, either.

There was also a much-needed constraint on the behaviour of Parliament itself; how would Parliament be held to its end of the bargain? Answer: 'by others in Parliament'. The Whigs and the Tories had different views on how governments should be run. The commerce-minded

Whigs, for example, instinctively preferred limited government and took a libertarian view, while the Tories were generally more sympathetic to the monarch. The diversity of views in Parliament itself provided built-in brakes on any extreme position being taken by any individual or groups of Parliamentarians on any issue—an important aspect of pluralism, so needed to sustain inclusive institutions.

Further, an independent and empowered judiciary was now as reluctant to brook any interference from Parliament as from the Crown, thus providing further checks on these institutions. Another important built-in check was the provision that only the Crown could propose an expenditure, which Parliament would consider and approve or reject. Parliament could not propose any expenditure on its own: it could say 'yea' or 'nay' only for the purposes proposed by the Crown.

We noted in Chapter 3 that a key characteristic of good governance is predictability. The institutional and political changes brought about by the Glorious Revolution did exactly that in Britain: they significantly enhanced the predictability of the government. In the pre-Revolution period, private citizens were always vulnerable to arbitrary 'impositions' by the monarch or worse (expropriations of wealth, non-payment of dues, unilateral reduction of interest rates, and/or rescheduling of loans, for example). These arbitrary royal attempts to raise additional revenues were now neither necessary (the Crown being on much sounder financial footing), but more importantly, nor allowed, for fear of consequences of Parliamentary censure or worse.

10.3.6 Transitioning to inclusive political and economic institutions

Cumulatively, these changes dramatically changed the political landscape of the country. Parliament held greater authority than ever before, and the absolutist powers so keenly sought by past monarchs (despite the Magna Carta) had been sufficiently trimmed after the bloodless Glorious Revolution of 1688. Through their elected representatives, ordinary folk now had access to the political institutions of the country, making them more pluralistic, if not still quite inclusive. Notice that under 2 per cent of the country's population, and that too only men, could vote in the eighteenth century, making the process of direct participation still very limited. However, anybody could petition Parliament, which was a way for the common subjects to influence Parliament and thus the political and economic institutions of the country. And quite significantly, Parliament listened: 'it is this more than anything that reflects the defeat of absolutism, the empowerment of a fairly broad-based segment of society, and the rise of pluralism in England after 1688'.[29]

In their comprehensive tour d'horizon of the impacts of the Glorious Revolution, North and Weingast observed that it simultaneously led to a fiscal revolution as well and laid the institutional foundations of modern capital markets and the emergence of inclusive economic institutions in Britain.[30] The increased credibility of the Government's commitments provided greater security of private property rights in general. It also resulted in greater confidence in the Government's promises to honour its financial agreements, since the Government's borrowings were now a liability of the state and not the monarch's. The state took responsibility for the future repayments, while earlier private wealth-holders would have been wary of lending to the government (i.e. the monarch personally). The government's ability to borrow from its citizens thus increased dramatically, as evidenced 'by the increase in the size of the government debt, which grew to nearly £17 million in 1697 from a mere £1 million nine years earlier on the eve of the Golden Revolution. This level of debt, approximately 40 per cent of GNP, was previously unattainable. By 1720, government debt was over fifty times the 1688 level and on the order of GNP' in that year.[31]

Incorporation of the Bank of England in 1694 was a big boost, not only to public capital markets but to private capital markets as well. From initially intermediating only public debt, the Bank of England soon started private operations too. This provided the necessary institutional structure for borrowing and lending between private parties also, based on their mutual confidence in the security of property rights and in the judicial system to intercede fairly, as needed.

The flourishing of both the public and private capital markets enabled the efficient mobilization of domestic savings around the country, and by the mid-eighteenth century they had started to provide financial services in an integrated manner at the national level. This large-scale mobilization of savings enabled large infrastructure projects (mainly in river transportation) with significant impacts on Britain's long-term economic growth. But even more exciting was the fact that the capital needs of a nascent Industrial Revolution, just beginning to happen then (around 1730) could be met, and indeed encouraged, by the growing capacity of the public and private capital markets.

Along with increased pluralism of political and economic institutions, the Glorious Revolution also catalysed the process of strengthening the State. Parliament, which now had the authority to approve and monitor expenditures by the monarch, was more willing to provide the necessary funds to increase state operations, which it had baulked at doing earlier, since it could not have been sure how the funds would be spent. Not only did the size of the state expand, but the quality of the national bureaucracy improved as well, as appointments were increasingly based on merit, rather than political or social connections. This is an important lesson to draw upon: enhancing pluralism and strengthening the state is not a zero-sum game. Enabling greater participation by the population (pluralism) can in fact strengthen the state as well, as we see in the case here in Great Britain following the Glorious Revolution and events thereafter.

10.4 Summary

Around the turn of the second millennium, Scandinavian countries, Denmark included, began their transition from a Viking to a feudal society, where the landed aristocracy held great sway even over the monarch, and common subjects had little say. Over the next five centuries, the monarch gradually chipped away at the power of the nobility, but the major institutional breakthrough in Denmark happened with the Lutheran Reformation of 1536 replacing the Catholic church as the prime keeper of spiritual faith in the country. The monarch was anointed as the head of the church as well. As head of the state and the church, the monarch now had greater authority (moral and legal) over his subjects, and fortuitously, he used it well to expand and strengthen the institutions of state administration, and the judiciary.

A new constitution was adopted in 1665 establishing absolute monarchy in Denmark. With the new powers now vested in him, the monarch embarked on some far changing institutional reforms. Property rights were recognized and the bureaucracy and judiciary strengthened. Simultaneously, the extractive powers of the nobility were also reduced who could no longer hold common peasants as virtual serfs on their lands. Labour mobility thus increased significantly, enabling the workers to participate more meaningfully in the country's growing economic opportunities. As a consequence, inclusive economic institutions gradually began to emerge in the country.

However, political institutions still remained extractive. But a few favourable factors began to emerge : first, the administration was centralized, but with an increasingly professionalized, efficient, and honest Weberian bureaucracy and judiciary, and the absolute monarchs, ruling as 'enlightened despots', operated within the bounds of the rule of law. Second, the absolutist rule was remarkably stable, lasting for almost two centuries till it was supplanted in 1849 by the liberal, constitutional monarchy of modern times, with the introduction of an elected bicameral Parliament. And third, all the succeeding monarchs under the absolutist regime fortunately continued with the bureaucratic, judicial, social, and political reforms of their predecessors. Thus, even though the emergence of inclusive political institutions began in earnest only after the transition to constitutional monarchy, the seeds of Denmark, the country with inclusive economic and political institutions had begun to be sown much earlier.

In Great Britain, politically inclusive institutions emerged much earlier than in Denmark, with the country's first elected Parliament in place by 1265, following the signing of the Magna Carta in 1215, and resulting in a broader section of society gradually becoming politically empowered.

Though the initial conditions for the emergence of inclusive institutions (greater pluralism and centralization of state powers) had begun to emerge as early as 1265, it is instructive that the transition took over 650 years to take root with frequent and sometimes even formidable setbacks along the way. Even as late as the early 1600s, Britain was still marked by extractive political and economic institutions, with the Crown continuing to encroach on the legislative and judicial powers of the State without much oversight from Parliament.

Tensions between the monarch and Parliament only began to be resolved with the Glorious Revolution of 1688, which ushered in some fundamental institutional changes in the country.

Some basic tenets of liberty were enshrined in the country's first Bill of Rights which also limited the Sovereign's power, declaring that 'no one, not even the sovereign [was] above the law'. It also reaffirmed the judiciary's independence, and Parliament's control over taxation and legislation.

The Glorious Revolution was an important step in the transition to inclusive institutions in Britain., laying the foundations for the first Industrial Revolution some seven decades later and the subsequent economic prosperity of the country.

Two pointsworth noting: in Denmark, first economic institutions gradually turned inclusive, while the political institutions took almost another two centuries to become so. The sequence in Great Britain was the reverse, but the important point is that institutions had to be both politically and economically inclusive to get to 'Denmark'. Notice too the long time (centuries) it took for inclusive institutions to emerge in both these countries, a point worth remembering as we travel from Here to Denmark. It is often a long and slow journey.

11

Some Asian Journeys

11.1 Introduction

Japan and Korea were both in ruins at the end of World War II. Japanese cities were wrecked, their stockpiles depleted, and their industries gutted. Undivided Korea suffered even more catastrophic losses in the Korean War, which followed a few years later, and the country split into two: the North (Democratic Republic of Korea, DRK) and the South (Republic of Korea, referred to as Korea here). However, while it seemed most improbable then, both Japan and Korea rose from the ashes spectacularly and achieved high income and human development status within a generation. Remarkably, Korea also joined the OECD in 1996, having been poorer than its northern cousin even as late as 1970. How such remarkable changes happened is the focus of this chapter.

11.2 Japan

The Japanese economy was devastated by World War II. Its per capita GDP had stood at $2,874 (in 1990 US dollars) in 1940—the year before Japan entered the war—but dropped by more than half to $1,346 in 1945, when the country surrendered. From being slightly over 40 per cent of both the US and the British per capita incomes before the war, the corresponding Japanese figure plummeted to 11 per cent and 19 per cent, respectively, by the end of it.[1]

However, by 1956, Japan's real per capita GDP had crossed the pre-war 1940 level. In impressively and impeccably hosting the 1964 Summer Olympic Games and joining the OECD in the same year, the country effectively announced its resurgence from the ravages of the war, and its per capita GDP now stood at 44 per cent of the corresponding US figure and

From Here to Denmark. Rajat M. Nag and Harinder S. Kohli, Oxford University Press.
© Rajat Mohan Nag and Harinder Singh Kohli 2023. DOI: 10.1093/oso/9780198893103.003.0011

almost 60 per cent of the British. By 1969, Japan had become the world's second largest economy (after the US).

Without a doubt, this was a very remarkable economic success and was rightly dubbed 'the Japanese miracle'. However, without taking anything away from the phenomenal achievements of this period, one must recognize that the seeds of fundamental political, social, and institutional reforms which had put Japan on a long-term economic-growth path had been sown almost three centuries back, which made all this possible.

11.2.1 The Tokugawa shogunate (1603–1868)

Since the seventh century BCE, the head of state in Japan has been the emperor, tracing his lineage as a descendant of the sun goddess Amaterasu. After over a millennium of reign by emperors, a new political force was taking root by the end of the twelfth century. In 1185, a successful military general, Minamoto Yoritomo, took control of Japan, and seven years later assumed the title of *seii taishogun* ('barbarian-quelling generalissimo') or *shogun* for short, a title occasionally bestowed on a general after a successful campaign. Shogun Yoritomo established the first military government in Kamakura, a small seaside village south of Edo (modern-day Tokyo). The government was his *shogunate* (or *bakufu*, literally tent government), perhaps trying to give the impression of a temporary event. In fact, the shoguns became a system of hereditary dictators that lasted for the next seven centuries.

The emperor, in turn, was reduced to a mere figurehead, reigning only in name as 'God on earth' with the shogun in complete control of governing the country. The shogunate appointed its own military governors, the *shugos*, one heading each province, to weave together a cohesive national apparatus of administration. Over time the *shugos* expanded their influence and for the better part of the next hundred and forty years, the Kamakura shogunate tried in vain to establish adequate control over them and ultimately, in 1338, lost power to a local governor, Ashikaga Takauji, based in Kyoto.

As it turned out, the Ashikaga shogunate was even less successful than its Kamakura predecessors in exercising its authority, and the country gradually slid into civil war. Beginning around 1467 and continuing through most of the 1500s, frequent warfare between competing *shugos* (now called *daimyos*, feudal lords with their own large land holdings and their samurai, their soldiers) paralyzed the country, with the various daimyos vying for land and control. By a process of attrition and constant shifts in alliances, the situation finally started to improve when one of the more powerful among them, Tokugawa Ieyasu, the daimyo from Edo, won a decisive battle in 1600 (the battle of Sekigahara). He rapidly consolidated his power and established the Tokugawa shogunate in 1603, bringing in a period of much welcome stability and relative peace in the country for the next two and a half centuries.

11.2.1.1 Consolidation of power

Having experienced the chaos of the constant fighting between the various daimyos, Tokugawa's topmost priority was to bring a sense of cohesiveness and stability to the country, and he did so, often with an iron hand. He created 'a centralized "feudal" system in which more than 200 domains or *han* maintained fiscal and military autonomy, while their lords (the daimyos) served an authoritarian government (led by him, i.e., the Shogun) in Edo'.[2]

A key guiding principle of governance for the new shogun was to limit the individual daimyos from acquiring too much land or power. He did so rather astutely by devising the alternative attendance (*sankin kotai*) system that required the daimyos to spend every alternate year in the shogun's court in Edo working for him directly. Not only did it prevent the daimyos from building strong alliances with their own people, particularly the more powerful warriors (the *samurai*), but it also built personal relationships between them and the shogun, and an appreciation of a national perspective. Of course, the daimyos didn't travel solo. A large retinue accompanied each daimyo, and another unintended but a very positive consequence of this 'alternative attendance' system was the gradual building of a national infrastructure of roads and towns, greater intra-country trade, and appreciation of the cultural diversities of the various regions in the country.

Wisely, while Tokugawa consolidated his overall authority over the daimyos, he didn't overextend himself, and granted the daimyos enough authority in ruling their regions to build a national system of semi-autonomous domains under the shogun's central authority.

On the darker side, the Tokugawa's constant concerns about possible efforts by others to disturb the still-nascent political stability spilled over into society at large with what often amounted to religious and social oppression. The dominant faith of the Tokugawa period was Confucianism, and people outside this faith, namely the Christians, were looked at with suspicion, and ultimately forced underground. Tokugawa also prohibited mobility between the four social classes which had evolved in Japanese society: the warriors (the samurais), artisans, farmers, and merchants. Farmers, for example, who constituted over 80 per cent of the population, were forbidden to engage in non-agricultural activities.

11.2.1.2 Act of Seclusion 1636: closing Japan to the West

Suspicions about foreigners were now even more heightened. Trade with the West was prohibited. An Act of Seclusion was proclaimed in 1636, and Japan effectively sealed off its borders (excepting with Korea and China, with whom relations continued to be close), particularly to the Western nations, for the next two centuries, excepting the Dutch, who were allowed a small trading post in Nagasaki. While both these factors (increased social rigidities and closing the country to the West) had some far-reaching, long-term negative effects, they enabled the country to enjoy a fairly stable political regime and peace for the next 250 years, and make significant economic and social progress.

The economy progressed significantly during the Tokugawa period, with per capita income more than keeping pace with increases in population.[3] Agricultural production grew significantly, as did commerce and manufacturing. Production of fine silk and cotton, manufacture of porcelain, and brewing of sake flourished. Widening use of currency and credit enhanced mercantile activity and a wealthy merchant class began to emerge in the increasingly urbanized population centres of Edo (Tokyo), Kyoto, and Osaka. Literature and art flourished, which saw the rise of haiku, Kabuki, and Bunraku puppet theatre, and woodblock printing.

11.2.1.3 Emphasis on education and improving living standards

Education was a priority for the Tokugawas. The traditional emphasis on education for the upper-class samurai continued and indeed grew under their regime. The daimyos were encouraged to build schools (*hanko*) in their respective domains for the education of the children of their samurai retainers. Special emphasis was put on Confucianism, believed to be essential for maintaining the ideology of the feudal regime, and the Confucian Academy, at the apex of the educational hierarchy, was administered directly by the shogunate from Edo and served as a model for the hankos throughout the country.

But the fundamental change was in extending the reach of education to the commoners, prompted to a large extent by the emerging merchant class, who demanded better education for their children. Temple schools (the *terakoya*) spread rapidly in most towns and villages.

By the early 1800s, the expanding educational system had led Japan to a literacy rate of about 40 per cent for boys and 10 per cent for girls, then among the highest in the world. It also created the framework of a national bureaucracy committed to the Confucian ideal of public service and provided a strong institutional base for the future development of the country.

Globally, Japan had also begun to compare favourably on other indicators. A study of the standard of living in the mid-1800s concluded that 'the evidence, taken together with life expectancy estimates, suggests that the standard of living in mid-19th century in Japan was not only higher than in the 1700s, but relatively high in comparison to most of the industrializing West'.[4]

11.2.1.4 Extractive institutions: feudal structure of society

Notwithstanding the positive economic and social changes described above, the Tokugawa regime continued to be deeply feudal. It monopolized foreign trade; the country was closed to foreigners and the economic and political institutions were extractive. In the name of plans to maintain social stability, mobility between various social classes had been prohibited. Peasants, who constituted almost 80 per cent of the country's population 'even though they held tenuous property rights, were bound to their land, denied free cropping, and forbidden the alienation of land, all of which are typically feudal arrangements'.[5] Even more oppressive was 'the right of the ruling class (the daimyos and the shogun) to a substantial part of the returns from land. In this sense, they (and not the peasants) held real economic property rights'.[6] The Tokugawa land tax was based on the estimated gross yield (in rice or rice equivalent) and they were very demanding, varying among 'over 55 percent in some parts of the country and less than 25 percent in others, with the modal burden around 40 percent'.[7,8]

Farmers, even the relatively wealthy among them, did not benefit much from the economic growth during the Tokugawa period. In fact, many got progressively poorer as the surplus in hand after paying the high land taxes was often not enough to meet their own subsistence needs. Many would thus periodically sell or pawn their land to moneylenders and often ultimately become tenants on their own holdings. Three major famines in the country during the mid-eighteenth to the mid-nineteenth centuries greatly exacerbated the misery of the general population, but particularly the farmers.[9] No wonder then that 'during the 265 years under the control of the Tokugawa Government, not less than 1,240 farmer insurrections broke out', with the average annual number of such uprisings increasing steadily, with as many as thirty-five farmer revolts in 1866, the year preceding the fall of the Tokugawa shogunate.[10] As Horie observes, 'the moving force, which brought about the Meiji restoration, was the anti-feudal activity and opposition among the farmers and the poor urban population'.[11]

Ironically, there was another group of the population who also did not fare very well under the Tokugawa regime: they were the warriors (samurai) who traditionally had been just below the shoguns and the daimyos in the Japanese social hierarchy (followed by artisans, farmers, and merchants). Historically, the samurai had often been a farmer warrior, tilling the land (which he usually owned) in times of peace, and following his lord to battle in times of war (which were quite frequent). Over time, as warfare became more demanding, it was considered too important to be a part-time occupation, and the samurai were grouped into garrisons in the exclusive service of their masters. This system was even more formalized during the Tokugawa regime. Most samurai lost their land and 'in return, received stipends from the domain treasury payable in rice or in some instances, in cash'.[12]

Paradoxically, it was the relative peace and stability brought on by the Tokugawas after centuries of internal conflict in Japan that boded ill for the samurai. He was no longer in demand as a warrior, and his traditional strong bond with the lord of the domain underwent profound changes during the 250 years of peace in Tokugawa Japan. The samurai moved

from the land or the village where they had lived to the castle towns controlled by the daimyos, losing their land base as independent warriors
on retainer with the lords (daimyos). From playing principally a military
role, the samurai gradually became civil servants in the service of the
daimyo: their 'basic character was transformed from that of the feudal
vassal to that of the patrimonial bureaucrat of the Tokugawa family or of
a particular daimyo'.[13]

While this growing predominance of the civilian role of the samurai
in the Tokugawa government ultimately bequeathed to modern Japan
the makings of a bureaucracy, its immediate effect on the samurai themselves was mostly negative, often disastrous. The samuraiwere warriors,
usually without any commercial, financial, or administrative skills. The
vast majority had to live on paltry salaries and stipends—usually paid in
rice. Perforce, the samurai gradually turned to the local merchants, who
not only bought their rice stipends for cash, but offered advances against
future income. Faced with high interest rates and low prices for their rice
stipends, the samurai were gradually overwhelmed with their debt burdens. Some formed ties with the merchant houses through marriage (effectively marketing their samurai rank). Some abandoned their samurai
status and returned to the villages to take up agriculture or trade (a huge
loss of face, and often not advisable because it risked incurring the wrath
of the daimyo). More often than not, however, 'they could decline into
genteel poverty, as many of them (sadly) did'.[14]

11.2.1.5 Decline of the Tokugawas

By the mid-1800s, some two hundred and fifty years after they had established their shogunate in Edo, the Tokugawas started to feel the pressures
of the office. The extractive nature of the institutions (both economic
and political, but particularly the latter) had started to take its toll. Not
only were the rumblings of discontent from the farmers and the samurai
growing, the shogunate itself began facing increasing fiscal challenges,
despite imposing harsh taxes. Its administrative capacity, staffed by officials 'who spent much of their time bluffing, too paralyzed by traditions,
mediocrity, and fear to act decisively',[15] also began to decline. Not surprisingly, the balance of power between the Tokugawas and some of the
daimyos began to shift 'with large and distant domains, such as Satsuma
(in southern Kyushu) and Choshu (on western Honshu), experiencing

political and economic growth even as the shogunate itself sunk even more deeply.[16]

Equally worrying were dangers appearing from abroad around the same time. Western naval powers—British, Dutch, French, and Russian—began to challenge the Tokugawan self-imposed isolation, which had held for more than two centuries. The shogunate was able to stave off the foreigners for a while, but when in 1853 the American Commodore Matthew C. Perry, with his flotilla of eight ships, made his way into the Edo Bay, carrying with him a letter from President Franklin Pierce requesting trade with Japan, the die was cast. The intentions of the 'request' were clear, and the shogunate was effectively forced to sign a convention with the Americans on 31 March 1854 at Kanagawa (at the entrance to the Edo Bay). This allowed for 'opening Shimoda and Hakodote as ports of call for American ships; authorizing the appointment of consuls at a later date; and making no unambiguous provision for trade.'[17] Other Western powers soon followed, with demands of their own to gain access to Japanese trade, and the country's more than two hundred years of self-imposed isolation was over.

The signing of these concessions to the Western powers, dubbed the 'unequal treaties'—particularly the Treaty of Kanagawa, signed with Commodore Perry—was taken as a sell-out by the Tokugawas and added considerably to their domestic woes and loss of public support. This was seriously exacerbated when it became known that the Emperor (even though merely a figurehead) and his courtiers in Kyoto were still personally in favour of seclusion, as were several of the greater daimyos, and that the shogun had signed the unequal treaties in defiance of the Imperial wish. Lower-ranked samurai and the peasants, already disturbed over the loss of their own economic and social power, also began agitating for the ouster of the Westerners under the emotionally charged slogan of 'Sonno joi' (Revere the Emperor! Expel the Barbarians!), an astute political ploy, as much to support the throne as to embarrass the shogunate.

Many of the larger daimyos cleverly capitalized on the growing sense of disenchantment with the Tokugawas on both domestic and foreign issues. Choshu became the centre for discontented samurai from other domains, and by 1866, it was in the hands of an anti-Tokugawa administration. With more than an approving nod from the Imperial Court for change, and an enlarging set of alliances involving the powerful and anti-Tokugawa south-western domains of Choshu and Satsuma and other major daimyos, the message to the last Tokugawa shogun, Yoshinobu, was clear. The days of the shogunate were numbered. In January 1868, he was summoned to Kyoto to be stripped of all his powers. An imperial decree was issued announcing that the responsibility for governing the country was to be restored to the fifteen-year-old emperor Mutsuhito. Later that year, the Emperor (taking the reign name Meiji, 'enlightened rule') moved into the Tokugawa castle in Edo, now renamed Tokyo ('Eastern capital'), and the Meiji era began.

11.2.2 The Meiji Restoration (1868–1912)

The young Emperor Mutsuhito and his immediate counsellors who took charge of governing the country faced two obvious challenges, which turned out to be major opportunities as well. They were all young (the principal samurai from the Choshu and Satsuma domains who joined the Emperor were in their twenties and thirties), and their hold on power was tenuous. That also made them very pragmatic and not bound by the burdens of custom or history to achieve their three immediate object-ives: centralize, be open to the world, and make Japan a modern nation which would be accepted as an equal by the world powers. As Huffman observed: 'One of their central slogans, "*kuni no tame*" (for the sake of the country) said it all: their overriding commitment was simply to enhance national strength, regardless of what customs or ideologies had to be vio-lated in the pursuit of that goal'.[18]

11.2.2.1 Modernization of Japan: transformative institutional changes
The ease with which the Americans had forced the last shogun to accede to their demands to open up foreign trade and presence had seared the Japanese collective psyche. Acutely resentful of the 'unequal treaties' the country had been forced to sign, the Meijis were acutely aware that without modernity and military power, Japan would not be taken seriously by the Western imperial powers. The fact that all of them had been ardent isola-tionists until recently did not prevent them from now adopting the West as their model of development, keen to abolish the old feudal institutions and establish a modern state. They sent a fifty-member, very high-level

mission to the West for a two-year (1871–1873) study tour to understand modern institutions such as banks, schools, political systems, and treaty structures. The objective was not to imitate them but to see how to adapt them to Japanese circumstances. The Meiji Constitution, for example, drew heavily on the Prussian-German-Austrian experiences.

The drive towards centralization of power and social changes was pursued with zeal with the power of new rules and regulations: class and status systems were abolished, and the feudal domains replaced with modern prefectures in 1871. Compulsory military draft was introduced in 1872, further diminishing the role of samurai as warriors; and a minimum of three years of schooling for boys and girls was required by law.

Transformative institutional changes began and gradually became inclusive. Feudalism was abolished through the Land Tax Revision Act of 1873. The daimyo lost feudal rights over the land and the people of his domains, and the four social classes were abolished. No longer bound to the land they tilled, peasants were now free to migrate and pursue vocations of their choosing. A private property system was established, and the rights of farmers to free cropping on all land recognized. All tax payments were to be paid in money and not in kind (rice), as had previously been the case; and the tax base was changed to land value instead of the estimated annual harvest, with the economic brunt borne not only by the farmers, but by the population at large.[19]

The samurai, who accounted for the largest proportion of the ruling class (the daimyos being the others), were also significantly affected by the land reforms of the Meiji era. They had already started losing influence during the Tokugawa regime and had been placed on a stipend usually paid in kind (rice). Under the Meiji land reforms, their stipends were first lowered to monthly pensions and then converted to bonds whose income values were significantly less than even the reduced pensions. By some estimates, the samurai incomes post-Meiji Restoration had collapsed to only about 15 per cent of their pre-restoration values.[20]

In spite of the heavy tax burden placed on the people and the significant reduction in payouts to the samurai, the new Meiji government faced severe fiscal constraints. By the early 1880s, the economic situation was dire. Rice and silk prices plummeted, pushing many into destitution. Peasants were pushed off the lands and into working in the rapidly expanding silk and cotton factories in neighbouring towns and urban centres at low wages, ironically helping Japan compete effectively on the world market.

Modern institutions, postal networks, and a banking system were established. Taxation was centralized and a modern bureaucratic state began to emerge to replace the old feudal one. The country's central bank, the Bank of Japan, was founded in 1882. Public schools, modern hospitals, railways, and roads started to emerge. The first Japanese daily newspaper (the Yokohama Mainichi Shinbun) that covered both foreign and domestic news started in 1871. Newspaper readership increased dramatically.

While the economic institutions increasingly turned inclusive with the above reforms, political institutions gradually became inclusive as well. Japan adopted a written constitution in 1890, the first country in Asia to do so, creating a form of mixed constitutional and absolute monarchy with an elected bicameral Parliament, the Diet, an independent judiciary and a Prime Minister and cabinet appointed by the emperor. Voting rights were gradually expanded to all adult (over 25) males by 1925 but became universal only after the new Post World War II constitution of 1947. At the same time, the country also moved to a pure constitutional monarchy with the emperor only as ceremonial head of state.As in the case of Britain, these moves to inclusivity of the political and economic institutions also laid the groundwork for Japan's subsequent economic prosperity.

11.2.2.2 Education

Education was already a high-priority agenda in the Tokugawa period. The Meijis continued this emphasis with great vigour and unequivocally reiterated the commitment in the Fundamental Code of Education adopted in 1872: 'There shall, in the future, be no community with an illiterate family, nor a family with an illiterate person'.[21]

However, there was a fundamental change in the Meiji approach: as in diplomatic ties and trade, the country had also isolated itself intellectually from the rest of the world. The Meijis made particular efforts to correct this. As a matter of fact, one of the five tenets in the Charter Oath adopted in early 1868, within a few months of the Meiji Restoration, categorically declares that: 'knowledge shall be sought throughout the world'.[22] The Meijis sent a large number of young students to study in American and European institutions and brought in hundreds of Westerners to teach English and science, create school systems, and build roads and railways, till the late 1870s. Kido Takayoshi, a well-regarded Japanese statesman and generally considered as one of the three key nobles who led the Meiji Restoration, said it all: 'Our people are no different from the Americans or the Europeans of today; it is all a matter of education or lack of education.'[23]

Pursuing this emphasis, 'between 1906 and 1911, education consumed as much as 43 percent of the budgets of the towns and villages for Japan as a whole ... and by 1910, Japan had, it is generally acknowledged, universal attendance in primary schools.'[24] Sen adds that by 1913, even though Japan was still very poor 'it had become one of the largest producers of books in the world, publishing more books than Britain and indeed more than twice as many as the United States.'[25]

11.2.2.3 Changing social norms

With these deliberate comprehensive reforms, new ideas and modern practices rapidly spread throughout Japanese society. In what Schelling[26] would have considered a dream situation of creating new focal points (discussed in Chapter 7), the emperor himself served as a norm entrepreneur for many of the social changes which followed. Western culture was strongly encouraged. Men's hair styling changed. Royal dress codes now included Western formals and long coat-tails.

An interesting example of change in Japanese social norms is its now well-known respect for, even obsession with, punctuality. Difficult as it might be now to imagine, the situation was quite different in the early Meiji period. Consider the plight and frustration of a Dutch scientist, Willem van Kattendyke, who had spent two years (1857–1859) at the naval training centre in Nagasaki teaching the principles of Western navigation and scientific technology. He laments: 'the supplies necessary to make repairs, which he had specifically ordered to be delivered at high tide, did not arrive in time. One worker showed up just once and never returned, and a stableman spent two whole days going around to make his New Year's greetings'. Kattendyke's frustrations were in fact 'shared by most of the foreign engineers in Japan in the latter half of the nineteenth century. They often found themselves vexed by the work habits of the Japanese, and the main reason for their vexation was the apparent lack of any sense of time. To these foreigners, the Japanese worked with an apparent indifference to the clock'.[27] Imagine this being said of Japan, where punctuality is so sacrosanct now that people regularly arrive ahead of schedule so as not to keep others waiting, and delays (or early departures) by train, even by seconds, produce immediate public indignation and apologies from senior officials.

How did this change happen? Wider use of cheap mechanical clocks obviously helped, but direct and continuous intervention from the top made the most difference. Three key institutions—schools, factories, and railways—were chosen as the first points of intervention. Consider the following directive of the Ministry of Education to new primary school students in 1873: 'Make sure that you are at school ten minutes before the start of class every day. If you are late for school, do not enter the classroom without permission; explain the reasons for your tardiness and wait for your teacher's instructions'.[28]

One directive obviously wouldn't make a systemic difference. What made the difference over time was a consistent communication and application of the principles of punctuality in all aspects of life by norm entrepreneurs till people started believing that others would be punctual, and it would be bad form to keep them waiting. New focal points emphasizing punctuality were created.

11.2.2.4 Changes in social structures: gradual move to open-access orders

Samurai, who suffered significant losses in income, also lost social status under the new regime and no longer enjoyed any special privileges by virtue of birth. They were treated as commoners, judged solely on their merits and 'irrespective of status, samurais and commoners, persons who were men of learning and talent should be promoted' and 'the regular samurai who cannot perform their duty should be permitted to take jobs as farmers, artisans, and merchants'.[29] These fundamental changes were transformational for Japanese society and essentially ushered in a culture of inclusivity, emphasizing meritocracy and competence as the principal criteria for joining, say, the military service. New rules for admission to the naval academy, for example, clarified that 'irrespective of place of origin or of social origin—be it nobility, samurai, or commoner—those who are over fifteen years old and pass the examination of the naval academy (which tested their physical condition, calligraphy, Japanese history, Chinese classics, and arithmetic) can become commissioned officers'.[30] Importantly, these new rules were strictly enforced too.

A striking change in the Meiji Restoration was that unlike it had been under the rule of the Shoguns and the daimyos, Japan was no longer ruled by a landed aristocracy. The Land Tax Revision Act of 1873 had effectively forced the daimyos off their land holdings: their domains were abolished and transformed to state ownership through the newly constituted prefectures, ownership of which reverted to the state. Neither the bourgeoisie nor landowners now controlled the state. Equally, though the emperor had been restored, it was also clear that he would not rule directly. Instead, the country was 'ruled by an oligarchy of ex-samurai, from the feudal domains of Satsuma and Choshu, the domains that had brought about the Meiji Restoration'.[31]

As the role of the samurai weakened as warriors during the Tokugawa rule, they had already started to transform themselves, largely as civil servants in the employ of the various daimyos. Japanese society had thus already begun to get bureaucratized during the Tokugawa shogunate, and 'many of the key features of the modern bureaucratic state emerged during those years'.[32] However, the Tokugawas had followed the decentralized daimyo model of governance. The institutions were not inclusive and thus, a centralized bureaucratic state did not emerge. This happened only with the Meiji Restoration and the structure of a truly modern national bureaucracy 'along the lines of Bismarck's Prussia, and a relatively close approximation of Max Weber's ideal bureaucracy' began to be put in place.[33] In perhaps the most fundamental legacy of the Meiji Restoration, 'the bureaucracy was modernized, and recruitment was now based not on status but on merit, as indicated by success in examinations.' The Imperial University was founded in Tokyo (in 1877) where admission was similarly merit-based and was a fertile recruiting ground of future bureaucrats and 'the graduates of this university, especially those of its law faculty, were given privileged access and have subsequently dominated the upper ranks of the bureaucracy'.[34]

It is quite puzzling why the transformative institutional changes brought about by the Meijis has been called a restoration rather than a revolution, which, in fact, it was. Perhaps this was to give a sense of historical continuity to the transfer of power to the new emperor and thus make it more acceptable in the context of domestic politics? Regardless, the changes were indeed revolutionary. The Meiji Restoration was the 'return to power to the emperor after a period of more than 600 years of feudal control under the feudal lords. It was the overthrow of the decentralized rule of feudal lords and the setting up of a strong centralized government with the emperor as its head'.[35] It enabled inclusive political and economic institutions to take root in the country and had a transformational effect on the future course of Japan's economic and social development.

11.3   South Korea

The three-year Korean War (1950–1953), following on the heels of World War II, ravaged both North and South Korea, with more than two million dead, the already poor economy in shambles, and their cities and towns in ruin. In the first few years after the war, North Korea made an impressive recovery and seemed to be on track to becoming a modern industrial society. On the other hand, South Korea (referred to as Korea here) was faced with political turmoil, pervasive corruption, a stagnant economy, and was heavily dependent on aid from the US. Even eight years on, in 1961, one could hardly foresee that Korea was on the brink of one of the most dramatic economic transformations in modern history.

The country's economic performance over the past six decades has been most striking. Having been poorer than its northern cousin even as late as 1970, with a per capita GDP (in constant 2010 US$) of only $932 in 1960 (even lower than Ghana at slightly over a thousand), Korea joined the OECD in 1996, with a GDP per capita i then of slightly over $14,000, (in constant 2015 US$) which had climbed to over $33,000 in 2022, making it one of the richest nations in the world.[36] It is also a High Human Development country as assessed by the UNDP, ranking nineteenth among 191 countries in 2021.[37]

Korea's performance in improving governance and fighting corruption has also been impressive. In 2022, Transparency International (TI) ranked Korea thirty-first out of 180 countries (in the top fifth) on its Corruption Perception Index (CPI). At the turn of the century (2000), Korea had been ranked in the lower half (48/90).[38] In 2021, the country was ranked nineteenth globally on the Index of Public Integrity (IPI) and very impressively at the top position in the Asia-Pacific region.[39]

In its 2017 survey (the latest survey available to date) to construct the Global Corruption Barometer, TI found that fewer than 5 per cent of Koreans had paid a bribe for any public service in the previous twelve months, bringing Korea into the company of the top ten best-performing countries in the world. By contrast, in 2003, almost 85 per cent of Koreans had reported that corruption significantly affected their personal life.[40] However, though corporate and political corruption are still a matter of concern, corruption is not accepted as a norm, and fighting it has become institutionalized in the country, an important marker of ethical universalism.

It is fair to assert that Korea's process of transition from particularism to ethical universalism of the open--access order (à la North) is well under way. It is remarkable that during 2018–2021 two ex-presidents and the head of a very large business house (chaebol) were charged, convicted, and sent to prison on corruption charges. You[41] captures the general assessment well: '[w]hile South Korea today is widely recognized as a rich and robust democracy with relatively good governance, many Western observers considered the country a poor and hopelessly corrupt autocracy in the 1950s.'

Obviously, no one particular cause can be attributed for this transition. There would certainly be several, which have interacted with each other, and without pretending in any way that this list is complete as an explanation of a process as complex as socioeconomic change in a country, several critical institutional reforms may be identified that have contributed to the significant economic and social progress in the country.

11.3.1 Historical context

Korea has a long history as a unified nation state, dating back to the Goryeo era (918–1392). During that time, the country saw an unprecedented flourishing of the arts and culture and included a generally centralized, but extractive, institutional arrangement of ruling the peninsula. Another long period of reign of more than 500 years (1392–1910) by the Chosuns followed. While the long uninterrupted rule of the two dynasties built in social stability, it also gradually ossified the system.

By the time Japan colonized the country in 1910, the Korean political system had become 'monarchical and patrimonial in nature, characterized by a highly inflexible, classified social system with slaves at the lowest social stratum'.[42] Even though the country had built a long tradition of government bureaucracy and a civil service examination system, these were far from being effective and impartial. The Japanese colonial government, headed by a governor-general, usually a military officer, replaced the dilapidated monarchical state with a centralized, and highly repressive, bureaucracy. Some scholars have argued that the Japanese introduced an effective, disciplined government bureaucracy into the country by transforming 'a relatively corrupt and ineffective agrarian bureaucracy into a highly authoritarian, penetrating organization'.[43] No doubt the provision of universal education at the primary level, and the fact that a large number of Koreans were recruited and trained by the colonial government (albeit at the lower levels of the bureaucracy) helped to ultimately build a cadre of Korean bureaucrats. However, it would be too much of a stretch to suggest that the 'Korean developmental state was solely (or even mainly) attributable to Japanese rule'.[44] The political and economic institutions continued to be extractive.

The partition of the peninsula into the two Koreas in 1948 followed by a devastating war (1950–1953) was disastrous for both Koreas. Levels of human capital and 'per capita income were higher in the North, which predominated in industry, mining, and power generation, as compared to the South, which was largely agricultural'.[45] Most of the middle-class Koreans in the North fled South, as did about half a million refugees from various parts of the Japanese empire. Unemployment swelled and inflation hit triple digits, dramatically exacerbating the economic and governance challenges in South Korea.

11.3.2 Land reforms

One of the first acts of the Provisional People's Committee in the (then) Soviet-controlled North Korea was a massive land reform programme in 1946, based on uncompensated confiscation and free redistribution of land to the peasants and tenants tilling the land. This posed an immediate challenge to the US Military Government (USMG) and the provisional political leaders in the South, where land distribution was even more skewed than in the North. In the undivided peninsula, the south was more agricultural than the north, and thus deep inequality in land ownership was more of a pressing issue. In the southern part of pre-reform Korea, 'the richest 2.7 percent of the rural households owned two-thirds of all the cultivated lands, while 58 percent owned no land at all'.[46] To counter the perception that the North was being more responsive to the peasant population than the South, the USMG, despite initial reservations about land reforms, redistributed about 240,000 ha (about 12 per cent of total cultivated land) of formerly Japanese-held lands to former tenants, even before the first South Korean government had been established.

Land reforms were also part of the political platform of all parties in the May 1948 elections and were formally written into the country's first constitution, adopted a couple of months later. The formal constitution unequivocally committed to the intention that 'Farmland shall be redistributed to farmers'. This commitment to land reforms, now enshrined in the constitution, had very significant positive effects on South Korea's future growth and welfare.[47]

The first president of South Korea, Syngman Rhee, expeditiously pursued the land reforms programme as much out of genuine commitment to the programme as for domestic political reasons. Restricting land ownership to no more than 3 ha per household, about 330,000 ha of excess farmland and that owned by absentee landlords were redistributed by the government by 1952. There was little, if any, domestic political support for the landowners in any case, many of them being perceived as having collaborated with the previous Japanese colonial power. Reading the writing on the wall and well aware of the impending land reforms, many landowners sold their land—often at well below market prices—directly to their tenants even before the land reform legislation was implemented. As a matter of fact, the land area thus transferred (about 500,000 ha) far exceeded the government's own redistribution programme.

Almost 90 per cent of the land, which had previously been cultivated by tenants, was transferred to them by the early 1950s, and the Government's pledge of 'land to the tiller' fulfilled. By 1965, 'the proportion of families

who owned all the land they farmed rose dramatically from 13.8 percent of the total in 1945 to 69.5 percent, and the proportion of tenants
similarly dropped sharply from 48.9 percent to 7.0 percent.[48] By the
mid-1960s, Korea had implemented one of the most radical land-reform
programmes in the non-communist world and fundamentally transformed its rural class structure.

Land reforms had a very significant role in reducing income inequality in Korea after the wars. Some estimates show that 'the top 4 percent of the rural population (previous landlords) lost 80 percent of their
income, while the bottom 80 percent (tenants and owner tenants) increased their income by 20 percent to 30 percent; this was all because
of land reform.'[49] Another recent study showed that while the top 1 per
cent garnered as much as 20 per cent of the income in 1930, this fell
steeply by the early 1950s to 7 per cent, again mainly due to the land reforms.[50] In 1953, the country's Gini coefficient was only 0.34, reflecting
low inequality (zero would imply perfect equality, with 1 at the other
extreme),[51] and laying the groundwork for political and economic institutions in the country gradually becoming more inclusive.

11.3.3   Education

Despite the Japanese colonial administration's efforts to provide universal
education, particularly at the primary level, the fact remains that at the
end of their rule, almost 80 per cent of the country's population had not
received any public schooling. Of those who had, more than 90 per cent
were only educated up to primary level.[52]

The most immediate and lasting impact of Korea's land reforms was on
education.

Traditionally, the *yangban* or landed aristocracy had held a monopoly
over access to higher education and the higher civil service examinations.
Even during Japanese rule, when education was made universal, higher
education was in fact open only to the few wealthy and landed elite. Land
reforms and the ensuing virtual elimination of the landed elite unleashed
a sense of empowerment and the aspirations of the common people for
better education for their children. There was thus a huge upsurge in
popular demand for more and better education.

A major boost for education also came on the supply side from an un-expected quarter: the wealthy landed elite who were in fact the target of the land reforms. An insightful provision of the land reforms was that land belonging to educational institutions was exempt from state appro-priation. Perhaps in a bid to be seen as good citizens and refurbish their tainted reputation, many of the landed elite donated their land to educa-tional institutions rather than let the government take it away.

Land reforms essentially increased both demand for and supply of edu-cation. The number of schools, colleges, and universities thus increased dramatically, resulting in almost universal education being achieved in the country by 1960.[53] However, contrary to general impressions, gov-ernment expenditure on education was low, imposing a heavy burden on private households. In 1960, for example, government expenditure on education was only 2 per cent of GNP, even lower than the average of 2.2 per cent for all developing countries as a whole at that time.[54] By the government's own account, it financed only slightly more than half (55 per cent) of the cost of elementary education and less than a quarter (22 per cent) of secondary education, leaving the rest to private households to finance on their own.

However, the belief that education is a prerequisite for later successes in life now permeated all classes in society, including the rural house-holds. The metaphor of the farmer selling his only ox or his best paddy field to finance his children's education wasn't just a metaphor any more, but a genuinely held aspiration driving people's focus on education—what Koreans often themselves call their 'education fever'.[55]

11.3.4 Bureaucracy

Bureaucracy in South Korea is generally considered to be meritocratic, competent, and honest. Corruption is the exception. As the bureaucracy became more meritocratic it also became less corrupt; not just bribery, but there was a decline in embezzlement, undue favours, and use of public office for private gains. While some have emphasized the Confucian trad-ition of bureaucracy as a reason, and others the Japanese colonial bureau-cracy as the motivator for meritocracy in Korean civil services, the facts are somewhat different. During a large part of the Japanese rule and the early years of the Rhee presidency, bureaucracy was marked by political patronage in recruitment (clientelism), which in turn encouraged bureaucratic corruption.

Rapid expansion of education increased the pool of eligible applicants for the civil-service examinations, and simultaneously built increased domestic political pressure for fairer and meritocratic recruitment. The elimination of the landed elite in Korea following the land reforms meant that there was no dominant political power to capture the process of bureaucratic appointments, and the situation began to improve during the later years of the Rhee administration and continued thereafter. The proportion of meritocratic recruitment through competitive civil-service examination went from under 5 per cent when Rhee took office to over 70 per cent in the 1990s.[56]

Till 1959, the civil-service examinations were limited to recruiting for only a few highly coveted elite bureaucrat cadres. The Student Democratic Revolution of April 1960 further increased the pressure for meritocracy in the bureaucracy, and the short-lived Chang Myon Government (1960–1961) started the expansion of the civil-service competitive examinations to include recruiting for lower-level entry level positions as well. Starting in 1960, 'the civil service examinations became a wide road to the bureaucracy open to thousands of youths every year'.[57]

In addition to meritocracy, largely ensured by the robust recruitment process at entry through the competitive civil-service examination, political neutrality and autonomy are the other key attributes of a professional bureaucracy. This was done through appropriate assurances provided in the civil-service regulations. Additional reforms, such as legalization and introduction of parliamentary hearings, were made by successive governments to fortify the Weberian type of professional bureaucracy.[58] Korea's meritocratic and honest bureaucracy evolved gradually as the political institutions became more inclusive.

11.3.5 State autonomy

A key attribute of a modern, open-access regime (ethically universal) is state autonomy—the power of a state not to be held hostage by any one vested-interest group (particularism) to act in its own interest alone, rather than the state as a whole. This requires greater centralization of state power to enforce the law in the larger interest of the state. Many scholars have identified land reforms as an important factor in this process of building state autonomy.[59,60,61]

In Korea, land reforms profoundly affected the political structure as well. The general empowerment of the populace and reduced inequality liberated the state from being dominated by any class, limiting the extent of political clientelism and patronage appointments. This, in turn, prevented rampant corruption and even state capture by powerful elite classes.[62] The elimination of the traditional landed aristocracy enhanced state autonomy in Korea, while in several other late-industrializing countries, large landholders challenged the state's authority or reduced it to rent-seeking.[63]

11.3.6 Transition to inclusive institutions

Despite the several reforms discussed above, it would be fair to say that the country's political institutions remained authoritarian. General Park Chung-hee had come to power in 1961 via a military coup and focused exclusively on the economic development of the country through a largely export-oriented policy. However, the economic institutions in the country were generally inclusive. This was happening partly at the insistence of the US, which was still deeply involved in the affairs of the country, and partly because the political and business elite, including the military, recognized that economic growth was key to their survival and let the economic institutions function accordingly. By the 1970s, 'economic institutions in South Korea had become sufficiently inclusive that they reduced one of the strong rationales for extractive political institutions—the economic elite had little to gain from their own or the military's dominance of politics.'[64] While domestic pressures for political liberalization and greater inclusiveness mounted, the country remained politically extractive under military rule till 1987, when President Roh Tae-woo was elected democratically. Political institutions gradually turned more inclusive as, in addition to centralization of power, which they already enjoyed; greater pluralism also emerged in society.

Successful land reforms had essentially eliminated the landed elite and greatly reduced inequality in the country. That in turn meant that the political elite had less to fear from pluralism. The land reforms also enhanced state autonomy, contained clientelism, dramatically enhanced education, leading to a meritocratic bureaucracy and more inclusive (programmatic as against particularistic) politics.

Interestingly, several other countries, such as Japan and Taiwan, also undertook significant land reforms at around the same time (after World War II), and their experiences were similar.[65] Such land reforms have been argued as major factors behind East Asian countries performing much better than South East Asia,[66] and also overtaking Latin American countries.[67]

A relevant lesson can be learnt from the obverse too: that of the Philippines, in striking contrast to Korea and Taiwan. Due to insufficient political will and the power of the landed oligarchy, land reforms failed in that country. As a result, domination of the landed elite in both politics and the economy continued, resulting in persistent political clientelism, increasing patronage in the bureaucracy, and policy capture. All three countries were generally similar in terms of their economic conditions at the time of their independence in the late 1940s, but while Korea and Taiwan grew rapidly, the Philippines did not. A principal reason was that the political and economic institutions remained extractive in the Philippines, as they did not in Korea and Taiwan.

Building on the country's ancient traditions and emphasis on learning, Korea's post-war public policy on education has played a major role in achieving its striking economic development. By the 1960s, the country had achieved a much higher literacy rate than many other countries at similar income levels. Not only did it contribute to a well-educated and competent bureaucracy, it laid strong groundwork for subsequent advances in high technology and scientific research in the country in the 1980s. This also led to the rise of political pressures to transform its institutions to be more inclusive.

11.4 Summary

The feudal era in medieval Japan (1185–1603) was beset with frequent internal strife between the various feudal lords. In 1603, Tokugawa Ieyasu, the daimyo from Edo, rapidly consolidated his power and established the Tokugawa shogunate. A long period of over two and half centuries of stability and peace in the country followed. During this time, the Tokugawas placed significant emphasis on education, resulting in the country's achieving high literacy levels, a professionalized merit-based bureaucracy, and impressive economic growth.

However, the Tokugawa regime continued to be deeply feudal, with extremely limited social mobility. And, the economic and political institutions remained extractive.

The modernization of Japan began in earnest with the Meiji Restoration in 1868, following the demise of the Tokugawa shogunate. Transformative institutional changes were made. Feudalism was abolished, social mobility allowed, and private property rights were recognized.

Modern institutions, postal networks, and a banking system were established, and economic institutions increasingly became inclusive. Political institutions also trended towards greater inclusivity. A new constitution (the Meiji Constitution) was adopted in 1890, limiting to a certain extent the powers of the monarch with an elected Parliament and an independent judiciary in place. Increased plurality and inclusivity in both economic and political institutions laid the groundwork for Japan's subsequent economic and social development.

The partition of the peninsula in 1948, followed by the Korean War (1950–1953) was disastrous for both Koreas. Land reforms were high-priority for both. By the mid-1960s, South Korea had implemented a radical land-reform programme which fundamentally transformed its rural class structure. A significant lasting impact of the land reforms was on education. A growing sense of empowerment in the common citizen led to increased demands for better education opportunities and push for meritocratic recruitment to the much-coveted civil service laying the groundwork for a competent and effective bureaucracy. Land reforms also virtually eliminated the landed elite, reduced inequality and liberated the state from domination by any particular section of society. This also enhanced state autonomy, a key attribute of a modern, open-access regime.

However, even with the above reforms and while the country's economic institutions became generally inclusive, political institutions remained extractive until the late 1980s, when President Roh Tae-woo was democratically elected as the country's president (in 1987). With this transition, political institutions also gradually turned inclusive, with greater pluralism now possible.

Emphasis on education has been a major hallmark of both Japan's and Korea's cultural antecedents and public policy. As people enhanced their human capabilities, the countries moved up the value chain to produce higher-value goods. Enhanced revenues and profitability enabled individual firms and the state to substantially increase their investments in technology, research, and development, generating transformational breakthroughs in electronic and information-technology products.

As Sen has noted, 'indeed, Japan's entire experience of economic development was, to a great extent, driven by human-capability formation, which included the role of education and training'.[68] Though Sen mentions only Japan in this quote, it would apply equally well to Korea. Indeed, it would not be an exaggeration to assert that the spectacular economic successes in East Asia were in no small part due to their consistent attention to education and health in their development strategy.

12

Some Other Journeys

12.1 Introduction

Turning our gaze away from the prosperous, developed, OECD countries, we also wanted to look at the development trajectories of other less-obvious examples that are making impressive progress on their journey to 'Denmark'. Fortunately, there were several examples to choose from. In the interest of spreading our learning spectrum widely across the world we looked at Botswana in Africa, and Uruguay in South America.

12.2 Botswana

A landlocked country in the centre of Southern Africa, Botswana (2.3 million population, 2019) was one of the poorest countries in the world at its independence in 1966. About forty years later, it was classified by the World Bank as an upper-middle-income country, and had a GDP per capita of over $6,5,00 (in constant 2015 US$).[1] Botswana was also categorized as the second highest Medium Human Development country by the UNDP, ranking 117th among 191 countries in 2021.[2]

Strikingly, Botswana does even better on global governance scores. TI ranked the country 35th (out of 180) in its 2022 Corruption Perception Index report, the second highest in sub-Saharan Africa, after Seychelles. It had a better score (60/100) than the average of Asia Pacific (45), Eastern Europe, and Central Asia (35), and only slightly worse than the average of Western Europe and the European Union (66).[3] In the latest available regional report on corruption in Africa, TI also reported that only 7 per cent of respondents in Botswana had paid a bribe in the last twelve months, compared to 55 per cent in Kenya, 44 per cent in Nigeria, and 18 per cent in South Africa.[4]

From Here to Denmark. Rajat M. Nag and Harinder S. Kohli, Oxford University Press.
© Rajat Mohan Nag and Harinder Singh Kohli 2023. DOI: 10.1093/oso/9780198893103.003.0012

These are all remarkable achievements for a young country that had started from scratch. Good governance and prudent macroeconomic management, particularly of the country's dominant diamond resources, which for many countries have in fact been a curse, have resulted in steady and significant reductions in poverty levels in the country, down from slightly under 42 per cent in 1985 to just over 15 per cent in 2015, at $2.15/day (2017 PPP).[5]

However, despite these significant economic and social improvements, low levels of job creation keep inequality still very high (0.533 in 2018; the higher the value between 0 and 1, the more unequal the society), with poor health conditions, and HIV/AIDS prevalence among the adult population (15–49 years of age) still over 20 per cent, the fourth highest in the world.

Botswana certainly did not start out with very favourable conditions at independence in 1966. The country's physical infrastructure was virtually non-existent (only 12 km of paved road) and the human capital was equally dismal (only twenty-two university graduates and 100 who had completed secondary level schooling).

So how did Botswana—perhaps the only uncontroversial success story in Africa—do it? Understandably, this question has been asked and studied by many and 'there is almost complete agreement that Botswana achieved this spectacular growth performance because it managed to adopt good policies. The basic system of law and contract worked reasonably well. State and private predation have been quite limited. Despite the large revenues from diamonds, this has not induced domestic political instability or conflict for control of this resource. The government sustained the minimal public service structure that it inherited from the British and developed it into a meritocratic, relatively non-corrupt and efficient bureaucracy ... Fiscal policy has been prudent, and the exchange rate has remained closely tied to fundamentals.'[6] In another incisive analysis, Leith observes that Botswana prospered because tribal economic interests, particularly regarding natural-resource management (read diamonds) were balanced by a wise leadership who, working within a democratic political system anchored in tradition, adopted good policies conducive to growth.[7]

But how did Botswana manage to choose good policies? It could possibly be because able, inclusive institutions were in place in Botswana.

Such institutions 'protect the property rights of actual and potential investors, provide political stability, and ensure that the political elites are constrained by the political system and the participation of a broad cross-section of the society'.[8] At the risk of sounding too Socratic, another question then follows: why did such institutions take root in Botswana, while not in many other developing nations in neighbouring sub-Saharan Africa, or around the world, starting from a similar base position?

Several factors were probably at play. While none of them can individually explain the evolution of inclusive institutions in Botswana, perhaps together they do. Without pretending to be comprehensive in any way, the five following factors may be considered.[9]

12.2.1 Botswana's tribal institutions

Ancestors of the modern *Tswana*[10] tribes (who make up almost 80 per cent of the country's population) practised a social structure where the chief was the central leader with authority to allocate land for cattle-grazing, growing crops, and building houses, but he could not make these decisions unilaterally. The decision process was consultative through a series of public forums, the *kgotla*, held around the community. The *kgotla* was an assembly of adult males in which issues of public interest were discussed. Botswana's tribal institutions encouraged broad-based participation in decision-making and placed constraints on the political elite. Though the *kgotlas* were only advisory in nature, they carried significant influence, since the king himself attended some of them to hear public grievances. An institution of public feedback thus evolved, which over time 'created a degree of trust in the government—the sense that the government exists to serve the people and promote development and is not the instrument of one group or individuals for the purpose of getting hold of the (community) wealth'.[11] *Tswana* tradition also respected private property, a factor which played a significant role in the later evolution of Botswana's inclusive economic institutions.

Botswana's stable political environment and regular election cycle also probably owe something to the old *Tswana* tradition of the *kgotlas*. Continuing its uninterrupted, free, and fair democratic elections since independence, the country held its latest general elections in October

2019. The voter turnout was an impressive 84 per cent. In a closely fought competitive election, the ruling Botswana Democratic Party (BDP) won over 52 per cent of the votes and Mokgweetsi Masisi took office as the country's new and fifth President.

Essentially, then, the *Tswana* states had over time built up a core set of pluralistic political institutions, particularly the *kgotla*, which encouraged political participation and placed constraints on the political elites, very much along the lines of how the Magna Carta had on the English monarchs and widened the political influence of the barons in the early thirteenth century. The *Tswana* tradition of selecting their chiefs on merit and competency rather than on strictly hereditary grounds also contributed to the inclusive nature of their political institutions. It is true that *Tswana* chieftaincy was often passed down through generations, but the processes they followed in doing so suggest that 'winning the chieftaincy was a matter of achievement but was then rationalized so that the successful competitor appeared to be the rightful heir'.[12]

12.2.2 Botswana's colonial past

Botswana was a protectorate, rather than a fully colonized state under the British, for about eighty years (1885–1966). British colonization thus did not destroy or supplant the traditional, pre-colonial institutions of the country, which served them well.

Ironically, it was the *Tswana* chiefs themselves who had sought out the British, as early as 1853, to ask for protection of the *Batswana* (people of Botswana) from the Boers of South Africa. They were initially rebuffed. However, as the prospect of diamonds in the region increased, and the scramble for Africa gathered steam, the British began to seriously look at Botswana as a route inward from the Cape Colony to Central Africa. The country's strategic location, ideal to thwart the Germans on one side, who had annexed South West Africa (now Namibia) in 1884, and the Boer states on the other, was not lost on the British. They thus declared Bechuanaland (erstwhile name of Botswana) as Britain's protectorate in 1885, to be administered from South Africa. Fortuitously for the *Batswana*, the British decided that their 'colonialism' in Botswana would be a light touch. Their intentions could not be clearer: 'We have no interest in the country to the north of the Molope (the Bechuanaland

Protectorate), except as a road to the interior. We might therefore confine ourselves for the present to preventing that part of the Protectorate being occupied by foreign powers doing as little in the way of administration or settlement as possible', declared the British High Commissioner.[13]

Just as well. The benign neglect of Bechuanaland by the British spared the *Batswana* from the ravages of extractive institutions in the country such as were usually set up by the colonial masters of the time elsewhere in Africa, and indeed, the rest of the world. The *Batswana* were thus able to continue to manage their own affairs and avoided becoming a source of cheap labour or natural resources for the Boers or the British to exploit.

There was another critical long-term benefit of the relatively benign colonization of Bechuanaland. The authority of the traditional *Tswana* chiefs was not much diluted. In addition to the pluralism of their societies through the *kgotlas*, the *Batswana* tribes had centralized a fair degree of political power and accountability in their chiefs. It is worth noting that Bechuanaland being a protectorate, the moral and political authority of the *Tswana* chiefs was not significantly compromised, unlike in other fully colonized states, in Africa and elsewhere.

Limited colonial rule allowed the continuity of traditional political institutions and customs of the *Batswana* and provided greater legitimacy to the new government immediately after independence. The traditional practice of consultation also allowed the first president, Seretse Khama, to form a broad-based coalition government within the BDP, including the tribal chiefs and cattle-owners, which helped build a much-needed political consensus in the early years of a new country.

12.2.3 Role of traditional *Batswana* elites

In 1966, Botswana started out as a very poor country with few assets and little infrastructure. To address these pressing issues, the early development plans of the new country focused on the rural sector, essentially cattle ranching. It was effectively the only sector of the economy which could be developed to export to the European market. Interestingly, more than two thirds of the members of the National Assembly in those years were large- or medium-sized cattle-owners themselves. Establishing and enforcing well-defined property rights were obviously very important for the cattle-owners and indeed the national economy as well.

Interestingly, though land was communally owned in the *Tswana* states, cattle-ownership was private property and property rights were thus already a part of the institutional framework, even in pre-independence Botswana. Given that the cattle-owners were themselves part of the political elites, economic and political interests converged, and they were all in support of well-established and -enforced property rights. The point is that traditional *Batswana* elite actively participated in the political life of the newly independent Botswana and that was a major contributing factor in further nurturing inclusive political and economic institutions in the country.

12.2.4   Avoiding the resource curse

By the mid-1970s, diamond revenues were fast becoming a major source of revenue for the government, overtaking cattle-ranching in importance. It would not have been surprising if the political elites found ways to capture such revenues for their own interest (as indeed it happened in many countries with natural resource finds, Venezuela's oil, for example). Fortunately, Botswana managed to avoid the feared resource curse. A big reason for this happy course of events was that the traditional *kgotla* institution placed effective constraints on the political elites. They could not do as they pleased and get away with it. And the broad coalition within the ruling BDP didn't allow the cattle-owners, for example, to insist on adequate property rights when it came to their interests, but at the same time expropriate the diamond revenues. Thus, the 'diamond rents were widely distributed, and the extent of this wealth increased the opportunity cost of undermining the good institutional path. No group wanted to fight to expand its rents at the expense of rocking the boat'.[14] Nobody wanted to kill the goose which laid the golden egg.

12.2.5   Leadership

Above all, human agency and the role of Botswana's leadership—particularly that of its first president, Seretse Khama—was critical and perhaps even decisive in putting Botswana on its way to 'Denmark'. This was especially true in the areas of mineral exploitation and the rights of the state versus those of the tribes. With great foresight, Khama had insisted that the BDP, 'even before independence, write into its platform its intention to assert the state's rights to all mineral resources'.[15] This enabled President Khama to reach an agreement with the tribal chiefs on fair sharing of the diamond revenues as they came in; but in return, he simultaneously extracted from them an arrangement which reduced their powers in favour of the national government. Both these moves were crucial in the evolution of successful inclusive institutions in post-independence Botswana, while many other resource-rich countries often got mired in internal conflict and even civil war over similar issues. These strategic statesmanlike actions are even more striking when in fact, the largest diamond mines were in Khama's own district of Bamangwoto, and he clearly chose the interests of the state over his tribe's.

Another fundamental policy decision was Khama's strong stance on the importance of an autonomous and competent civil service in the country. While acknowledging the scarcity of human capital resources in the country, he stuck to his policy of not prematurely 'indigenizing' the bureaucracy until suitably qualified *Batswana* were available. With adequate compensation and clear guidelines for authority and accountability, Khama could thus build a relatively effective bureaucracy. Although there have certainly been several instances of corruption, the country's bureaucracy has been, on the whole, meritocratic and 'corruption and mismanagement in Botswana is relatively pale and restricted. It is almost entirely an elite phenomenon'.[16]

Khama served as the country's president till his death in 1980, having won four free and fair multiparty national elections. He was succeeded by Quett Masire, who, in addition to serving out Khama's remaining term, went on to win three elections on his own. Masire's succession marked a very important milestone in institutionalizing electoral democracy and peaceful transition of power in the country.[17] Between the two of them, Khama and Masire presided over the country for thirty-two years, providing remarkable political stability and policy continuity.

Without a doubt, Botswana is surely but slowly transiting from particularism to a regime aspiring to ethical universalism (à la Mungiu-Pippidi) or from limited to open-access orders (à la North). Political and economic institutions are more inclusive than not, but the process is far from over. Corruption is certainly low, but there are concerns that the process is fraying at the edges. Favouritism and nepotism are on the rise. While public spending is generally transparent, and use of digital technology in public procurement increasing, 'most government tenders for the supply of goods and services from government are won by members of the "tenderpreneurs" group, linked to the ruling party'.[18] Scores on TI and CPI, while still high, have deteriorated in the past few years, as have several components of the Index of Public Integrity (IPI).[19] Ranked forty-fourth out of 109 countries in 2015 on the IPI, the country slipped to the eighty-third position four years later. Scores on judicial independence, freedom of the press, and budget transparency all slipped.

The BDP has ruled Botswana continuously since independence in 1966, albeit by free and fair elections held every five years as mandated by the Constitution. While there is no indication that the rule of law has been compromised in the country, single-party rule even in a multiparty democracy can inhibit the transition to an open-access regime, and that indeed seems to be the case in Botswana. A remarkable journey, but a journey still in progress.

12.3   Uruguay

12.3.1 A contemporary transition to open-order access

A country of about 3.5 million people with gradually increasing political commitment to inclusive economic growth in recent decades, Uruguay is classified by the UN as a 'Very High Human Development' country in the world. Globally, it ranked fifty-eighth in 2021 (out of 191 countries), and third among the Latin American countries (behind Chile and Argentina).[20] At an annual per capita income of just over $20,000 (in 2019), the country has virtually eliminated extreme poverty—down from 0.6 per cent in 2006 to 0.1 per cent in 2022, at $2.15/day (2017 PPP)—while moderate poverty reduced dramatically.[21]

In terms of inequality, Uruguay performs best, with the lowest Gini coefficient in the region (though still rather high at 0.397), and income levels among the poorest 40 per cent of its population increased much faster than the national average growth rate of income during 2006–2019.

However, the country still suffers from significant spatial, demographic, and racial differences. People in the north, the youth (below seventeen) and African descendant population are significantly poorer.[22]

The country also performs well on governance issues, ranked by TI as the world's fourteenth least corrupt country in 2022, and the best in the Americas (tying with Canada and remarkably, ahead of the US).[23] Similar analyses by the Americas Barometer[24] and the World Bank[25] (on not only corruption but other dimensions of governance as well, such as voice and accountability, political stability, government effectiveness, regulatory quality, and rule of law) confirm these conclusions.

However, this generally positive assessment of the country's current governance profile was not always the case. In fact, Uruguay is generally considered to be a contemporary achiever in terms of transparency, a country that has only recently come to be called an 'open-access order' à la North,[26] in which politicians' corrupt behaviour is penalized by citizens and meritocracy, rather than the privilege of wealth or the accident of birth, is the only criterion for access to economic and political opportunities.

A striking feature of the phenomenon of corruption in Uruguay's history, particularly in the nineteenth and twentieth centuries, was often not an issue of widespread misuse of public funds for private gain. Instead, Uruguay has a long history of political particularism, also referred to as clientelism. In such a situation, the state would use its discretionary powers to distribute public resources, jobs, and other benefits to specific groups and individuals in exchange for electoral support.[27] Only in recent decades has the country made the transition from a regime of political particularism to universalism.

12.3.2   An old democracy but with clientelism

Though Uruguay has a long tradition of democracy since its independence in 1825, governing the country was essentially monopolized by two principal political parties for almost 150 years. These were the Partido Colorado, 'Red' (PC), with a relatively liberal urban base; and the Partido Nacional, 'Blanco' (PN), comprising the more conservative landowners. Between them they maintained partisan control of all areas of the government machinery, public sector jobs, and resources. Thus, through this practice, euphemistically known as 'co-participation', even though the PN formed the government for the first time in 1958 (since 1865), they had not been fully frozen out of the advantages of the office during that period.

Interestingly, these understandings were often enshrined in law, even in the constitution itself.[28] A constitutionally approved method of practising clientelism was the 'multiple simultaneous voting system (MSV)'. In effect, this was a form of 'open list proportional representation (PR) in which a voter would vote first for a party, and then for a list or a candidate within that party. This essentially turned votes into a currency that second-line politicians could exchange with party leaders in return for government posts'.[29] Both parties also had allotted positions in statutory bodies such as the Election Board (Corte Electoral, established in 1924), or the Accounting and Auditor General's office (Tribunal de Cuentas, established in 1934). The country's top judicial bodies, the Supreme Court and the Administrative Contentious Court, created in 1952, required a super-majority (two thirds of the General Assembly) to be appointed. Similar sharing of high offices in public-service organizations, including in their boards of directors, was formally provided for in the country's revised constitution in 1952. Although this was ultimately removed in another constitutional revision in 1966, the practice continued.

While such sharing of offices in the legislature, the executive, and the judiciary, provided remarkable political stability, it also meant that 'Uruguayan democracy and the political institutions that supported it tended to distribute power', creating the perfect ecosystem for political patronage in the country.[30]

Unsurprisingly, a sense of clientelism permeated the whole society, and until the 1960s, particularism rather than ethical universalism (à la Mungiu-Pippidi) ruled the governing regime's behaviour in all dealings between the government and the common citizen. Citizens needed a broker for any service from the government, nationally or locally, whether it was a business licence, a phone connection, or access to health services, and of course, for public-sector jobs (the most significant source of employment in the country).[31]

12.3.3 Mounting pressure for change

Things began to change in the 1960s in response to two interrelated factors: one, economic, and the other, political. It was getting too expensive for the state to maintain a clientelist regime, and disaffection with the present political arrangements in the country had started to gather momentum, forcing the political institutions to become more pluralistic.

The post-World War II boom around the world had been good for the Uruguayan economy, particularly its beef exports. But things got progressively worse from the mid-1950s: economic growth fell from a high of almost 8 per cent in 1954 to almost zero by 1968. The state's pension burdens, and payroll costs, became increasingly unsustainable, labour unrest ensued, and living standards dropped. These factors, plus a general sense of disillusionment with the clientelist system which was increasingly unable to meet people's expectations and aspirations, led the citizens to see just how extractive their economic and political institutions in fact were. In turn, this led to the creation of a third political party in the country—the leftist Broad Front (Frente Amplio or FA)—a broad coalition of Christian democrats, socialists, communists, and dissident members of the two traditional parties. Reflecting the general frustration of the citizens with the status quo, the FA did surprisingly well in the 1971 elections. A viable three-party political system, with significant implications for the country's future, was born.

The economic and political challenges of the sixties prompted some quarters of the ruling parties and the intelligentsia to begin considering that some fundamental institutional reforms in the country were necessary. A Commission on Investigation and Economic Development, an inter-ministerial body,[32] toiled for seven long years to produce a blueprint forf much-needed reforms aimed squarely at reducing the clientelist influence of the state. Fortunately for the country, this blueprint significantly influenced the new constitution that Uruguay adopted in 1967, considered by many as the first major step towards building a modern, rationally functioning governance apparatus based on principles of ethical universalism.

12.3.4 The dark years of military rule and subsequent transition to greater political plurality

Unfortunately, there was a more immediate crisis to be faced first. The growing disenchantment of the people, seriously exacerbated by the worsening economic situation in the country and the general political and social milieu in the regional neighbourhood, spawned Uruguay's own homegrown urban guerrilla movement (the Tupamaros). The old bipartisan clientelist equilibrium was unable to cope with the new political force, that is, the FA, and even less the urban guerrilla movement, leading to a military takeover in the country from 1973 to 1985.

The trauma of these dozen brutal and murderous years seared the urgency of reforms into the country's political and economic institutions. Public spending, particularly on the unsustainable public pension schemes, was trimmed through a 'Public Enterprises Law' (adopted in 1992), which also mandated the privatization of major publicly held companies and the ending of state monopolies in certain sectors. Bureaucratic reforms were undertaken, and public-service delivery to the citizens was streamlined and made less discretionary. Technology, for example, getting a phone connection, helped in cutting out the brokers in certain cases.

There were major changes in the political domain as well. All through the 1970s and 1980s, the FA had grown as a political force. In the 1994 national elections, it emerged as a viable challenger to both the established political parties, and the three parties (FA, PC, and PN) ended up in a virtual dead heat, with the PC eking out a very narrow victory. The message was clear: the social agenda of the FA and their demand to move from political particularism to universalism was gathering traction around the country.

On the political side, electoral reforms introduced the system of majority run-offs to presidential elections. Multiple simultaneous votes were eliminated. Politicians could no longer use the votes they garnered as bargaining chips to extract particularistic rewards from other parties to get them past the finish line. Pension reforms were undertaken to ensure that social security would remain fiscally viable in the long term, while also making it more difficult for politicians to manipulate pensions as a clientelist resource.

Even as the traditional parties (the PC and the PN) adjusted their governance strategies to become more universal rather than clientelist, the political influence of the FA continued to rise. Their politics, which was based on what may be called competition for ideas or 'programmatic' competition (or a universal rather than a clientelist logic), had taken root in the Uruguayan society. The FA won a majority in the national elections in 2004, the first time in the nation's history that neither of the two traditional parties were in power. Multiparty democracy had truly arrived in the country. What was even more impressive was that they won the next two elections as well, while the conservative PC won back power by a rather narrow margin in a run-off election against the FA in 2019.

The FA is a coalition of ideologically diverse parties, with views and beliefs ranging from slightly left of centre to extreme left. While they disagree on much, especially on the role of the state in the economy and levels of public ownership, there is clear convergence on one issue: total opposition to clientelism. The party's electoral base was not built on the particularistic distribution of state resources, and thus while the traditional parties had always had to fight their own core support groups whenever they tried to limit the discretionary use of government resources, the FA did not have to face such internal oppositions.[33]

Consequently, the FA could pursue policies based on universal competition. They were able to focus on the relative merits and consequences of the individual programmes, and thus had greater success in undertaking reforms, say on pension or taxes, or expanding access to public services, while cutting out the parasitic role of intermediating agents.

It would be an exaggeration to say that Uruguay has eliminated clientelism in its public affairs. However, it would be fair to claim that the country has made the transition from particularism to universalism to become what North would call an 'open-access regime'. Uruguayan experience of the last sixty years or so shows 'how a change in the competitive equilibrium of the political party system (from clientelism to programmatic competition) can transform a country into an open access regime'.[34]

Two principal existential factors drove this change: one, fiscal challenges which made continuing with particularism unaffordable; and two, the political challenges of accommodating a third party in a traditional two-party system. It is ultimately to the great credit of the response of the

288 FROM HERE TO DENMARK

country's traditional political parties (the PC and the PN) to proactively respond to the new social forces demanding an end to clientelism and accommodation of a new political party (the FA) into the mainstream politics of the country.

12.4 Summary

From being one of the poorest countries in the world at its independence in 1966, Botswana had become an upper-middle-income and a High Human Development country barely four decades later.

Botswana was fortunate that its tribal institutions had traditionally been remarkably inclusive. While the community chiefs were vested with the authority to decide issues of public interest, the process (the *kgotla*) was consultative and involved the community thereby suitably constraining the political elites. The country's tribal institutions were also fortunate to be spared the ravages of extractive colonization, as Botswana was a protectorate, rather than a fully colonized state, under the British for about eighty years.

Traditionally, while land was communally owned, cattle were considered private property and more than two thirds of the members of the National Assembly in independent Botswana were themselves large or middle-class cattle-owners. It was in the legislators' personal, and indeed the national, interest to develop the cattle sector, as it was the only sector of the economy which could generate exports to European markets. Economic and political interests thus converged and well-defined property rights continued to be part of the institutional framework in the country.

The inclusive nature of the traditional *kgotla* institutions in the country also constrained the elites from unfairly capturing the windfall profits of the booming diamond finds in the post-independence period and thus avoiding the feared resource curse.

Enlightened leadership, particularly that of its first president, Seretse Khama, played a critical role in Botswana's journey. He was instrumental in setting the stage for an equitable share of diamond revenues between all tribes across the nation, but in return got the tribal leaders to agree to greater power-sharing with the national government. Greater equity and centralization of power led in turn to the evolution of successful inclusive institutions in post-independence Botswana, including an autonomous and competent Weberian bureaucracy. Aided by the interplay of the above factors, and constitutionally mandated free and fair elections every five years, Botswana is slowly transiting to an open-access system.

Even though Uruguay had been a democracy for almost two centuries (with a damaging period of military rule for over a decade, starting in the mid-1970s), its principal challenge in assuring good governance was its equally long history of political particularism (clientelism). From its independence in 1825 till the mid-1960s, Uruguay's political system was monopolized by only two political parties, Partido Colorado, 'Red' (PC), and the Partido Nacional, 'Blanco' (PN). Between them, the two parties shared the spoils of the government administration, even when the party was not in power.

Particularism, rather than ethical universalism, thus characterized the country's social structure and political institutions.

By the mid-1960s, these cosy clientelist practices started to come under pressure caused principally by the economic slowdowns the country faced. The government's fiscal space to afford the clientelist regime began to shrink and the state's pension burdens and rising payroll costs became increasingly unsustainable. Labor unrest ensued, living standards dropped, and in the midst of a general sense of disillusionment with the current economic and political institutions, a third political party, a left-oriented Broad Front, the Frente Amplio (FA), emerged to capture popular support. The FA did surprisingly well in the 1971 general election and a genuine political plurality with three viable political parties took root in the country.

The people now had a stronger voice and pressures began to build for some fundamental institutional reforms in the country to move it away from the privileged clientelism enjoyed by the elite. The situation was further compounded by similar demands for political and social changes. This volatile mix spawned Uruguay's own home-grown urban guerrilla movement (the Tupamaros) leading to a brutal military takeover in the country in 1973, lasting a long and murderous twelve years. The trauma of these years led to significant economic reforms, including in the bureaucracy and public service delivery, but more importantly in the country's political institutions which gradually turned inclusive.

Part III: Key messages

1. *There is no unique road map for the journey to Denmark, though some common features may be identified.*
2. *Institutions have to be both politically and economically inclusive. Just one or the other won't do.*
3. *It can take very long (even centuries) for inclusive institutions to emerge.*
4. *Participation of the citizens in the process of governance is important for a successful journey.*
5. *Human capabilities (particularly, education and health) are crucial enablers for people to effectively participate in such a process.*

PART IV
THREE FELLOW TRAVELLERS

Overview

Our social order and well-being are influenced and affected by three principal institutions that comprise our society: the state, the markets, and the community. However, it is not only a matter of how well or poorly these institutions work on their own, but even more importantly, how well they work together and balance each other. Think of these three institutions as fellow travellers. How the journey 'From Here to Denmark' will turn out depends on how well the three travellers travel together: not as individual adventurers but as fellow travellers, supporting each other along the way and not leaving either of the other two behind.

The state includes the government and other institutions of political governance in the country, such as the legislature and the judiciary, but for the most part, we will focus on the national government and often refer to it synonymously as the state. At its core, the role of the state is to provide good governance, ensuring security and justice for its citizens and establishing a foundation of law and order.

The markets include a broad array of market-related institutions in the country, be it the neighbourhood vegetable market, the street hawker, or the large private-sector corporations. It includes markets for goods and service, labour, and the financial institutions. A society needs well-functioning, competitive markets to enable it to efficiently produce, buy and sell, and consume goods and services. These in turn generate economic growth, expand opportunities for its citizens and enhances prosperity.

The community is we, the people. It is our neighbours, with whom we interact regularly, and our fellow citizens we associate with. Our community extends to include our local government, the municipality, the local school board, our local hospital, and even the residents' welfare association in our neighbourhood and other similar groups. The community lies at the heart of the development process. Ultimately, the journey from Here to Denmark is to achieve a better life for all citizens in the community, nothing more, nothing less.

In Part IV of this book, we will discuss each of these three travellers separately but with a focus on their interactions with each other. The interplay of the state, market, and community at large in any society forms a very important part of any enquiry into how that society could build inclusive institutions, and thus deliver inclusive development to its people.

Achieving this delicate balance between the three fellow travellers to ensure that they are travelling in tandem is a principal challenge in the journey From Here to 'Denmark'.

13

The STATE, the Markets, and the Community

13.1 Introduction

A recurring refrain heard in many countries around the world, particularly in those devastated by war and violence, is fear: people living in fear. Fear of violence, fear of the neighbourhood goons, fear of the knock on the door in the dead of night. This fear can be as debilitating as the actual violence itself, as it puts one under the control of another person or group. Such threats could be external as well as internal, from other countries across borders as much as the dark forces within.

Sen[1] has suggested that the fundamental premise of a decent, fulfilling life must be freedom from such fear, dominance, and insecurity. According to the Irish philosopher, Philip Pettit, it would surely be unacceptable for society if one has to 'live at the mercy of another, having to live in a manner that leaves you vulnerable to some ill that the other is in a position arbitrarily to impose'.[2] Dominance does not just originate from brute force or threats of violence. As Acemoğlu and Robinson have observed, 'any relation of unequal power, whether enforced by threats or by other social means such as customs, will create a form of dominance'.[3] Even if one's fundamental rights and liberties are assured by, say, the constitution, as is now the case in most countries (no constitution would state 'you will not have liberty'), freedom requires more than only such an assurance; one should be able to express and exercise that freedom safely and fearlessly. Otherwise, the assurance is just ink on paper.

Unfortunately, untold millions of people around the world still live in such a state of domination and injustice. As a matter of fact, for most of human history, dominance and the consequent insecurity people have

From Here to Denmark. Rajat M. Nag and Harinder S. Kohli, Oxford University Press.
© Rajat Mohan Nag and Harinder Singh Kohli 2023. DOI: 10.1093/oso/9780198893103.003.0013

lived in is what Thomas Hobbes, writing during the English Civil War of the 1640s, graphically described as 'continual fear and danger of violent death; and the life of man, solitary, poor, nasty, brutish and short'.[4] Hobbes attributed this as a situation which emerges 'when there is no visible power to keep them [*the people*] in awe and tie them by fear of punishment to the performance of their covenants'. He obviously held a rather dim view of human nature and suggested that it was the 'natural passion of man' to partiality, pride, revenge, and the like. And 'Covenants, without the sword are but words, and of no strength to secure a man at all'.[5] Hobbes thus proposed the need for an all-powerful central authority which he called the *Leviathan*, the feared and powerful sea monster in the Bible's Book of Job: 'there is no power on earth to be compared to him' (Job 41:24).

The Leviathan would be feared, yes, but on the other hand it would ensure that people don't 'endeavour to destroy, or subdue one another' and having been thus assured, a citizen could go about her daily life with her 'head held high'.[6] The idea of the state emerged precisely from the keen desire of the citizenry for such an assurance: the need for a social structure which would legally monopolize the use of violence so that ordinary citizens are free of fear. Much is expected of the state. While providing security and assuring freedom from violence is key, an effective state is also vital to put such rules and institutions in place that would allow markets to operate, for people (the community) to have a voice in their governance and to pursue their lives productively, peacefully, and with dignity.

But herein lies a fundamental dilemma. Would the Leviathan as the state not be unreliable as well? Would citizens not have traded the domination of many for the domination of one, though it might have theoretically reduced the scope of random violence or threats of it? Surely, it should be a matter of great concern that the same coercive power which protects the citizens could also act against them, confiscate their property, and abuse their rights.

As Fukuyama notes, 'the task of modern politics has been to tame the power of the state, to direct its activities towards ends regarded as legitimate by the people it serves, and to regulate the exercise of power under a rule of law'.[7] The key word here is 'legitimate', very much in line with the Weberian definition of the state as: 'a human community that claims the monopoly of the legitimate use of physical force within a given territory.[8] The ultimate essence of stateness is, in other words, legitimate enforcement.

Try to do too much, the state runs the risk of becoming the feared Hobbesian despotic Leviathan whose power overwhelms society. Do too little, the state falters, the society is ruled haphazardly by an absent Leviathan, and chaos reigns. Thus, the state needs to find a balance of power and function in what Acemoğlu and Robinson have called the 'Narrow Corridor' in their very insightful book, where the Leviathan does not have so much power as to be despotic but is also not so marginalized as to be effectively absent.[9] Rather, the state is constrained enough by the fellow travellers (the markets and the community) to become what they call the 'Shackled Leviathan'.

13.2 The role of the State: at its core, to provide good governance

Among the key functions of the state are ensuring security and freedom from fear, establishing a foundation of law and property rights, and justice, which will provide social order. Without such an order, under-pinned by institutions, markets cannot function, society cannot survive, and freedom cannot thrive.

Human society has survived and evolved to its present form having realized that under many circumstances, working together rather than individually is much more effective. A community working together can protect its members much better than any individual could alone. People can also be more productive and prosperous collectively than in-dividually. Ancient rice-growing societies in Bali recognized the key role of 'collective action' in constructing and maintaining the irrigation ca-nals. Collectively, they could irrigate their rice lands, which individually they could not. But how would people do things 'together'? Sometimes, it could be through voluntary associations; sometimes through mar-kets; but oftentimes, societies would need an orchestra conductor, the state (government). Hence, 'societal well-being was advanced not just by farmers and merchants pursuing their own dreams in a libertarian dream, but also through a strong government, with clearly specified but limited powers'.[10] Notice again the need to clearly circumscribe the government, lest it become a Leviathan, but also for it to be strong enough to be able to govern effectively.

But note, too, the need for the government to be involved in managing collective goods. Without pollution-control rules and regulations, an individual producer will not include (internalize) the costs of the pollution they cause (e.g. by discharge of waste into the river) in their own cost-benefit assessments. Markets on their own could produce excessive pollution and unemployment, but too little basic research.

National defence is perhaps the most obvious example of collective action. Everyone benefits, but individually we would be unable (and hopefully, unwilling too) to hire our own private militia (well, almost all of us). In addition to the obvious impracticality of the cost, it would also be most ineffective, resulting in Hobbes's version of a 'nasty, brutish, and short life'. Such 'public goods' are best collectivized and provided by the state, paid for by all (through taxes) and benefitting all.[11] Markets (or private provision) of public goods will be undersupplied because of the pervasive discrepancies between private and social returns.

Good public infrastructure such as roads, ports, airports, electricity, water, sanitation, and basic health and education are other examples of public goods, which benefit society at large. Their lack or under-provision hampers economic development and social welfare. Basic and advanced research in science and technology carried out in universities, research labs, and national science institutions is another instance. The invention of the X-ray, the polio and smallpox vaccine, the Internet, space travel, have all been pathbreaking global public goods, benefitting humanity as a whole. A recent and affirming example of this has been the development and distribution of covid-19 vaccines, which have single-handedly helped the human race fight a pandemic, an exercise in symbiotic collective action.

But the examples above all depend on some central authority to provide the public goods. That central authority is the state and thus, perhaps the most important public good is an efficient and fair state, working in the interest of all and providing a level playing field. Laws have to be written, adopted, and equally importantly, enforced. Easier said than done, but these are indeed the crucial functions of the state. So would be ensuring social justice for all, taking care of the weak and the old, the sick, and those with special needs who can't do it on their own and cannot be left only to the workings (mercy) of the market or charity.

But this does not mean that the government needs to (or even should) provide such services all on their own. As a matter of fact, they shouldn't. Public policy areas such as taxation, criminal justice, immigration, and so on, obviously have to be in the hands of the state. But there are many other areas where public–private partnerships in both physical (toll roads, airports, power grids) and social infrastructures (schools, hospitals, even prisons) have been tried around the world, with varying degrees of success. Local communities need to be drawn in, too. Most production activities are best carried out by the private sector, but it has to be regulated. Rules, regulations, fair play, and standards of safety have to be specified and again, more importantly, enforced; this is where the state steps in. Recall our earlier point: 'the ultimate essence of stateness is legitimate enforcement'.

We have noted in previous chapters the critical importance of human capability formation as a key driver of human development and modernization of society. As a society modernizes, its people adopt modern attitudes, which are the 'essential building blocks of an advanced society and indeed an advanced economy'.[12] People in a modern society are characterized by 'a stronger sense of personal and social efficacy, more open to new ideas, new experiences, and new people ... they valued science more and accepted change more readily'.[13] Based on a seminal multi-country study, sociologists Inkeles and Smith concluded that the two key sources of modernity were the school and the factory. No other factor—gender, residence, family background, occupation, income—comes close.

The influence of schooling on developing as an individual is well-known and thus to be expected. But at first glance, the influence of the factory in fostering modernity might not appear to be so obvious. However, on further reflection, working in a factory is a serious business: workers have to follow a regular schedule, regularly learn and upgrade their skills to keep up with technology, work in teams and cooperate with colleagues, and focus as much on efficacy (doing the right thing) as on efficiency (doing it with minimum inputs of resources and time), while producing quality product with an eye on the bottom line. Inkeles and Smith's unequivocal conclusion: 'the factory is unmistakably a school in

modernity ... the organizational experience it provides serves consistently to change men (sic) in ways which qualify them as more modern in
attitude, value, and behaviour.'[14]

In our observation above that the schools and factories are the two key
modernizers, it does not follow that the state needs to build and run all
the schools and all the factories. As a matter of fact, it usually should not,
certainly not the latter. It possibly can't, and certainly not in a sustainable, inclusive, and proficient fashion. But the state has to provide the
necessary legal and policy framework—a level playing field—along with
assurances of fair and consistent enforcement, which would enable entrepreneurs and communities to invest in the schools and factories as they
see fit.

The important point here is that the government is the key institution
for collective action in a society. How the production and delivery of
services will be organized is a matter of detail; the government's resources
and capability, cultural practices, norms, and beliefs of a particular society will influence the choice. And the choices need not be binary; it
doesn't have to be all government or all private sector or all community.
There has to be a balance of the three fellow travellers. As Stiglitz correctly
observes: '[i]deology here and elsewhere is unhelpful. The near-religious
belief that private firms are always and everywhere better is wrong and
dangerous'; just like believing that the state can or should do it all.[15]

The above is already a long and demanding list of what a state is expected to do. But it could perhaps all be summarized into a single overarching role: provide good governance. A modern state, to varying
degrees of success, depending on its own capability, provides this under
two broad categories of institutional support: political and judicial, and
to these we now turn.

13.3 A generalized institutional framework of the State

The political institutions create a framework for drawing clear checks and
balances on the various constituents of a society, including on the state itself, preventing it from exercising its powers arbitrarily. Together with the
economic institutions, they set out the rules of the game while the judicial

and regulatory institutions are designed to see that the rules are enforced fairly, and justice prevails.

13.3.1 Political and Economic institutions

If the state is to provide good governance, as it is expected to do, it fundamentally needs to have the power to carry out programmes and policies in the larger interests of the society. It cannot, for example, provide the necessary public goods without the authority of taxation to raise public revenues. It cannot ensure the sanctity of property rights or law and order if it does not have the power to constrain and punish those who flout them. It cannot provide a stable macroeconomic environment without the power to implement the necessary fiscal and monetary measures which the state would deem appropriate

On the other hand, the state needs to assure its citizens that such power will not be misused and arbitrarily applied to benefit a favoured few or punish those it finds inconvenient. Such constraints on the state's powers are particularly important to build credible commitment on the part of the state to respect and enforce the rights assured to the citizens. In the absence of credibility, assurances in the form of laws or regulations are meaningless.

Political and economic institutions in a society help maintain this balance between power in the hands of the state and the risks of its arbitrary use by politicians and bureaucrats. They do so 'by delineating property rights between the state and the private sector and providing for their enforcement'.[16] We have earlier seen the example of the 1688 Glorious Revolution in England bringing about changes in political institutions by imposing limits on the powers of the Crown to expropriate property and thus ensuring the sanctity of property rights.

Political institutions also delineate the division of power and accountability between various levels of national, regional, and local governments. These could take the form of formal institutions, say the constitution, defining the formal division of powers between the legislative, executive, and judicial branches of government or between the different chambers of the legislature. They could also be informal arrangements, say, based on local traditions of authority being vested in the village chiefs as in

Botswana. Formal or not, they all essentially provide a society with a political framework of self-government, with built-in mechanisms of checks and balances and accountability.

13.3.2 Judicial institutions

A recurring theme in this book is the basic human desire for justice. Through the wide spectrum of voices that we have reported in the book, talking of people's longing to live a life of peace and dignity, freedom from want and violence, runs the common thread of justice. Justice forms the basis of lasting social order and social peace. Justice distinguishes Denmark from Here.

Political institutions, formal and informal, set out the rules for how the members of a society may engage with each other in a fair and productive fashion to foster development and maintain order; this also applies to how the markets will operate in that society. But ultimately, whether such rules, expressed as formal laws and regulations, will be more than just ink on paper will depend on what people, from the common citizen to the leader, believe that others believe about whether or not those rules will be applied fairly and consistently.

Judicial institutions are key to ensuring that both the citizens and the state alike follow such rules and bear the consequences if they do not. Societies develop norms and informal means of conflict resolution, but as economies become larger and more complex, such informal means may not be adequate. Under such circumstances, the society needs to impose more formal, legitimate arrangements. Institutions such as courts need to be in place which will be responsible for a two-stage process: ascertaining the facts of the issue at hand, do an independent assessment, and in keeping with the law of the land, decide on the appropriate recourse as its resolution. Providing such a rule-based assessment and decision, and then enforcing it, will then become a state-backed, institutional process, not dependent on private individuals, no matter how powerful. But just as we saw in the case of political institutions, judicial institutions will be credible and effective only if the rulers are subject to their oversight as well. Justice will prevail only if the judicial system imposes adequate checks and balances on the state as much as on the citizens. The reality (and indeed the perception as well) of fair play and all being equal in the eyes of the law is a necessary support for market institutions, improving the business climate, and developing market economies.

While political and judicial institutions need to be mutually reinforcing, the latter must be independent of any political interference. A judiciary 'independent from both government intervention and influence by the parties in a dispute provides the single greatest institutional support for the rule of law',[17] and in turn for society at large, including well-functioning markets.

Remember: '[w]e are all citizens of the Republic of Beliefs'. What we believe others will believe who in turn are influenced by what they think we will believe is very significantly influenced by the actions of the judiciary. If the law or the courts are seen to be biased and unfair, if the state is not constrained in its actions, if the powerful are treated more leniently than the powerless, then the effectiveness of the judiciary will be compromised both in fact and in the beliefs about it. But, here again, a balance is necessary: judicial independence will have to be matched by society demanding accountability of the judicial system. As in the case of the political institutions, transparency is key in doing so and civil society organizations and the media play a key role in monitoring judicial performance. To be effective, judicial institutions also need to be efficient: they must be accessible to all, particularly the poor and the weak; they must also be affordable and provide speedy resolution. A major challenge for the functioning of courts in many countries is the predominance of written over oral procedures, which by their very nature are costly, cumbersome, and complicated not only for the poor and the disadvantaged but also for small businesses. Simplifying procedures to encourage more oral hearings makes the process cheaper, quicker, and more accessible, as in the case of small claims courts and specialized tribunals in many countries. Simplification of procedures has another important side benefit: it also enhances transparency and reduces the opportunities for corrupt court officials to seek bribes.

Important as they are, procedural reforms to enhance the efficiency of judicial systems can only go so far. A greater constraint often is in the law itself. In many developing countries, for example, a major rural development challenge is the insecure land tenure. As most of the land is untitled, the rights of sharecroppers are uncertain, and courts are too slow and unpredictable about what views they might take on a particular dispute. A major rural land reform programme (Operation Barga) in India, in the late 1970s, was possible only when a newly elected state government made legal changes guaranteeing inheritable rights to share-cropping tenants and eliminated absentee landlordism to a large extent.[18,19] A land titling programme in Peru brought about legal changes in land tenures which then enabled the courts to respond to property-right challenges which it had earlier been unable to do expeditiously and meaningfully.[20]

Judicial reforms, like other institutional reforms, are easier said than done. Not only is it a matter of financial resources, particularly in the poorer countries which come in the way, but also the social dynamics in a society. Judicial institutions are also influenced by the distribution of political power in a society, and what would work in open-access-order (or universally ethical) societies would not readily function in limited-access-order (or particularistic) societies. The basic principles of judicial independence and accountability need to be balanced with existing social orders in a country.

13.4 Changing expectations of the role of the State in recent times

The appropriate role and size of the state is a source of much controversy and political contestation. At the beginning of the twentieth century, the role of the state was rather limited, even in the leading liberal states of that time, Great Britain and other European countries, and even narrower in the US. The pendulum began to swing to the other side with the beginning of the First World War, but the role of the state grew more dramatically as a response to the economic and social catastrophe of the Great Depression in the 1930s.

The unbridled reign of the free market was perceived to be the main culprit behind the Great Depression, and 'many societies blamed corrupt capitalism for the prolonged downturn and turned to fascism or socialism instead. Even in the US there was a broad groundswell of opinion that market competition was to blame, and that capitalism would be more stable if it were muzzled'.[21] President Roosevelt's New Deal programme, particularly the Social Security Act of 1935, which established state-level unemployment insurance, a contributory retirement pension, and selective welfare benefits, further enhanced the role of the state in the US economy. So did large public-sector infrastructure projects, such as the Lincoln Tunnel and New York City's first airport, later to be named the LaGuardia Airport.

This trend towards greater state involvement continued, and indeed expanded, in the post-Second World War era. Developed countries grew spectacularly in the three decades or so after that war. Not just the US, but Japan and Western Europe, too, as they rebuilt themselves out of the rubble of the war, helped by the generosity of the American Marshall Plan. Countries behind the Iron Curtain saw growth and development as well.

The euphoria of state-led growth in the post-Second World War decades was fed by a combination of factors. In addition to reconstruction, many parts of Europe and even the US were not uniformly developed and suffered from serious infrastructure deficits (including old and aged machinery) even before the war, which needed to be built up. Resumption of global trade, technological upgrading, widespread education, and higher labour force participation were among other factors which helped fuel growth.

But perhaps the most important of all was a broad political consensus for economic growth, and this consensus was not limited to simply rebuilding lost or missing infrastructure. It included significant expansion of social spending on health care, education, and social security in the strengthened democracies in the West and the newly independent countries elsewhere.

A measure of the expanding role of the State can be gleaned from the growing share of the state in a country's gross domestic product (GDP). Accounting for only about a tenth of GDP at the beginning of the twentieth century in most Western European countries and the United States, the state sectors accounted for almost half of GDP by the 1980s (and an even higher 70 per cent in the case of social democratic Sweden).[22]

The growing role of the state could be accommodated while the economies grew, but this started to stagnate in the 1970s. A combination of factors such as the growing inefficiencies of state interventions, increased private sector cartelization limiting competition, oil price shocks, rising inflation, and gradual diminishing of the remaining benefits of the Second Industrial Revolution, cramping the market with onerous rules and regulations, undue involvement of the state in production and provision of services, restricting competition and trade, led to considerable slowing of growth. Fiscal deficits ballooned and many countries began to roll back the welfare state. With that started the dialling down of the role of the state, and the vigorous pushback in the form of Reaganism ('the government is the problem')[23] and Thatcherism in the 1980s.

The emphasis now shifted to deregulating the economy—liberalizing to reduce, if not remove, the competitive barriers, allow freer movement of capital and people, and integrate economies further, particularly in Europe. The fall of the Berlin Wall in 1989 and the break-up of the Soviet Union within a couple of years of that only served to bolster the idea of 'an unabashed victory of economic and political liberalism'.[24] As the initial liberalizations proved successful, the pervasive sentiment on regulation among the liberalizing governments was 'less is more'. Social attitudes, which had in the post-war decades held that the state could do no wrong, now swung to believe that the state could do no right.[25]

Adding further lustre to the market was the China–India growth story. China continued to grow at phenomenal rates (averaging about 10 per cent since its turn to market-oriented reforms in the late 1970s), but under the banner of 'socialism with Chinese characteristics'. Beginning in 1991, India also finally woke up from its long economic slumber, and implemented deep, structural reforms unshackling the economy from the grip of the 'licence raj'.

The situation in the non-communist developing world was more complex. The state had grown, often unsustainably, in many such countries. For example, the share of the Mexican government's expenditures (as percentage of GDP) more than doubled over the period 1970–1982, and the fiscal deficit soared to 17 per cent of GDP. The Mexican debt crisis followed later in 1982.[26] Similar stories emerged elsewhere in Africa, Asia, and South America as well, where the state had become involved in running large corporations and parastatals, and more often than not, rather inefficiently and unproductively.

The sensible path to take at that time was to reduce and preferably even remove state involvement in many areas of the economy: production, prices, and trade. However, in the frenzied wave of liberalization and the adoption of market-friendly strategies (the government is the problem, so get the government out approach), state involvement was recklessly cut back across the board. And, unfortunately, a host of essential services that a society expects and needs to be provided by the state fell into this category: primary health care, education, infrastructure, particularly rural, the social safety net, and perhaps most importantly, law and order. While indeed the state needed to cut back in certain areas (such as the bloated civil service or money-losing state enterprises), it needed to be simultaneously strengthened in others. This did not happen: the state retracted across the board, often more on the social needs of the poor; and the liberalized economic reforms did not deliver the promised results either. The 1997 World Development Report summed it up well: '[s]tate dominated development has failed, but so will stateless development. Development without an effective state is impossible'.[27]

The role of the State needs to be defined with some fundamental expectations: (i) provide public goods including protection from internal and external threats, (ii) supply merit goods that markets do not provide in adequate quantities, and (ii) ensure proper functioning of markets. But in many successful economies around the world, the State has played a much more active role to promote development—characterised as the developmental state. While the regulatory role of the State is clearly important, its developmental role is no less important either. This role envisages the state to be more actively involved in (but not dominate) developing policies to determine the structure of domestic economy and enhance the nation's competitiveness in the global market.

In the post WWII era, Germany, Japan, and Korea all adopted this hybrid-market-based policy with strong under underpinnings of state guided indicative planning supported by public financial institutions. Under strong state guidance, these countries relied on export driven growth built on effective industrial and external policies focusing on technological transformation to enhance efficiency in the chosen thrust sectors, internal competition, and transient protection from foreign competition. Their governments actively supported production-oriented research and development infrastructure with public-private partnerships to promote innovation. As history has proven, all such measures contributed to strong and sustainable economic growth in each of these countries.

13.5 Limitations of State capability

Fukuyama defines stateness as the 'functions, capability, and grounds for legitimacy of governments'.[28] Most, if not all, developing countries do concern themselves with the issue of 'grounds of legitimacy', perhaps with varying degrees of success. Let us first focus on the first two: functions and capability, and the two are distinctly related. The first element (functions) asks: what is the appropriate role of the State in any country? And the second (capability) asks: how can a State's capability be enhanced? The answers to these two questions could serve as a two-part strategy to make a state a credible, effective partner in a country's development.[29]

13.5.1 Matching the State's role to its capability

A fundamental challenge all governments face is that there is always so much to do. The state obviously has a major responsibility in providing public goods such as defence, security of its citizens, foundations of law and property rights, assured justice, basic health, and education, setting macroeconomic and other public policies, and enforcing contracts, which all directly influence the market failures common in many countries, particularly the developing ones. These too call for state intervention. But an important lesson from global experience is that states need to work in partnership with markets to correct their failures, not replace them.

Over and above all of this, an imperative responsibility of a functioning state is to work towards equity. The State must try to ensure fairness and justice in the society, so that no one person or group dominates the others, particularly the poor and the disadvantaged. Experiences around the world have confirmed that economic growth and equity are not mutually exclusive. As a matter of fact, inequality is a deterrent to growth. Keeping people safe, healthy, educated, and empowered enhances economic growth, reducing both poverty and inequality.

Given such far-ranging demands, it is obvious that there cannot be a template defining the roles and functions of an effective State. However, an important guiding principle for the State should be to provide the enabling environment for the markets and the community to be productive and thrive and only take on roles which these other two actors cannot and should not, for example, provision of public good or law and order. But even there, it will critically depend on the capability—defined as the ability to undertake and promote collective actions efficiently—of a particular state.[30] A common mistake that developing countries make is that the State tries to do too much, well beyond its capability, and ends up doing nothing well. Often the result of such unfocused attempts is gross underperformance, lack of effectiveness, even in basic public goods like security, protection of property rights, health care, and education, and ultimately damage to the state's credibility. The first priority of any state must therefore be to recognize the limitations of its capabilities and then prioritize among its many functions.

The State should function along a continuum of capability. Those with limited capability should focus at least on the minimal functions, which only the State can provide—pure public goods, such as defence and law and order—and try to protect the poor. Notice that public health (for instance, control of infectious diseases) is included here. Setting broad public policies is another primary role that the State can't ignore. States with some more capability can undertake intermediate functions, such as addressing externalities like environmental degradation. And even higher on the capability continuum would be states that can take on even more complex activist functions, such as coordinating private activity by more sophisticated regulatory processes, as in some East Asian countries.

The issue is not whether the functions outlined above are needed or not. They all are. The important issue is one of prioritizing by matching role to the capability of the State. Naushad Forbes, a leading intellectual industrialist in India, in his very thoughtful book *The Struggle and The Promise: Restoring India's Potential*, argues for a strong role for the State in providing public goods such as an enabling environment, an effective police and judicial system, but urges the state to be selective: do less but do it well. Speaking for India, he cautions that 'the Indian state must focus its energy on a very limited set of things it can do and rely on the private sector and NGOs to fill in the gaps. We struggle when the state either overplays or underplays its role.'[31] This message applies equally well to others.

13.5.2 Enhancing State capability

We have established that the State need not and indeed cannot do everything. In fact, monopoly public providers may not be the most effective or efficient. Public–private partnerships in the provision of large, physical infrastructure with separation of the financing of infrastructure and services from their delivery are standard practice in most countries now. Unbundling the competitive and the monopoly segments of the utility markets to allow private-sector involvement is also now quite common around the world, even in developing countries.

Social programmes can also be structured to let in the markets and civil society to ramp up the delivery of services (health and education), while the state focuses on the policy aspects. These partnerships, while somewhat successful, are not always inclusive, so the State needs to keep its eyes on the ball and protect the larger public interests. The State must build on the relative strengths of the markets, civil society, and the public institutions, emphasizing the concept of balance. That said, the challenges many developing countries with limited state capability face need to be addressed and the State's institutional capability enhanced. A key lesson from many institutional strengthening efforts around the world (many failures, and a few modest successes born out of our own experiences) is clear: 'find rules and norms that create incentives for state agencies and officials to act in the collective interest, while restraining arbitrary action'.[32]

Three basic incentive mechanisms would be: articulate clear rules and restraints, expose the state to greater competitive pressures, and increase citizen voice and participation.

13.5.2.1 Articulate clear rules and restraints

Predictability and accountability, which in turn establish the government's credibility, are key expectations of any functioning state and a major enabler of market development. Sadly, many countries lack these basic institutional capabilities, giving rise to what is generally referred to as the 'lawlessness syndrome'. In such a scenario, citizens are not protected from violence or theft. To make matters worse, the government itself may be capricious and unpredictable, undertaking arbitrary actions such as ad hoc changes to rules and regulations, including taxes;

there might be corruption, and the judiciary might be weak or even non-existent. Correcting these issues is indeed very challenging, particularly in states with limited state capacity. Designing appropriate rules and restraints to address the lawlessness syndrome (restoring trust) must thus be the first order of business for any government.

Writing the laws, rules, and regulations, and even formally adopting them is relatively easy; enforcing them effectively is not. And without enforcement, they remain nothing but ink on paper. The challenge of exercising enough restraint on itself is greater for a state with limited institutional capacity. Matching role to capability would mean adopting simpler rules (rather than copying more complex ones from more advanced countries) appropriate to their situation. Limiting the discretionary authority of public officials is an obvious starting point. Adopting policies which reduce controls on the economy, (say, entry barriers for the private sector), reduces such discretionary authority and scope for arbitrary actions by the state.

Formal rules and the 'stick' of prescribed punishments for unacceptable arbitrary actions by public servants help, but also need to be balanced by 'carrots' of incentives. Reforming the civil service is thus a high priority, but again, easier said than done. Clearly defining responsibilities demanding greater accountability, but with better pay, helps. Equally, civil servants need greater oversight by the formal institutions of the state but also through monitoring by individual citizens and the community at large.

Several countries have tried fighting corruption by establishing formal institutions, with varying degrees of success. Hong Kong's Independent Commission Against Corruption, established in 1974 to fight the growing surge of corruption in the colony from the 1960s into the 1970s, is generally hailed as a remarkable success story. With strong leadership, complete autonomy granted to it by successive governments, and the close involvement of the local community, Hong Kong is now one of the least corrupt regions in the world, ranking eleventh (out of 180 countries) in Transparency International's Corruption Perception Index in 2020. But as discussed earlier in the book, corruption is a much deeper challenge than can be addressed just by setting up formal institutions to fight it.

Political scientists have long advised that corruption should not only be seen as a social malady to be eradicated, but rather understood as a built-in feature of governance interactions between the powerful elite and the rest of society. Control of corruption needs to be thus seen as a balance of power and 'constraints that an autonomous society is able to inflict on the ruling elites through an independent judiciary and a mass of enlightened citizens who put up a strong demand for good governance'.[33] Corruption is controlled when this balance is right, and not because a particular top-down policy or institution is in place.

A novel experiment of citizen-monitoring was started in 1994 in Bengaluru, a thriving metropolis in India (often called the 'Silicon Valley' of India). A citizens' group, later formalized into a non-profit community organization, the Public Affairs Centre (PAC), sought feedback from the residents on their assessment of the quality of various public services (usually uniformly poor) provided by different municipal departments of the city. The survey results were presented publicly in the form of a 'Citizen's Report Card', giving the scores by department and shared with all citizens, the senior bureaucrats, and the local government. At first this was ignored by officialdom, but as the media gave it wide coverage and average citizens started comparing their neighbourhoods with others and demanding better service, the bureaucrats took note. An instrument had been created 'that civil society could use to hold the state accountable for its performance, one that hopefully could nudge the state to act'.[34] And it worked. Nearly thirty years later it is still going strong.

13.5.2.2 Expose the State to greater competitive pressures

In many developing countries, the state takes it on itself to deliver services. Generally, they are provided poorly, with political interference in day-to-day operations, seeking personal favours, or for a select group of vested interests. Management has limited authority and even less accountability. And in many situations where the public-service provider enjoys a monopoly position, the performance is usually even worse with no competitive pressures for better performance. The key role of the State should be to ensure that the necessary services are provided to the populace; they don't necessarily have to be provided by the State itself.

And even when the State needs to be involved (say, in the case of market failures), opening the public sector to some competitive pressures from the private sector could improve incentives and performance. Technology and appropriate legal arrangements can enable segmenting of operations in the power sector, water utilities, and telecommunications, making it feasible to introduce private players, which usually results in enhanced competition, lower unit costs, and expansion of services. The opening up of the telecommunications sector in India in the late 1990s to private participants has been a stellar success, providing wireless services across the sprawling nation with per-unit cost of services among the lowest in the world. Public–private partnerships in the development and operation of infrastructure facilities (roads, ports, railways, and airports) are common around the world. Significant private-sector capital invested in these sectors has made infrastructure projects possible which could not have been undertaken with public resources alone.

Contracting out services through competitive bids and auctions even if the public sector retains ownership (in the management of airports or utilities, for example) enhances competition and the quality of service. Simultaneously, public agencies are more accountable if their objectives are clearly articulated, and operations focused on performance. New Zealand was one of the earliest and most dramatic reformers along these lines in the early 1990s. Government ministries and departments were restructured into focused business units and 'headed by chief executives on fixed-term, performance-based contracts with the authority to hire and fire and to bargain collectively'.[35] Singapore's meritocratic civil service with strict accountability and performance-based assessments has long been held as a model of public-sector management that delivers.

It is true that such performances might well be beyond the institutional capacity of many developing countries, but the model is valid; and in fact, such mechanisms (to varying degrees of success) are used around the world. Airport management is now widely let out to the private sector in India, as is road maintenance in several parts of Africa, Asia, and Latin America. Some countries, such as Bolivia and Uganda, have even begun contracting out the delivery of social services, particularly in education and health, to the private sector and non-governmental organizations.

Undoubtedly, there are risks in this approach, particularly for states with limited institutional capacities. In neo-patrimonial societies, giving greater authority and flexibility to the managers of public agencies could further increase arbitrary actions, clientelism, and corruption. Working with the private sector is often challenging for the public sector, as there is usually a huge asymmetry of skills and sectoral competence. Legal contracts are complex to structure and execute and need specialized skills, which the public agencies often do not have. Sequencing thus becomes important. Some initial capacities in financial management and rules-based compliance need to be built first.

However, even while recognizing the capacity constraints public agencies face, the general point remains valid: exposing the public sector to greater competitive pressures is an effective incentive for state agencies to become more efficient, accountable, perhaps more profitable, and come closer to their objective of serving the society better.

13.5.2.3 Increase citizen voice and participation

A third important incentive for state agencies to improve their performance is feedback from end users. Even when such feedback is unwelcome, the state is more effective when it hears, and more importantly, listens to its citizens, particularly the marginalized and the poor. Recall the vivid and often desperate cries for help from many of the intended beneficiaries of state public services noted in Chapter 3.

However, the end users should not be considered simply as passive beneficiaries of state largesse. They are important stakeholders as well, and state agencies will fare much better if they work in partnership with civil society. The example of PAC in Bengaluru, India (discussed earlier) is a case in point, and there are many such all over the developing world.

It's not always as straightforward, though. The real challenge here is the lack of safe, direct, and effective channels of communication that can amplify the real concerns and suggestions of the citizenry. Once again, the role of the powerful elite in any country in subverting this process of allowing increased citizen voice and participation cannot be ignored or minimized. It is no surprise that this voice is distributed rather unevenly in any society, but particularly so in neo-patrimonial ones. Even the well-intentioned states need to find ways to engage with citizens to really know and understand their needs and aspirations. Greater transparency (through a freer media and greater accessibility to digital technology and social media, for example) is thus vital for more informed and involved public debates on issues of collective interest.

Experiences around the world convincingly demonstrate the benefits of such citizen engagement. Projects are better conceptualized and designed, there are fewer roadblocks in implementation, and projects have a higher chance of achieving their intended goals with participation and feedback from the intended beneficiaries. From forest management in Nepal, hydropower development in Laos, sanitation projects in Brazil, to health-care projects in Sudan and Cambodia, the experience of partnerships with civil society is overwhelmingly positive. Not that projects with participation by the beneficiaries and feedback are always an unmitigated success. Far from it, but it would be fair to assert that they succeed more often than not in contrast to those generated with the top-down approach, which fail more often.

We noted at the beginning of this chapter that a society's well-being is shaped and influenced by three principal institutions: the State, the markets, and the community. In this chapter, we have discussed the State as an institution and the key role it plays in a society, and we will come back to the this later too. But before doing so, let us discuss the other two institutions in more detail, the markets and the community, to which we shall now turn.

13.6 Summary

To paraphrase Sen, freedom from fear of being dominated by others is a fundamental premise for a decent and fulfilling life in a society. Hobbes argued that this can only be ensured if there is a visible central authority, which he called the Leviathan, that is powerful enough to keep people in line, through fear of severe consequences if they don't. This central authority is the State, which would legally monopolize the use of violence, ensure law and order, and assure justice, so that ordinary citizens could go about their daily life without fear.

But this Leviathan itself needs to be shackled and the power of the State appropriately tamed to operate within the bounds of the rule of law, lest it itself becomes the feared despot. Balance is thus the basic challenge for the State.

At its core, the role of the State is to provide good governance. A key element of doing so is for the State to equitably and efficiently manage collective public goods working in the interest of all and not just a select few. The State must ensure security and justice for everyone, especially the weak, the disadvantaged, the marginalized, and those with special needs. Thus, perhaps the most important public good is an efficient and fair State, working in the interest of all and not just a select few. Laws must be written and adopted, but equally importantly enforced and applied equally to all without fear or favour. Experiences around the world have confirmed that economic growth and equity are not mutually exclusive. As a matter of fact, inequality is a deterrent to growth. Keeping people safe, healthy, educated, and empowered enhances economic growth, reducing both poverty and inequality. Setting macroeconomic and other public policies, and enforcing contracts, which all directly influence the market failures which are common in many countries also call for State intervention.

A fundamental challenge for all governments is that there is always much to do. Priorizing is thus key. An important lesson from global experience is that states need to work in partnership with markets to correct their failures, not replace them. Experience around the world also convincingly demonstrate the benefits of increased community engagement as active participants in the development process, not merely the recipients of State largesse. The State thus needs to work closely with the community as well.

The appropriate role and size of the State is a source of much controversy and political contestation. Much is expected of the State, but what it can do effectively is a function of its capability. The two must be matched. Trying to do too much results in mediocrity and systems failures, damages State credibility, and erodes trust. The State must therefore prioritize what it can do well and let the markets and society step in and do their bit. The principal role of the State should be to enable the ecosystem for the markets to operate in and communities to thrive in peace and security with the assurance of justice.

14

The State, the MARKETS, and the Community

14.1 Introduction

Earlier in this book we argued that some of the underlying assumptions in neoclassical economics, such as that institutions do not matter, individuals are fully rational and omniscient, and transactions are costless, need to be adjusted taking realistic human behaviour into account. However, despite these reservations, one fundamental premise of neoclassical economics, of the critical importance of the marketplace, remains valid. Markets matter. A country needs well-functioning markets to enable its citizens to buy and sell goods and services, which in turn generates economic growth and enhances opportunities and prosperity for its citizens.

Markets play a critical role in a society's journey from Here to Denmark. When the State provides adequate and credible assurances of respect for property rights and protection against arbitrary actions, say expropriations, markets can flourish. But, just as the State has to be prevented from committing excesses and misusing its authority, the 'behemoth of the markets', fuelled by the spirit of laissez faire, has to be tamed as well.

14.2 The evolution of the State and the markets

Recall our earlier discussion of the Stuart monarchy in Great Britain in the early seventeenth century. We noted their imposition of 'forced loans' on the unwilling subjects of the realm who had no recourse if the terms of a loan were unilaterally changed by the monarch or even not repaid. The monarch could arbitrarily expropriate land and rights,

From Here to Denmark. Rajat M. Nag and Harinder S. Kohli, Oxford University Press.
© Rajat Mohan Nag and Harinder Singh Kohli 2023. DOI: 10.1093/oso/9780198893103.003.0014

sell hereditary titles and monopoly rights, or dismiss judges who ruled against the Crown. Such egregious disregard of property rights led to the Civil War of 1642 and the beheading of Charles I in 1649. While the arbitrary exercise of sovereign power was thus curtailed, the reprieve was only temporary, as the same excesses continued with the restoration of the monarchy. Markets could not function effectively or efficiently under such circumstances.

The fundamental changes in England's political institutions happened only after the Glorious Revolution of 1688. The principal achievement of this revolution was that the monarch was prevented from exercising absolute and arbitrary power through greater parliamentary and judicial oversight. But rather than losing influence, the Crown now enjoyed greater legitimacy among the subjects, particularly among the landed elite and the gentry, with its commitment to respect property rights and honour its social contract with its citizens and investors.

It was only after the Crown restrained its behaviour and actions that the power balance started to shift. The gentry were empowered, exercising greater political influence (by their numbers rather than any individual power base of their own), rule of law emerged, and competitive markets started to evolve, protected by a stronger Parliament and a more independent judiciary. Markets could now operate (both financial and for goods and services) with greater confidence that they would no longer be easily subjected to arbitrary actions by the monarch. The monarch now had access to the market and did not have to grant any special favours to anyone to raise funds. Cronyism now 'steadily gave way to a more open business environment, which in turn created many more independent entities that could check state power'.[1]

A lesson that clearly emerges from this is that the 'existence of vibrant competitive markets that allow productive and independent owners to emerge help constrain the state and protect property as part of the balance of power'.[2]

However, it is interesting to note that the State did not shrink even as the markets grew. In fact, they grew together. With assurances of far fewer domestic threats to his rule and greater access to finances, the British Crown expanded its military capabilities and grew as well.

A better balance between the markets and the State developed to the benefit of both, and hence, to society at large. The key takeaway in a broader context is that how institutions develop in a country is fundamentally dependent on how political power is distributed within that society, and sound political, economic, and ultimately social institutions determine the trajectory of development in a country.

14.3 Institutions to support and manage the markets

With the state restrained from arbitrary actions, and the consequently greater confidence of the wealthy in the security of their life and property, a spirit of laissez-faire preaching the virtue of free and unfettered markets began to take hold in Great Britain. In 1776, Adam Smith published his *An Inquiry into the Nature and Causes of the Wealth of Nations*, making the intellectual case for a competitive market where producers did what was in their own best interest; but in the process, as if guided by an invisible hand, maximized the wealth of the nation, benefitting all.[3] Building on this, it has often been suggested that competition is the 'only guarantee in a free market where the producer would be solicitous to customers, whether through innovation, better customer service, or low prices.'[4]

While extolling the virtues of the market, indeed its indispensability, Smith was no starry-eyed fan of the businessman. He recognized that free markets are not perfect, far from it. He correctly foresaw that competition would drive down profits and suspected that producers would thus be tempted to attempt cartelization rather than face the consequences of unfettered competition. Expressing his strong concerns about monopolies and guilds, Smith went so far as to cynically suggest that 'people of the same trade seldom meet together even for merriment and diversion, but the conversation ends in a conspiracy against the public or in some contrivance to raise prices.'[5]

John D. Rockefeller, an American oil magnate, would be a perfect confirmation of Smith's concerns. Starting in Cleveland, near where oil had first been discovered in the US, he focused on refining rather than prospecting for it, by far a riskier business. By a combination of cajolery, threats, and violence, Rockefeller began consolidating the local refiners, and over time, bought up twenty-two of his twenty-six Cleveland competitors. He struck a deal for discounts from the railroads for the crude and refined oil they shipped. However, 'more egregious, the railways agreed to pay the cartel for every barrel shipped by the competing, independent non-cartel refiners'.[6]

By 1870, Rockefeller had founded the Standard Oil Company and soon controlled 90 per cent of the oil refined in the US, and soon after, became the world's wealthiest man. Rockefeller's rationalization would naturally be that his actions were beneficial to the industry (closing inefficient plants, achieving economies of scale), and customers would thus benefit in the long run. He considered competition as causing busts and booms, which was good for neither the producers nor the consumers in the long run. His logic holds some merit, if the behemoth could be trusted. But could it? Experience, not only in Rockefeller's case, but around the world over time, would cast doubt on it.

Fast forward to the 2008 global financial crisis. It was obvious that the spate of deregulations in the financial sector in the US (many of them aggressively lobbied for by the large banks themselves) had encouraged them to take excessive risks. They grew aggressively, knowing full well that since they would have become too big to fail, the State would ultimately bail them out, a classic case of moral hazard. Heads they win, tails the State loses. And this is exactly what happened.

Unregulated markets will gradually tend towards concentration. Thus, just as the Leviathan of the authoritarian state has to be tamed, so must the behemoth of the monopoly enterprises. Society needs 'regulations to make markets work like they're supposed to in a competitive way, with transactions between well-informed parties, where one party isn't a party trying to take advantage of another'.[7] This is not to argue for undue constraint of the market. Rather, it is an argument to make the markets work better and more effectively. As a matter of fact, the danger is the converse: 'without confidence that markets are reasonably well-regulated, markets might even disappear'.[8]

Markets thus need to be encouraged, but also managed. In modern societies, many of the institutions to do so are publicly provided, as we saw in the previous chapter.

However, such economic institutions (say, the regulatory agencies) will have little credibility with markets in the absence of simultaneous checks and limits on the state's capacity for arbitrary action. As discussed in the previous chapter, political institutions in the country would need to ensure and assure the markets that such agencies would not be biased in favour of the state, nor be anti-market. They need to ensure a level playing field for all, particularly in simultaneously constraining the state (from becoming a Leviathan) and the markets (from becoming the dreaded behemoth). Similarly, decentralization efforts in a country (either between the various levels of the government or between the various agencies of the government) will be ineffective if the credibility of the national government in ensuring the necessary checks and balances on the behaviour of their public officials is compromised.

The State needs resources to provide services, which in turn requires strong and effective tax-collection institutions. Weak tax-collection institutions have a 'double whammy' effect. They not only result in reduced revenues for the State but also weaken markets. Consider the effect of taxes on international trade, a more easily collected source of taxes for governments with weak tax institutions. Taxes on international trade protect inefficient domestic firms, thus limiting competition. Perversely, diminished tax revenues and rising fiscal deficits often create domestic political pressures to raise tax rates, rather than improving tax-collection efforts. Higher tax burdens, coupled with corrupt tax officials, serve as major disincentives for firms, with adverse effects for competition and the functioning of markets.

As we noted in an earlier chapter, corruption seriously hinders the development of well-functioning markets in an economy. When firms have to pay bribes, not only do their costs go up, but more detrimentally, so does the uncertainty of doing business. New firms might thus be reluctant to start operations and existing ones leave for better climes, reducing competition in domestic markets. In a more insidious way, corruption also compromises the legitimacy of the State itself, with its agents taking the bribes having lost the fundamental ethical basis of representing the State and exercising power on its behalf.

Particularly extreme, though unfortunately not too uncommon, is the phenomenon of 'State capture', by which the official State apparatus is completely bypassed in collusion between the players in the market (individuals or firms) and the agents of the state. Political and judicial institutions which 'restrain politicians and bureaucrats from arbitrary exercise of power and hold them accountable for their actions can help reduce the opportunities and incentives for corruption.'[9] Greater decentralization, enhanced transparency, a free media, and an active civil society are all key enablers in this process of providing better governance.

14.4 Challenges of taming the behemoth

Presciently, Adam Smith warned about the dangers of producers wishing to circumvent the pressures of competition by attempting cartelization. We have seen the example of John Rockefeller's great success in doing so. Evidently, this would not have been possible without the active support (or at least the malevolent indulgence) of the state, including the bribing of entire legislatures, or worse.[10] Close and cosy ties between big business and politicians are at the heart of political corruption around the world where 'manipulating government was just another means to business success',[11] but the willingness of the government to be manipulated (or its inability to resist such manipulation) is just as much of a problem. The history of how US institutions evolved to manage the process of letting the market work well and efficiently and yet not become a behemoth in its own right is instructive.

High levels of political corruption had taken root in the United States by the late 1890s. Even though egregious in its conduct at times, with great costs inflicted on the local communities, Standard Oil was by no means alone. It had the company of giants such as the United States Steel Corporation and large-scale financial houses, such as that of J. P. Morgan, who were corporate behemoths with significant influence on governments.

In 1862, the US Congress had passed the Pacific Railway Act, authorizing the construction of a transcontinental railway. Millions of acres of public land were provided to the rail companies to lay the tracks but also to finance the construction of the railways by selling off some of the land given to them. Rail companies were particularly influential in securing land grants, tax exemptions, municipal and state subsidies, and public loans. Without taking away from the stellar achievements of the dramatic expansion of the rail network (quadrupling the network over the thirty-year period 1871–1900), the relevant issue for our discussion is the significant political collusion which accompanied this expansion.

The state was obviously unable to tame the behemoth. In fact, it was often in collusion with it, in a classic case of crony capitalism. Enter two successive grass-roots reform movements—the Populists and then the Progressives, over the thirty-year period 1890–1920—to make the difference. The Populists were a coalition of agrarian reformers demanding a greater political voice for farmers. The Progressive movement which succeeded the Populists was more urban in its orientation, with a principal objective of encouraging competition in the marketplace and fighting state corruption.

Though both these popular movements had petered out by the early 1920s, they had lasting political impact. Enough political momentum had been built up to restore the balance between the state and the markets, principally through legislative and regulatory means which then also created appropriate institutions to enforce them. As a matter of fact, all these institutions have since become the bedrock of the American system of governance and have served as models for similar institutions around the world, including those in many developing countries.

It was clear that monopolies and collusive practices which reduced competition had not served US society well and these were early targets of the reform movements. This resulted in very significant, landmark legislation passed by the US Congress: the Sherman Antitrust Act of 1890, which outlawed monopolies and cartels and emphasized the role of enhanced competition within the economy. Rockefeller's Standard Oil was one of the first behemoths to be broken up under this legislation. The Sherman Act was further strengthened in 1914 (the Clayton Act) prohibiting anticompetitive mergers and acquisitions, predatory and discriminatory pricing, and interlocking directorships. The Federal Trade Commission was established in the same year to enforce the provisions of the antitrust legislation.

A major responsibility of the State is to assure the ordinary citizen of the quality and safety of products sold by the market, particularly when it comes to food and drugs. Even under the best circumstances, it would be a stretch to rely exclusively on the assurances of the producers alone. In 1906, the Pure Food and Drug Act was passed, and a strong institutional base created to enforce it, which later became the Food and Drug Administration. The Federal Reserve Act (passed in 1913) was a similar critical legal measure taken by the state to balance the potential for excesses of the behemoth in the financial system of the country, and created the country's central bank, the Federal Reserve Board.

Legal and institutional measures are ways for the State to contain the behemoth of monopoly enterprises and big business. But it would be fair to ask that just as the State is subject to the possibility of political capture, how can one be sure that regulators would not be subject to the same? And the answer, of course, is that one cannot. In 1982, American economist George Stigler was honoured with the Nobel Prize for his seminal work in developing the Economic Theory of Regulation, more commonly called 'regulatory capture'. The basic premise of this theory is that the regulated use their financial means and consequent political muscle to not only influence the regulators to protect their interests over the greater good of the society's, but even more insidiously, they influence the State (the executive and the legislature) itself to shape laws and regulations in ways that benefit big business.[12,13]

It is certainly fair to ask: *quis custodiet ipsos custodes?* ('Who will guard the guards themselves?'). Not an easy one to answer, but two considerations are relevant. That to a large extent it would depend, one, on the State's capability, which we discuss briefly in the next section, and two, on the vigilance of the population at large (the community), which is the focus of our next chapter.

14.5 State capacity to manage the behemoth

Let us circle back to our discussion in the previous chapter about matching the scope of the State's activities with its capability. Designing and enforcing a good, efficient regulatory system is complex and difficult, and many developing countries have limited capacity. Complicating the situation further, the regulated entities (large banks, utilities, producers) have far larger resources to afford expensive lawyers and lobbyists to argue their case. This asymmetry of knowledge, wealth, and power cannot be wished away.

Recognizing their institutional constraints, states with limited capacity may need to err on the side of less flexibility and more restraint in designing regulations. They can be based on simple rules, which would reduce the discretionary power of a regulator to (mis)interpret rules and regulations and could be easily enforced. For example, 'take or pay' contracts with independent power producers are relatively standard and simple utility regulations to follow.

As the State's institutional capabilities increase, regulations can be made more complex but also more flexible. In the financial sector, for example, detailed regulations—possibly including some deposit insurance monitored and enforced by competent, impartial supervisory bodies—could gradually be brought in.

The key message is that adopted regulations should match with State capability so that they can be enforced fairly and consistently. However, using laws and regulations to contain big business has its limits even in states with strong institutional capability. Regulatory bodies can collude with the powerful among the regulated, and in fact, use the regulations to grant undue favours.

But just as the State must balance the markets, so must the converse apply too, and it achieves this by its productive efficiency. A healthy, competitive private sector keeps the state's possible authoritarian tendencies in check. Competition is key. When a few firms dominate the private market, the interests of the few behemoths can coalesce with each other, and collusive arrangements with the State (the Leviathan) can emerge. The experience of Stuart England and other countries show that there is obvious safety in numbers of participants in the market. When the gentry gathered economic power in England following the Glorious Revolution, there were too many of them with divergent interests, and it was hard for the state to serve them all. Self-interest would dictate that each producer would keep a watch on others, serving as a check on each other and the State.

It is realistic to recognize, however, that there are limits to how well and how much the markets and the State can balance each other. The private sector does depend on the government for a wide variety of support measures and is influenced, for better or worse, by the government. Similarly, even in states with strong capabilities, there are limits to the extent to which big business can be tamed. And in any case, the answer to an expansion of the markets cannot simply be an expansion of the State. Rather, the third leg of the stool—the community—needs to be strengthened, through drawing in the 'centripetal forces within the local community to offset the centrifugal forces of the global market'.[14]

14.6 Summary

Markets matter. A society needs well-functioning, competitive markets to enable it to efficiently produce, buy and sell, and consume goods and services. These in turn generate economic growth, expand opportunities for the citizens, and enhance prosperity. Markets are thus critically important in a society's journey from Here to Denmark. While Adam Smith made the case for a competitive market where even while all actors (buyers and sellers, producers and consumers) did what was in their own self-interest, the process also maximized the collective benefits for all, as if guided by an invisible hand.

However, free markets are far from perfect. Smith correctly foresaw that competition would drive down profits and producers would be tempted to form cartels rather than operate in a truly competitive manner. Thus, just as the Leviathan of the state has to be shackled, the behemoth of the markets has to be tamed as well. This is not to unduly constrain the markets but to ensure that they work better and efficiently without unduly inhibiting competition. In modern societies, many of the institutions to do so are provided by the State, which usually does it through its political and judicial institutions. Legal and institutional measures are ways for the State to contain the monopoly enterprises and big business.

However, the State is usually limited in its capability of taming the behemoth. Designing and enforcing a good, efficient regulatory system is complex and difficult, and many developing countries have limited capacity. The situation is further exacerbated by the fact that the regulated entities usually have far larger resources at their disposal than the regulators themselves creating an asymmetry of knowledge, wealth and power in their favour. This raises the distinct possibility of 'regulatory capture'.

Recognizing their institutional constraints, States with limited capacity may need to err on the side of less flexibility and more restraint in designing regulations. As the States' institutional capabilities increase, the regulations can be made more complex but also more flexible. The key message is that adopted regulations should match with the State capability so that they could be enforced fairly and consistently.

Just as the State must balance the markets, so must it be the other way around too. Markets achieve this by their productive efficiency. A healthy, competitive private sector keeps the State's possible authoritarian tendencies in check. Self-interest would dictate that each producer would be a watch on others, serving as a check on each other and the State.

History shows that the mutual constraint of the State and the markets on each other has usually not been detrimental to either.

Of course, there are limits to how well and how much the markets and the State can balance each other. This is where our third traveller, the community comes in to complete the triad, and to that we turn in our next chapter.

15

The State, the Markets, and the COMMUNITY

15.1 Introduction

More than anything, a community is a feeling: a feeling of belonging, of being accepted, and solidarity based on some common identity, interest, shared history, or life experience. This largely positive feeling is entirely intrinsic to human existence. In fact, human society evolved from the community: neighbours watched and protected the children while the parents went food gathering. The community was the first port of call and mutual support for all; and even if weakened over time, it continues to be a key support structure in most societies around the world, some more than others.

For the longest time in human history, the community played the role of the State and markets as well, all rolled into one. Over time, the State and the markets began to emerge as distinct institutions. The latter enabled distant communities to trade, making everyone more prosperous. The former could aggregate the power and the resources of the many, regulate the markets, enforce law and order, while also defending the realm against foreign aggressors.[1]

From Plato (fifth century BCE) to Chanakya (third century BCE), and through the ages, the role of the State as 'arising from the need of men for one another's assistance'[2] was recognized, and in fact, grew steadily. As we saw earlier in Chapter 13, by the second half of the twentieth century, the State was seen as the powerful agent to take care of all: the economy, and more importantly, the welfare of the people. This was true not only in the emerging developing, newly independent countries, but in the developed world as well. We also saw how over time, by the early 1980s, the limitations of the top-down State as the agent to deliver everything that a

From Here to Denmark. Rajat M. Nag and Harinder S. Kohli, Oxford University Press.
© Rajat Mohan Nag and Harinder Singh Kohli 2023. DOI: 10.1093/oso/9780198893103.003.0015

society needs began to show. The importance of the markets began to re-emerge, but equally, the critical role of the community, which had faded somewhat into the background, began to be appreciated again.

Failed or partially successful programmes and investment projects, particularly large infrastructure development projects in several developing countries, led to a rethink in how such projects were being designed and implemented. While there would be several reasons for their failures, one common cause stood out: most of these were top-down projects, conceived and designed in distant capitals without much consultation or input from the local communities, which would be directly affected or supposedly benefitted by them. Essentially, the community had been left out of the process, or at least marginalized.

Gradually, attention began to shift to what came to be known as community-driven development (CDD), which emphasizes the involvement of the local community in planning and investment decisions. We interpret 'the local community' to include not just the immediate physical neighbourhood, but also the local government, that is, the municipality, small-town civic bodies, local school board, or the mayor. In ancient times, the tribe would be the community, and the manor in medieval times.

Of course, community-driven development is not a new concept. Aristotle had talked about the virtues of a community as a self-governing political entity in his *Politics* as early as the fourth century BCE.[3] In more modern times, Gandhi's *swaraj* (self-rule) movement in the 1920s, and later his fight for India's independence from the British, were built on mobilizing the community, as was Martin Luther King's civil rights movement in the US in the 1960s.

Paradoxical as it may sound, getting a community mobilized to get involved in, let alone take charge of its own development is not easy. Two possible obstacles usually come in the way. One is internal to the community, and the other, to the State; and we consider them in turn below.

15.2 Challenges of inadequate social capital: amoral familism

In Chapter 8, we observed the persistence of cultural influences over long periods of time. Recall the example of the long-term pernicious effects of the slave trade seen in the low levels of trust in some African societies even today. Levels of anti-Semitism in Germany in the early to mid-twentieth century were strongly influenced by similar sentiments from some five hundred years ago. The diffusion of the plough in agriculture in some societies gave men a comparative advantage over women, resulting in the perpetuation of gender discrimination in those societies.

We also discussed Banfield's pioneering study (1958) of a village in Southern Italy (with the fictitious name of 'Montegrano') characterized by glaring poverty, inadequate physical infrastructure, and more importantly, a striking lack of social capital. Banfield called this 'amoral familism'—complete apathy to all, except the immediate family. This general feeling of lack of self-empowerment or self-efficacy—the belief that the individual holds very little agency, if any, to positively affect situations around them[4]—has persisted over generations in Montegrano.

The above are examples of the influence of negative shocks which persisted over time in a community. Guiso et al.[5] provide similar evidence of a positive lasting shock. They find that northern cities in Italy which achieved self-government in the Middle Ages have relatively higher levels of social capital today.[6] They also found that 'fifth graders in former free city states consistently exhibit stronger self-efficacy beliefs, and that these beliefs are correlated with a higher level of civic capital'.[7]

These are rather significant findings, appearing to confirm Ostrom's[8] and Putnam's[9] observations that direct participation in public life (such as in the management of common irrigation facilities) boosts a sense of self-efficacy in the members of the community.

The key takeaway here is that a community's history has long-term persistence effects which linger on, for better or for worse, in their collective and individual beliefs. The influence of the past on a community's current behaviour needs to be recognized and studied as a society seeks to strengthen itself.

15.3 The need to hear the voice of the community

The State needs to internalize the fact that not only are people the final intended audience of development, but they are also the means to deliver it. People should not be seen just as passive recipients of state policies, actions, and largesse, but also need to be active participants in the process.

This is of course, easier said than done. A leading impediment to this is the imbalance of the power structure in most societies, particularly in developing countries. In almost all societies, the wealthy always manage to get their voices heard, and their preferences and interests well-reflected in government policies and actions. Not so for the poor and the marginalized. There is significant asymmetry of power and voice for such people.

The voices of the poor systematically get drowned and are rarely heard in the corridors of power.

15.4   Devolving power to the community: the subsidiarity principle and inclusive localism

The principal finding of the Guiso study is that enhanced self-government produces a more confident, involved, and productive citizenry. This is a strong indication that decentralizing powers to communities may reduce apathy and get them to take responsibility for their own well-being.

For generations, the usual hierarchy of political authority in most countries has seen the national governments sitting at the apex, followed by the regional governments being granted some clearly delineated authority, and the local communities (cities and municipalities) at the bottom of the heap. These local communities have often acted as administrative agents for the higher levels of the government rather than as agents responsible for the future of the communities they ostensibly serve. In fact, as markets have globalized, power and resources have moved up the chain from the community to the region to the national government and in some cases, even to the supra-state institutions such as the European Union or the World Trade Organization (WTO), governed by international agreements.

Decentralization would seek a reversal of this trend: returning power to the communities, adopting the subsidiarity principle—powers (and corresponding accountability) should be vested at the lowest level where it can work most effectively. In their insightful book, *The New Localism: How Cities Can Thrive in the Age of Populism*, urban experts Katz and Nowak 'reimagine power' as it shifts downwards to a new locus of cities, communities, and civic actors, aka 'the problem solvers'.[10]

Throughout the world, communities face serious social, economic, and environmental challenges. Katz and Nowak argue that solving problems at the local level is not only more practical, but it can also produce better and sustainable results with greater community participation and buy-in. Pittsburgh, for example, reinvented itself from a rust-belt victim of de-industrialization in the mid-1970s to become a high-tech global leader in advanced robotics and autonomous vehicles. As a sign of this trans-formation, Pittsburgh had earned the moniker of 'Roboburgh' by 2015, and dozens of world-class companies in the high-tech field had moved in, creating thousands of jobs.

By the mid-1970s, Indianapolis was on the verge of bankruptcy, dev-astated by deindustrialization and excessive suburbanization. Local lead-ership and its creative dynamism first targeted sports as a potentially winning strategy to revitalize the city and rebuild the urban core, and then gradually moved 'from basketball to biotech'. Both moves paid off handsomely.

By the mid- to late 1980s, the unemployment rate in Copenhagen, Denmark's capital, was in the high teens and the city carried an annual unsustainable budget deficit of almost $750 million. The local economy was stagnant and the traditional manufacturing industry in the country had been badly hit by the growing wave of globalization causing huge losses of local jobs. The situation in Copenhagen was further exacerbated by government policies which had, in effect, subsidized the outmigration of families from the city to its suburbs. The city's tax base had dwindled, 'leaving a city overrepresented by pensioners and college students, nei-ther of whom contributed greatly to the city's tax revenue'.[11] Beginning in 1990, a remarkable partnership of the city and the federal government created a new publicly owned, privately managed entity. It was mandated to rejuvenate the city core's large tracts of underutilized public lands into attractive high value housing and state of art commercial facilities. It did so spectacularly well significantly strengthening the city's tax and rev-enue base in the process.

However, in making a case for devolution of power down the ladder to make a self-governing community an empowered player in its own right, it is also important to note that devolution of power and problem-solving to the local level—inclusive localism—is not an argument against the na-tional level governments. As Katz and Nowak put it: 'local action is not a replacement for the vital roles the federal government plays as a distri-butional and regulatory platform; rather, it is the ideal complement to an effective government'.[12]

15.5 Empowering the community through consultation and information sharing

A common grievance of many local communities is that they are not consulted in advance on the various programmes being undertaken in their name and ostensibly, for their benefit. In fact, they often are totally unaware of the programmes or projects being planned for them until these are being implemented. Communication cannot just be passive, one-way, top-down from the State to the affected people. It has to flow the other way too, from the community to the State. The first step to correct this could be to transparently share as much information as possible in advance with the public and the intended beneficiaries. Available Information Technology (IT) facilities make this quite possible if there is a political and bureaucratic will to do so. But, while sharing information would be a major step forward, that would not be enough. There would need to be an easy, accessible forum for the affected people to air their views and concerns in good time, well before the bulldozers roll in.

Legislation to empower the citizens to seek information on federal and state government actions (e.g. through the Right to Information Act adopted in India in 2005) or public information disclosure policies can also strengthen accountability and responsiveness. By requiring public agencies to announce and enforce service standards, citizens know the standards of service they can expect and demand. Information is power and sharing information on government actions as widely as possible in a transparent manner is thus one of the most potent tools of empowering local communities.

Why did the just constructed road near my house crumble at the first onset of the monsoon showers? The answer is obvious: it was poorly constructed, sub-standard materials were used and the asphalt cover much less than what was specified. And, of course this happened because of the unholy collusion between the contractor and the roads inspector who had certified that all was fine.

India's RTI Act defines the 'Right to Information' as including the right 'inspection of work, documents, records ... even taking certified samples of material'.[13] Using this provision, residents of a community in Ahmedabad, Western India forced the local municipal corporation (through the State Information Commissioner's office) to provide them with samples from the material used on the collapsed road, test results of their quality from a reputable third party lab, and details of the contractor's procurement bills for them (the residents) to examine.[14]

Consultation and deliberations with stakeholders in the local community can be time-consuming and difficult, but these are often critical for success. Some countries establish formal deliberative mechanisms, often backed by law, to seek advice and feedback on proposed government actions. In East Asia, public–private deliberation councils comprising members of the labour unions, industry, local communities, and the government help in reaching broad agreement on key policy issues, which later helps in smoother implementation. More than the specifics of any particular programme or policy issue, a direct benefit of such a consultation process is that it gradually builds people's trust and confidence in the various institutions in society and thus, social capital.

To systematically gather citizens' views on a variety of national policies and initiatives, Singapore established its 'Feedback Unit' as early as 1985. Some twenty years later, the government expanded the Unit's mandate to go beyond just seeking public feedback, renamed it 'REACH' (Reaching Everyone for Active Citizenry @Home) and made it the lead agency for directly engaging and connecting with citizens on a wide range of national and social issues. This is inclusive localism in action.[15]

Such information-sharing, feedback, and consultation mechanisms introduce more openness and transparency into the system. As more citizens 'become aware of the performance of specific agencies or officials, they are more likely to exert collective pressure on the agency to perform better. At the same time, public agencies will have less opportunity for arbitrary action'[16]

Drawing on our earlier example in Chapter 13 of the 'report cards' given by the Public Affairs Centre, a civil society organization in Bengaluru, India with the job of rating the various public service agencies in the city—initially the Bangalore Development Authority, responsible for housing and other services, was defensive and even indifferent to the ratings, but later used the reports' findings to launch a joint citizen–government initiative to address the service-delivery problems. Several other public agencies in Bengaluru also took corrective action; inspiring other cities in the country, including the megalopolis of Mumbai, to also start using the report-card approach.[17]

15.6 The need for more than consultation—need a more active participation

While improved consultations and feedback obviously help, they would still be more in the mould of the passive role of the beneficiaries discussed earlier, essentially accepting what the state is offering them. Inclusive localism expects more from its citizens than just consultation and feedback. It calls for active participation by the local community in the design and implementation of public services or programmes, to influence planning decisions and investment resources and in some instances ultimately even have control over them.

Ostrom's groundbreaking work on collective action showed how community participation in the management of common-property natural resources, such as grazing lands or forests or water resources (irrigation systems) improved sustainability and performance. India's National Forestry Policy mandates increased the participation of local communities in managing forests. Beneficiary participation in the design and management of rural water supply projects is now a standard requirement in many countries. Using data from 121 rural water-supply projects spread over forty-nine countries in Africa, Asia, and Latin America, a World Bank assessment had concluded that of the forty-two projects with high levels of beneficiary participation, 64 per cent had been judged to be successful. In sharp contrast, of the forty-nine projects with low levels of participation, only 8 per cent were successful.[18]

As noted earlier, the subsidiarity principle (i.e. that public goods and services should be provided by the lowest levels of government, that can better capture the costs and benefits) is the guiding philosophy of inclusive localism. This does not mean that the local community will have no accountability. It will be balanced by the other two travellers, the State and the markets, which will necessitate openness and inclusion so that local communities do not become 'islands unto themselves'.

But simply passing down the responsibility to the local communities for providing public services without simultaneously transferring the resources and political power would not work. Decentralization of responsibilities and the devolution of tax revenues (financial resources) to the community would have to go hand in hand, and this has often been a major stumbling block in greater decentralization efforts in many developing countries.

15.7 Challenges of governance at the local government level: the need for balance between the State and the community

Institutional capabilities in local governments are usually weaker than at the national level, which itself is often limited in many developing countries. There are also genuine concerns that local governments may be more susceptible to local influences and corruption. A study comparing the level of corruption in piped-water-supply schemes run by centralized and decentralized agencies in two large states of India (Madhya Pradesh and Chattishgarh) found that corruption increases significantly at least in the immediate aftermath of decentralization. Although the increase persists in the medium term, it reduces significantly with time.[19]

It is possible that the more discretion the local government has, the more the potential for abuse. But that by itself is not reason enough to not devolve power and resources to the local community. The answer will have to be close monitoring and accountability, exerted lightly by the national government (the State), and more rigorously by the community itself.

The State should clearly lay out credible rules of engagement with the local governments and then enforce them. The local governments need to be accountable for delivering and ensuring fiscal prudence and integrity. However, it would defeat the whole purpose of decentralization if the State were to control the local governments with a heavy hand. Of course, the local governments need to be accountable for delivering and ensuring fiscal prudence and integrity. The State should focus on assessing whether the larger development goals of the programmes being undertaken by the local governments contribute meaningfully to the national goals and whether the objectives of the State are being met, and probe more minutely only on instances of egregious deviation, including corruption. The State shouldn't get lost in the weeds of local community development but keep an eye on the big picture instead. Follow the subsidiarity principle.

The important thing is to 'maintain balance' between the State and the community: 'not so much power with the state that the community has little sense of self-determination, and not so little that it cannot discipline obviously corrupt local governments or create the common assets that drive a strong nation'.[20]

The primary responsibility of monitoring the local government should be with the local community. After all, the local government is working for the community, funded by resources which, at least partly, come from the community itself through taxes. For communities to perform this role, relevant information—particularly on the flow of funds—must be easily and routinely accessible to them, rather than their having to claw it out of reluctant local-government officials.

Modern IT makes this easily possible. Individual citizens can now readily report the state of services (potholes, broken water pipes) or misgovernance (police harassing motorists, public servants asking for bribes) to the local governments and authorities from their mobile phones. In fact, app-based platforms to do so are now commonly available in many countries around the world. A website started in India by community activists—ipaidabribe.com—encourages people to report acts of corruption by public servants.[21] A mobile-phone-based app allows residents in Gurgaon, in India's national capital region, to report on instances of service failures: waterlogged drains and roads during the monsoon season, dark streets, and broken roads are among the most common complaints.[22]

The benefits of inclusive localism go well beyond the better delivery of services. It helps build and revive communities, creating a sense of civic engagement and social capital. The dramatic rejuvenations of Copenhagen, Indianapolis, and Pittsburgh, discussed earlier, attest to the value of such inclusive localism.

Inclusive localism provides a platform to debate a diversity of views, including political positions. A new political party committed to good governance, the Aam Aadmi Party (Common Persons' Party), emerged through a grass-roots community movement in Delhi in 2012. By 2015, they swept into power to form the local government and handily won again five years later.

Italy had gone through a fairly tumultuous period in the 1970s and 1980s, marked by widespread political and economic failures. However, even within this milieu, the northern regions (with their significantly higher social capital) continued to perform reasonably well, responding innovatively to the crises with leading-edge job-training centres, day-care programmes, and promoting investments in both traditional and new technology. The social capital poor, southern regions of the country, by contrast, were much less able to meet the challenges and faltered.

Studies have attributed regional differences to societal structures, with horizontal structures common in the north and hierarchical forms in the south, and also differences in the extent of collective action, citizen involvement, and governmental efficiency, that is, social capital.[23] Based on his landmark studies of civic traditions in Italy, Putnam[24,25] draws a bold conclusion: certain communities enjoy a more vital civic life not because they are prosperous, but because they have greater social capital.

But decentralization is no panacea. Nothing ever is. Decentralization should not be a rigid, doctrinaire policy: it should be a matter of balance between the various levels of government, following the subsidiarity principle as far as is practical. Of course, the extent of decentralization will depend on the institutional capacity of the local governments to take on greater responsibilities and absorb greater financial resources, and on whether national governments can monitor them adequately. As the World Bank noted, 'experience suggests that decentralization is unlikely to work without effective institutional arrangements to foster accountability at the local level and fiscal restraint on the part of both local and national governments'.[26]

This is when a gradual approach is better. Decentralization might begin with certain priority areas such as education and health, which benefit considerably from local community involvement. As capacity builds at the local and national levels and experience is gathered, greater decentralization may be phased in.

Several studies in Latin America concluded that 'decentralization and especially school autonomy can improve the delivery of schooling'.[27] However, they also cautioned that simply changing the organization of education—creating school councils or delegating responsibilities to local governments—is barely enough. Giving the schools control over the budget and involving parents in school governance is what really affects the delivery of education. Randomized field experiments in Bangladesh found that 'parent-teacher meetings in schools have significant and positive effects on test scores'.[28]

Decentralization also allows the schools and teachers to engage the local community in providing some much-needed education services in an efficient and cost-effective manner.

Consider the case of a large-scale remedial education programme started in 2001 for poor and marginalized children in Mumbai and Vadodora in India. Instead of using teachers from the local schools (who were stretched anyway with their regular teaching load), the schools engaged Pratham, a leading non-governmental organization in the country, dedicated to learning and education. They hired young women from the community (at a fraction of the cost of regular schoolteachers) to teach basic literacy and numeracy to children who had reached grade three or four, but without having learnt much. Evaluation of this programme by Banerjee et al. was very encouraging. They reported that 'the program had substantial positive impacts on children's academic achievement. In both Vadodara and Mumbai, the program significantly improved overall test scores. Moreover, the weakest students who were the primary target of the program gained the most'.[29] The programme has since been adapted, re-evaluated, and scaled up across India.

15.8 Shackling the Leviathan

Earlier in Chapter 13, we discussed Hobbes's concern about a society at 'Warre' where it lived in 'continuall feare and danger of violent death; And the life of man, solitary, poore, nasty, brutish, and short'.[30] Hobbes's proposed solution to avoid the state of 'Warre' was an all-powerful Leviathan to ensure order and security in society. But the Leviathan who ends 'Warre' can also turn despotic. And life under the yoke of such a Despotic Leviathan without any liberty can be equally 'nasty, short and brutish' too.

It follows then that neither the Despotic Leviathan nor the Absent Leviathan will do in generating a society of liberty, freedoms, and justice. What we need is a State which would be, in Acemoğlu's and Robinson's words: the 'Shackled Leviathan'. This is a more dramatic and graphic way of saying that what we need is a balanced State 'that has the capacity to enforce laws, control violence, resolve conflicts and provide public services but is still tamed and controlled by an assertive, well-organized society'.[31]

Ancient Athens provides an interesting instance of successfully creating a Shackled Leviathan. In 594 BCE, Solon, a wealthy trader, an accomplished military commander, and a man widely respected for his integrity, was elected as Athens' Archon (Chief Magistrate) for a year. From all appearances Solon was a part of the local elite, but he turned out to be a very significant reformer. His genius lay in recognizing that the way forward for Athens to prosper and indeed survive was to ensure a balance between the powers and interests of the elites and those of the common citizens. His reforms focused on strengthening the people's voices and rights against any injustices and violations by elites, but at the same time, he assured the elites that he would respect their property rights and ensure that their interests were not unfairly compromised. He constrained the State's powers while simultaneously increasing its capacity to ensure peace, provide security, and resolve conflicts.

Until the time of Solon, all loans were secured by the person of the debtor, essentially a servitude till the debt was cleared. Often unable to repay the loans owing to economic hardship, people became bonded labourers in the personal service of their creditors. Aside from the issue of unfreedom which this caused, the debt servitude also had a significant impact on the political institutions of the State, which consisted of two assemblies, the Ekklesia and the Areopagus. The former was open to all free male citizens who were free of any debt servitude. However, by being debt defaulters, many Athenians were effectively disenfranchised. Solon cancelled all outstanding debt-servitude contracts and banned future borrowings against one's own self as security. All Athenian male citizens (unfortunately, no mention of females at all in the reforms of even someone as enlightened as Solon) were now empowered to participate in the political processes of the State and society.

Solon also undertook far-reaching land reforms to improve the economic circumstances of the poor. He abolished the land tenancy arrangements in place which required all tenants farming the land to pay a sixth of their produce to the landowners. These two reforms made fundamental changes to the power dynamics of society, in effect achieving a better balance between the community and the state. The poor, now free of debt servitude and with better economic opportunities were able to participate more fully in the affairs of society and had increasingly greater stakes and ability in keeping a closer watch on the state.

Solon balanced these pro-people reforms by giving concessions to the elites as well. He altered the process of selecting the Archon, so that the elites would continue to control the appointment of the Archon and membership in the Areopagus. He also created a new executive council of 400 members with more positions for the elites. Simultaneously, Solon instituted several judicial reforms, reduced the role of the political elite in implementing the laws, and enhanced the role of state bureaucrats (the magistrates) in doing so, effectively strengthening the state institutions in the process.

Among the most striking and effective judicial reforms was the Hubris Law, under which anybody, elite or not, could be charged with an act of hubris (behaviour which humiliates or intimidates) against any individual (man or woman, slave or free) and taken to court. This was a remarkable empowering of the individual Athenian 'to enjoy liberty from dominance of powerful individuals'.[32]

We have discussed the Athenian example not so much to give a historical account as to draw some lessons of relevance for the appropriate balancing of the State and society in creating the Shackled Leviathan. By ending the system of debt servitude, expanding economic opportunities, and providing greater access to justice to the common citizens, Solon empowered the common citizens. He also enhanced some political rights of the elite and protected their property rights, but then cleverly built in a constraint on their possible domination through the Hubris Law. Notice that the more Solon empowered the Athenians (the community), the more he could strengthen the state as well. Notice too the interplay of institutional reforms and norms. Prior to Solon's time, rules and laws were usually not codified in writing. They were enforced by society through an elaborate system of norms of expected behaviour and using means such as ostracism or social exclusion. Solon built on these norms by codifying and strengthening them (as in the Hubris Law) but 'in the process he also changed these norms, so that hubristic behaviour became far less acceptable in Athenian society'.[33]

Fast-forward to the early twenty-first century and from Athens to New York for another unique and bold international initiative to bring the community and the State to walk in tandem. On the sidelines of the UN Annual General Assembly Meeting in New York of global leaders in September 2011, eight heads of state (Brazil, Indonesia, Mexico, Norway, the Philippines, South Africa, the United Kingdom, and the United States) and nine civil society leaders around the globe launched the Open Government Partnership (OGP).[34] Presidents Obama and

Rousseff (of Brazil) were the first co-chairs of this multilateral initiative to create a global platform where government leaders and civil society would meet as equals to promote transparency, fight corruption, strengthen accountability, and empower citizens in participating countries in the OGP. Though bold and critically relevant for human development, this initiative was seen even by its most ardent protagonists as an experiment, an aspiration to achieve better and open communication between the community and the State, with the outcome uncertain.

But led by a group of deeply committed and competent social reformers right from the start, and currently by a dynamic and infectiously enthusiastic Chief Executive, Sanjay Pradhan, the experiment so far has turned out to be remarkably successful. From the initial eight countries and nine civil society leaders who launched the OGP in 2011, the membership has now grown to a very impressive seventy-five countries, 106 local governments, and thousands of civil service organizations, reaching over two billion people worldwide.

In urging governments around the world to deepen their partnerships with civil society, President Obama had articulated well why such partnerships are so important: 'Open and honest collaboration with citizens over the long term, no matter how uncomfortable it is, makes the country stronger and more successful, and it creates more prosperous economies and more just societies and more opportunities for its citizens'.[35] Cautioning that progress will only be in small instalments, his words captured the hope and aspirations of many that a stronger partnership between governments and their citizens will produce 'better governments and stronger civil society and over time that means that not only will individual countries be stronger and not only will the citizens in those countries have greater opportunities and be less prone to injustice, but that translates into a world that is more just and more fair'.[36]

The fundamental guiding principle of OGP is to help transform the relationship between the State and the community into one of equality, as fellow travellers and not as the ruler and the ruled. Restoring trust between the two travellers is key to transforming this relationship, and it is done in a simple but bold fashion by the OGP members. Member governments commit themselves to a series of actions they plan to undertake over the next two years to make them more open, transparent, partici-patory, inclusive, and accountable. But to be credible these cannot just be rhetorical expressions of aspirations and promises of best efforts by governments, which often go unfulfilled. It is easy to dismiss such bold assertions and the scepticism is understandable. But, in the case of OGP members, there are specific actions the governments commit to under-take, which the civil society can monitor and hold the governments accountable for. What is also fundamentally different about the OGP ex-periment is that such commitments are not made by the governments unilaterally or working in isolation. On the contrary, 'working together, governments and civil society co-create action plans with concrete com-mitments across a broad range of issues'.[37] There is then a buy-in from civil society to what these actions will be and the government is aware, ex ante, how their commitments will be watched and monitored by the citi-zens who will hold them accountable.

One could argue that ten years is too short a period in which to as-sess whether the OGP model works. Such transformative changes take not months, or even years, but decades to materialize. But based on inde-pendent, third-party reviews by leading international experts of OGP's operation, the evidence is encouraging. Drawing on a database of dozens of available indicators, the review compared the performance of forty-two OGP countries who have been a part of OGP for at least five years with non-OGP countries, in five policy areas, namely, civic space, cor-ruption, transparent policymaking, access to information, and fiscal openness. In each case, 'the OGP countries earned higher scores than non-OGP countries'.[38]

Evidence also shows that when the governments and civil society co-create the action plans together, not only are such plans more ambitious, but the results are also better. Of the 2,000 odd OGP reforms reviewed by the independent experts, over 20 percent were assessed to have made governments significantly more open to citizens.[39] In Ukraine prior to the war, for example, reformers from the government, civil society and business joined forces to leverage OGP to openly disclose procurement contracts that were earlier handed out in corrupt backroom deals cap-tured by powerful oligarchs. Not only did this result in savings of about US$1 billion to the public purse in two years, about 80 percent of busi-nesses reported reduced corruption in government procurement and there was a dramatic 50 percent increase in new businesses now bidding for government contracts due to the level playing field.[40]

In Kaduna Nigeria, when an audit revealed that a hospital promised to citizens and paid for by the government only existed on paper, the Budget Director partnered with citizens to create a mobile app, using which citizens could upload photos and feedback on public projects, that would go directly to the state legislature and governor's office for corrective actions. This led to a record completion of roads and health clinics in two years.[41]

A more recent assessment by independent researchers concluded that in spite of initial scepticisms, the OGP has emerged as a successful transnational multistakeholder initiative that has indeed impacted policy, helped to produce progressive reforms, and expand open government norms.[42]

The Athenian and the OGP experiences go on to show that the Leviathan needs to be shackled to achieve the delicate balance of the State and the community operating effectively and for the greater good, and facilitate the journey from Here to Denmark.

15.9 Exit, voice, and loyalty

Achieving the optimal working balance between the three fellow travellers—the State, the markets, and the community—is a moving target, requiring open communication, accountability, and constant re-evaluation. The feedback loop should be productive and flow freely between the travellers.

In a fascinating book, *Exit, Voice, and Loyalty: Responses to Decline in Firms, Organizations, and States*, social scientist Albert Hirschman articulates the importance of this communication (voice) in enabling this balance and the serious consequences of a breakdown in this process.[43] His basic argument is as simple as it is insightful: in the case of a firm or an organization in response to a decline in the quality of a product or service, a consumer has two choices. She can convey her dissatisfaction to the firm or the merchant (voice) or she can go elsewhere (exit). Which of these two options she will exercise will depend on the responsiveness of the firm to her complaint (taking responsibility, acknowledging the defect, offering to replace the product, or ensuring better service next time) and her loyalty to the product or the organization. If she is a loyal customer, she might not choose the exit option too readily. If she is not, and if her voice has not been readily heard, she will go elsewhere, if she can. The same is true of an employee who is dissatisfied with his non-responsive employer and feels that the only option is to look for a job elsewhere and quit.

Hirschman's thesis applies to states as well. A citizen can vote with her feet. If she feels that the state does not give her a meaningful voice (once every five years at the voting booth, if that, is not enough), is not responsive to her concerns, then she will emigrate if she can, often illegally if she must, for the sake of her family and children.

How long she will stay on in the country (or stick with the firm) will depend to a large extent on her loyalty. If the citizen's protests are ignored, or worse suppressed, by muzzling the media or (ab)using state institutions to harass or intimidate protestors, exit may be the only option. And until then, the citizens will become passive and withdraw from the process of active engagement with the state. Without this feedback loop, the state institutions will falter and wither.

On the contrary, if the voice is strong and encouraged as contemplated in the experiments of the OGP discussed earlier, the state and the community will both be stronger, with the mutually reinforcing forces of better communication and robust accountability.

How readily one chooses 'exit' over 'voice' depends on 'loyalty'. And loyalty in turn depends on a citizen's trust in her state. Trust builds social capital. If she feels that in spite of periodic incidents when the state appears to be treating her or her communities rather unfairly, still overall, the state is fair, then she will trust the state and be loyal. She will raise her voice, not be passive in her role as a citizen, and will not readily choose the exit option. Conversely, if her trust in the state is low, then the exit option will be her preferred choice, over voice.

Though this section has been devoted almost entirely to the relationship between the State and the community, the same is true of the market as well. A citizen can as easily exit the market (or a participant in it, that is, a firm or an organization) if she feels that her voice is not being heard and the organization is not willing to be held accountable. Similarly, if the private sector does not trust the state to be fair and consistent in enforcing the rules and regulations, if the tax laws are changed retroactively, if political connections and bribery win contracts rather than price and quality consideration, then an organization can exit the market and indeed, so can domestic and foreign investors. The same factors of exit, voice, and loyalty are at play.

15.10   Leadership

In 1965, Lee Kuan Yew took office as the first prime minister of Singapore, a newly independent country, so resource-poor that it didn't even have its own water sources. At the same time, the Philippines, then seen as the leading light of Asia after Japan, elected Ferdinand Marcos as its tenth president. Coincidentally, both ruled for about the same period of time, but their end points could not be more divergent. Marcos was overthrown by a People's Revolution in 1986 against his corrupt regime and fled into exile where he died, unwept and unsung. Lee left office in 1990, exalted and venerated by his fellow citizens and the world at large till his death in 2015.

Singapore might not have become Singapore were it not for Lee; he took the country to great heights. The Philippines, too, might not have become today's Philippines were it not for Marcos; he drove it into the ground.

Evidently, it all boils down to leadership. But where do good leaders come from? Is it just a matter of chance or circumstances or timing? The truth is, we do not know, and it is probably not a very fruitful exercise to engage in philosophical debates about whether leaders are born or made.

In his fascinating and insightful book, *The 10 Rules of Successful Nations*, Ruchir Sharma identifies the nature of politics, more specifically leadership, as one of the titular criteria. He writes, 'while politics can shape the economy of developed nations, it matters even more for emerging countries, where institutions tend to be weaker, and one man or woman at the top can make all the difference'[44] and goes on to add that 'successful nations throw their weight behind a reformer, frequently one new to office'.[45] Note the qualifier: 'new to office', and it is an important one. Sharma expands: 'the probability of successful reforms is higher under fresh leaders than stale leaders, under leaders with a mass base than well credentialed technocrats and under democratic leaders than autocrats'.[46] A lot is packed into that sentence, and it would help to un-bundle that a bit.

A crisis is the most opportune time for reforms. Reforms become a necessary condition for survival and not just good-to-have which will ul-timately improve the well-being of a country. Be it in India in the early 1990s, when the country was reeling under the burdens of an overbearing 'license raj', or Russia tottering after the break-up of the Soviet Union and the ensuing financial crisis, or the imminent collapse of the South Korean economy during the Asian financial crisis in 1998, the solution in each case was the same: reform or perish. And in each case, it was the emer-gence of fresh leaders that saved the day: Prime Minister Narasimha Rao and his able Finance Minister (and a future prime minister) Manmohan Singh in India, Vladimir Putin in Russia, and Kim Dae-jung in South Korea were all fresh leaders, willing to take risks, clear-headed about the necessary reforms, and motivated to undertake them.

Rao and Singh brought in massive deregulations, releasing hamstrung entrepreneurs, brought down debilitating import controls, and opened the country to foreign and domestic competition. Putin dramatically simplified the tax code, aggressively pursued tax collection, and ration-alized state expenditures to stabilize government finances. Kim head-on confronted the unholy alliance of the politicians, the state banks, and the large conglomerates (the chaebols), which together had allowed these companies to run up massive debts which they could not possibly repay.

The most dramatic of all, of course, were the fundamental reforms ush-ered in by Deng Xiaoping in China in the early 1980s. Couching his ap-proach in a Confucian saying that 'it did not matter whether the cat was black or white, so long as it caught mice, it is a good cat', he pioneered the transformational economic reforms in China known as the 'socialist eco-nomic reforms'. To counter any charges that he was veering away from socialism, he astutely declared that China was practising socialism with Chinese characteristics and immediately made the reforms more politic-ally palatable to the ruling class and the masses.

But leaders turn stale. Their zeal and commitment to reforms wanes with time, their passionate stances get compromised owing to political pressures, and personal ambitions to cling on to power, including bla-tant efforts to enrich themselves or their families, take over the service ideal. Hubris begins to set in, and the originally reform-minded leaders gradually cut themselves off from any meaningful, critical feedback, increasingly sheltering themselves in a cocoon of 'yes men and women' and sycophants. Calling this the 'second term curse', Sharma cites some revealing statistics: 'by 2013, seven of the twenty most emerging countries were suffering political unrest (Russia, India, South Africa, Egypt, Turkey, Brazil and Argentina)' and in each of these cases, the ruling 'regime had been in power more than eight years; this was a revolt against stale leaders'.[47]

President Suharto in Indonesia, Prime Minister Mahathir in Malaysia, and President Erdogan in Turkey were all reform-minded leaders to begin with, but then succumbed to the temptations of the office. They ultimately became impediments to further reforms and increasingly turned autocratic the longer they stayed in office, and clung on to power, sometimes even by the nominally democratic processes of elections. Singapore's Prime Minister Lee Kuan Yew, who governed the country for more than three decades, was an exception to prove the rule.

A major reason why leaders turn stale and either sow the seeds of their demise from power or turn increasingly autocratic is essentially that they gradually and intentionally begin to disrupt the balance of power between the three fellow travellers. They start to behave as if they are the only player that matters, curbing the voice of the other two. And, once the balance is disturbed, a vicious cycle of more imbalance results, as the leaders turn further into their own echo chambers and mute the voice of their fellow travellers.

An argument often offered in support of well-intentioned autocratic leaders (the 'benevolent autocrat' hypothesis) is that they are good for economic growth. Yes, they rule with an iron hand, denying what many ordinary citizens would consider their fundamental rights, but this might be a small price to pay, so the argument goes, particularly for poor countries, for the economic growth such leaders can unleash. As a matter of fact, according to this school of thought 'too much democracy' is a cause for underdevelopment, which well-intentioned autocratic leaders can turn around with their insistence on discipline and strict enforcement of rule and order. A recent study debunks this ' "benevolent autocratic leader" being good for economic growth' hypothesis.[48]Based on a sample of 133 countries over the period 1858–2010 (it would be hard to argue that the sample size was small or the period of analysis too short), the authors conclude that 'autocratic leaders with positive effects (on the economy) are found, at best, only as frequently as one would expect due to chance alone'.[49] That is econ speak for 'there is no merit in the "benevolent autocratic leader" hypothesis'. And, in the few cases where the effect is positive, the authors further conclude that such 'infrequent growth positive autocrats largely "ride the wave" of previous success'.

But there is yet another striking finding of the study: that 'autocratic leaders with negative effects are found more frequently than chance would predict'.[50] This is a very significant conclusion: not only is an autocratic leader NOT good for economic growth, but his (yes, almost universally a 'he') rule is bad for the economy. So much for the benevolent autocrat.

Our usual search for leadership is probably limiting, since we instinctively think of a national leader. While some countries have been fortunate enough to produce exceptional and transformational leaders who have guided their country through very challenging times, evidence points to many worse or indifferent ones. But perhaps we need to think of leadership through a wider lens than just a single national leader alone: competent and charismatic, honest, and committed, the mythical King Arthur or the real-life Mandela.

When we ask who is leading the country, we usually mean, who is leading the State? But the State is only one traveller on this journey to Denmark. There are two others: the market and the community; and we need leadership in those two areas too, and society must look for collective leadership and direction. We should start to reimagine leadership not as a single national leader, or even a few, collectively. Our search for leadership must widen to be society-wide, and the thousands of leaders who will emerge from the State, the markets, and the community.

In an intertwined society of the state, market, and community—in balance—power cannot be restricted to any one of them alone. With greater involvement of the community, power is 'drifting downwards from the nation state to cities and metropolitan communities, and horizontally from government to networks of public, private, and civic actors ... In sum, power increasingly belongs to problem solvers',[51] and leadership is abundant in those layers of society.

Since there are no easy answers to our question, 'where do good leaders come from?', perhaps the solution is better found in 'empowering a multiplicity of problem solvers rather than hoping that one problem solver at the apex of the state gets it right.[52]

15.11 The Three Travellers: travelling in tandem

Let us go back again to the history of Great Britain (Chapter 10) where post the Glorious Revolution, as the power of the State was constrained, markets grew. But it also emerged that the State was not weakened in the process, in fact it grew stronger.

However, while this was all ultimately to the benefit of society as whole, there were some immediate losers in the process as well. With greater security of property rights, a market for the sale of produce and sale of land began to emerge. As landowners converted (sold or let out their land) to more productive and profitable uses, many long-standing tenancy agreements were terminated, and tenants thrown off the land. Adding to the woes of the peasants was the fact that many no longer had access to the commons, where they had grazed their cattle for generations. The feudal community started to disintegrate, and the protection thus far provided to the poor peasants began to disappear.

The young migrated to the towns looking for work in polluted and overcrowded manufacturing establishments and factories, which had begun to mushroom in the wake of the emerging industrial revolution. Though the working conditions in the new factories were hellish as were the appalling, living arrangements, at least the young could feed themselves and put food on the table for the rest of the family back in the countryside who could not move out. And, with the large number of unemployed peasants, the new urban industrialists were under no competitive pressure to improve the working or squalid living conditions of the factory workers. They were under no political pressure either. With property ownership being a requirement to have the right to vote, Parliament consisted only of the wealthy landed gentry whose interests occupied it most. The peasants, the equally hapless urban workers, and the middle class, were disenfranchised and thus had no political influence to change matters.

But changes did happen, slowly but surely. And they happened not because the new industrialists and the political elite suddenly became

350 FROM HERE TO DENMARK

altruistic and enlightened, but out of their fear of social unrest and threats to their own economic well-being. Acemoğlu and Robinson argue that the ensuing political reforms were essentially 'strategic decisions by the political elite to prevent widespread social unrest and revolution'.[53]

Several violent political agitations in the early nineteenth century shook the political establishment. The Swing Riots in 1830, led by impoverished and dispossessed agricultural labourers, finally ushered in expanded voting rights in England. Obviously done very grudgingly and slowly and out of fear, but at least the cause was honestly admitted by Prime Minister Earl Grey, when introducing the electoral reform bill to the British Parliament in 1831: 'There is no one more decided against annual parliaments, universal suffrage, and the ballot, than am I ... The principle of my reform is to prevent the necessity of revolution. I am reforming to preserve, not to overthrow'.[54]

The British franchise was extended in 1832 to include the middle class, in 1867 to include the urban workers, in 1884to include the rural workers, in 1919 to include women but only with property ownership and ultimately became universal only in 1928, when the property requirement for women was lifted.

Similar expansion of voting rights happened in some other countries in Europe, such as in France, Germany, and Sweden, also in the face of social turbulence as in Great Britain. However, in some countries, such as the United States, voting rights were extended out of a different motivation altogether: sheer economic necessity. In a country with plentiful land and insufficient population to use it productively, additional settlers could be attracted only with the promise of being in charge of their own affairs. Having the right to vote (albeit by no means universal) was the first step in that process. As Rajan notes, 'perhaps this was why none of the states that entered the Union after the initial thirteen had a property requirement for voters—would be settlers usually came without property'.[55]

The expanded franchise was usually accompanied, both in the United States and the United Kingdom, by an increase in local spending on public goods. For example, in England spending by local governments 'rose from 17 percent of total government spending in 1790 to 41 percent in 1890, much of it in spending on public health infrastructure like sewerage systems, filtered water, and paved and drained roads'.[56]Evidently, the increased community powers due to the expanded franchise resulted in greater attention to the needs of new urban migrants.

Interestingly, contrary to some fears that expanding the franchise would result in the masses demanding and getting more of the 'economic pie' at the expense of the rich, 'the spending on welfare decreased during the nineteenth century—from a peak of 2 percent of GDP in 1820 to less than 1 percent of GDP through most of the rest of the century … And total taxation as a fraction of GNP decreased between 1800 and 1870, and in 1900 had not yet reached the 1800 level'.[57]

We had seen earlier in this section that acceding some powers to Parliament had not weakened the State. Instead, both the State and the markets had grown. Similarly, expanding voting rights strengthened the communities to articulate and influence affairs on the national stage, rather than simply 'accept top-down commands from the state'.[58] However, this did not in any way threaten either the State or the markets, since property rights were now, if anything, even stronger, with fears of social unrest abated and a greater buy-in by the non-elites in the country's political processes.

We had noted in Chapter 2 that civic society (the community) has gained a greater voice in most countries in recent years. There is no evidence that states have weakened as a result. On the contrary, as we saw above, a community becoming stronger through being given increased voice and more space, or the markets becoming stronger with recognition of property rights can also strengthen the state, not weaken it. There is an important lesson here. The strengthening of one institution does not have to be at the cost of another. It is not a zero-sum game.

However, it does not follow that the three institutions—the State, the markets, and the communities—would always be instinctively inclined to stay in balance and mutually support each other. Quite the contrary: each of these fellow travellers might wish to become more powerful and dominate the others. The State might, for example, see the rising voice of the civic society as a challenge to its authority and try to curb it. The community might see the markets as acting in its own interests at the cost of the community's welfare and try to influence the State to tame the behemoth. Tempting as these steps might initially appear, they usually turn out be counterproductive and even detrimental for society.

Rajan articulates this dilemma well and it is perhaps best to quote him at length to conclude this chapter: 'Too weak the markets and society becomes unproductive, too weak a community and society tends towards crony capitalism, too weak the state and the society turns fearful and apathetic. Conversely, too much market and society become inequitable; too much community and society become static; and too much state and society become authoritarian. A balance is essential.'[59]

15.12 Summary

The community lies at the heart of the development process. Denmark is marked by the well-being of its people, that is, its communities, which are served by the State and the markets. In our book we focus on political and economic institutions, but with the overarching goal of empowering our communities and our formal and informal social institutions to help achieve a better life for all citizens. In Denmark, people are rich as well as free; they have the freedom to embrace all their identities with dignity and the opportunity to choose and change their station in life.

Getting a community involved in, not to mention taking charge of, its own development is not easy. For the State, the challenge is to overcome its frequent tendency to consider people (the community) as only passive recipients of State action, rather than as active participants in the process as well. One major impediment to achieving this is the unequal power structure in most societies, particularly in developing countries, where the voices of the poor and the marginalized systematically get drowned and are rarely heard in the corridors of power.

The virtues of a community as a self-governing political entity were recognized as far back as ancient Greece and extolled by Aristotle. Writing in the early 12th century, King Someshvara III of the Chalukya dynasty in present day Karnataka, in southern India had penned his *Manasollasa*, an eyclopedic treatise, where he similarly emphasized decentralization as a major plank of his governance philosophy. But, over time in the process of evolution of the nation state, and more lately as markets have globalized, power has devolved up the chain from the community to the top.

Strengthening communities would require devolving political power to them through a process of decentralization. Decentralization would seek to reverse this trend, adopting the principle of subsidiarity: power (and corresponding accountability) should be vested at the lowest level where it is best put to effective use, in a process aptly described as inclusive localism.

Often a community is weakened by simply being ignored by the State. This can be corrected by transparent sharing of as much information as possible in advance with the affected parties and intended beneficiaries, by legislative means, if necessary. But there would also need to be an easy forum for people to air their views and concerns. Communication has to be a two-way street.

However, inclusive localism demands more than just exchange of information. It would involve active participation by the community in the design and implementation of public services or programmes, and ultimately have control over planning decisions and investment resources. But simply passing down the responsibility to the local communities would not work either. The communities would have to have the necessary resources to carry them out as well. Thus, decentralization of responsibilities would also require the simultaneous devolution of financial resources to the community. Inclusive localism also calls for the State to hold the community accountable for the tasks and resources devolved to it. There is no single right answer or formula to achieve this. If the State becomes too powerful, the Leviathan turns despotic and authoritarian. Too strong a community, the Leviathan becomes absent. It cannot then prevent chaos in society or ensure justice, particularly for the poor and the marginalized. When the markets become too strong, society become inequitable. But equally, when markets become too weak, society becomes unproductive. The key point is balance.

Essentially then, in the journey from Here to Denmark, the three fellow travellers must walk in tandem. And just as every developing country is at a unique and distinct 'Here', so unique and distinct will their 'Denmark' be. It is not a one-size-fits-all Denmark that we are after, but the three fellow travellers moving in tandem will hopefully find their way to their own different Denmark, their own version of 'that heaven of freedom'.

Part IV: Key messages

1. *A society's welfare depends on how well the three institutions comprising it - the state, the markets and the community- work together in tandem.*

2. *The State (Hobbes's Leviathan) would legally monopolize the use of violence, ensure law and order, assure justice for all and provide a supportive eco system for markets to thrive and the community to go about its daily life without fear. But the State's power must also be appropriately tamed, lest it itself becomes the feared despot.*

3. *Markets matter, but free markets are far from perfect. Just as the Leviathan of the state has to be shackled, the behemoth of the monopoly enterprises has to be tamed as well.*

4. *Strengthening communities requires devolving political power to them through a process of inclusive localism (decentralization) adopting the principle of subsidiarity: powers and corresponding accountability should be vested at the lowest level, where it is most effective.*

5. *These three institutions (fellow travellers) need to be in balance. Achieving this delicate balance is a principal challenge in the journey from Here to 'Denmark'.*

16

Some Concluding Thoughts and the Way Forward

16.1 Introduction

The defining thesis of this book has been that life in Denmark is characterized by good governance. While there can be many paths for the journey from Here to Denmark, the success of that journey will ultimately be tested by a single metric: has the state been able to provide good governance to its citizens? The book has argued that delivering good governance ultimately depends on whether the country has good, inclusive institutions. The quest in this journey is thus a quest for such robust institutions: how they evolve, how they need to be nurtured, and how they can satisfactorily mediate the interests of various segments of society, particularly how they protect the weak and the vulnerable from the might of the powerful.

Insights from the relatively new and exciting field of behavioural economics on how humans think and act individually and collectively as members of a society demonstrate that institutions critically depend on the distribution of political power in that society. Politics matters, as do the social contexts. Institutions would thus vary greatly from society to society and, therefore, transplanting best practices from elsewhere would not work.

At the same time, past experiences of countries, including of Denmark itself, as it made its journey to 'Denmark', point to some key essentials which appear to be universally valid: strong human capital (an educated and healthy population) and effective community participation by citizens have a strong influence on the state of well-being of the society they live in. In each successful case of the journey to Denmark, another key lesson emerges: a sense of harmony between the three institutions (the

From Here to Denmark. Rajat M. Nag and Harinder S. Kohli, Oxford University Press.
© Rajat Mohan Nag and Harinder Singh Kohli 2023. DOI: 10.1093/oso/9780198893103.003.0016

State, the markets, and the community) in a society, where each complements the other, as fellow travellers is essential.

While study of the past experiences of countries around the world is no doubt relevant and instructive, it is also important to remember that 'history is not destiny'. The book has thus made some efforts to peer into the future and identified ten megatrends which we believe will influence the world in the future. Collectively, they will increase demands for better governance and accountability, but also, hopefully, accelerate change for the better.

We have intentionally not called this chapter, as one might expect, 'Conclusions'. The enquiry into the challenges of economic and social development is complex and far from complete. Seeking answers to questions about why some countries are rich and others poor, what leads some countries to develop sound, inclusive institutions, and others not, is work in progress. It would perhaps be premature and even presumptuous to suggest conclusions. We thus offer below a broad summary, including some concluding thoughts, and a look into the future which could influence the trajectory of the journey of various countries from Here to Denmark.

While many challenges and roadblocks undoubtedly remain on this journey, our book ends on a note of hope. People around the world today are richer, more literate, are healthier and live longer than they did even a few decades back. Even though the destination seems distant at times, and the path zig zag and tortuous, most countries, on all continents, are closer to Denmark now than they have ever been before. And, there is no reason to despair that that trend will not continue despite obvious challenges ahead.

16.2 Critical importance of good governance

Good governance is a necessary condition for good development. On the other hand, lack of good governance, particularly owing to corruption, forms a major bottleneck in the course of development.

By 'development' we mean not just economic development, nor increases in incomes, alone, important as they are. Good development is much broader in scope: it embraces freedom from injustices, freedom from deprivations of hunger, freedom from discrimination based on race, gender, creed, sexual orientation or religion, freedom to choose and live a life of equal opportunity and dignity.

There is convincing evidence that good governance leads to superior economic performance, including higher GDP growth and faster poverty reduction. It also yields better social outcomes, such as higher human capital (better education outcomes, lower infant and maternal mortality), and overall better living conditions. In addition, by giving people a greater say in how they are ruled, the society is better off on the whole. The net result is that globally better-governed countries have higher incomes and better social development, and the converse is also true. This is because countries that are well-governed make better use of their resources (human and capital) and attract additional resources, further accelerating their growth and well-being. Unfortunately, the reverse is true for poorly governed countries: poor governance keeps them poor and condemns their people to misery. In short, good governance is critical for good development.

Governance is the process of how a society steers or governs itself. It is a complex amalgam of multidimensional and multidisciplinary considerations. Not only is governance multidimensional, but it also involves multiple stakeholders. Governance is not only about governments. Governments undoubtedly have a key role to play, since good governance implies managing public affairs in a transparent, accountable, participatory, and equitable manner. But good governance also requires close interaction between governments, the markets, and the community.

Good governance essentially comprises four basic elements: predictability, transparency, participation, and accountability, which must work in tandem to produce good governance. They reinforce each other; the absence or dilution of any one of them undermines the entire structure of governance.

16.3 Institutions are key

Robust institutions are crucial for improving governance.

Institutions are the rules—formal and informal—which define the framework within which human interaction takes place in a society.

These various sets of rules guide and place constraints on the behaviour of members in a society, the governors and the governed alike, for the overall welfare of the community.

Formal rules such as constitutions, laws, regulations define the legal and formal structure within which a society expects to conduct itself and the standards it hopes to uphold. However, even the world's best-written constitutions and laws are nothing but 'ink on paper' if not implemented in both word and spirit. Informal rules, shared beliefs, social norms, and cultures define the context within which a society functions. A constant interaction of formal and informal rules influences how effective institutions are in that society. Institutions must also thus be tailored to fit local social norms and circumstances, and therefore, as mentioned, cannot be transplanted from elsewhere.

16.4 Human behaviour as catalyst of change

Policies and institutional practices must be designed on the premise that human decision-making and actions are significantly influenced by norms, beliefs, and mental models of the world around them.

Studies around the world confirm that poor governance in most countries is not because there aren't enough laws and regulations on the books. The challenge is in their adequate implementation. Well-crafted, culturally sensitive, and elegant laws are important, but equally important are people's beliefs about them. For the laws to be truly effective, ordinary citizens have to believe not only in the laws and the need to follow them, but more importantly, that others will follow them too. Compared to beliefs, which are individualistic, norms are a social construct and are important for their contribution to social order. They are the language a society speaks as an embodiment of its collective values and social desires. Social life would not be feasible without norms. Our beliefs are shaped by what we believe others believe, who in turn believe what they think we believe, in a mutually reinforcing spiral. We are all 'citizens of the republic of beliefs', and this has significant implications for the state of good governance in a society.

Social norms influence collective behaviour, for better or for worse. For example, evidence shows that while humans can be altruistic and kind, they are not always so. Instead, humans are conditional co-operators. 'I won't play sucker, and will be good to you only if you are good to me.' This is a valuable insight, which can be used to enhance the relevance of existing social norms and nudge them to lead to better social outcomes.

By the very nature of their evolution, norms and mental models have long staying power. They can have positive effects, of collective knowledge and ancestral wisdom being bequeathed to successive generations. But they can also outlive their relevance and be counterproductive.

While changing negative social norms and mental models is not easy, they are not immutable either. Changing norms and mental models needs collective actions. Participatory deliberations, empowering the affected people through better education and health raising their social awareness, or offering a counter norm to anchor the change, are some such possible actions. Making space for human behavioural insights can make a big difference to successful policy design and institutional practices. And indeed, historical experiences of countries such as Denmark and Great Britain some centuries back, or Japan since the Meiji Restoration, all show that changes for the better, difficult as they might be, are indeed possible.

16.5 Importance of open societal systems and inclusive institutions

Broadly, societies may be categorized as either limited- or open-access orders, also referred to as particularistic or universalistic societies. In the former, access to economic and political opportunities is limited to the elites rather than being open to all. While there are no magic bullets, past experiences around the world have shown that open societal systems and inclusive institutions are central to developing better governance. These two systems must fit together for effective governance.

Open-access-order societies rely on competition, open access to organizations, and the rule of law to hold the society together. In such societies, all citizens are empowered to form economic, political, and social organizations to pursue any activity (except violence). They can pursue their own interests and open entry induces competition, which in turn dissipates rents. By their very construct, political and economic transactions are impersonal in the open-access order and based on transparent and predictable criteria. In contrast, and obviously less desirable, is the limited-access-order society, where powerful individuals or the elite possess privileges and means to create limits on access by others to resources and economic functions in order to generate rents. These elites have privileged access to social tools enabling them and only them to form powerful organizations, and they manage to keep others (i.e. most of the society) out. Elites actively manipulate the social order to regulate access and economic competition, thereby creating economic rents which only they enjoy. The elites also use these rents to create social order, control violence, and establish social cooperation for their own, narrow advantage and welfare.

The second concept is that of 'inclusive institutions' as distinct from 'extractive institutions'. Inclusive economic institutions create the incentives and opportunities for a large majority of the people in a society to innovate, adopt new technology, and aspire to achieve prosperity because they believe they can. This would include the standard neoclassical requirements of secure property rights, rule of law, and the uninhibited entry and exit of new entrepreneurs in any enterprise. The critical requirement for inclusivity is that these incentives and rights must be available to a large majority of the people.

Inclusive economic institutions 'require secure rights and economic opportunities not just for the elite but for a broad cross section of society'. Even if the institution of secure property rights, governed by instruments of law, and enforced by the courts were indeed available but only for the minority elites, these institutions wouldn't be inclusive for society as a whole and hence would not create widespread and sustainable prosperity for all. Inclusive institutions must include the population at large in the process of governing in a predictable, transparent, and accountable manner, thereby reducing—if not eliminating—the process of exploitation by a few. Extractive institutions do the opposite: they extract incomes and wealth from many to benefit a few.

An institutional arrangement which will function effectively in an open-access society will not do so in a limited-access, particularistic society. If the institutions do not serve their ends, the elite will exercise their power to sabotage the workings of those institutions. A good example would be the limited success of many anti-corruption commissions set up by many countries. Even if the intentions of the governments setting them up are serious (and many are not), whether such anti-corruption bodies will be effective will depend on the power balance of the affected elites in that society. While such bodies worked very well in Hong Kong and Singapore, for example, they did not in many other places.

Institutions are context-specific and thus institutional arrangements must also be tailored to the specific circumstances of that context. Unbridled faith in transplanting best practices from elsewhere is unproductive. Designing appropriate institutional arrangements thus requires local knowledge, particularly of the local political power dynamics in that society.

How strong or weak the institutions are in a society has a decisive influence on the state of its governance and economic performance. But it is not economic institutions alone which matter. Political institutions are just as important. As a matter of fact, how the economic institutions evolve and perform in a society critically depends on the nature of political institutions and the distribution of political power in that society.

16.6 Three fellow travellers

A society's well-being is shaped and influenced by the three principal sets of institutions comprising it: the State, the markets, and the community. For an effective, prosperous, caring and just society to emerge, not only must each of these work well individually, but they must also do so together. It is as much a question of balance as it is of their individual performances. The essence of this balance is inclusive localism and active participation by the citizens at the community level. Each is needed to support but also check the excesses of the other two. Essentially then, in the journey from Here to Denmark, the three fellow travellers must walk in tandem. And just as every developing country is at a unique and distinct Here, so unique and distinct will their Denmark be. It is not a one-size-fits-all Denmark that we are after, but the three fellow travellers who moving in tandem will hopefully find their way to their own Denmarks, their own version of 'that heaven of freedom'.

16.7 Improving governance takes patience
and time

Historically, achieving sustainable improvements in governance has taken much trial and error, patience, and time, even centuries, and yes, luck as well as the experiences of many have shown.

Moving to an open-access society is a complex, and time-consuming process in the journey from Here to Denmark. Powerful vested interests who monopolize the levers of political and economic power under limited-access orders would naturally be unwilling to cede their powers too readily and would resist that for as long as possible.

In countries such as Denmark, the UK, and Japan, it took centuries to gradually create open-access societies. In some countries (such as France and the US), a revolution or a civil war was the trigger point. Even in their cases it took a long time before all their people (men and women, blacks, and whites) had equal rights under liberal democratic regimes.

On the other hand, in most emerging and developing countries liberation from colonial rule and the move to universal suffrage under some form of democracy came almost simultaneously during the 1950s and 1960s (Latin American countries have been independent much longer but many were military dictatorships even until the 1970s). As a result, almost all such countries now have the fundamental conditions in place to create open-access systems. It is now up to the citizens of each country to bring about the needed changes.

Creating formal inclusive institutions that fit local social conditions is challenging and takes time, as they require not only a close fit with local circumstances, but also much trial and error. Institutions also take time to mature. Finally, they must evolve as the economies develop and become more complex, as well as respond to technological changes. Changing the informal norms, habits, and behaviour of a society, to complement and reinforce the formal rules and laws enshrined in the formal institutional framework, is equally challenging and time consuming. Indeed, in most countries it would be the pace of these desired changes that would most likely determine the effectiveness of the overall institutional framework, and therefore the pace of the journey from Here to Denmark.

16.8 Hopeful signs from recent examples and lessons learnt

While, as noted above, institutional changes take time, some recent examples show that major progress can also be achieved over shorter periods under the right circumstances—over a few generations instead of several centuries. The examples of Korea and Botswana demonstrate that it is indeed possible, under some circumstances and with political will, to compress that time period significantly and achieve major improvements in a couple of decades. However, sustaining progress remains a constant challenge, even in the best of circumstances; backsliding is a risk that must always be watched.

The six countries studied in Part III of this book, divided by geography, politics, history, and culture, are each on a journey to a fairer, more equal, more just, and more developed state. Their challenges, circumstances, chances, and solutions are unique to their specific position in time and place. One success can't simply be replicated elsewhere. But there are some broad lessons to be learnt and ideas to be gleaned from their experiences as they travel on their individual paths to reach their Denmark.

A common thread in each case is the idea of balance. The State should be powerful enough to run the state, but must simultaneously allow for pluralism in running the affairs of the state and impose constraints on the Leviathan, as needed. The State should essentially be a 'Shackled Leviathan'. In each case, inclusive political and economic institutions emerged only when a centralized state ruled with authority but was also constrained by the citizens, who enjoyed space and voice to participate. The end of feudalism in Denmark and Great Britain, and land reforms in Japan and Korea, empowered the common citizen to gradually demand and obtain the right of voice. Uruguay expanded the space for peoples' voice in the country by accommodating a third national political party to break the stranglehold of the traditional two parties, who had dominated the political space for almost a century and a half. Recognition of property rights, building an accountable, meritocratic bureaucracy, and ensuring not only the rule of law but rule by law as well, were key milestones in each of the countries we studied.

Human capability formation is key to progress in the journey to Denmark. Japan's and Korea's significant and historic emphasis on education has been a major factor in their development.

The much-needed balance between the three travellers we have emphasized throughout needs active participation by the citizens in having adequate voice in running the affairs of the state. But meaningful participation would require an informed and empowered citizen, educated and healthy.

Social norms have a key role to play, for better or for worse, in how well (or not) institutions function in a society. As we noted earlier, while changing negative social norms is not easy, they are not immutable either. But that again needs to draw on an informed citizenry who will be able to challenge norms (buck the trend) and lead the way (be norm entrepreneurs).

Enlightened leadership matters. The remarkably long and consistent pace of reforms in Denmark for almost two hundred years was possible because successive monarchs built on the reform agenda of their predecessors, principally for better governance ... Emperor Meiji managed a social revolution in Japan while maintaining social cohesiveness. President Seretse Khama in Botswana was an inspirational leader who restored trust in society and established the much-needed credibility of the state. But a society cannot simply wait for the (fortunate) emergence of a good, enlightened leader. When they do, that can make a big difference and is a blessing, but a broad-based participation of the general population in the governance of society is key.

16.9 Peering into the future

While learning from the past is helpful, looking at the future is even more important.

We also recognize that it is obviously risky, if not foolhardy, to try to predict the future, especially on a matter as complex and multidimensional as governance. But given the importance of good governance to the future well-being of billions of people living in the emerging world today, it is still useful to peer into the future, based on what we have learned in earlier chapters of the book, combined with our prognostication of some relevant global megatrends that could have a fundamental impact on the long-term trajectory of governance worldwide.

The pace of change is accelerating in almost all aspects of life all over the world. Over the past seventy five years, almost all countries which were still under the yoke of colonization gained independence. People around the world are becoming more politically aware of their basic rights. Most of the young today know how to read and write. There has been very significant progress in poverty alleviation, which continues to this day (though there was a short interruption due to the covid19 pandemic). The rate of technological progress and breakthroughs is accelerating. Though much remains to be done, all these political, economic, and technological changes are in turn leading to faster societal changes (such as the increasing role of women, drops in population growth rates in most parts of the world, greater mobility of people, revulsion against corruption, more vocal calls for improved governance, rise of civic societies, etc.).

In most countries, **the fundamental conditions for better governance** have been put in place.

Billions of people, though not all, live under open democratic systems and have a voice in electing their leader. Clearly, the democratic regimes are still imperfect in many countries. But it is also true that local people and communities have a much greater say and freedom today to choose their political leaders at all levels and remove them from office than they did some decades back. While most countries cannot yet boast of having realized the open-access-order societies, which 'rely on competition, open access to organizations, and the rule of law to hold the society together', there is hope with democracy taking root around the world.

Many emerging countries have also established another critical building block for good governance in a remarkably short time, something which took Denmark and the UK so much longer (centuries). They have put in place, to varying degrees, formal institutions (constitutions that protect the basic rights and privileges of all, basic laws and rules, civil service, police, judiciaries, regulatory bodies, central banks, etc.) that, at least on paper, meet the definition of inclusive institutions.

In most countries, however the biggest challenge now is how to make these formal institutions more effective and, even more critically, how to change people's beliefs and behaviour so that informal societal rules complement what the formal rules and laws heroically proclaim.

Unlike past experiences in countries such as Denmark, UK, and Japan, future improvements in the emerging countries would most likely be driven from the bottom (by communities, the youth, and/or civic groups). There are two fundamental reasons for this. First, unlike Denmark, the UK, and pre-World War II Japan, countries today generally do not have any imperial power (an all-powerful king) to impose changes from the top. And second, future changes will be driven by the more energetic youth and grass-roots (community) groups motivated by existential causes (like climate change) and social ills (like corruption, inequality, gender, injustices), which they feel intensely passionate about.

16.9.1 Ten global megatrends

We believe that the above fundamental conditions, which have emerged over the last few decades around the world, will be shaped and driven by the ten following global trends (but which will obviously influence each country differently and at a different pace in each).

1. First, widespread growth of education of younger people, and their access to the Internet and social media. Indeed, compared to where their grandparents and even parents were (often under colonial rule) in the 1960s and 1970s, first mostly the boys, and then, gradually, the girls enrolled in schools in practically every emerging economy (with some exceptions in sub-Saharan Africa). Today, primary education is almost universal. While there is legitimate and much-needed debate about the quality of education and the actual learning outcomes, particularly in science and mathematics, it is fair to say that most young people today have the basic skills to read in their native language. With all emerging economies continuing to give high priority to education at least to secondary-school level, and with young people having ready access to news from around the world as well as the ability to communicate via social media, they will exert a powerful influence on the demand for improved governance, going forward.

2. Second, the ongoing explosion in the size of the middle (and upper middle) income group classes. One of the distinguishing features of the twenty-first century will be the emergence of a large—and in many countries even a dominant—middle class worldwide. 2022 marked a major historic milestone as a majority of the world population reached middle income or higher levels above. By 2060, the world will have been further transformed in terms of people's income levels and consumption, provided the world economy stays on its current course following a trend of the past several decades. By the 1960s, the vast majority of North Americans and Western Europeans had become middle-income earning, or higher, benefiting from the post-WWII economic recovery. This trans-Atlantic transformation was followed by Japan and the so-called newly industrializing countries (NICs) in Asia—South Korea, Taiwan, Hong Kong, and Singapore. In parallel, Latin America, historically the richest of the developing regions, also greatly increased the size of its population classified as middle-income. After the major economic reforms in China in the 1980s and in India in the 1990s, these two most populous countries in the world exhibited some of the highest economic growth rates in the world, their poverty rates fell sharply, and the size of their middle income groups started to grow rapidly. Finally, in Europe, the fall of the Berlin Wall led to the economic revival of most emerging economies in Eastern Europe (after a lag of a few years), boosting incomes and middle-income population.

All these developments combined have brought the world to a stage today when it appears to be on the cusp of another major transformation. By 2060, by some estimates, 80 per cent of the world population would be classified as middle-income or higher.[1] By then, about four billion more people would have joined this group, almost exclusively in the emerging economies. In addition to the current three developed regions (North America, Europe, and Oceania), East Asia too will have almost all its population in the ranks of middle-income or higher (when measured by current international standards). Past experiences in many countries suggest that these large emerging middle-income groups could play a very positive role by demanding greater transparency and accountability from their governments and other institutions in both private and public sectors.

3. Third, the coming surge in urbanization mostly in Asia and Africa. The majority of the world's population (4.36 billion or 56 per cent) lives in urban areas today. Greater economic development in the emerging

economies has been accompanied by an acceleration in rural–urban migration, particularly in Asia. In terms of urbanization, some emerging economies already exhibit characteristics similar to those of the advanced economies. For example, Latin America is now the most urbanized region of the world, after Europe and North America, followed by the Middle East and East Asia. South Asia and sub-Saharan Africa are still mostly rural. By some estimates, global urban population would rise to 7.25 billion (72 per cent of the total) by 2060. For all emerging economies, particularly for countries in sub-Saharan Africa and South Asia, challenges involved in urban management will be exacerbated. Agglomeration of larger numbers of restless people in urban centres would be another powerful force for improvements in governance at all levels.

4. **Fourth, rising inequalities within countries.** While inter-country inequalities have gradually been decreasing in recent decades owing to the higher per capita GDP growth of emerging economies relative to the advanced economies, intra-country inequalities have widened. From the perspective of the average citizen of a country, these intra-country disparities in income (urban–rural, regional, by ethnic group, by gender) are more relevant. Such intra (within) country inequalities are already a major political issue and will become even more pronounced in the coming years Reducing (if not eliminating) them will require sustained policy and institutional actions at individual country level. They cannot be ignored any more. Beyond the issues of income inequities at the national level is the much more vexing issue of broader social disparities in most emerging economies There are very wide disparities faced by citizens within countries in getting access to basic public services such as education, health care, clean water, sanitation, transportation, and public safety. As in the case of income inequities, these disparities in access to social services vary by region, ethnic group, gender, and so on. Again, they can be remedied only by actions at national levels. People, including civic groups, will demand action from national political leaders. Such demands will act as a powerful force to improve governance.

5. **Fifth, climate change.** This is an existential challenge the world faces over the medium to long term. This megatrend also has fundamental implications for governance at all levels—local, national, as well as global. The Sixth Intergovernmental Panel on Climate Change (IPCC) report, released by the UN in August 2021,[2] warned that our planet is already on

a trajectory to warm by 1.5 degrees Celsius by 2040. In that scenario, almost every human being is likely to be adversely affected by more frequent extreme weather events, including heavy floods, droughts, and melting of glaciers. Overall, the emerging economies and within them the poorest segments of societies, will be hurt the most. They will face a diverse set of environmental issues, including extreme flooding due to rising seas, heavy rainfall, and storm surges from typhoons. These changes in weather patterns have fundamental implications for billions of people as to where and how they will live. A rise in global temperature of two degrees Celsius (a question of when and not if) is projected to lead to a rise in sea levels of fifty to 100 centimetres, directly impacting between 190 and 480 million people currently living in affected areas. In Asia alone, many cities in which millions of people live will be almost entirely submerged. Similarly, millions in sub-Saharan Africa will have to abandon their current homes as droughts choke off their supply of water. Such developments will result in perhaps hundreds of millions of environmental refugees worldwide. Additionally, the ongoing changes in climate could have a major adverse impact on agriculture and food production as well as rural employment. Further, over the longer term as glaciers melt (e.g. in the Himalayas), even agricultural production on irrigated lands would suffer as water-flows in rivers begin to ebb. A recent study[3] concluded that at least 85 per cent of the world's population and 80 per cent of the world's land area has already been affected by human-induced climate change. It is clearly in the interest of everyone—in advanced countries as well as the emerging ones—to work together to mitigate and adapt to climate change by taking actions at local, national, regional, and global levels. The coming decades will be the ultimate test of the ability and willingness of the global community—governments, businesses, local communities, civic societies, as well as international institutional institutions—to act together to preserve the planet for future generations. As was evident at the COP26 and COP27 summits, grass-roots civic groups could successfully exert a powerful influence on national political leaders to be more forthcoming in pursuit of their commitments on Net Zero targets. Such grass-roots pressures are likely to increase in the future to improve related governance aspects at local, national, and global levels.

   6. Sixth, the accelerating pace of technological progress. This would also simultaneously accelerate the demand for and hopefully the pace

of improvements in governance in many societies by complementing other conducive conditions fermenting therein. New scientific discoveries are leading to technological breakthroughs that have the potential to help the world tackle current and future global challenges such as climate change, pandemics, inequality, and to promote inclusive growth. They—including the so-called breakthrough technologies—will be key to pushing the global productivity frontier further during the coming decades, and hopefully reverse the recent trend of sagging productivity growth in most economies.

During our lifetime, massive breakthroughs in information technology—including computing power—have already revolutionized the use of computers in the daily lives of people and in businesses. So far, every eighteen months, technical progress has doubled the speed of microprocessors. Simultaneously, costs have come down dramatically. The buzzwords in the computer world are smaller, faster, cheaper, pipelined, super-scalar and parallel. Laboratories around the world are busy exploring novel technologies that may one day herald the arrival of a new generation of computers and microelectronic devices. Quantum techniques, which capitalize on the non-classical behaviour of the devices, are being rapidly developed. Other scientists are actively pursuing non-silicon routes by developing data-storage systems that can potentially use photonically activated biomolecules. Yet others are exploring nano-mechanical logic gaps. Future developments in information technology offer exciting potential benefits. These in turn will help improve all aspects of governance, including effectiveness and efficiency, transparency, and accountability of all three sets of institutions: the state, markets, and community.

Technological developments, particularly over the past few decades, show that the potential impact of technology—particularly public sector digital infrastructure—on governance will be significant. India provides an encouraging case study of such a phenomenon. Commonly referred to as 'India Stack', the country has developed a well-functioning public sector digital infrastructure in recent years which has dramatically enhanced financial inclusion and improved governance. Building on a country wide unique digital identity system, Aadhaar (which means foundation), a significantly large proportion of the country's households (including the poor) have been able to open even zero balance Bank accounts. This in turn has enabled a remarkably robust United Payments Interface (UPI) to take root which is widely used from the street hawker to transact her daily business to the government to transfer any government sponsored benefits directly to her bank account. Needless to say, the leakages in such transfer payments were significant and cause of much grief in the past which are now gradually reducing.

Use of AI (artificial intelligence) and data analytics enable governments to leverage their limited resources to improve public service delivery. In India, for example again, use of such digital tools has allowed the government to introduce faceless income tax assessments which not only makes the process more efficient but also significantly reduces the scope for bribes and harassment by corrupt officials.

7. **Seventh, Information sharing and Communications Revolution.** A critically important ongoing revolution in our lifetimes involves information-sharing that could further empower people, combined with other megatrends highlighted above, to demand and realize changes in governance. Satellites, television, mobile telephony, and the Internet—leveraged by new social media—have already revolutionized the way in which information is shared within and across national boundaries. Emergence of the World Wide Web, the rapid rise of new global business giants like Google, Apple, Facebook, and Twitter have further transformed information-sharing. The latest examples of how the communication revolution can be harnessed to deliver superior, or even totally new, products and services to the consumers are the likes of Uber, YouTube, Netflix, Instagram and TikTok. Many more will certainly emerge in future.

The International Telecommunications Union estimated that in 2020 some 85 per cent of people in the world had access to mobile Internet. By 2060, practically all Internet connections could be through mobile devices. The mobile world will be omnipresent by 2060, including to most new Internet users and billions of consumers in today's emerging economies. A few years ago, digital communications were primarily the preserve of advanced countries. In the past ten years this revolution has spread to emerging economies. Just twenty years ago, only three of every 1,000 in India had access to a telephone (mainly fixed lines). In 2021, India had over 1.1 billion mobile-phone connections, or over eight out of every ten. This communications revolution is fast spreading throughout the developing world, including Africa. Similarly, Internet penetration is beginning to explode; introduction of low-cost Internet services via satellite to remote areas (including in Africa) could be a major game-changer. The pace of change of this communication revolution will only accelerate. The fast spread of information and communication technologies around the world continues, connecting people globally and making them aware of how people live and are governed elsewhere.

Instant and universal communications and access to information are a powerful social force, for better and for worse. Events in Egypt and Tunisia about a decade ago, as well as the dramatic rise of Daeshin the Middle East and Africa earlier this century have demonstrated the power of the communications revolution in even more traditional societies and politics. However, while the immense power of the unfolding communications revolution can facilitate human progress, it can also be misused to disrupt communities, sow discord and even disturb national and global peace and harmony. Societies need to be keenly aware of such potential downsides and proactively take measures to counter them.

8. Eighth, emergence of civic society as an agent of empowerment of the community. Though not always readily apparent given the recent onslaughts and crackdowns on civic society in many places around the world, a significant positive development of the past decades has in fact been the emergence of civic society. It has become a major voice of ordinary citizens and an important force in public affairs in many countries. The reach of the Internet and the ability to amplify one's voice outside of physically limited areas has allowed a new wave of activism and engagement to take root around the world. This new global and interconnected civic society has taken many shapes in recent years, ranging from Western 'Slacktivism' to the revolutions of the Arab Spring, to the emergence of undesirable extremist groups in many countries. As technology progresses, the barriers to entry to engage with these other citizens—and civic society as a whole—will continue to decrease. The rise of civic groups worldwide, and their protests against corruption and poor governance will inevitably lead to widespread demands for greater accountability. Powerful elites who had managed to monopolize power in the past will find it increasingly difficult, if not impossible, to hold back change. As a result, in future changes are likely to come faster than was the case in the past.

9. Ninth, accelerated spread of social media. A major global phenomenon of the past two decades is the phenomenal spread of social media which can only be expected to accelerate even further. It is rapidly becoming a major force both for peer-to-peer communications and for social activism. The explosion in the use of social media in the past decade or so has been driven by four factors. First, wide availability of (lower-cost) mobile connectivity—including in rural areas—not just in advanced countries, but also in most emerging economies. Second, almost universal use of mobile phones. Third, the continuing growing diaspora of populations in urban centres seeking to retain some connection with their communities. And fourth, availability of multiple, easy-to-use, newer platforms such as WhatsApp, WeChat, Signal, TikTok, Telegram, and so on, in addition to the more mature platforms such as Facebook, Twitter, and YouTube. The result is billions of messages being exchanged daily amongst millions of chat groups. While most are for sharing personal information, many are also actively used to discuss social and political issues, and how to organize to influence policies at the national or even global level. Social media's influence is likely to increase exponentially over time and it could potentially become an even more powerful force in improving governance, both domestic and global This explosive use of social media, allowing average citizens to communicate with each other with minimum risk of censorship and organize could be a powerful tool in forcing people in power to listen to average citizens. All these developments again strongly reinforce the above eight megatrends, suggesting that societies may see improvements in governance occurring much faster in the future than they have in the past. However, such excitement over the upside potential of social media in improving governance must also be tempered by potential downsides recognizing, as noted earlier, its ability to spread false information, undercut the rule of law, sow discords and polarize society.

10. And finally, Tenth, Rise of the Emerging Economies. During the next forty years, further major transformation of the global economy is anticipated that gives hope for an acceleration in social and political reforms in the emerging economies. This coming transformation will lead to major shifts in the structure and size of the global economy, as the world economy potentially triples in size. According to some recent estimates, by 2060, the absolute size of the global economy could reach

US\$409 trillion (in 2018 prices) in PPP terms and \$276 trillion in market-exchange[4] terms, compared to \$128 trillion and \$82 trillion, respectively, in 2020. Average global per capita income could reach \$41,000 in PPP terms and \$28,700 in market-exchange rates, compared to \$16,600 and \$12,200, respectively, today. As a result, the world would be much more prosperous then than it is today. By 2060, 54 per cent of the global population in as many as eighty-five countries would have income levels equal to or higher than those enjoyed by an average citizen in southern Europe (Greece, Italy, Spain, and Portugal) in 2020. Almost all people in four regions of the world—North America, Europe (including developing Europe), Oceania, and East Asia—would be either middle- or upper-income by today's standards. Given the strong strides being made by East Asia, the current distinction between that region and advanced countries is likely to diminish. Given such a scenario—and leaving aside the cause-and-effect issue of incomes on demand for good governance debated earlier in this book—the demand for better governance and stronger and more inclusive institutions can only be expected to grow.

16.10   From Here to Denmark

The combination of the existence of the basic foundations necessary for good governance established in most emerging countries in the past fifty years or so, with the forces being unleashed by the ten global megatrends summarized above, suggests that demands from people at large for better governance is likely to increase in most societies in the coming decades, perhaps even explosively in some cases. This will in turn will reinforce demand for better, stronger institutions. While many factors influence the evolution of institutions, and they will vary from country to country, enhanced human capital through improved education and health, will continue to be key for all. This will empower citizens to exercise greater human agency and enable them to participate more effectively and extensively in decisions and activities critical for their well-being.

Given our observations above about the achievements of the past several decades and the global mega trends, we are hopeful that faster progress from Here to Denmark is plausible. At the same time, we recognize that such breakthroughs are by no means preordained. Nor should such changes be expected to occur in most countries quickly, given the complex and multidimensioned nature of changes required in societies to achieve sustainable improvements in governance.

While striving for steady improvements in governance and the continuous hard work that goes with institution building, countries should be ready to take advantage of 'black swan' events. When unexpected opportunities arise, national and community leaders can make a huge difference, as exemplified by country cases cited in this book. Changes can happen in non-linear ways. Such opportunities, combined with enlightened leadership, led to non-linear changes in countries as diverse as Denmark, Japan, Botswana, and South Korea in the past, and there is no reason why they can't happen in the future in other places.

Undoubtedly, the journey from Here to Denmark will neither be easy nor quick. Given each country's distinct political and social milieu, and its own historical experiences, each will have to find its own way. There is no easy blueprint. But history also tells us that the arc of the journey does bend towards Denmark, and we end this book with the hope that each country will indeed, paraphrasing Tagore, 'awake into that heaven of freedom ... where the mind is without fear and the head is held high'.

Key messages of the book

1. *The journey from Here to Denmark is essentially a journey seeking good governance for all.*
2. *This in turn needs robust, inclusive economic and political institutions—both formal and informal—in the country.*
3. *Each country has to develop its institutions in its own unique way to achieve good governance. They cannot be transplanted from elsewhere.*
4. *In the past seventy-five years, most emerging market economies have made impressive economic and social progress, and put formal institutions in place.*
5. *The key challenges now are to: change peoples' behaviors, build public trust, and develop informal institutions (to complement the formal ones) so crucial for better governance.*
6. *Enhanced human capital through improved education and health will also be crucial to empower citizens to exercise greater human agency and enable them to participate more effectively in decisions critical for their well-being.*
7. *The ten megatrends outlined in the book give hope that many countries will be able reach Denmark sooner than was conceivable by their ancestors a century ago.*
8. *History tells us that the arc of the journey bends towards Denmark.*

Notes

Chapter 1

1. Daron Acemoğlu, Simon Johnson, and James Robinson (2005) 'Institutions as a Fundamental Cause of Long Run Growth' in *Handbook of Economic Growth Volume 1A* (edited by Philippe Aghion and Steven Durlauf), Elsevier BV, 2005, 400.
2. Jeffrey Sachs (2001) Tropical Underdevelopment. *Working Paper 8119, National Bureau of Economic Research, USA*, February 2001, 15.
3. Ibid., 18.
4. World Health Organization (2020) *World Malaria Report 2020* (Geneva: WHO).
5. Abhijit V. Banerjee and Esther Duflo (2020) 'How Poverty Ends: The Many Paths to Progress and Why They Might Not Continue', *Foreign Affairs*, January/February.
6. William Easterly (2002) *The Elusive Quest for Growth: Economists' Adventures and Misadventures in the Tropics* (Cambridge, MA: The MIT Press).
7. R. Rajan (2019) *The Third Pillar: How Markets and the State Leave the Community Behind* (India: Harper Collins).

Chapter 2

1. Centennial Group (2021). In-house Growth Model, Unpublished.
2. www.oxfam.org/en/press-releases/vaccine-monopolies-make-cost-vaccinating-world-against-covid-least-5-times-more
3. Centennial Group (2021).
4. Kohli, H., Nag, R., & Vilkelyte, I., (eds) (2022). Envisioning *2060: Opportunities and Risks for Emerging Markets* (India: Penguin Random House) p. 36–37.
5. Ibid., 36.
6. Within a range of annual per capita income of $ 4,595–$ 41,345 (constant 2018 PPP US$).
7. International Panel on Climate Change (IPCC), 2021.
8. Eckstein, Kunzel, and Schafer (2021).
9. Tridimas (2011).
10. Muhlberger (1998).
11. Herre, Ortiz-Ospena, and Roser (2013).
12. Luhrmann, Tannberg, and Lindberg (2018).

Closed autocracy: citizens do not have the right to choose either the chief executive of the government or the legislature through multi-party elections

Electoral autocracy: citizens have the right to choose the chief executive and the legislature through multi-party elections; but they lack some freedoms, such as the freedoms of association or expression that make the elections meaningful, free, and fair

Electoral democracy: citizens have the right to choose the chief executive and the legislature in meaningful, free and fair, and multi-party elections

Liberal democracy: electoral democracy and citizens enjoy individual and minority rights, are equal before the law, and the actions of the executive are constrained by the legislative and the courts

13. Herre, Ortiz-Ospena, and Roser (2013).
14. World Justice Project (2019). Global Insights on Access to Justice—Findings from the World Justice Project General Population Poll in 101 Countries, https://worldjusticeproject.org/sites/default/files/documents/WJP-A2J-2019.pdf

Chapter 3

1. D. Narayan et al (2000) *Voices of the Poor: Can Anyone Hear Us?* (Oxford: Oxford University Press), 3.
2. World Development Report, (2017), 43.
3. A. Sen (2009) *The Idea of Justice* (New York: Allen Lanexxx), 21–2.
4. A. Sen (1999) *Development as Freedom* (New York: Anchor Books), 37.
5. W. Easterly (2013) *The Tyranny of Experts: Economists, Dictators, and the Forgotten Rights of the Poor.* (New York: Basic Books), 340
6. WDR, (2017), 43.
7. A. Cárcaba et al. (2017) 'How Does Good Governance Relate to Quality of Life?', *Sustainability*, 9 (631), 1.
8. M. G. Quibria (2014) 'Governance and Developing Asia: Concepts, Measurements, Determinants, and Paradoxes'. *ADB Economics Working Papers Series No. 388*, March 2014.
9. Quibria, (2014), 3.
10. F. Fukuyama (2013) 'What is Governance?'Center for Global Development, Working Paper 314, (Washington, D.C) , 4.
11. Quibria, (2014), 3.
12. Asian Development Bank (1995), Governance: Sound Development Management (ADB), 8.
13. Asian Development Bank, (1995), 10.
14. Ibid.
15. Asian Development Bank, (1995), 8.

16. D. Kaufmann and A. Kraay (2008) 'Governance Indicators: Where Are We, Where Should We Be Going?', *The World Bank Research Observer*, 23 (1), 4.

17. Global Corruption Barometer (2019) Africa, 10th edition, July.

18. Global Corruption Barometer, (2019), 9.

19. There were some disturbing allegations in September 2021 of the World Bank having succumbed to pressures from China and Saudi Arabia to alter their rankings on this indicator. In response, the World Bank decided to suspend the future preparation of the *Doing Business* indicators (DBIs). While the WB's very open investigation of these serious allegations and prompt response are very praiseworthy, suspending the publication of these indicators is perhaps an over-reaction, akin to throwing the baby out with the bathwater. The DBI serves a very useful purpose, and we understand that that the WB is looking at ways to enhance the integrity of the process and resume the publication of these indicators.

20. Quibria, (2014), 5.

21. Kaufmann and Kraay, (2008), 10.

22. Or indeed, could there be other factors which could lead to countries being richer and also enjoying better governance? Per capita incomes across the world were not very different about 200 years back. They are widely different now., The prime reason for this difference is that the richer countries grew much faster than the poorer ones for most of the past two centuries, with a reversal of the growth rates in favour of the emerging and developing countries in the past three decades. And a large portion of this differential can be explained by deep historical differences in institutional quality, tracing back to colonial origins, among others. A very rich body of academic work over the past three decades '[has] identified the powerful effects of initial institutional quality on growth in the very long run' (Kaufmann, D. 2003. *Governance Redux: The Empirical Challenge*. MPRA Paper 8210, University Library of Munich, Germany, p. 12).

23. Ibid.

24. D. Kaufmann and A. Kraay (2002) 'Growth Without Governance'. *Policy Research Working Paper 2928* (World Bank Institute and Development Research Group).

25. D. Kaufmann, A. Kraay, and P. Zoido-Lobaton (1999) *Governance Matters* (Washington, DC: The World Bank), 12.

26. Kaufmann et al., (1999), 15.

27. A. Banerjee. and E. Duflo (2019) *Good Economics for Hard Times* (New Delhi: Juggernaut Books), 205.

28. Kaufmann et al., (1999), 17.

29. D. Acemoğlu and J. Robinson (2012) *Why Nations Fail: The Origins of Power, Prosperity, and Poverty* (New York: Crown).

30. G. Ofer (1988) 'Soviet Economic Growth: 1928–1985' (Los Angeles, CA: RAND/UCLA, Center for the Study of Soviet International Behaviour).

31. M. G. Quibria (2006) 'Does Governance Matter? Yes, No or Maybe: Some Evidence from Developing Asia', *Kyklos*, 59 (1), 99–114.

32. World Bank: https://data.worldbank.org/indicator

33. S. Devarajan (2008), 'Two Comments on "Governance Indicators: Where Are We, Where Should We Be Going?" by Daniel Kaufmann and Aart Kraay', *World Bank Research Observer* 23, 3–34.

34. Quibria, (2014), 30.

Chapter 4

1. BBC (2010) Report on UN International Anti Corruption Day December 9, 2010 http://news.bbc.co.uk/2/shared/bsp/hi/pdfs/09_12_10_world_speaks.pdf.Accessed July 26, 2019.

2. B. Buchan and Lisa Hill (2014) *An Intellectual History of Political Corruption* (UK: Palgrave Macmillan).

3. Laura Underkuffler (2009) 'Defining Corruption: Implications for Action' in Robert Rotberg, ed., *Corruption, Global Security, and World Order* (Washington, DC: Brookings).

4. https://johnsonsdictionaryonline.com/views/search.php?term=corruption. Accessed 2 May 2023.

5. Concise Oxford Dictionary, 10th edition, 1999.

6. R. Rotberg (2017) *The Corruption Cure: How Citizens and Leaders can Combat Graft* Princeton, NJ and Oxford: Princeton University Press), 19.

7. Henk Brasz (1978) 'The Sociology of Corruption' in Arnold J. Heidenheimer (ed.), *Political Corruption: Readings in Comparative Analysis* (New York: Holt, Rinehart, and Winston), 42.

8. Michael Johnston (2006) 'From Thucydides to Mayor Daley: Bad Politics and a Culture of Corruption?' *PS: Political Science and Politics,* 39, 4, 810. JSTOR, www.jstor.org/stable/20451822.

9. J. Patrick Dobel (1978) 'The Corruption of a State'. *American Political Science Review,* 72, 3, 958.

10. Richard Mulgan (2012) 'Aristotle on Legality and Corruption' in Manuhuia Barcham, Barry Hindess, and Peter Larmour, eds, *Corruption: Expanding the Focus* (Australia: ANU Press), 25.

11. J. S. Nye (1967) 'Corruption and Political Development: A Cost-Benefit Analysis', *The American Political Science Review,* 61, 2 (June). American Political Science Association, 417–27. www.jstor.org/stable/1953254

12. Ibid.

13. R. Klitgaard (1988) *Controlling Corruption.* (Berkeley, CA: University of California Press), 24.

14. Pranab Bardhan (1997) 'Corruption and Development: A Review of Issues', *Journal of Economic Literature,* 35, 3, 1320–46, 1321

15. Ibid.

16. John T. Noonan Jr. (1984) *Bribes: The Intellectual History of a Moral Idea* (New York: Macmillan), 702–3.

17. Robert Klitgaard (2017) 'What Do We Talk About When We Talk About Corruption?' *Working Paper LKYSPP-17-17* (Lee Kuan Yew School of Public Policy, August), p. 5.

18. Syed Hussain Alatas (2015) *The Problem of Corruption* (First published in 1968 as *The Sociology of Corruption*, Singapore: Donald Moore Press). Rev. edition. (Selangor, Malaysia: The Other Press), 95–6.

19. Ibid., 20–2.

20. A. Banerjee, S. Mullainathan, and R. Hanna (2012) 'Corruption', NBER *Working Paper 17968*, April (NBER, Cambridge, MA), 7.

21. Ibid.

22. Rotberg (2017), 1.

23. Hyperides, *Against Demosthenes*, , Fragment 3. www.perseus.tufts.edu/hop per/text?doc=Perseus%3Atext%3A1999.01.0140%3Aspeech%3D5%3Afragm ent%3D3

24. Hyperides, *Against Demosthenes*, Fragment 9. www.perseus.tufts.edu/hop per/text?doc=Perseus%3Atext%3A1999.01.0140%3Aspeech%3D5%3Afragm ent%3D9

25. Kautilya (2016) *The Arthashastra*, Edited, rearranged, translated, and introduced by L. N. Rangarajan (India: Penguin Random House), 2.9–36.

26. Kautilya (2016), 2.8.4–19, 21.

27. Lewis, Naphtali (1954) 'On Official Corruption in Roman Egypt: The Edict of Vergilius Capito', *Proceedings of the American Philosophical Society,* 98, 2 (15 April), 153–8. www.jstor.org/stable/3143647, p. 153.

28. John T. Noonan, Jr. (1984) *Bribes: The Intellectual History of a Moral Idea* (New York: Macmillan).

29. See, for example, Dev Kar and Sarah Freitas (2011) *Illicit Financial Flows from Developing Countries Over the Decade Ending 2009* (Global Financial Integrity).

30. Nicholas Ambraseys and Roger Bilham (2011) 'Corruption Kills' *Nature* 469, (7329), 153; DOI: 10.1038/469153a

31. Ibid.

32. A. Mungiu-Pippidi and Till Hartmann (2019) 'Corruption and Development: An Overview' in *Oxford Research Encyclopedia of Economics and Finance* (Oxford: Oxford University Press), http://dx.doi.org/10.1093/acrefore/9780190625979.013.237.

33. E. Shils (1960) 'Political Development in the New States', *Comparative Studies in Society and History,* 2, 3, April, 265–92. Published online 2009, Cambridge University Press, p. 271. DOI:10.1017/S0010417500000724.

34. N. H. Leff (1964) 'Economic Development through Bureaucratic Corruption', *American Behavioural Scientist*, 8, 3, 8–14; p. 11. https://doi.org/10.1177/0002764 26400800303

35. Colin Leys (1965) 'What is the Problem about Corruption?' *The Journal of Modern African Studies*, 3, 2 (August), 215–30. www.jstor.org/stable/158703

36. Nye (1967).

37. S. P. Huntington (1968) *Political Order in Changing Societies.* (New Haven, CT: Yale University Press), 386.

38. *The Telegraph* (2019) 6 December; www.telegraph.co.uk.

39. *The New York Times* Archives (1992) 30 August, Section 1, p. 14.

40. Asian Development Bank (1995) *Governance: Sound Development Management* (ADB).

41. https://documents.worldbank.org/en/publication/documents-reports/documentdetail/135801467993234363/people-and-development-annual-meetings-address-by-james-d-wolfensohn-president. Accessed 2 May 2023.

42. Transparency International, www.transparency.org/en. Accessed 22 September 2020.

43. Pranab Bardhan (1997) 'Corruption and Development: A Review of Issues', *Journal of Economic Literature,* 35, 3, 1320–46, p. 1323.

44. Gunnar Myrdal (1968) *Asian Drama, Vol. II* (New York: Random House).

45. Abhijit Banerjee (1997) 'A Theory of Misgovernance', *The Quarterly Journal of Economics*, 112, 4, 1289–1332November.

46. D. Kaufmann and Shang-Jin Wei (2000) 'Does "Grease Money" Speed Up the Wheels of Commerce?' *IMF Working Paper WP/00/64*, March 2000.

47. Andrei Shliefer and Robert Vishny (1993) 'Corruption', *The Quarterly Journal of Economics*, August, 599–617.

48. Pierre Landell-Mills (2013) 'Citizens Against Corruption', Partnership for Transparency Fund, 13.

49. Paolo Mauro (1995) 'Corruption and Growth', *The Quarterly Journal of Economics*, 110, 3, August, 681–712.

50. Kevin Murphy, Andrei Shleifer, and Robert Vishny (1993) 'Why is Rent Seeking so costly to Growth?' *AEA Papers and Proceedings* 83(2) (May), 409–14.

51. Ibid., 409.

52. Murphy, Shliefer, Vishny, (1993), 612.

53. Murphy, Shleifer, Vishny, (1993), 409.

54. Hongyi Li, Lixin Xu, and Heng-Fu Zou (2000) 'Corruption, Income Distribution, and Growth', *China Economics and Management Academy (CEMA), Central University of Finance and Economics Working Paper 472*, 18. Subsequently published in *Economics and Politics*, 12(2), July.

55. Ibid., 8.

56. Sanjeev Gupta, Hamid Davoodi, and Rosa Alonso-Terme (2002) 'Does Corruption Affect Income Inequality and Poverty?' *Economics of Governance*, 3, 23–45, p. 40.

57. Asian Development Bank (2012) 'Chapter 2: Rising Inequality Concerns in Asia', *Asian Development Outlook*, 41.

58. R. Nag (2017) *The 21st Century: Asia's?* (India: Sage Publications), 18.

59. Vito Tanzi and Hamid Davoodi (1997) 'Corruption, Public Investment and Growth'. *IMF Working Paper WP/97/139*.

60. International Monetary Fund (2015) 'Current Challenges in Revenue Mobilization: Improving Tax Compliance'. *IMF Staff Report*, Washington, DC, April, 17.

61. Ramnath Subbaraman et al. (2013) 'The Social Ecology of Water in a Mumbai Slum: Failures in Water Quality, Quantity, and Reliability', *BMC Public Health*, 13, 173, 7–9.

62. Transparency International (2017b) 'People and Corruption: Citizens' Voices from Around the World'. *Global Corruption Barometer*, 7.

63. Transparency International (2017a) *Corruption in Service Delivery Topic Guide*. Compiled by the Anti-Corruption Desk, TI.

64. Kaushik Basu (2011) 'Corruption and Bribery-Summary' (April) "Why, for a Class of Bribes, the Act of Giving a Bribe Should be Treated as Legal?' Published in Ministry of Finance Government of India, *Working Paper 1/2011-DEA*, March.

65. Rotberg, (2017), 51.

66. Transparency International (2019) *Corruption Perception Index* www. transparency.org/en/cpi. Accessed 17 September 2020.

67. *World Justice Project* (2020) Website: www.worldjusticeproject.org. Accessed 17 September 2020.

68. Daniel Kaufmann, Aart Kraay, and Massimo Mastruzzi (2010) 'The Worldwide Governance Indicators: Methodology and Analytical Issues'. *Policy Research Working Paper 5430* (World Bank, September), 3.

69. Ibid., 20.

70. Daniel Kaufmann and Aart Kraay (2008) 'Governance Indicators: Where Are We? Where Should We Be Going?' *The World Bank Research Observer*, 23 (1), 1–30, pp. 18–19.

71. Ibid., 20.

72. Robert Klitgaard (2017) 'What Do We Talk About When We Talk About Corruption?' *Working Paper LKYSPP-17-17* (Lee Kuan Yew School of Public Policy, August), 10.

73. Transparency International (2017a).

74. Bo Rothstein and Jan Teorell (2008) 'What Is Quality of Government? A Theory of Impartial Government Institutions' *Governance*, 21, 2, 165–190.

75. Laarni Escresa and Lucio Picci (2015) 'A New Cross-National Measure of Corruption'. *Policy Research Working Paper No. 7371* (World Bank, Washington, DC, July).

76. A. Mungiu-Pippidi and Ramin Dadasov (2016) 'Measuring Control of Corruption by a New Index of Public Integrity', *European Journal of Criminal Policy and Research*, 22, 1–28.

77. Transparency International, CPI Website, (2019). www.transparency.org/en/cpi. Accessed 17 September 2020.

Chapter 5

1. Alfred Marshall (1920) *Principles of Economics*, 8th edition (London: Macmillan), 158.
2. Erik G. Furubotn and Rudolf Richter (2005) *Institutions and Economic Theory*, 2nd edition (Ann Arbor, MI: The University of Michigan Press), 1.
3. Ronald H. Coase (1937) 'The Nature of the Firm', *Economica* 4, 386–405.
4. Armen Alchian (1965a) 'The Basis of Some Recent Advances in the Theory of Management of the Firm', *The Journal of Industrial Economics* 14, 1 (November), 30–41. JSTOR, https://doi.org/10.2307/2097649. Accessed 18 Feb. 2023.
5. Armen Alchian (1965b) 'Some Economics of Property Rights', *Il Politico*, 30, 4 (December), 816–29.
6. Douglass C. North (1981) *Structure and Change in Economic History* (New York and London: Norton).
7. Douglass C. North (1990) *Institutions, Institutional Change, and Economic Performance* (Cambridge: Cambridge University Press).
8. Douglass C. North (1993) 'Institutions and Credible Commitment', *Journal of Institutional and Theoretical Economics*, 149, 11–23.
9. Oliver E. Williamson (1979) 'Transaction-Cost Economics: The Governance of Contractual Relations', *Journal of Law and Economics* 22, 233–61.
10. Oliver E. Williamson (1991) 'Economic Institutions: Spontaneous and Intentional Governance', *Journal of Law, Economics, and Organization* 7, 159–87. JSTOR, www.jstor.org/stable/764962. Accessed 18 Feb. 2023.
11. Gary D. Libecap (1989) *Contracting for Property Rights* (Cambridge: Cambridge University Press).
12. Thrainn Eggertsson (1998) 'Limits to Institutional Reforms', *Scandinavian Journal of Economics* 100, 335–57. JSTOR, www.jstor.org/stable/3440782. Accessed 18 Feb. 2023.
13. Thrainn Eggertsson (2005) *Imperfect Institutions: Possibilities and Limits of Reform* (Ann Arbor, MI: University of Michigan Press).
14. Furubotn and Richter, (2005).
15. Ronald H. Coase (1984) 'The New Institutional Economics', *Journal of Institutional and Theoretical Economics*, 140, 229–31.
16. Douglass C. North (1994) 'Economic Performance Through Time', *American Economic Review*, June, 359. This article is North's Nobel Prize Lecture, delivered in Stockholm, Sweden on 9 December 1993.)
17. Ibid.
18. Douglass C. North and Robert Paul Thomas (2009) *The Rise of the Western World: A New Economic History* (Cambridge University Press, [1st edn1973], 23rd Printing), 1.
19. Ibid.
20. Kenneth Arrow (1970) *Essays in the Theory of Risk-Bearing* (Amsterdam: North Holland), 200.

21. Douglass C. North (1990) *Institutions, Institutional Change, and Economic Performance* (Cambridge: Cambridge University Press), 3.
22. Ibid.
23. Adam Smith (1776) *The Wealth of Nations* (1902 edition, New York: P. F. Collier & Son), Chapter III, 502 (Kindle).
24. Elinor Ostrom (1990) *Governing the Commons: The Evolution of Institutions for Collective Action* (Cambridge: Cambridge University Press), 51.
25. Ibid.
26. North, (1990), 4.
27. North, (1994), 361.
28. Ibid.
29. World Development Report (WDR), (2017), 5.
30. Dani Rodrik, Arvind Subramanian, and Francesco Trebbi (2002) 'Institutions Rule: The Primacy of Institutions over Geography and Integration in Economic Development' *National Bureau of Economic Research, Working Paper 9305, DOI 10.3386/w9305*, November, 1.
31. Daron Acemoğlu and James Robinson (2012) *Why Nations Fail: The Origins of Power, Prosperity, and Poverty* (New York: Crown).
32. Pranab Bardhan (2005) 'Institutions Matter, But Which Ones?' *Economics of Transition* 13 (3), 499–532, pp. 499–500.
33. Ibid.
34. Daron Acemoğlu and James Robinson (2008) 'The Role of Institutions in Growth and Development', *Commission on Growth and Development Working Paper No. 10.* (Washington, DC: World Bank).*https://openknowledge.worldbank.org/han dle/10986/28045*, p. v.
35. Bibek Debroy (2000) *In the Dock: Absurdities of Indian Law* (New Delhi: Konark).
36. Kaushik Basu (2018) *The Republic of Beliefs* (Princeton, NJ: Princeton University Press), 11.
37. WDR, (2017), 7.
38. Francis Fukuyama (2005) *State Building: Governance and World Order in the Twenty-First Century* (UK: Profile Books), 58.
39. R. Rajan (2019) *The Third Pillar: How Markets and the State Leave the Community Behind* (India: Harper Collins), 71.
40. Douglass C. North, John J. Wallis, Steven B. Webb, and Barry R. Weingast (2007) 'Limited Access Orders in the Developing World: A New Approach to the Problems of Development' *Policy Research Working Paper 4359* (Washington, DC: World Bank), 2.
41. Ibid., 3.
42. Ibid., 4.
43. Ibid., 26.
44. Alina Mungiu-Pippidi (2006) 'Corruption: Diagnosis and Treatment', *Journal of Democracy*, 17 (3), 86–99, p. 88.
45. Daron Acemoğlu and James Robinson (2012) *The Wealth of Nations*, 75.

46. Acemoğlu and Robinson, (2012), 80.
47. Jack Barbalet (2020) 'Violence and Politics: Reconsidering Weber's "Politics as a Vocation"', *Sociology*, 55 (1), 56–70; *Online first*, 10 January, 2020 DOI: 10.1177/0038038519895748.
48. Acemoğlu and Robinson 2012, 80.
49. Ibid., 82.
50. Douglass C. North, John J. Wallis, and Barry R. Weingast (2008) 'Violence and Social Orders: A Conceptual Framework for Interpreting Recorded Human History', in *Governance, Growth, and Development Decision Making* (Washington, DC: World Bank), 16.
51. North et al., (2007), 44.
52. Dani Rodrik (2008) 'Thinking about Governance', in *Governance, Growth, and Development Decision-Making* (Washington, DC: World Bank),22.
53. Daron Acemoğlu (2008) 'Interactions Between Governance and Growth' in *Governance, Growth, and Development Decision-Making.* (Washington, DC: World Bank), 3.

Chapter 6

1. Adam Smith (1776, 1902) *The Wealth of Nations*, 14 (New York: P. F. Collier & Son).
2. Kaushik Basu (2010) Beyond *the Invisible Hand*: *Groundwork for a New Economics*, 10 (London: Penguin Books).
3. R. Thaler and C. Sunstein (2008) *Nudge: Improving Decisions About Health, Wealth, and Happiness.* 6-7 (Penguin).
4. Herbert Simon, one of the early winners of the Economics Nobel Prize (in 1978), had raised exactly these issues about Econs vs Humans as far back as 1947 in his book, *Administrative Behavior: A Study of Decision-Making Processes in Administrative Organizations.* (First Edition, New York: Macmillan). He elaborated them further in the second edition of this book in 1957 and introduced the concept of Bounded rationality in his book, *Models of Man*, John Wiley, 1957.

   Some three decades after Simon first raised these issues, Daniel Kahneman and Amos Tversky (both psychologists) published their paper, 'Prospect Theory: An Analysis of Decision under Risk', *Econometrica*, March 1979. This work laid the foundation for the field of *Behavioural Economics*—a multidisciplinary subfield of economics drawing on psychology, sociology, and law—in addition to, of course, economics. The Prospect Theory essentially challenged and exposed the shortcomings of the tillthen-prevalent classical thinking based on the Utility Theory, starting from Bernoulli's work all the way back in 1738.

   Kahneman was awarded the Nobel Prize in Economics in 2002 for this work, a prize which certainly would have been shared with Tversky, but for his very untimely death in 1996. (Nobel Prizes are not awarded posthumously).

5. R. Thaler (2015) *Misbehaving: The Making of Behavioral Economics*, (Penguin). He won the Nobel Prize for Economics in 2017 for his work in Behavioural Economics.

6. Jeremy Freese (2011) 'Preferences' in *The Oxford Handbook of Analytical Sociology* Oxford, 98.

7. Milton Friedman (1966) 'The Methodology of Positive Economics' in *Essays in Positive Economics*, University of Chicago Press, 3–16, 30–43.

8. Milton Friedman (1970) 'The Social responsibility of Business is to Increase its Profits' *The New York Times Magazine*, 13 September.

9. World Development Report (2015) *Mind, Society, and Behavior* (Washington, DC: World Bank). This is a most relevant and useful exercise to comprehensively consider the psychological, social, and cultural influences on decision-making and human behaviour, as they clearly have significant impacts on development outcomes. We draw extensively on this report in our book.

10. D. Kahneman (2002) 'Maps of Bounded Rationality: A Perspective of Intuitive Judgment and Choice'. Nobel Prize Lecture, 8 December.

11. J. S. B. T. Evans and K. Frankish (eds) (2009) *In Two Minds: Dual Processes and Beyond* (Oxford University Press).

12. D. Kahneman (2003) 'Maps of Bounded Rationality: Psychology for Behavioral Economics' *American Economic Review*, 93, December.

13. J. S. B. T. Evans (2008) 'Dual-Processing Accounts of Reasoning, Judgment, and Social Cognition'. *Annual Review of Psychology*, 59.

14. D. Kahneman (2011) *Thinking Fast and Slow*. (New York: Farrar, Straus, and Giroux), 20–1.

15. Kahneman, (2011), p. 24.

16. WDR, (2015), p. 27.

17. Christopher Carpenter (2010) 'A Meta-Analysis of the Effectiveness of Health Belief Model Variables in Predicting Behaviour', *Health Communication*, 9 December, 25, 8, 661–9, DOI: 10.1080/10410236.2010.521906

18. Peter Todd and Gerd Gigerenzer (2000) 'Precis of *Simple heuristics that make us smart*', *Behavioural and Brain Sciences* 23, 727–80, 727.

19. L. Breiman, J. Freidman, R. Olshen, and C. Stone (1993) *Classification and Regression Trees* (Chapman and Hall) (Referred to in Todd and Gigerenzer (2000), p. 727).

20. WDR, (2015), 30.

21. Marianne Bertrand and Adair Morse (2011) 'Information Disclosure, Cognitive Biases, and Payday Borrowing', *Journal of Finance* 66 (6), 1865–93. www.jstor.org/stable/41305179.

22. WDR, (2015), 30.

23. Daniel Kahneman and A. Tversky (1979) 'Prospect Theory: An Analysis of Decision Under Risk', *Econometrica*, 47, 2 (March), 263–91.

24. Thaler and Sunstein (2008), 39.

25. Kahneman, (2011), 119.

26. Ibid.

27. Donald Philip Green, Daniel Kahneman, and Howard Kunreuther (1994) 'How the Scope and Method of Public Funding Affect Willingness to Pay for Public Goods', *The Public Opinion Quarterly* 58, 1, 49–67. www.jstor.org/stable/2749423.)

28. Brigitte Desaigues, Ari Rabl, Dominique Ami, Boun My Kene, Serge Masson, Marie-Anne Salomon, and Laure Santoni (2007) 'Monetary Value of a Life Expectancy Gain due to Reduced Air Pollution: Lessons from a Contingent Valuation in France' *Revue d'économie politique*, September–October, 675–98. (Editions Dalloz Stable) www.jstor.org/stable/24702540.

29. Kahneman, (2011), 127.

30. Thaler, (2015), 153–4.

31. Kahneman and Tversky, (1979).

32. Thaler, (2015), 12–19.

33. W. Samuelson and R. Zeckhauser (1988) 'Status Quo Bias in Decision-Making', *Journal of Risk and Uncertainty* 1, 1, 7–59.

34. R. Fryer, S. Levitt, J. List, and S. Sadoff (2012) 'Enhancing the Efficacy of Teacher Incentives Through Loss Aversion: A Field Experiment', *NBER Working Paper 18237*, July.

35. WDR, (2015), 38.

36. Kahneman, (2011), 127.

37. R. Thaler, C. Sunstein, and J. P. Balz (2014) 'Choice Architecture' (10 December) in *The Behavioural Foundations of Public Policy* SSRN: https://ssrn.com/abstract=2536504 or http://dx.doi.org/10.2139/ssrn.2536504.

    Also, Thaler and Sunstein, (2008).

38. Thaler, (2015), 325.

39. Thaler and Sunstein, (2008), 5.

40. Thaler and Sunstein, (2008), 6.

41. Thaler and Sunstein, (2008), 5.

42. Karthik Tennankore, Scott Klarenbach, and Aviva Goldberg (2021) 'Perspectives on Opt-Out Versus Opt-In Legislation for Deceased Organ Donation: An Opinion Piece', *Canadian Journal of Kidney Health and Disease*, June, https://doi.org/10.1177/20543581211022151).

43. Thaler, (2015), 327–8.

Chapter 7

1. Joan Robinson (1979) 'Morality and Economics: Commencement Speech, University of Maine, 1977'in her *Collected Economic Papers, 5* (Oxford: Blackwell), 43.

2. World Development Report (2015) *Mind, Society, and Behavior* (Washington, DC: World Bank) [WDR], 42.

3. T. Schelling (1960) *The Strategy of Conflict* (Harvard University Press).

4. Schelling was awarded the Nobel Prize in Economics in 2005 'for having enhanced our understanding of conflict and cooperation through game-theory analysis' (Fact Sheet: Thomas C. Schelling, The Nobel Prize, 2005). Interestingly, his entire Nobel Prize speech (8 December 2005) was devoted to the critical issue of non-use of nuclear weapons.

5. R. Myerson (2004) *Justice, Institutions, and Multiple Equilibria*, p. 3 (University of Chicago). http://home.uchicago.edu/~rmyerson/research/jistice.pdf. Accessed 20 June 2019.

6. Schelling, (1960), 54.

7. Ibid.

8. Ibid.

9. It is fascinating to think that the term 'focal point', which has subsequently become such a commonly used and important term in behavioural economics, was rather downplayed by Schelling himself. In typical understatement, he heads the section in his book first describing the concept of focal point rather dryly as 'Tacit Coordination (Common Interests)'.

10. Schelling, (1960), 97.

11. See, for example, Axelrod (1984), Basu (2018), Binmore (2020), Sugden (1989), Sunstein (1996).

12. Schelling, (1960), 55.

13. K. Binmore (2020) *Crooked Thinking or Straight Talk? Modernizing Epicurean Scientific Philosophy* (Springer).

14. Basu, (2018), 42.

15. In his own inimitable style of humour, Basu advises his readers that '[i]n game theory, when we consider abstract, illustrative examples, it is good policy not to waste time asking how and why such a strange situation arose'.

16. Myerson, (2004), 3–4.

17. Ibid.

18. 'Who was the person who just walked in, placed the crown on someone's head and left? Is she just somebody of the street, or a friend or accomplice of the person she "crowned?" Is the choice purely random or a coup? Is she a "behind the scenes" king maker? These are all very relevant questions (because they happen quite frequently around the world) with serious issues of legitimacy and fairness.' Ibid.; R. McAdams, *The Expressive Powers of Law: Theories and Limits* (Harvard University Press (Ch. 3)); Basu, (2018), 46.

19. Note that it might not always be possible to find a unique equilibrium, and it might not always be a good equilibrium either. In the island game, there might be chaos if the two islanders fail to choose between one of the two options (drive left or drive right) or settle into a bad equilibrium if one 'believes' they have agreed on the drive left option and the other believes the opposite.

20. Ken Binmore and Larry Samuelson (2002) 'The Evolution of Focal Points', *Economics Working Papers 0017*, 20. Institute for Advanced Study, School of Social Science, (Princeton, NJ: Princeton University).

21. R. Sugden (1989) 'Spontaneous Order', *Journal of Economic Perspectives*, 3, 4, 90–1.

22. H. Peyton Young (1993) 'The Evolution of Conventions', *Econometrica*, 61, 1, 58. https://doi.org/10.2307/2951778.

23. A. Greif (2014) 'Do Institutions Evolve?' *Journal of Bio-economics*, 16, 1. DOI:10.1007/s10818-013-9173-5

24. Schelling, (1960), 57.

25. Garrett Hardin (1968) 'The Tragedy of the Commons', *Science*, 162, 3859, 1243–8. Accessed 26 June 2021. http://www.jstor.org/stable/1724745, 1244.

26. Ibid., 1244–5.

27. M. Olson (1971) *The Logic of Collective Action: Public Goods and the Theory of Groups* (Harvard University Press).

28. R. Duncan Luce and Howard Raiffa (1983) *Games and Decisions: Introduction and Critical Survey* (New York: Dover) (originally published by John Wiley and Sons, New York, 1957).

29. A. Sen (1977) 'Rational Fools: A Critique of the Behavioural Foundations of Economic Theory', *Philosophy and Public Affairs*, 6, 4 (Summer), 317–44.

30. Basu, (2018), 27.

31. R. Dawes and R. Thaler (1988) 'Anomalies Cooperation', *Journal of Economic Perspectives*, 2, 3 (Summer), 187–97.

32. C. Bicchieri (2002) 'Covenants Without Swords: Group Identity, Norms, and Communication in Social Dilemmas', *Rationality and Society*, May, 14 (2), 192–228.

33. J. Hirschleifer (1985) 'The Expanding Domain of Economics', *American Economic Review*, December, 75, 6, 53–70.

34. H. Gintis et al. (eds) (2005) 'Moral Sentiments and Material Interests: Origins, Evidence, and Consequences' in their *Moral Sentiments and Material Interests: The Foundations of Cooperation in Economic Life* (Cambridge, MA: MIT Press), 12.

35. S. Blount (1995) 'When Social Outcomes Aren't Fair: The Effect of Causal Attributions on Preferences', *Organizational Behaviour and Human Decision Processes*, 63 (2), 131–44. https://psycnet.apa.org/doi/10.1006/obhd.1995.1068

36. J. List (2007) 'On the Interpretation of Giving in Dictator Games', *Journal of Political Economy*, 115, 3 (June), 482–93.

37. Dawes and Thaler, (1988), 189.

38. G. Marwell and R. Ames (1981) 'Economists Free Ride, Does Anyone Else?' *Journal of Public Economics*, 15 (1981), 295–310.

39. M. Isaac, K. McCue, and C. Plott (1985) 'Public Goods Provision in an Experimental Environment' *Journal of Public Economics*, 26, 51–74.

40. J. Andreoni (1988) 'Why Free Ride? Strategies and Learning in Public Goods Experiments', *Journal of Public Economics*, 37, 291–304.

41. R. Axelrod (1984) *The Evolution of Cooperation* (New York: Basic Books). The Tit for Tat strategy, proposed by Anatol Rapoport of the University of Toronto, was the winner of a global competition Axelrod had organized in 1979 to find the best strategy to solve the iterated prisoner's dilemma game.

42. Peter Martinsson, Nam Pham-Khanh, and Clara Villegas-Palacio (2012) 'Conditional Cooperation and Disclosure in Developing Countries', *Working Paper in Economics, No 541*, University of Gothenburg, September.

43. E. Ostrom (1990) *Governing the Commons: The Evolution of Institutions for Collective Action* (Cambridge University Press), 59.

44. D. Rustagi, S. Engel, and M. Kosfeld (2010) 'Conditional Cooperation and Costly Monitoring Explain Success in Forest Commons Management' *Science*, 330 (6006), 961–5.

45. N. Joshi, E. Ostrom, G. Shivakoti, and W. F. Lam (2000) 'Institutional Opportunities and Constraints in the Performance of Farmer Managed Irrigation Systems in Nepal', *Asia-Pacific Journal of Rural Development*, 10 (2), 67–92.

46. T. Hobbes (1651) *Leviathan, or the Matter of Forme and Power of a Commonwealth Ecclesiastical and Civil* (Sweden: Wisehouse Classics), 65.

47. D. Hume (1996 [1740]) *Of the Dignity or Meanness of Human Nature: Selected Essays*. Oxford World's Classics, 47.

48. A. Smith (2016 [1759]) *Of Sympathy, The Theory of Moral Sentiments*. (Enhanced Media Publishing), 2

49. Axelrod, (1984), 3.

50. E. Ostrom, J. Walker, and R. Gardner (1992) 'Covenants with and without a Sword: Self Governance Is Possible', in *American Political Science Review*, 86, 2 (June).

51. Hobbes, (1651), 85.

52. Richard Titmuss (2018 [1970]) *The Gift Relationship: From Blood Donations to Social Policy* (Bristol: Policy Press), 22.

53. Samuel Bowles and Sandra Polania-Reyes (2011) 'Economic Incentives and Social Preferences: Substitutes or Complements?', *Quaderni del Dipartimento di Economia Politica Statistica*, 617, October, 2.

54. James Heyman and Dan Ariley (2004) 'Effort for Payment: A Tale of Two Markets', *Psychological Science*, 15 (11),787–93.

55. Uri Gneezy and Aldo Rustichini (2000b) 'Pay Enough or Don't Pay at All', *Quarterly Journal of Economics*, 115 (3),791–810.

56. Joyce Berg, John Dickhaut, and Kevin McCabe (1995) 'Trust, Reciprocity and Social History', *Games and Economic Behaviour*, 10 (1), 122–42.

57. Armin Falk and Michael Kosfeld (2006) 'The Hidden Costs of Control', *American Economic Review*, 96 (5), 1611–30.

58. Lisa Shu, Francesca Gino, and Max H. Bazerman (2009 'Dishonest Deed, Clear Conscience: Self-Preservation through Moral Disengagement and Motivated Forgetting', *Harvard Business School, Working Paper 09-078*.

59. Uri Gneezy and Aldo Rustichini (2000a) 'A Fine is a Price', *Journal of Legal Studies*, XXIX (January).

60. Thomas Kinnaman (2006) 'Policy Watch: Examining the Justification for Residential Recycling', *Journal of Economic Perspectives*, 20 (4), 219–32.

Chapter 8

1. World Bank, World Development Report (2015), 42.

2. V. Havel (1978) 'The Power of the Powerless', *International Center of Non-violent Conflict*, www.nonviolent-conflict.org/wp-content/uploads/1979/01/the-power-of-the-powerless.pdf. Accessed on 26 June 2021.

3. D. Hume (1758) 'Essay IV: Of the First Principles of Government', in his *Essays, Moral, Political, and Literary, Volume 1, Essays and Treatises on Several Subjects in Two Volumes*. Kindle edition, Location 425, Hard Press, 2017).

4. Kaushik Basu (2018) *The Republic of Beliefs: A New Approach to Law and Economics* (Princeton University Press), 40.

5. K. Binmore (2020) *Crooked Thinking or Straight Talk? Modernizing Epicurean Scientific Philosophy* (Springer), p. 90.

6. Bibek Debroy (2000) *In the Dock: Absurdities of Indian Law* (New Delhi: Konark).

7. Basu (2018), 9.

8. G. Becker (1968) 'Crime and Punishment: An Economic Approach', *Journal of Political Economy*, 76, 2. Accessed 15 October 2020. http://www.jstor.org/stable/1830482.

9. Basu, (2018), 20–1.

10. Under standard neoclassical assumptions of complete rationality and information, well-defined utility functions (with clear preference for more rather than less of anything, uncharitably perhaps attached to the 'Selfish Gene'), governed by the principle of diminishing marginal utility and intent only on maximizing their individual utilities.

11. Though we have spoken of the Becker model in this context, there have been other significant thinkers as well. See, for example, H. Kelsen (1945) *General Theory of Law and State* (Harvard University Press).

12. L. Hurwicz. (2007) *But Who Will Guard the Guardians?* Nobel Prize Lecture.

13. Basu, (2018), p. 49.

14. A. Greif (1996) *Institutions and the Path to the Modern Economy: Lessons from Medieval Trade* (Cambridge University Press).

15. A. Greif (1993) 'Contract Enforceability and Economic Institutions in Early Trade: The Maghribi Traders Coalition', *American Economic Review*, 83, 3. 525–48. www.jstor.org/stable/2117532.

16. K. Basu (2000) *Prelude to Political Economy: A Study of the Social and Political Foundation of Economics* (Oxford University Press).

17. R. Ellickson (1991) *Order Without Law* (Harvard University Press).

18. R. Sugden (1989) 'Spontaneous Order', *Journal of Economic Perspectives*, 3, 4, 90–1.
19. R. McAdams (2015) *The Expressive Powers of Law: Theories and Limits* (Harvard University Press).
20. G. Hadfield (2016) *Rules for a Flat World: Why Humans Invented Law and How to Reinvent it for a Complex Global Economy* (Oxford University Press), p. 289.
21. Hadfield, (2016), 291.
22. A. Sen (1967) 'Isolation, Assurance, and the Social Rate of Discount', *The Quarterly Journal of Economics*, 81, 1 (February), 112–24.
23. C. Bicchieri and H. Mercier (2014) 'Norms and Beliefs: How Change Occurs', *The Jerusalem Philosophical Quarterly*, 63 (January), 60–82.
24. Jon Elster (1989) *The Cement of Society: A Study of Social Order* (Cambridge University Press).
25. C. Bicchieri (2006) *The Grammar of Society: The Nature and Dynamics of Social Norms* (Cambridge University Press), p. ix.
26. Ibid.
27. C. Sunstein (1996) 'Social Norms and Social Roles *96 Columbia Law Review*, 903–68.
28. E. Posner (2000) *Laws and Social Norms* (Harvard University Press), p. 3 (quoted in K. Basu, *Republic of Beliefs*, 88).
29. Kaushik Basu and Jorgen Weibull (2002): 'Punctuality: A Cultural Trait as Equilibrium', MIT Department of Economics, *Working Paper Series, WP 02-26*, (Cambridge, MI), 2.
30. Alina Mungiu-Pippidi (2015) 'When corruption is the norm', Spotlight 1: World Development Report, *Mind, Society, and Behaviour*, 60.
31. Odd-Helge Fjeldstade (2005) 'Corruption in Tax Administration: Lessons from Institutional Reforms in Uganda' *Working Paper 10* (Chr. Michelson Institute, Bergen, Norway).
32. Robert Wade (1985) 'The Market Rate for Public Office: Why the Indian State is not better at Development' *World Development* 13 (4), 467–97 https://doi.org/10.1016/0305-750X(85)90052-X
33. Raymond Fisman and Miguel Edward (2007) 'Corruption, Norms and Legal Enforcement: Evidence from Diplomatic Parking Tickets', *Journal of Political Economy*, 115 (6), 1020–48.
34. Transparency International (2015) *Successful Anti-Corruption Reforms* (Berlin: Anti-Corruption Helpdesk TI).
35. Republic Of Lebanon (2020) *The Anti-Corruption National Strategy (2020–2025)* (Beirut: Government of Lebanon).
36. Transparency International (2020) *Corruption Perception Index*.
37. Mancur Olson (1971) *The Logic of Collective Action, Public Policy, and the Theory of Groups* (Cambridge, MA; London: Harvard University Press).
38. A. Sen (1967) 'Isolation, Assurance, and the Social Rate of Discount', *The Quarterly Journal of Economics*, 81, 1 (February), 112–24.

39. Bo Rothstein and Jan Teorell (2015) 'Getting to Sweden, Part II: Breaking with Corruption in the Nineteenth Century', *Scandinavian Political Studies* 38 (3), 238–54.

40. Anna Persson, Bo Rothstein, and Jan Teorell (2012) 'Why Anticorruption Reforms Fail—Systematic Corruption as a Collective Action Problem', *Governance: An International Journal of Policy, Administration and Institutions*, 26 (3), 449–71. https://doi.org/10.1111/j.1468-0491.2012.01604.x

41. Persson et al., (2012), 458.

42. Bo Rothstein (2000) 'Trust, Social Dilemmas, and Collective Memories', *Journal of Theoretical Politics*, 12 (4), 477–501, p. 477.

43. Ibid., p. 478.

44. H. Wechsler, J. E. Lee, M. Kuo, and H. Lee (2000) College Binge Drinking in the 1990s: A Continuing Problem, Results of the Harvard School of Public Health 1999 College Alcohol Study. *Journal of American College Health*, 48 (5) (March), 199–210. doi: 10.1080/07448480009599305. PMID: 10778020.

45. R. Muldoon (2018) 'Understanding Norms and Changing Them' *Social Philosophy and Policy*, 35 (1), 128–48. doi:10.1017/S0265052518000092, Published online by Cambridge University Press, 4 December 2018.

46. R. Thaler and C. R. Sunstein (2008) *Nudge* (New Haven, CT: Yale University Press), 73–4.

47. BIT (Behavioural Insights Team, UK) (2012) *Applying Behavioural Insights to Reduce Fraud, Errors, and Debt* (London: Cabinet Office, BIT).

48. World Bank, (2015), 52.

49. James Habyarimana and William Jack (2009) 'Heckle and Chide: Results of a Randomized Road Safety Intervention in Kenya', *Working Papers 169*, (Center for Global Development).

50. G. Mackie and J. LeJeunne (2009) 'Social Dynamics of Abandonment of Harmful Practices: A New Look at the Theory' *UNICEF Innocenti Research Center, Working Paper IWP-2009-06*.

51. V. Gauri, T. Rahman, and I. Sen (2020) 'Shifting Normal Norms to Reduce Open Defecation in Rural India' *Behavioural Public Policy*, 1–25.

52. Ibid.

53. D. Acemoğlu and J. Robinson (2019) *The Narrow Corridor: How Nations Struggle for Liberty* (UK: Penguin Books), p. 19.

54. Ibid.

55. R. McAdams (2015) *The Expressive Powers of Law: Theories and Limits* (Cambridge, MA: Harvard University Press), p. 22.

56. L. Lessig (1995) 'The Regulation of Social Meaning', *University of Chicago Law Review*, 62, 3, 968.

57. J. Gusfield (1993) 'The Social Symbolism of Smoking and Health' in R. Rabin and S. Sugarman,ed *Smoking Policy: Law, Politics, and Culture*, 53. (Oxford).

58. Gusfield (1993) 'The Social Symbolism of Smoking and Health' in R. Rabin and S. Sugarman, ed *Smoking Policy: Law, Politics, and Culture*, 65 (Oxford).

59. L. Friedman (2016) *Impact: How Law Affects Behavior* (Cambridge, MA: Harvard University Press).

60. World Bank, (2015), 53.

61. A. Kinzig, P. Ehrlich, L. Alston, K. Arrow, Scott Barrett, Timothy G. Buchman, Gretchen C. Daily, Bruce Levin, Simon Levin, Michael Oppenheimer, Elinor Ostrom, and Donald Saari (2013) 'Social Norms and Global Environmental Challenges: The Complex Interaction of Behaviors, Values, and Policy', *BioScience*, 63, 3 (March), 164–75.

62. W. Stuntz (2000) 'Self-Defeating Crimes', *Virginia Law Review*, 86, 8, *Symposium: The Legal Construction of Norms* (November), 1871–99.

63. J-P. Platteau (2000) *Institutions, Social Norms, and Economic Development* (London and New York: Routledge).

64. G. Aldashev, J-P Platteau, and Z. Wahhaj (2010, 2011) 'Legal Reform in the Presence of a Living Custom: An Economic Approach'. *Proceedings of the National l Academy of Sciences of the United States.* Epub 2011.

65. Stuntz, (2000), 1872.

66. Bicchieri et al., (2014), 64.

67. Sunstein, (1996), 909.

68. A. Bisin and T. Verdier (2001) 'The Economics of Cultural Transmission and the Dynamics of Preferences', *Journal of Economic Theory*, 97 (2), 298–319.

69. World Bank, (2015), 62.

70. N. Nunn and L. Wantchekon (2011) 'The Slave Trade and the Origins of Mistrust in Africa', *American Economic Review*, 101 (7) (December), 3221–52.

71. World Bank, (2015), 65.

72. Nunn and Wantchekon, (2011), 3222.

73. E. Banfield (with the assistance of Laura Fasano Banfield) *The Moral Basis of a Backward Society* (Glencoe, IL: Free Press), 1958.

74. P. Jones (1997) *The Italian City-State: From Commerce to Signoria* (Oxford University Press).

75. R. Putnam, with R. Leonardi and R. Nanetti (1993) *Making Democracy Work: Civic Traditions in Modern Italy* (Princeton University Press).

76. L. Guiso, P. Sapienza, and L. Zingales (2016) 'Long Term Persistence', *Journal of the European Economic Association*, 14, 6, 1401–36.

77. *Times Atlas of World History*, 124. Quoted in Putnam, (1993), 123.

78. Putnam, (1993), 123–24.

79. Guiso et al., (2016), 1406.

80. Ibid., 1433.

81. Nico Voigtländer and Hans-Joachim Voth (2012) 'Persecution Perpetuated: The Medieval Origins of Anti-Semitic Violence in Nazi Germany', *Quarterly Journal of Economics*, 127 (3), 1339–92. Available at SSRN: 2021 http://dx.doi.org/10.2139/ssrn.1824744. Downloaded on 23 July.

82. A. Alesina, P. Giuliano, and N. Nunn (2013) 'On the Origin of Gender Roles: Women and the Plough', *Quarterly Journal of Economics*, 128, 469–530.

83. K. Hoff and P. Pandey (2006) 'Discrimination, Social Identity, and Durable Inequalities', *American Economic Review*, 96, 2 (May), 206–11.

84. N. Nunn (2008) 'The Long-term Effects of Africa's Slave Trades', *Quarterly Journal of Economics*, 123 (1), 139–76.

85. WDR, (2015), 69.

Chapter 9

1. World Development Report (WDR) (2015) *Mind, Society, and Behaviour* (Washington DC: World Bank), 30.

2. Anandi Mani, Sendhil Mullainathan, Eldar Shafir, and Jiaying Zhao (2013) 'Poverty Impedes Cognitive Function'. *Science*, 341, 976–80.

3. Florencia Devoto, Esther Duflo, Pascaline Dupas, William Pariente, and Vincent Pons (2012) 'Happiness on Tap: Piped Water Adoption in Urban Morocco', *American Economic Journal: Economic Policy, American Economic Association*, 4 (4), 68–99.

4. WDR, (2015), 81.

5. Deepa Narayan, Robert Chambers, Meera K. Shah, and Patt Petesch (2000) *Voices of the Poor: Crying Out for Change* (Washington, DC: World Bank), 2.

6. WDR, (2015), 84.

7. Esther Duflo, Michael Kremer, and Jonathan Robinson (2011) 'Nudging Farmers to Use Fertilizer: Theory and Experimental Evidence from Kenya'. *American Economic Review*, 101 (6), 2350–90. DOI: 10.1257/aer.101.6.2350.

8. Ibid., 2355.

9. Ibid., 2366.

10. WDR, (2015), 38.

11. Abhijit Banerjee and Esther Duflo (2011) *Poor Economics* (India: Random House).

12. Ibid., 191.

13. Richard Thaler and Cass Sunstein (2008) *Nudge: Improving Decisions About Health, Wealth and Happiness* (New Haven, CT: Yale University Press).

14. WDR, (2015), 71.

15. UNICEF (2021) https://data.unicef.org/topic/child-protection/female-genita lmutilation/).

16. Duncan Green (2016) *How Change Happens* (Oxford: Oxford University Press), p. 63.

17. Alison Byrsk (2013) 'Changing Hearts and Minds: Sexual Politics and Human Rights' in Thomas Risse, Stephen Ropp, and Kathryn Sikkink, *The Persistent Power of Human Rights: From Commitment to Compliance,*(Cambridge: Cambridge University Press), p. 273.

18. Byrsk, (2013), 272.

19. Richard Pascale, Jerry Sternin, and Monique Sternin (2010) *The Power of Positive Deviance: How Unlikely Innovators Solve the World's Toughest Problems* (Boston, MA: Harvard Business Press).

20. Cass Sunstein (1996) 'Social Norms and Social Roles' *96 Columbia Law Review*, 903–68; p. 909.

21. Sunstein, (1996), 912.

22. L. Lessig (1995) 'The Regulation of Social Meaning', *University of Chicago Law Review*, 62,3.

23. WDR, (2015), 47.

24. M. Shinada and T. Yamagishi (2007) 'Punishing free riders: Direct and indirect promotion of cooperation', *Evolution and Human Behavior*, 28, 330–9. https://doi.org/10.1016/j.evolhumbehav.2007.04.001

25. Samuel Bowles and Sandra Polania-Reyes: (2011) 'Economic Incentives and Social Preferences: Substitutes or Complements?', *Quaderni del Dipartimento di Economia Politica Statistica, University of Sienna, WP No 617*, October 2011, 28.

26. Ibid., 39.

27. Ibid.

28. B. Herrmann, C. Thoni, and S. Gachter (2008) 'Antisocial Punishment Across Societies', *Science*, 319, 7 March, 1362–67.

29. E. Rosenthal (2008) 'Motivated by a Tax, Irish Spurn Plastic Bags', (New York: *New York Times*).

30. Bowles and Polania-Reyes, (2011), 39.

31. Ibid.

32. I. Bohnet, B. Herrmann, M. Al-Ississ, A. Robbett, K. Al-Yahia, and R. Zeckhauser (2010) 'The Elasticity of Trust: How to Promote Trust in the Arab Middle East and the United States'. *Faculty Research Working Paper Series, RWP10-031*, Harvard Kennedy School: Cambridge.

33. Bowles and Polania-Reyes, (2011), 40.

34. Rohini Pandey and Deanna Ford (2011) 'Gender Quotas and Female Leadership', background paper, *World Development Report 2012 Gender Equality and Development* (Washington, DC: World Bank), 3.

35. J-PAL Update (2018) *Improving women's representation in politics through gender quotas* www.povertyactionlab.org/policy-insight/improving-womens-representation-politics-through-gender-quotas accessed 16 May, 2023.

36. Rikhil R. Bhavnani (2009) 'Do Electoral Quotas Work After They Are Withdrawn? Evidence from a Natural Experiment in India', *American Political Science Review*, 103 (1), 23–35 DOI: https://doi.org/10.1017/S0003055409090029

37. Eric T. Rosenthal (2011) 'Betty Ford's Momentous Contributions to Cancer Awareness', *Oncology Times*, 33, 15 (10 August), 7–8. doi: 10.1097/01.COT.0000403839.34558.e7)

38. Richard Pace (1993) 'First-Time Televiewing in Amazônia: Television Acculturation in Gurupá, Brazil', *Ethnology*, 32, 2 (Spring), 187–205. www.jstor.org/stable/3773772

39. Robert Jensen and Emily Oster (2009) 'The Power of TV: Cable Television and Women's Status in India', *The Quarterly Journal of Economics*, 124, 3 (August), 1057–94 URL: www.jstor.org/stable/40506252).

40. E. M. Rogers, P. W. Vaughan, R. M. Swalehe, N. Rao, P. Svenkerud and S. Sood (1999) 'Effects of an entertainment-education radio soap opera on family planning behavior in Tanzania', *Studies in Family Planning*, 30 (3),193–211. doi: 10.1111/j.1728-4465.1999.00193. x. PMID: 10546311).

41. Sen (1999) *Development as Freedom* (New York: Anchor Books).

42. World Bank (2018) World Bank, World Development Report 2018, *Learning: To Realize Education's Promise* (Washington, D.C.: World Bank 2018).

43. World Bank (2018): 42.

44. Wantchekon, Klasnja, Novta (2015): 'Education and Human Capital Externalities: Evidence from Colonial Benin'. *Quarterly Journal of Economics* 130 (2), 703–57.

45. Larreguy, Horacio A., and John Marshall (2017). 'The Effect of Education on Civic and Political Engagement in Non-consolidated Democracies: Evidence from Nigeria'. *Review of Economics and Statistics*. http://www.mitpressjournals.org/doi/abs/10.1162/REST_a_00633

46. Chzhen, Yekaterina, 2013. 'Education and Democratisation: Tolerance of Diversity, Political Engagement, and Under-standing of Democracy'. Background paper, Report 2014/ED/EFA/MRT/PI/03, United Nations Educational, Scientific, and Cultural Organization, Paris.)

47. Borgonovi, F. and T. Burns (2015), 'The educational roots of trust', OECD Education Working Papers, No. 119, OECD Publishing, Paris, https://doi.org/10.1787/5js1kv85dfvd-en.)

48. World Bank (2018): p. 43.

49. Sen, A. (2002) 'Why Health Equity?', *Health Econ* 11, 659–666, Published online in Wiley Interscience (www.interscience.com) doi:10.1002/hec.762.

Chapter 10

1. L. Pritchett and M. Woolcock (2004) 'Solutions When the Solution is the Problem: Assessing the Disarray in Development'. World Development, 32.2.

2. F. Fukuyama (2011) *The Origins of Political Order: From Pre-Human Times to the French Revolution* (New York, NY: Farrar, Strauss, and Giroux), p. 14.

3. Daron Acemoğlu and James Robinson (2012) *Why Nations Fail: The Origins of Power, Prosperity, and Poverty* (New York: Crown), p. 174.

4. Lars Bo Kaspersen (2004) 'How Denmark Became Democratic: The Impact of Warfare and Military Reforms' *Acta Sociologica*, 47 (1) (March), 71–89. DOI:10.1177/0001699304041552, p. 78.

5. Kaspersen, (2004), 81.

6. Kaspersen, (2004), 79

7. Matte Frisk Jensen (2018) 'Building of the Scandinavian States: Establishing Weberian Bureaucracy and Curbing Corruption from the Mid-Seventeenth Century to the End of the Nineteenth Century', *Bureaucracy and Society in Transition* (*Comparative Social Research*, 33) Bingley: Emerald Publishing Limited, 179–201.

8. G. Lind (2012) 'Beyond the Fiscal-Military Road to State Formation: Civil Society, Collective Identities, and the State of the Old Danish Monarchy. 1500–1850', *Balto-Scandia*, 18, 1–11.

9. Jensen, (2018), 5. (This page number refers to a post print versión of Jensen's paper which we used.) https://doi.org/10.1108/S0195-631020180000033013

10. Jensen, (2018), 7. https://doi.org/10.1108/S0195-631020180000033013

11. A. Mungiu-Pippidi *Becoming Denmark: Understanding Good Governance. Historical Achievers.* www.againstcorruption.eu

12. Jensen, (2018), 11. https://doi.org/10.1108/S0195-631020180000033013

13. Ibid., 20 https://doi.org/10.1108/S0195-631020180000033013

14. Ibid. https://doi.org/10.1108/S0195-631020180000033013

15. Ibid., 21 https://doi.org/10.1108/S0195-631020180000033013

16. Acemoğlu and Robinson (2012), 185.

17. C. Hill (1961) *The Century of Revolution (1603–1714).* Routledge Classics (referred to in D. North and B. Weingast (1989) 'Constitutions and Commitment: The Evolution of Institutions Governing Public Choice in Seventeenth Century England', *The Journal of Economic History*, XLIX, 4, 812.

18. North and Weingast. (1989), 812–14.

19. Hill observes that 'in the eighteenth century, Blackstone (Sir William Blackstone, an English Jurist, Judge, and Tory politician) called this Act a greater boon to property owners than the Magna Carta itself'. (Referred to in ibid., p. 814.)

20. The Exclusion Crisis (1679–1681) is often considered as to have spawned the first political parties in England. Sensing the strong feeling in support of ex-clusion, King Charles II had dissolved Parliament indefinitely. Those who sup-ported the passage of the Exclusion Bill and regularly petitioned the King to recall Parliament were called the 'Petitioners' and later the 'Whigs' ('Horse Thief' in Scottish Gaelic), and were ultimately incorporated into the Liberal Party under William Gladstone in 1859. Those opposing the Bill were the Abhorrers, who grew into the Tories (with no less dramatic a meaning: 'thieving outlaws' in Irish).

21. North and Weingast, (1989), 815.

22. A. Zuvich (2016) *A Year in the Life of Stuart Britain* (England: Amberley Publishing).

23. www.britannica.com/place/United-Kingdom/The-early-Stuarts-and-the-Commonwealth
    www.britannica.com/place/United-Kingdom/The-later-Stuarts
    www.britannica.com/place/United-Kingdom/The-Revolution-of-1688

24. This, of course, is an oversimplification: various other factors, including colonization and the extraction of significant wealth from the colonies, were also at play. But that is not the subject of our interest in this book.
25. North and Weingast, (1989), 816.
26. Maitland (see note 29, ibid.).
27. Dickson (note 28, ibid., 815.
28. Jones (note 30, ibid., 817).
29. Acemoğlu and Robinson, (2012), 192.
30. North and Weingast, (1989), 816.
31. North and Weingast, (1989), 823.

Chapter 11

1. A. Maddison (2006) *The World Economy, Vol 1: A Millennial Perspective, Vol 2: Historical Statistics* (OECD).
2. J. Huffman (2003) 'The Meiji Restoration Era, 1868–1889', *Japan Society*.
3. Over the period 1600–1850, per capita income grew by 31 per cent in Japan, though the population had grown even more (73 per cent). Source: A. Maddison, *The World Economy: Historical Statistics 1–2003 AD*. The historical data were originally developed in three books: (1995) *Monitoring the World Economy 1820–1992*, (Paris: OECD), (2001) *The World Economy: A Millennial Perspective* (Paris: OECD Development Centre); (2003) *The World Economy: Historical Statistics* (Paris: OECD Development Centre). GGDC databases (www.ggdc.net/).
4. S. Hanley (1983) 'A High Standard of Living in Nineteenth Century Japan: Fact or Fantasy?', *The Journal of Economic History*, 43, 1 (March), 183–92.
5. J. Nakamura (1966) 'Meiji Land Reform, Redistribution of Income, and Saving from Agriculture', *Economic Development and Cultural Change*, 14, 4 (July), 428–39.
6. Ibid., 429.
7. R. Bird (1977) 'Land Taxation and Economic Development: The Model of Meiji Japan', *Journal of Development Studies*, January, 162–74.
8. Nakamura, (1966), 429, cites an even more dramatic range: 'The percentage of the total product claimed by the ruling class has been variously estimated to have ranged from 20 to over 90 percent of the reported harvest in different parts of the country'.
9. A. B. Jannetta (1992) 'Famine Mortality in Nineteenth Century Japan: The Evidence from a Temple Death Register', *Population Studies*, 46, 3 (November), 427–43. JSTOR. www.jstor.org/stable/2175288. Accessed 18 August 2021. These famines, named for the eras in which they occurred, are known as the Kyoho famine (1732–1733), the Tenmei famine (1783–1787), and the Tenpo famine (1833–1837).

10. Hideichi Horie (1952) 'Revolution and Reform In Meiji Restoration', *Kyoto University Economic Review*, 22, 1 (52), 23–34. www.jstor.org/stable/43216962.

11. Ibid., 25.

12. W. G. Beasley (1990) *The Rise of Modern Japan* (New York: St Martin's Press).

13. H. Sonoda (1990) 'The Decline of the Japanese Warrior Class, 1840–1880', *Japan Review*, 1, 73–111.www.jstor.org/stable/25790888. Accessed 16 April 2019.

14. Beasley, (1990), 13.

15. J. L. Huffman (2019) *Politics of the Meiji Press: The Life of Fukuchi Gen'ichirō* (United States: University Press of Hawaii), 30.

16. Huffman, (2003), 2.

17. Beasley, (1990), 29.

18. Huffman, (2003), 2.

19. Bird, (1977), 165.

20. G. Sansom (1950) *The Western World and Japan: A Study in the Interaction of European and Asiatic Cultures* (New York: Alfred A. Knopf). https://ia804603.us.archive.org/30/items/westernworldandj012243mbp/westernworldandj012243mbp.pdf

21. Benjamin Duke (2014) '4. The Gakusei: The First National Plan for Education, 1872' in his *The History of Modern Japanese Education: Constructing the National School System, 1872-1890*, 61–76. (Ithaca, NY: Rutgers University Press). https://doi.org/10.36019/9780813546483-008.

22. John Breen (1996) 'The Imperial Oath of April 1868: Ritual, Politics, and Power in the Restoration.' *Monumenta Nipponica* 51, 4, 410 https://doi.org/10.2307/2385417.

23. A. Sen (2006) *Identity and Violence: The Illusion of Destiny* (UK: Penguin), 110.

24. Ibid., p. 111.

25. Ibid.

26. T. Schelling (1960) *The Strategy of Conflict* (Cambridge, MA and London, England: Harvard University Press).

27. T. Hashimoto (2008) 'Japanese Clocks and the History of Punctuality in Modern Japan', *East Asian Science, Technology and Society: An International Journal*, 2, 124. DOI 10.1007/s12280-008-9031-z

28. Ibid., 127.

29. Sonoda, (1990), 99.

30. Kaigun Heigakkō, ed. (1919) *The History of Japanese Naval Academy* (in Japanese). Quoted in Sonoda (1990), 100.

31. J. Fulcher (1988) 'The Bureaucratization of the State and the Rise of Japan', *The British Journal of Sociology*, 39, 2 (June), 228–54.

32. Ibid., 230.

33. T. J. Pempel (1992) 'Bureaucracy in Japan', *PS: Political Science and Politics*, 25,1 (March), 19–24.

34. J-P. Lehmann (1982) *The Roots of Modern Japan*. Macmillan Asian History Series. (London: Macmillan).

35. Horie, (1952), 23.

36. World Bank Data:https://data.worldbank.org/NY.GDP.PCAP.KD?locations=KR

37. UNDP (2021–22) *Human Development Report 2021–22*. Human Development Composite Indices, Table 1, 272 (New York: UNDP https://hdr.undp.org/cont ent/human-development-report-2021-22

38. Transparency International (2022a) *Corruption Perception Index 2022*. www. transparency.org/cpi/2022

39. European Research Centre for Anti-Corruption and State-Building (ERCAS), Hertie School of Governance, Berlin (2021) *The Index of Public Integrity (IPI)*. https://corruptionrisk.org/ipi-ranking

40. Transparency International (2003a and 2017b) *Global Corruption Barometer*. https://www.transparency.org/en/gcb/global/global-corruption-barometer-2003, https://www.transparency.org/en/gcb/global/global-corruption-barome ter-2017

41. Jong-Sung You (2017a) 'South Korea: The Odyssey to Corruption Control' in A. Mungiu-Pippidi and M. Johnson (eds), *Transition to Good Governance: Creating Virtuous Circles of Anti-Corruption*. (UK, USA: Edward Elgar Publishing), 129.

42. Jiyoung Kim (2015) 'Aid and State Transition in Ghana and South Korea', *Third World Quarterly*, 36, 7, 1336. https://doi.org/10.1080/01436597.2015.1038339

43. A. Kohli (2004) *State Directed Development: Political Power and Industrialization in the Global Periphery. Part 1 Galloping Ahead* (Korea: Cambridge University Press).

44. Kim, (2015), 1336.

45. M. Noland (2011) 'Korea's Growth Performance: Past and Future', *East West Center Working Papers, Economics Series*, 123 (November), 2.

46. Jong-sung You (2014) 'Land Reform, Inequality, and Corruption: A Comparative Historical Study of Korea, Taiwan, and the Philippines', *The Korean Journal of International Studies*, 12-1 (June), 191–224, p. 203. http://dx.doi.org/10.14731/ kjis.2014.06.12.1.191

47. Ibid., 72.

48. Jong-Sung You, (2016) 'Demystifying the Park Chung-He Myth: The Critical Role of Land Reform in the Evolution of Korea's Developmental State'. Available at SSRN: https://ssrn.com/abstract=2505810 OR http://dx.doi.org/10.2139/ ssrn.2505810, 1–35, p. 17

49. You, (2014), 204, referring to a study by S. P. Moon Ban and D. Perkins (1980) *Rural Development: Studies in the Modernization of the Republic of Korea, 1945–1975* (Cambridge, MA: Harvard University Press).

50. Nak Nyeon Kim and Jongil Kim (2015) 'Top Incomes in Korea, 1933–2010: Evidence From Income Tax Statistics'. *Hitotsubashi Journal of Economics 56*, 1, 1–19. www.jstor.org/stable/43610998.

51. Jong Il You (1998) 'Income Distribution and Growth in East Asia', *Journal of Development Studies*, 34 (6), 37–65.

52. Hankie Lee (2001) 'School Expansion in North Korea and South Korea: Two Systems, Two Approaches', *Asia Pacific Education Review*, 2, 1, 101–10.

53. Jong-Sung You, (2016), 18.

54. World Bank (1993) *The East Asian Miracle: Economic Growth and Public Policy* (USA: Oxford University Press).

55. M. Seth (2002) *Education Fever: Society, Politics, and the Pursuit of Schooling in South Korea*. Hawaii Studies on Korea. (Honolulu: University of Hawaii Press).

56. You, Jong-Sung, (2017), 143.

57. You, Jong-Sung, (2016), 12.

58. You, Jong-Sung, (2017b), p. 144. Based on G. Ju and M. Kim (2006) *Understanding of Personnel Administration System in Korean Bureaucracy* (in Korean) (Seoul: Gyongsewon).

59. A. Amsden (1989) *Asia's Next Giant: South Korea and Late Industrialization* (New York: Oxford University Press).

60. J. Campos and H. Root (1996) *The Key to the East Asian Miracle: Making Shared Growth Credible* (Washington, DC: Brookings Institution).

61. D. Rodrik (1995) 'Getting Interventions Right: How South Korea and Taiwan Got Rich', *Economic Policy*, 10, 20, 55–107. https://doi.org/10.2307/1344538.

62. Ibid.

63. Amsden, (1989), 147.

64. Daron Acemoğlu and James Robinson (2012) *Why Nations Fail: The Origins of Power, Prosperity, and Poverty* (New York: Crown), p. 92.

65. P. W. Kuznets (1988) 'An East Asian Model of Economic Development: Japan, Taiwan, and South Korea' *Economic Development and Cultural Change*, 36, 3, S11–43. www.jstor.org/stable/1566537.

66. W. Kim (2009) 'Rethinking Colonialism and the Origins of the Development State in East Asia', *Journal of Contemporary Asia*, 39, 3 (August), 382–99.

67. C. Kay (2002) 'Why East Asia Overtook Latin America: Agrarian Reform, Industrialization and Development', *Third World Quarterly*, 23, 6 (December), 1073–102.

68. A. Sen (2006), op cit, p.111.

Chapter 12

1. World Bank Data Base $6,657 in 2022, GDP per capita (constant 2015 US$). *Source*: https://data.worldbank.org/indicator/NY.GDP.PCAP.KD?locations= BW&name_desc=false

2. UNDP (2021–22) *Human Development Report 2021–22*. Human Development Composite Indices, Table 1, 272 (New York: UNDP). https://hdr.undp.org/content/human-development-report-2021-22

3. Transparency International (2022b) *Corruption Perception Index 2022* www.transparency.org/en/cpi/2022

4. Transparency International (2019) *Global Corruption Barometer-Africa (Tenth Edition)* www.transparency.org/en/gcb/africa/africa-2019

5. World Bank Data Base: Poverty headcount ratio at $2.15 a day (2017 PPP) (% of population), Botswana. https://data.worldbank.org/indicator/SI.POV. DDAY?locations=BW

6. D. Acemoğlu, S. Johnson, and J. Robinson (2001) 'An African Success Story: Botswana'. MIT Department of Economics, *Working Paper Series*, WP-01-37 (July), 1–2. See also K. Good (1992) 'Interpreting the Exceptionality of Botswana'. *The Journal of Modern African Studies*, 30 (1), 69–95. doi:10.1017/S0022278X00007734.

7. C. Leith (2005) *Why Botswana Prospered* (McGill-Queen's University Press).

8. Acemoğlu, Johnson, and Robinson, (2001), 2.

9. Ibid., 32–3.

10. 'Tswana' is the root word of the country's name, Botswana. A single Tswana person is a Motswana, two or more are *Batswana*.

11. M. Lewin (2011) 'Botswana's Success: Good Governance, Good Policies, and Good Luck' in P. Chuhan-Pole. and M. Angwafo (eds), *Yes, Africa Can: Success Stories from a Dynamic Continent* (World Bank), 82.

12. Daron Acemoğlu and James Robinson (2012) *Why Nations Fail: The Origins of Power, Prosperity, and Poverty* (New York: Crown), 407.

13. L. Picard (1987) *The Politics of Development in Botswana: A Model for Success?* (Boulder, CO: L. Rienner Publishers). Quoted in Acemoğlu, Johnson, and Robinson, (2001), 13.

14. Acemoğlu, Johnson, and Robinson, (2001), 24.

15. Lewin, (2011), 85.

16. K. Good (1994) 'Corruption and Mismanagement in Botswana: A Best-Case Example' *The Journal of Modern African Studies*, 32, 3 (September), 499–521, p. 516. www.jstor.org/stable/161986

17. Acemoğlu, Johnson, and Robinson (2001), 25, recounts a very striking and revealing incident. Masire, unlike Khama, was neither a Bangwato nor of royal descent. When his photo was printed on national banknotes, large protests erupted in the Bangwato tribal area. This potentially explosive political situation was defused when Bangwato tribal leaders joined other national leaders to quell the move.

18. D. Sebedubudu, L. Khatib., and A. Bozzini (2017) 'The Atypical Achievers: Botswana, Qatar, and Rwanda' in A. Mungiu-Pippidi and M. Johnson (eds), *Transition to Good Governance: Creating Virtuous Circles of Anti-Corruption* (UK, USA: Edward Elgar Publishing), 34.

19. The Index of Public Integrity (IPI) is compiled and published by a team of researchers at the European Research Centre for Anti-Corruption and State-Building at the Hertie School of Governance in Berlin.

20. UNDP (2021–22) *Human Development Report 2021–22*. Human Development Composite Indices, Table 1, 272 (New York: UNDP) https://hdr.undp.org/content/human-development-report-2021-22

21. World Bank Data Base: Poverty headcount ratio at $2.15 a day (2017 PPP) (% of population), Uruguay. https://data.worldbank.org/indicator/SI.POV.DDAY?locations=UY

22. World Bank. www.worldbank.org/en/country/uruguay/overview.

23. Transparency International (2022) *Corruption Perceptions Index, 2022*. www.transparency.org/en/cpi/2022

24. M. Cohen, N. Lupu, and E. J. Zechmeister (eds) (2017) 'The Political Culture of Democracy in the Americas 2016–17: A Comparative Study of Democracy and Governance', *Americas Barometer (Barometro de las Americas) Latin American Public Opinion Project (LAPOP)*, August.

25. World Bank (2020) World Governance Indicators info.worldbank.org/governance/wgi/.

26. D. North, J. Wallis, and B. Weingast (2012) *Violence and Social Orders: A Conceptual Framework for Interpreting Recorded Human History* (New York: Cambridge University Press).

27. A. Mungiu-Pippidi and M. Johnston (eds) (2017) *Transitions to Good Governance: Creating Virtuous Circles of Anti-Corruption* (UK., USA: Edward Elgar Publishing).

28. D. Buquet and R. Piniero (2016) 'Uruguay's Shift from Clientelism', *Journal of Democracy*, 27, 1 (January), 139–51, p. 143. *Project MUSE*, doi:10.1353/jod.2016.0008.

29. Ibid.

30. D. Buquet and R. P. Rodriguez (2019) 'Party System Change and Transparency in Uruguay', *Taiwan Journal of Democracy*, 15, 1, 113–29.

31. Buquet and Piniero, (2016), 141.

32. The Commission was coordinated by a bright young economist, Enrique V. Iglesias, who later headed the Inter-American Development Bank.

33. D. Buquet and R. Piniero (2015) *The Uruguayan Way from Particularism to Universalism*. EU Grant Agreement Number 290529, Anti-Corruption Policies Revisited, Hertie School of Governance, Berlin; and German Institute of Global and Area Studies (May 2015). (www.againstcorruption.eu/wp-content/uploads/2015/05/D3-Uruguay_Buquet_Pi%23U00f1. eiro.pdf)

34. Buquet and Piniero (2016), 149.

Chapter 13

1. A. Sen (1999) *Development as Freedom* (New York: Anchor Books).

2. P. Pettit (1999) *Republicanism: A Theory of Freedom and Government* (UK: Oxford University Press).

3. D. Acemoglu, J. Robinson (2019) *The Narrow Corridor: How Nations Struggle for Liberty* (UK: Penguin Books), p. 6.

4. T. Hobbes (1651 [2016]) *Leviathan or The Matter, Forme and Power of a Commonwealth Ecclesiasticall and Civil* (Sweden: Wisehouse Classics), p. 65..

5. Ibid., 85. Note that this thought is very much akin to Basu's expression, 'ink on paper', discussed in Chapter 8.

6. Ibid., 64.

7. F. Fukuyama (2005) *State Building: Governance and World Order in the Twenty-First Century* (UK: Profile Books), p. 2.

8. M. Weber (1946) *From Max Weber: Essays in Sociology* (New York: Oxford University Press).

9. Acemoğlu and Robinson, (2019), 40.

10. J. Stiglitz (2019) *People, Power, and Profits: Progressive Capitalism in an Age of Discontent* (UK: Penguin Random House), p. 139.

11. A distinguishing feature of the public goods is that once provided, nobody can be excluded from its benefits. Paul Samuelson, winner of the Economics Nobel Prize in 1970, first introduced the concept, distinguishing such goods and ordinary private goods in the following short but ground-breaking paper of only three pages.

    P. Samuelson (1954) 'The Pure Theory of Public Expenditure', *The Review of Economics and Statistics*, 36, 4 (November), 387–9.

12. N. Forbes (2022) *The Struggle and the Promise: Restoring India's Potential* (India: Harper Collins), p. 43.

13. A. Inkeles and D. SmithD (1974) *Becoming Modern* (Cambridge, MA: Harvard University Press), p. 143.

14. Inkeles and Smith, (1974), 174.

15. Stiglitz, (2019), 142.

16. World Bank (2002) *World Development Report 2002: Building Institutions for the Markets* (New York: Oxford University Press), 100.

17. Ibid., 129.

18. Ajitava Raychaudhuri (2004) 'Lessons from the Land Reform Movement in West Bengal, India'.
    A case study from 'Scaling Up Poverty Reduction: A Global Learning Process and Conference', Shanghai, 25–27 May 2004, World Bank.

19. Debabrata Bandyopadhyay (2003) 'Land Reforms and Agriculture: The West Bengal Experience' *Economic and Political Weekly*, 38, 9 (1–7 March), 879–84: www.jstor.org/stable/4413274.

20. Hernando De Soto (2000) *The Mystery of Capital. Why Capitalism Triumphs in the West and Fails Everywhere Else* (New York: Basic Books).

21. Rajan, (2019), 138.

22. Fukuyama, (2005), 4.

23. R. Reagan (1981) *President Ronald Reagan's Inaugural Address*. 20 January 1981, USA: 'the government is not the solution to our problem; government is the problem'.

24. F, Fukuyama (1989) 'The End of History', *The National Interest No. 16* (Summer), 3.

25. Rajan, (2019), 167.

26. A. Krueger (1993) *Political Economy of Policy Reform in Developing Countries* (Cambridge, MA: MIT Press), p. 11.

27. World Bank (1997) *World Development Report 1997: The State in a Changing World* (New York: Oxford University Press), 25.

28. Fukuyama, (2005), p. xx.

29. This section on the two-part strategy draws on concepts presented in World Bank, (1997).

30. World Bank, (1997), 3.

31. Forbes, (2022), 22.

32. Ibid., 28.

33. A. Mungiu-Pippidi (2017) 'Corruption as Social Order' *Background Paper, Governance and the Law, World Development Report* 2017, 2.

34. S. Paul (2012) *A Life and its Lessons—Memoirs* (Bangalore: Public Affairs Centre).

35. World Bank, (1997), 10.

Chapter 14

1. R. Rajan (2019) *The Third Pillar: How Markets and the State Leave the Community Behind* (India: Harper Collins Publishers), 74.

2. Ibid., 71.

3. A. Smith (1776 [1902]) *An Inquiry into the Nature of and Causes of the Wealth of Nations* (New York: P. F. Collier and Son), 14. Page numbers refer to the Kindle edition of this text.

4. Ibid., 86.

5. Ibid., 76.

6. Rajan, (2019), 85.

7. J. Stiglitz (2019) *People, Power, and Profits: Progressive Capitalism in an Age of Discontent* (UK: Penguin Random House), 145.

8. Ibid.

9. World Bank (2002) *World Development Report 2002: Building Institutions for the Markets* (New York: Oxford University Press), 108.

10. Ron Chernow (1998) *Titan: The Life of John D. Rockefeller, Sr.* (Random House).

11. Rajan, (2019), 111.

12. George J. Stigler (1971) 'The Theory of Economic Regulation', *The Bell Journal of Economics and Management Science*, 2, 1, 3–21, https://doi.org/10.2307/3003160.

13. Sam Peltzman (1993) 'George Stigler's Contribution to the Economic Analysis of Regulation', *Journal of Political Economy*, 101, 5, 818–32, www.jstor.org/stable/2138597.

14. Rajan, (2019), 284.

Chapter 15

1. R. Rajan (2019) *The Third Pillar: How Markets and the State Leave the Community Behind* (India: Harper Collins Publishers), p. xiv–xv.

2. L. Ferrari (1956) 'The Origin of the State according to Plato', *Laval théologique et philosophique*, 12 (2), 145–51 https://doi.org/10.7202/1019942ar. Accessed on September 27, 2021.

3. T. Sinclair (1981) *Aristotle: The Politics*. Translated by T. Sinclair (UK: Penguin Books,1962, revised edition 1981).

4. A. Bandura (1977) 'Self-efficacy: Toward a Unifying Theory of Behavioural Change', *Psychological Review*, 84, 2, 191–215. https://doi.org/10.1037/0033-295X.84.2.191.

5. L. Guiso, P. Sapienza, and L. Zingales (2016) 'Long-Term Persistence', *Journal of the European Economic Association* July, 1–36.

6. Social capital as measured by more non-profit organizations per capita, the presence of an organ bank, and fewer children caught cheating in national examinations.

7. Guiso et al., (2016), 34.

8. E. Ostrom (1990) *Governing the Commons: The Evolution of Institutions for Collective Action* UK: Cambridge University Press.

9. R. Putnam (2000) *Bowling Alone: The Collapse and Revival of American Community* (New York: Simon and Schuster).

10. B. Katz and J. Nowak (2017) *The New Localism: How Cities Can Thrive in the Age of Populism* (Washington, DC: Brookings Institution Press).

11. Ibid., 121.

12. Ibid., 2.

13. Right to Infiormation (RTI) Act, India (2013), Para 10, p. 6.

14. Times of India, Ahmedabad (April 3, 2021) https://timesofindia.indiatimes.com/city/ahmedabad/roads-in-bad-shape-seek-material-sample-under-rti/articles how/8187740.cms

15. Singapore REACH.

16. World Bank, (1997), op. cit., p. 117.

17. Paul, S. (2012). *A Life and its Lessons—Memoirs* (Bangalore: Public Affairs Centre).

18. World Bank, (1997), op. cit., Box 7.5, p. 119.

19. A. Asthana, (2008). 'Decentralization and Corruption: Evidence from Drinking Water Sector'. *Public Administration Development*,28, 181–189. Published online in Wiley InterScience.

20. Rajan, op. cit. (2019), p. 305.

21. http://ipaidabribe.com

22. https://onemapggm.gmda.gov.in

23. J. Helliwell and R. Putnam (1995). 'Economic Growth and Social Capital in Italy'. *Eastern Economic Journal*, 21, 3, 295–307, Palgrave Macmillan.

24. R. Putnam (1993). 'What Makes Democracy Work?' *National Civic Review*, 82, 2, Spring 1983, Wiley Online Library, pp. 101–7.

25. R. Putnam (1993). *Making Democracy Work: Civic Traditions in Modern Italy* (Princeton, NJ: Princeton University Press).

26. World Bank, (1997), op. cit., p. 122.
27. D. Winkler and B. Yeo (2007). *Identifying the Impact of Education Decentralization on the Quality of Education* (Washington, D.C.: EQUIP2, USAID).
28. A. Islam (2016). 'Parent-Teacher Meetings and Student Outcomes: Evidence from Field Experiments in Remote Outcomes'. *Working Paper, F-31022-BGD-1* (International Growth Centre, LSE, and University of Oxford).
29. A. Banerjee, S. Cole, E. Duflo and L. Lindon (2007). 'Remedying Education: Evidence from Two Randomized Experiments in India', *The Quarterly Journal of Economics,* 122(3), 1235–1264.
30. T. Hobbes (1651). *Leviathan, or the Matter of Forme and Power of a Commonwealth* Ecclesiastical and Civil Wisehouse Classics. Sweden, 2016, p. 65.
31. D. Acemoğlu, and J. Robinson (2019). *The Narrow Corridor: How Nations Struggle for Liberty.* (UK: Penguin Books)., p. 34.
32. Ibid., p. 38.
33. Ibid., p. 40.
34. The White House, Office of the Press Secretary (2011): 'Fact Sheet: The Open Government Partnership' The Office of the Press Secretary, September 20, 2011).
35. B. Obama (2014): 'Speech at the Open Government Partnership Meeting at the United Nations', (Office of the Press Secretary, The White House, on You Tube, September 24, 2014).
36. Ibid.
37. Open Government Partnership (2022), 'The Skeptic's Guide to Open Government', *OGP Washington, 2022.*
38. Open Government Partnership (2019), *Open Government Partnership Global Report: Democracy Beyond the Ballot Box* (First Edition, Vol I and II, March 2019).
39. Open Government Partnership (2021).
40. Ibid.
41. Ibid.
42. Piotrowski, Berliner, Ingrams (2022).
43. A. Hirschman (1969), *Exit, Voice and Loyalty: Responses to Decline in Firms, Organizations and States* (Harvard University Press, Cambridge, Massachusetts and London, England).
44. R. Sharma (2017), *The 10 Rules of Successful Nations* (Penguin UK, 2017), p. 32 Kindle Edition.
45. Ibid.
46. Ibid., p. 33.
47. Ibid., p. 39.
48. Stephanie M. Rizio and Ahmed Skali (2020), 'How often do dictators have positive economic effects? Global evidence, 1858–2010'. *The Leadership Quarterly,* 31(2020), 3, 101302. Elsevier.
49. Ibid., p. 17.
50. Ibid.
51. Katz and Nowak, (2017), op cit, p. 1.

52. Y. Levin (2016). *The Fractured Republic: Renewing America's Social Contract in the Age of Individualism* (New York: Basic Books), p. 5.

53. Daron Acemoğlu and James Robinson (2000) 'Why did the West Extend the Franchise? Democracy, Inequality and Growth in the Historical Perspective', *Quarterly Journal of Economics*, p. 1167.

54. Ibid., p. 1182.

55. Rajan (2019), p. 120.

56. Lizzeri, Alsssandro and Persico, Nicola (2004). 'Why did the Elites Extend the Suffrage? Democracy and the Scope of Government, with an application to Britain's Age of Reform'. *Quarterly Journal of Economics*, p. 711.

57. Ibid., pp. 710–711.

58. Rajan (2019), p. 122.

59. Rajan (2019), p. xviii.

Chapter 16

1. Kohli, Nag & Vilkelyte (2022), 35.

2. Intergovernmental Panel on Climate Change (IPCC), August 2021.

3. *Nature* 'Climate Change' (October 2021).

4. Kohli, Nag & Vilkelyte (2022), 46.

Bibliography

Acemoğlu, D., 2008, 'Interactions Between Governance and Growth', in Douglass North, Daron Acemoğlu, Francis Fukuyama, and Dani Rodrik, eds, *Governance, Growth, and Development Decision-Making* (Washington, DC: World Bank), 1–8.

Acemoğlu, D. and Robinson, J., 2000, 'Why did the West Extend the Franchise? Democracy, Inequality and Growth in the Historical Perspective', *Quarterly Journal of Economics*, 115 (4) (November), 1167–99.

Acemoğlu, D. and Robinson, J., 2008, 'The Role of Institutions in Growth and Development', in *Commission on Growth and Development Working Paper No. 10* (Washington, DC: World Bank), https://openknowledge.worldbank.org/handle/10986/28045.

Acemoğlu, D. and Robinson, J., 2012, *Why Nations Fail: The Origins of Power, Prosperity, and Poverty* (New York: Crown).

Acemoğlu, D. and Robinson, J., 2019, *The Narrow Corridor: How Nations Struggle for Liberty* (UK: Penguin Books).

Acemoğlu, D., Johnson, S., and Robinson, J., 2001, 'An African Success Story: Botswana', MIT Department of Economics, *Working Paper Series, WP-01-37* (July).

Acemoğlu, D., Johnson, S., and Robinson, J., 2005, 'Institutions as a Fundamental Cause of Long Run Growth', in Philippe Aghion and Steven Durlauf, eds, *Handbook of Economic Growth*, 1A (Amsterdam, Netherlands: Elsevier BV), 385–472.

Alatas, S.Hussain., 2015, *The Problem of Corruption*. (First published 1968 as *The Sociology of Corruption*.) (Singapore: Donald Moore Press, 1986; Malaysia: The Other Press Sdn. Bhd. Selangor, rev. edn, 2015), 95–6.

Alchian, A., 1965a, 'The Basis of Some Recent Advances in the Theory of Management of the Firm', *The Journal of Industrial Economics*, 14 (1) (November), 30–41.

Alchian, A., 1965b, 'Some Economics of Property Rights', *Il Politico*, 30 (4) (December, 816–29.

Aldashev, G., Platteau, J.-P., and Wahhaj, Z., 2011, 'Legal Reform in the Presence of a Living Custom: An Economic Approach', *Proceedings of the National Academy of Sciences of the United States*, 108 (supplement 4), 21320–5.

Alesina, A., Giuliano, P., and Nunn, N., 2013, 'On the Origin of Gender Roles: Women and the Plough', *Quarterly Journal of Economics*, 128, 469–530.

Ambraseys, N. and Bilham, R., 2011, 'Corruption Kills', *Nature*, 469 (7329), 153; DOI: 10.1038/469153a.

Amsden, A., 1989, *Asia's Next Giant: South Korea and Late Industrialization* (New York: Oxford University Press).

Andreoni, J., 1988, 'Why Free Ride? Strategies and Learning in Public Goods Experiments', *Journal of Public Economics*, 37, 291–304.

Arrow, K., 1970, *Essays in the Theory of Risk-Bearing* (Amsterdam: North Holland).

Asian Development Bank, 1995, *Governance: Sound Development Management* (ADB: Manila).

Asian Development Bank, 2012, 'Chapter 2: Rising Inequality Concerns in Asia', *Asian Development Outlook 2012: Confronting Rising Inequality in Asia* (ADB: Manila) 1–298.

Asthana, A., 2008, 'Decentralization and Corruption: Evidence from Drinking Water Sector', *Public Administration and Development*, 28, 181–9. (online publication: Wiley).

Axelrod, R., 1984, *The Evolution of Cooperation* (New York: Basic Books).

Ban, S. P. Moon and Perkins, D., 1980, *Rural Development: Studies in the Modernization of the Republic of Korea*, 1945–1975 (Cambridge, MA: Harvard University Press).

Bandura, A., 1977, 'Self-efficacy: Toward a Unifying Theory of Behavioral Change', *Psychological Review*, 4 (2), 191–215.

Bandyopadhyay, D., 2003, 'Land Reforms and Agriculture: The West Bengal Experience', *Economic and Political Weekly*, 38 (9) (1–7 March), 879–84, www.jstor.org/stable/4413274.

Banerjee, A., 1997, 'A Theory of Misgovernance', *The Quarterly Journal of Economics*, 112 (4) (November), 1289–1332.

Banerjee, A. and Duflo, E., 2011, *Poor Economics* (India: Random House).

Banerjee, A. and Duflo, E., 2019, *Good Economics for Hard Times* (New Delhi: Juggernaut Books).

Banerjee, A. and Duflo, E., 2020, 'How Poverty Ends: The Many Paths to Progress and Why They Might Not Continue', *Foreign Affairs*, 99 (1), 22.

Banerjee, A., Mullainathan, S., and Hanna, R., 2012, 'Corruption', NBER *Working Paper 17968*, April (NBER, Cambridge, MA).

Banerjee, A., Cole, S., et al., 2007, 'Remedying Education: Evidence from Randomized Experiments in India', *The Quarterly Journal of Economics*, 122 (3), 1235–64.

Banfield, E. (with the assistance of Laura Fasano Banfield), 1958, *The Moral Basis of a Backward Society* (Glencoe, ILL: Free Press).

Barbalet, J., 2020, 'Violence and Politics: Reconsidering Weber's "Politics as a Vocation"', *Sociology Online First* (10 January 55(1) 56–70); DOI: 10.1177/0038038519895748.

Bardhan, P., 1997, 'Corruption and Development: A Review of Issues', *Journal of Economic Literature* 35 (3), 1320–46.

Bardhan, P., 2005, 'Institutions Matter, But Which Ones?', *Economics of Transition* 13 (3), 499–532.

Basu, K., 2000, *Prelude to Political Economy: A Study of the Social and Political Foundation of Economics* (New York: Oxford University Press).

Basu, K., 2010, *Beyond the Invisible Hand: Groundwork for a New Economics* (London, UK: Penguin Books), pp. 1–15.

Basu, K., 2011, 'Corruption and Bribery-Summary (April 2011): Why, for a Class of Bribes, the Act of Giving a Bribe Should be Treated as Legal?' Published in Ministry of Finance Government of India, *Working Paper 1/2011-DEA* (March 2011).

Basu, K., 2018, *The Republic of Beliefs: A New Approach to Law and Economics* (Princeton, NJ: Princeton University Press).

Basu, K. and Weibull, J., 2002, 'Punctuality: A Cultural Trait as Equilibrium', MIT Department of Economics, *Working Paper Series, WP 02–26* (Cambridge, MA).

BBC, 2010, Report on UN International Anti Corruption Day December 9, 2010. http://news.bbc.co.uk/2/shared/bsp/hi/pdfs/09_12_10_world_speaks.pdf. Accessed July 26, 2019

Beasley, W. G., 1990, *The Rise of Modern Japan* (New York: St Martin's Press).

Becker, G., 1968, 'Crime and Punishment: An Economic Approach', *Journal of Political Economy* 76 (2), 169–217, accessed 15 Oct. 2020.

Behavioural Insights Team, UK (BIT), 2012, *Applying Behavioural Insights to Reduce Fraud, Errors, and Debt* (London: Cabinet Office, BIT).

Benartzi, S. and Thaler, R., 2013, 'Behavioral Economics and the Retirement Crisis', *Science*, 339 (6124), 1152–3.

Berg, J., Dickhaut, J., and McCabe, K., 1995, 'Trust, Reciprocity and Social History', *Games and Economic Behavior*, 10 (1), 122–42.

Bertrand, M. and Morse, A., 2011, 'Information Disclosure, Cognitive Biases, and Payday Borrowing', *Journal of Finance* 66 (6), 1865–93.

Bhavnani, R., 2009, 'Do Electoral Quotas Work After They Are Withdrawn? Evidence from a Natural Experiment in India', *American Political Science Review* 103 (1), 23–35.

Bicchieri, C., 2002, 'Covenants Without Swords: Group Identity, Norms, and Communication in Social Dilemmas', *Rationality and Society*, 14 (2) (May), 192–228.

Bicchieri, C., 2006, *The Grammar of Society: The Nature and Dynamics of Social Norms* (Cambridge University Press).

Bicchieri, C. and Mercier, H., 2014, 'Norms and Beliefs: How Change Occurs', *The Jerusalem Philosophical Quarterly* 63 (January), 60–82.

Binmore, K., 2020, *Crooked Thinking or Straight Talk? Modernizing Epicurean Scientific Philosophy*, (Cham: Springer); p. 31

Binmore, K. and Samuelson, L., 2002, 'The Evolution of Focal Points', *Economics Working Papers 0017*, Institute for Advanced Study, School of Social Science (Princeton University).

Bird, R., 1977, 'Land Taxation and Economic Development: The Model of Meiji', *Japan Journal of Development Studies* (January), 162–74.

Bisin, A. and Verdier, T., 2001, 'The Economics of Cultural Transmission and the Dynamics of Preferences', *Journal of Economic Theory* 97 (2),298–319.

Blount, S., 1995, 'When Social Outcomes Aren't Fair: The Effect of Causal Attributions on Preferences', *Organizational Behavior and Human Decision Processes* 63 (2), 131–44.

Bohnet, I. et al., 2010, 'The Elasticity of Trust: How to Promote Trust in the Arab Middle East and the United States', *Faculty Research Working Paper Series*, RWP10-031 (Cambridge, MA: Harvard Kennedy School).

Borgonovi, F. and T. Burns., 2015, 'The educational roots of trust', OECD Education Working Papers, No. 119, OECD Publishing, Paris, https://doi.org/10.1787/5js1k v85dfvd-en

Bovaird, T. and Löffler, E., 2002, 'Moving from Excellence Models of Local Service Delivery to Benchmarking Good Local Governance', *International Review of Administrative Sciences* 68 (1), 9–24.

Bowles, S. and Polania-Reyes, S., 2011, 'Economic Incentives and Social Preferences: Substitutes or Complements?', *Quaderni del Dipartimento di Economia Politica Statistica*, *WP No. 617* (University of Sienna, October).

Brasz, H., 1970, 'The Sociology of Corruption' in Arnold J. Heidenheimer (ed.), *Political Corruption: Readings in Comparative Analysis* (New York: Holt, Rinehart, and Winston), 41–46.

Breen, J., 1996, 'The Imperial Oath of April 1868: Ritual, Politics, and Power in the Restoration', *Monumenta Nipponica*, 51 (4) (Winter407–29).

Breiman, L. et al., 1993, *Classification and Regression Trees* (Boca Raton, FL: Chapman and Hall). Referred to in Todd and Gigerenzer, 2000.

Buchan, B. and Hill, L., 2014, *An Intellectual History of Political Corruption* (UK: Palgrave Macmillan).

Buquet, D. and Piniero, R., 2015, The Uruguayan Way from Particularism to Universalism. EU Grant Agreement Number 290529, Anti-Corruption Policies Revisited, Hertie School of Governance, Berlin; and German Institute of Global and Area Studies (May 2015). (https://www.againstcorruption.eu/wp-content/uploads/2015/05/D3U-ruguay_Buquet_Pi%23U00f1eiro.pdf).

Buquet, D. and Piniero, R., 2016, 'Uruguay's Shift from Clientelism', *Journal of Democracy*, 17 (1), 139–51.

Buquet, D. and Rodriguez, R. P., 2019, 'Party System Change and Transparency in Uruguay', *Taiwan Journal of Democracy*, 15 (1), 113–29.

Byrsk, A., 2013, 'Changing Hearts and Minds: Sexual Politics and Human Rights' in Thomas Risse, Stephen Ropp, and Kathryn Sikkink, *The Persistent Power of Huan Rights: From Commitment to Compliance* (Cambridge: Cambridge University Press), 259–274.

Campos, J. and Root, H., 1996, *The Key to the East Asian Miracle: Making Shared Growth Credible* (Washington, DC: Brookings Institution).

Cárcaba, A., González, E., Ventura, J., Arrondo, R. et al., 2017, 'How Does Good Governance Relate to Quality of Life?', *Sustainability*, 9 (631), 1–16.

Cardenas, J.C., 2004, 'Norms from outside and from inside: An experimental analysis on the governance of local ecosystems', *Forest Policy and Economics* 6 (3), 229–41; DOI:10.1016/j.forpol.2004.03.006.

Carpenter, C., 2010, 'A Meta-Analysis of the Effectiveness of Health Belief Model Variables in Predicting Behavior', *Health Communication* (9 December), 25: 8, 661–9; DOI: 10.1080/10410236.2010.521906.

Centennial Group, Washington, D.C. 2021, In-house Growth Model, Unpublished.

Chernow, R., 1998, *Titan: The Life of John D. Rockefeller, Sr.* (New York: Random House).

Chung, Y., 2007, *Korea in the Fast Lane* (UK: Oxford University Press).

Chzhen, Y., 2013, 'Education and Democratisation Tolerance of Diversity, Political Engagement, and Under-standing of Democracy', Background paper, Report 2014/ED/EFA/MRT/PI/03, United Nations Educational, Scientific, and Cultural Organization, Paris.

Coase, R., 1937, 'The Nature of the Firm', *Economica* 4, 386–405.

Coase, R., 1984, 'The New Institutional Economics', *Journal of Institutional and Theoretical Economics*, 140, 229–31.

Cohen, M., Lupu, N., and Zechmeister, E. J. (eds), 2017, 'The Political Culture of Democracy in the Americas 2016-17: A Comparative Study of Democracy and Governance', *Americas Barometer (Barometro de las Americas) Latin American Public Opinion Project (LAPOP)* (August).Cooper, A., 2021, '360 Special, 2021,'

President Barack Obama in Conversation with Anderson Cooper (CNN, 7 June, 2021).

Dawes, R. and Thaler, R., 1988, 'Anomalies Cooperation', *Journal of Economic Perspectives*, 2 (3) (Summer), 187–97.

Debroy, B., 2000, *In the Dock: Absurdities of Indian Law* (New Delhi: Konark).

Desaigues, B., et al., 2007, 'Monetary Value of a Life Expectancy Gain due to Reduced Air Pollution: Lessons from a Contingent Valuation in France', *Revue d'économie politique*, 117 (5); *Numéro spécial en Hommage à Brigitte Desaigues* (Editions Dalloz Stable, September–October), 675–98. Available at www.jstor.org/stable/24702540.

De Soto, H., 2000, *The Mystery of Capital. Why Capitalism Triumphs in the West and Fails Everywhere Else* (New York: Basic Books).

Devarajan, S., 2008, ' "Two Comments on Governance Indicators: Where Are We, Where Should We Be Going?", by Daniel Kaufmann and Art Kraay', *World Bank Research Observer* 23, 3–34.

Devoto, F., et al., 2012, 'Chapter 7: Institutions Matter Happiness on Tap: Piped Water Adoption in Urban Morocco', *American Economic Journal: Economic Policy*, 4 (4) (November), 68–99.

Dixit, A., 2009, 'Governance, Institutions and Economic Activity', delivered as *Presidential Address to the American Economic Association* (4 January).

Dobel, P.J., 1978, 'The Corruption of a State', *American Political Science Review*, 72 (3), 958–73.

Duflo, E., Kremer, M., and Robinson, J., 2010, 'Nudging Farmers to Use Fertilizer: Theory and Experimental Evidence from Kenya', *Working Paper* (October), https://economics.mit.edu/files/6170 , p. 6. Also published in *American Economic Review*, 2011, 101 (6): 2350–90; DOI: 10.1257/aer.101.6.2350

Duke, B., 2009, 'The Gakusei: THE FIRST NATIONAL PLAN FOR EDUCATION, (1872)' in B. C. Duke, *The History of Modern Japanese Education, 1872–1890* (UK: Rutgers University Press), 61–76.

Easterly, W., 2002, *The Elusive Quest for Growth: Economists' Adventures and Misadventures in the Tropics* (Cambridge, MA: The MIT Press).

Easterly, W., 2013, *The Tyranny of Experts: Economists, Dictators, and the Forgotten Rights of the Poor* (New York: Basic Books).

Eckstein, D., Kunzel, V., and Schafer, Laura, 2021. 'Global Climate Risk Index 2021—Who Suffers Most from Extreme Weather Events? Weather-Related Loss Events in 2019 and 2000–2019', Briefing Paper, Germanwatch, Bonn January 2021. https://germanwatch.org/sites/default/files/Global%20Climate%20Risk%20Index%202021_1.pdf

Eggertsson, T., 1998, 'Limits to Institutional Reforms', *Scandinavian Journal of Economics*, 100, 335–57.

Eggertsson, T., 2005, *Imperfect Institutions: Possibilities and Limits of Reform* (Ann Arbor, MI: The University of Michigan Press).

Ellickson, R., 1991, *Order Without Law* (Cambridge, MA: Harvard University Press).

Elster, J., 1989, *The Cement of Society: A Study of Social Order* (UK: Cambridge University Press).

Escresa, L. and Picci, L., 2015, 'A New Cross-National Measure of Corruption', *Policy Research Working Paper, No. 7371* (Washington, DC: World Bank, July). 1–43.

European Research Centre for Anti-Corruption and State-Building at the Hertie School of Governance, Berlin, 2019, *The Index of Public Integrity,* https://integrity-index.org/.

Evans, J. S. B. T., 2008, 'Dual-Processing Accounts of Reasoning, Judgment, and Social Cognition', *Annual Review of Psychology,* 59, 255–278.

Evans, J. S. B. T. and Frankish, K. (eds), 2009, *In Two Minds: Dual Processes and Beyond* (UK: Oxford University Press).

Falk, A. and Kosfeld, M., 2006, 'The Hidden Costs of Control', *American Economic Review,* 96 (5), 1611–30.

Ferrari, L., 1956, 'The Origin of the State according to Plato', *Laval théologique et philosophique,* 12 (2), 145–51. Available at https://doi.org/10.7202/1019942ar, accessed 27 Sept. 2021.

Fisman, R. and Edward, M., 2007, 'Corruption, Norms, and Legal Enforcement: Evidence from Diplomatic Parking Tickets', *Journal of Political Economy,* 115 (6), 1020–48.

Fjeldstad, O., 2005, 'Corruption in Tax Administration: Lessons from Institutional Reforms in Uganda', *Working Paper 10* (Bergen, Norway, Chr. Michelson Institute).

Forbes, N., 2022, *The Struggle and the Promise: Restoring India's Potential* (India: Harper Collins).

Freese, J., 2011, 'Preferences', in *The Oxford Handbook of Analytical Sociology* (Oxford: Oxford University Press), 94–114.

Friedman, L., 2016, *Impact: How Law Affects Behavior* (Cambridge, MA: Harvard University Press).

Friedman, M., 1966, 'The Methodology of Positive Economics' in M. Friedman, *Essays in Positive Economics* (Chicago, IL: University of Chicago Press), 3–16, 30–43.

Friedman, M., 1970, 'The Social responsibility of Business is to Increase its Profits', *The New York Times Magazine* (September), 17.

Fryer, R. et al., 2012, 'Enhancing the Efficacy of Teacher Incentives Through Loss Aversion: A Field Experiment', *NBER Working Paper 18237* (NBER, July).

Fukuyama, F., 1989, 'The End of History', *The National Interest,* 16, 1–18. Center for the National Interest (Summer).

Fukuyama, F., 2005, *State Building: Governance and World Order in the Twenty-First Century* (UK: Profile Books).

Fukuyama, F., 2011, *The Origins of Political Order: From Pre-Human Times to the French Revolution* (New York, NY: Farrar, Strauss, and Giroux).

Fukuyama, F., 2013, 'What is Governance?', Center for Global Development, Working Paper 314 (Washington, DC), 1–18.

Fulcher, J., 1988, 'The Bureaucratization of the State and the Rise of Japan', *The British Journal of Sociology,* 39 (2) (June), 228–54.

Furubotn, E. G. and Richter, R., 2005, *Institutions and Economic Theory* (2nd edn, Ann Arbor, MI: The University of Michigan Press).

Gauri, V., Rahman, T., and Sen, I., 2020, 'Shifting Normal Norms to Reduce Open Defecation in Rural India', *Behavioural Public Policy* 7(2), 1–25.

Gintis, H., Fehr, E.et al. (eds), 2005, 'Moral Sentiments and Material Interests: Origins, Evidence, and Consequences', in H. Gintis, E. Fehr et al., *Moral Sentiments and Material Interests: The Foundations of Cooperation in Economic Life* (Cambridge, MA: MIT Press), 3–39.

Global Corruption Barometer, *Africa* (10th edn, July 2019).

Gneezy, U. and Rustichini, A., 2000a, 'A Fine is a Price', *Journal of Legal Studies*, XXIX (I), 1–17.

Gneezy, U. and Rustichini, A., 2000b, 'Pay Enough or Don't Pay at All', *Quarterly Journal of Economics*, 115 (3), 791–810.

Good, K., 1992, 'Interpreting the Exceptionality of Botswana', *The Journal of Modern African Studies*, 30 (1), 69–95; DOI:10.1017/S0022278X00007734.

Good, K., 1994, 'Corruption and Mismanagement in Botswana: A Best-Case Example?', *The Journal of Modern African Studies*, 32 (3), 499–521.

Green, D., 2016, *How Change Happens* (Oxford: Oxford University Press).

Green, D.P., Kahneman, D., and Kunreuther, H., 1994, 'How the Scope and Method of Public Funding Affect Willingness to Pay for Public Goods', *The Public Opinion Quarterly* 58 (1), 49–67, www.jstor.org/stable/2749423.

Greif, A., 1993, 'Contract Enforceability and Economic Institutions in Early Trade: The Maghribi Traders', *American Economic Review*, 83 (3), 525–48.

Greif, A., 1996, *Institutions and the Path to the Modern Economy: Lessons from Medieval Trade* (UK: Cambridge University Press).

Greif, A., 2014, 'Do Institutions Evolve?', *Journal of Bio-economics*, 16 (1), 1–9.

Guiso, L., Sapienza, P., and Zingales, L., 2016, 'Long Term Persistence', *Journal of the European Economic Association*, 14 (6) (2016), 1401–36.

Gupta, S., Davoodi, H., and Alonso-Terme, R., 2002, 'Does Corruption Affect Income Inequality and Poverty?', *Economics of Governance* (3), 23–45.

Gusfield, J., 1993, 'The Social Symbolism of Smoking and Health' in R. Rabin and S. Sugarman, eds, *Smoking Policy: Law, Politics, and Culture* (United Kingdom: Oxford University Press), 49–68.

Habyarimana, J. and Jack, W., 2009, 'Heckle and Chide: Results of a Randomized Road Safety Intervention in Kenya', *Working Papers 169* (Center for Global Development).

Hadfield, G., 2016, *Rules for a Flat World: Why Humans Invented Law and How to Reinvent it for a Complex Global Economy* (UK: Oxford University Press).

Hanley, S., 1983, 'A High Standard of Living in Nineteenth Century Japan: Fact or Fantasy?', *The Journal of Economic History*, 43 (1) (March), 183–92.

Hardin, G., 1968, 'The Tragedy of the Commons', *Science*, 162 (3859), 1243–8. Available at www.jstor.org/stable/1724745, accessed 26 June 2021.

Hashimoto, T., 2008, 'Japanese Clocks and the History of Punctuality in Modern Japan', *East Asian Science, Technology and Society: An International Journal*, 2 (1), 123–133.

Havel, V., 1978, 'The Power of the Powerless', *International Center of Non-violent Conflict* (October). Available at www.nonviolent-conflict.org/wp-content/uplo ads/1979/01/the-power-of-the-powerless.pdf, accessed 26 June 2021.

Helliwell, J. and Putnam, R., 1995, 'Economic Growth and Social Capital in Italy', *Eastern Economic Journal*, 21 (3) (Summer), 295–307.

Herre, B., Ortiz-Ospina, E., Roser, M., 2013, Democracy, Published online at OurWorldInData.org. https://ourworldindata.org/democracy

Herrmann, B., Thoni, C., and Gachter, S., 2008, Antisocial Punishment Across Societies', *Science*, 319 (7 March), 1362–7.

Heyman, J. and Ariley, D., 2004, 'Effort for Payment: A Tale of Two Markets', *Psychological Science*, 15 (11), 787–93.

Hill, C., 'The Century of Revolution (1603–1714)', 1961, Routledge Classics (referred to in D. North. and B. Weingast, 1989, 'Constitutions and Commitment: The Evolution of Institutions Governing Public Choice in Seventeenth Century England'), *The Journal of Economic History*, XLIX (4), 803–32.

Hirschleifer, J., 1985, 'The Expanding Domain of Economics', *American Economic Review* 75 (6) (December), 53–70.

Hirschman, A., 1969, *Exit, Voice and Loyalty: Responses to Decline in Firms, Organizations and States* (Cambridge, MA and London, UK: Harvard University Press).

Hobbes, T., 2016 [1651], *Leviathan, or the Matter of Forme and Power of a Commonwealth Ecclesiastical and Civil* (Sweden: Wisehouse Classics).

Hoff, K. and Pandey, P., 2006, 'Discrimination, Social Identity, and Durable Inequalities', *American Economic Review*, 96 (2) (May), 206–11.

Horie, H., 'Revolution and Reform in Meiji Restoration', 1952, *Kyoto University Economic Review*, 22 (1), 23–34, https://doi.org/10.11179/ker1926.22.23.

Huffman, J., 2003, 'The Meiji Restoration Era, 1868–1889', *Japan Society*.

Huffman, J., 2019, *Politics of the Meiji Press: The Life of Fukuchi Gen'ichirō* (Honolulu, HA: University Press of Hawaii).

Hume, D., edited with an introduction by Stephen Copley and Andrew Edgar, 1996 [1740], 'Essay 9: Of the Dignity or Meanness of Human Nature' in D. Hume, *Selected Essays* (Oxford World's Classics, Kindle Edition)].

Hume, D., 2017, 'Essay IV: Of the First Principles of Government' in D. Hume, *Essays, Moral, Political, and Literary, Volume 1, Essays and Treatises on Several Subjects in Two Volumes* (Hard Press, Kindle Edition).

Huntington, S. P., 1968, *Political Order in Changing Societies* (New Haven, CT: Yale University Press).

Hurwicz, L., 2007, *But Who Will Guard the Guardians?* Nobel Prize Lecture.

Hyperides, *Against Demosthenes*, Fragment 3. From *Minor Attic Orators in two volumes, 2*, with an English translation by J. O. Burtt, 1962 (Cambridge, MA, Harvard University Press; London, William Heinemann Ltd.) www.perseus.tufts.edu/hopper/text?doc=Perseus%3Atext%3A1999.01.0140%3Aspeech%3D5%3Afragment%3D3.

Hyperides, *Against Demosthenes*, Fragment 9. From *Minor Attic Orators in two volumes, 2*, with an English translation by J. O. Burtt, 1962 (Cambridge, MA, Harvard University Press; London, William Heinemann Ltd.) www.perseus.tufts.edu/hopper/text?doc=Perseus%3Atext%3A1999.01.0140%3Aspeech%3D5%3Afragment%3D9.

Inkeles, A. and Smith, D., 1974, *Becoming Modern* (Cambridge, MA: Harvard University Press).

Intergovernmental Panel on Climate Change (IPCC). Summary for Policymakers. Climate Change 2021: The Physical Science Basis. Contribution of Working Group I to the Sixth Assessment Report of the Intergovernmental Panel on Climate Change. [Valerie Masson-Delmontte et al., eds.]. Geneva, Switzerland: Intergovernmental Panel on Climate Change (IPCC), 2021.

International Monetary Fund, 2015, 'Current Challenges in Revenue Mobilization: Improving Tax Compliance', *IMF Staff Report* (April).

International Monetary Fund, 2017, 'G-20 Report', *Fostering Inclusive Growth.*

Isaac, M., McCue, K., and Plott, C., 1985, 'Public Goods Provision in an Experimental Environment', *Journal of Public Economics*, 26, 51–74.

Islam, A., 2016, 'Parent-Teacher Meetings and Student Outcomes: Evidence from Field Experiments in Remote Communities', *Working Paper, F-31022-BGD-1* (International Growth Centre, LSE, and University of Oxford).

Jannetta, A. B., 1992, 'Famine Mortality in Nineteenth Century Japan: The Evidence from a Temple Death Register', *Population Studies*, 46 (3) (November), 427–43. Available at www.jstor.org/stable/2175288, accessed 18 Aug. 2021.

Jensen, M.F., 2018, 'Building of the Scandinavian States: Establishing Weberian Bureaucracy and Curbing Corruption from the Mid-Seventeenth Century to the End of the Nineteenth Century' (Aarhus University).

Jensen, R. and Oster, E., 2009, 'The Power of TV: Cable Television and Women's Status in India', *The Quarterly Journal of Economics*, 124 (3) (August), 1057–94. Available at www.jstor.org/stable/40506252).

Johnston, M., 2006, "From Thucydides to Mayor Daley: Bad Politics and a Culture of Corruption?" *PS: Political Science and Politics* 39 (4), 809–12; available at www.jstor.org/stable/20451822, accessed 2 May 2023.

Jones, P., 1997, *The Italian City-State: From Commerce to Signoria* (New York: Oxford University Press).

Jong-sung, Y., 2014, 'Land Reform, Inequality, and Corruption: A Comparative Historical Study of Korea, Taiwan, and the Philippines', *The Korean Journal of International Studies*, 12-1 (June), 191–224, http://dx.doi.org/10.14731/kjis.2014.06.12.1.19

Joshi, N. et al., 2000, 'Institutional Opportunities and Constraints in the Performance of Farmer Managed Irrigation Systems in Nepal', *Asia-Pacific Journal of Rural Development* 10 (2), 67–92.

J-PAL Update, 2018, *Improving Women's Representation in Politics Through Gender Quotas*, www.povertyactionlab.org/policy-insight/improving-womens-representation-politics-through-gender-quotas.

Kagan, R. and Skolnick, J., 1993, 'Banning Smoking: Compliance without Enforcement' in R. Rabin and S. Sugarman, *Smoking Policy: Law, Politics, and Culture* (Oxford: Oxford University Press; Referred to in Lessig, 1995).

Kahneman, D., 2002, 'Maps of Bounded Rationality: A Perspective of Intuitive Judgment and Choice', Nobel Prize Lecture (8 December).

Kahneman, D., 2003, 'Maps of Bounded Rationality: Psychology for Behavioral Economics', *American Economic Review*, 93 (December), 1449–75.

Kahneman, D., 2011, *Thinking Fast and Slow* (New York: Farrar, Straus, and Giroux).

Kahneman, D., 2013, *Thinking Fast and Slow* (New York: Farrar, Straus and Giroux; paperback edition).

Kahneman, D. and Tversky, A., 1979, 'Prospect Theory: An Analysis of Decision Under Risk', *Econometrica* (March), 47 (2), 263–92.

Kaigun H., ed., 1919, *The History of Japanese Naval Academy* (in Japanese) (Hiroshima: Kaigun Heigakkō; Quoted in Sonoda, 1990).

Kar, D. and Freitas, S., 2011, *Illicit Financial Flows from Developing Countries Over the Decade Ending 2009*. (Washington, D.C.: Global Financial Integrity).

Kaspersen, L., 2004, 'How Denmark Became Democratic: The Impact of Warfare and Military Reforms', *Acta Sociologica*, 47 (1) (March), 71–89; DOI:10.1177/0001699304041552.

Katz, B. and Nowak, J., 2017, *The New Localism: How Cities Can Thrive in the Age of Populism* (Washington, DC: Brookings Institution Press).

Kaufmann, D., 2003, *Governance Redux: The Empirical Challenge*. MPRA Paper 8210 (University Library of Munich, Germany), 1–39.

Kaufmann, D., 2005, 'Back to Basics-Ten Myths about Governance and Corruption' Finance and Development, (Washington: IMF) 42(3).

Kaufmann, D. and Kraay, A., 2002, 'Growth Without Governance', *Policy Research Working Paper 2928* (World Bank Institute and Development Research Group).

Kaufmann, D. and Kraay, A., 2008, 'Governance Indicators: Where Are We, Where Should We Be Going?', *The World Bank Research Observer*, 23 (1), 1–30.

Kaufmann, D. and Wei, S., 2000, 'Does "Grease Money" Speed Up the Wheels of Commerce?', *IMF Working Paper WP/00/64*, 1–21 (March).

Kaufmann, D., Kraay, A., and Mastruzzi, M., 2009, Governance Matters : Learning from Over a Decade of the Worldwide Governance Indicators (Washington, DC: The Brookings Institution).

Kaufmann, D., Kraay, A., and Mastruzzi, M., 2010, 'The Worldwide Governance Indicators: Methodology and Analytical Issues', *Policy Research Working Paper 5430* (World Bank, September).

Kaufmann, D., Kraay, A., and Zoido-Lobaton, P., 1999, *Governance Matters* (Washington, DC: The World Bank).

Kautilya, 2016, *The Arthashastra*, Edited, rearranged, translated, and introduced by L. N. Rangarajan (India: Penguin Random House).

Kay, C., 2002, 'Why East Asia Overtook Latin America: Agrarian Reform, Industrialization and Development', *Third World Quarterly*, 23 (6) (December), 1073–102.

Kelsen, H., 1945, *General Theory of Law and State* (Cambridge, MA: Harvard University Press).

Kim, J., 2015, 'Aid and State Transition in Ghana and South Korea', *Third World Quarterly*, 36 (7) 1333–48.

Kim, N. and Kim, J., 2015, 'Top Incomes In Korea, 1933-2010: Evidence From Income Tax Statistcs', *Hitotsubashi Journal of Economics* 56 (1), 1–19. www.jstor.org/stable/43610998.

Kim, W., 2009, 'Rethinking Colonialism and the Origins of the Development State in East Asia', *Journal of Contemporary Asia*, 39 (3) (August), 382–99.

Kinnaman, T., 2006, 'Policy Watch: Examining the Justification for Residential Recycling', *Journal of Economic Perspectives*, 20 (4), 219–32.

Kinzig, A. et al., 2913, 'Social Norms and Global Environmental Challenges: The Complex Interaction of Behaviors, Values, and Policy', *BioScience*, 63 (3) (March), 164–75.

Klitgaard, R., 1988, *Controlling Corruption* (Berkeley, CA: University of California Press).

Klitgaard, R., 2017, 'What Do We Talk About When We Talk About Corruption?', *Working Paper LKYSPP-17-17* (Lee Kuan Yew School of Public Policy, August).

Kohli, A., 2004, 'Part 1. Galloping Ahead: Korea' in A. Kohli, *State Directed Development: Political Power and Industrialization in the Global Periphery* (UK: Cambridge University Press), 27–126.

Kohli, H., Nag, R., & Vilkelyte, I., (eds), 2022, *Envisioning 2060: Opportunities and Risks for Emerging Markets* (India: Penguin Random House).

Krueger, A., 1993, *Political Economy of Policy Reform in Developing* Countries (Cambridge, MA: MIT Press).

Kuznets, P. W., 1988, 'An East Asian Model of Economic Development: Japan, Taiwan, and South Korea', *Economic Development and Cultural Change*, 36 (S3), 11–43.

Landell-Mills, P., 2013, *Citizens Against Corruption*, Partnership for Transparency Fund. (UK: Matador, Troubador Publishing Ltd.).

Larreguy, H., and Marshall, J., 2017, 'The Effect of Education on Civic and Political Engagement in Non-consolidated Democracies: Evidence from Nigeria', *Review of Economics and Statistics*. http://www.mitpressjournals.org/doi/abs/10.1162/REST_a_00633

Lee, H., 2001, 'School Expansion in North Korea and South Korea: Two Systems, Two Approaches', *Asia Pacific Education Review*, 2 (1), 101–10.

Leff, N. H., 1964, 'Economic Development through Bureaucratic Corruption', *American Behavioral Scientist*, 8 (3), 8–14.

Lehmann, J.-P., 1982, *The Roots of Modern Japan*, Macmillan Asian History Series (London: Macmillan).

Leith, C., 2005, *Why Botswana Prospered* (Montreal, Que: McGill-Queen's University Press).

Lessig, L., 1995, 'The Regulation of Social Meaning', *University of Chicago Law Review*, 62 (3) 943–1045.

Levin, Y., 2016, *The Fractured Republic: Renewing America's Social Contract in the Age of Individualism* (New York: Basic Books).

Lewin, M., 2001, 'Botswana's Success: Good Governance, Good Policies, and Good Luck' in P. Chuhan-Pole and M. Angwafo (eds), *Yes, Africa Can: Success Stories from a Dynamic Continent* (Washington, DC: World Bank), 81–90.

Lewis, N., 1954, 'On Official Corruption in Roman Egypt: The Edict of Vergilius Capito', *Proceedings of the American Philosophical Society* 98 (2) (15 April), 153–8. ww.jstor.org/stable/3143647.

Leys, C., 1965, 'What is the Problem about Corruption?', *The Journal of Modern African Studies*, 3 (2) (August), 215–30.

Li, H., Xu, L., and Zou, H., 2000, 'Corruption, Income Distribution, and Growth', *China Economics and Management Academy (CEMA), Central University of Finance and Economics Working Paper 472*, 18. Subsequently published in *Economics and Politics*, 12 (2) (July 2000),155–82.

Libecap, G.D., 1989, *Contracting for Property Rights* (Cambridge: Cambridge University Press).

Lind, G., 2012, 'Beyond the Fiscal-Military Road to State Formation: Civil Society, Collective Identities, and the State in the Old Danish Monarchy, 1500–1850', *Balto-Scandia*, 18, 1–11.

List, J., 2007, 'On the Interpretation of Giving in Dictator Games', *Journal of Political Economy* 115 (3) (June), 482–93.

Lizzeri, A. and Persico, N., 2004, 'Why did the Elites Extend the Suffrage? Democracy and the Scope of Government, with an application to Britain's Age of Reform', *Quarterly Journal of Economics* (May).

Luce, R.D. and Raiffa, H., 1983, *Games and Decisions: Introduction and Critical Survey* (New York: Dover Publications); originally published by New York: John Wiley & Sons, 1957).

Lührmann, A., Marcus T., and Staffan L., 2018, 'Regimes of the World (RoW): Opening New Avenues for the Comparative Study of Political Regimes', *Politics and Governance*, 6 (1), 60–77.

Mackie, G. and LeJeunne, J., 2009, 'Social Dynamics of Abandonment of Harmful Practices: A New Look at the Theory', *UNICEF Innocenti Research Center, Working Paper IWP-2009-06*.

Maddison, A., 2006, *The World Economy Volume 1: A Millennial Perspective and Volume 2: Historical Statistics* (Paris: OECD).

Madrian, B. and Shea, D., 2000, 'The Power of Suggestion: Inertia in 401(k) Participation and Savings Behavior', *NBER Working Paper 7682* (May).

Mani, A., Mullainathan, S., Shafir,E. and Zhao, J., 2013, 'Poverty Impedes Cognitive Function', *Science* 341, 976–80.

Marshall, A., 1920, *Principles of Economics* (8th edn, London: Macmilllan).

Martinsson, P., Pham-Khanh, N., and Villegas-Palacio, C., 2012, 'Conditional Cooperation and Disclosure in Developing Countries', *Working Paper in Economics, no. 541* (University of Gothenburg, Sep. 2012).

Marwell, G. and Ames, R., 1981, 'Economists Free Ride, Does Anyone Else?', *Journal of Public Economics* 15, 295–310.

Mauro, P., 1995, 'Corruption and Growth', *The Quarterly Journal of Economics*, 110 (3) (August), 681–712.

McAdams, R., 2015, *The Expressive Powers of Law: Theories and Limits* (Cambridge, MA: Harvard University Press).

Muhlberger, S., 1998, Democracy in Ancient India, unpublished paper on World History of Democracy site. https://www.infinityfoundation.com/mandala/h_es/h_es_muhlb_democra_frameset.htm

Muldoon, R., 2018, 'Understanding Norms and Changing Them', *Social Philosophy and Policy*, 35 (1), 128–48; DOI:10.1017/S0265052518000092 (Published online by Cambridge University Press, 4 December 2018).

Mulgan, R., 2012, 'Aristotle on Legality and Corruption' in Manuhuia Barcham, Barry Hindess, and Peter Larmour, eds, *Corruption: Expanding the Focus* (Australia: ANU Press), 25–36.

Mungiu-Pippidi, A., 2006, 'Corruption: Diagnosis and Treatment', *Journal of Democracy* 17 (3), 86–99.

Mungiu-Pippidi, A., 2011, Becoming Denmark: Understanding Good Governance Historical Achievers. www.againstcorruption.eu

Mungiu-Pippidi, A., 2015, 'When corruption is the norm', Spotlight 1: World Development Report, *Mind, Society, and Behavior* (Washington, DC: World Bank), 60.

Mungiu-Pippidi, A., 2017, 'Corruption as Social Order', Background Paper, *World Development Report 2017—Governance and the Law* (Washington, DC: World Bank).

Mungiu-Pippidi, A. and Dadasov, R., 2016, 'Measuring Control of Corruption by a New Index of Public Integrity', *European Journal of Policy and Research,* (July), 22 (3), 1–28.

Mungiu-Pippidi, A. and Hartmann, T., 2019, 'Corruption and Development: An Overview', in *Oxford Research Encyclopedia of Economics and Finance* (Oxford: Oxford University Press), http://dx.doi.org/10.1093/acrefore/9780190625979.013.237.

Mungiu-Pippidi, A. and Johnston, M. (eds), 2017, *Transitions to Good Governance: Creating Virtuous Circles of Anti-Corruption* (UK, USA: Edward Elgar Publishing,).

Murphy, K., Shleifer, A., and Vishny, R., 1993, 'Why is Rent Seeking so costly to Growth?', *AEA Papers and Proceedings* 83 (2) (May), 409–14.

Myerson, R., 2004, *Justice, Institutions, and Multiple Equilibria* (Chicago, IL: University of Chicago) Available at http://home.uchicago.edu/~rmyerson/research/jistice.pdf., accessed 20 June 2019.

Myrdal, G., 1968, *Asian Drama, II* (New York: Random House).

Nag, R, 2017, *The 21st Century: Asia's?* (India: Sage Publications).

Nakamura, J., 1966, 'Meiji Land Reform, Redistribution of Income, and Saving from Agriculture', *Economic Development and Cultural Change*, 14 (4) (Chicago, IL: University of Chicago Press), 428–39.

Narayan, D., Patel, R., Schaft, K., Rademacher, A., and Koch-Schulte, S., 2000, *Voices of the Poor: Can Anyone Hear Us?* (Oxford: Oxford University Press).

Narayan, D., Chambers, R., Shah, M., Petesch, P., 2000, *Voices of the Poor: Crying Out for Change* (Washington, DC: World Bank).

Nature, 2021, 'Climate Change', 598(7882).

The New York Times Archives, 1992, Section 1 (30 August).

Noland, M., 2011, 'Korea's Growth Performance: Past and Future', *East West Center Working Papers, Economics Series, no. 123* (November).

Noonan, J.T. Jr., 1984, *Bribes: The Intellectual History of a Moral Idea* (New York: Macmillan).

North, D. C., 1981, *Structure and Change in Economic History* (New York and London: Norton).

North, D. C., 1990, *Institutions, Institutional Change, and Economic Performance* (Cambridge: Cambridge University Press).

North, D. C., 1993, 'Institutions and Credible Commitment', *Journal of Institutional and Theoretical Economics*, 149, 11–23.

North, D. C., 1994, 'Economic Performance Through Time', *American Economic Review* (June) 84 (3), 359–80.

North, D. C. and Thomas, R.P., [1973] 2009, *The Rise of the Western World: A New Economic History* (New York: Cambridge University Press, 23rd printing).

North, D. C. et al., 2007, 'Limited Access Orders in the Developing World: A New Approach to the Problems of Development', *Policy Research Working Paper 4359* (Washington, DC: World Bank).

North, D. C., Wallis, J., and Weingast, B., 2008, 'Violence and Social Orders: A Conceptual Framework for Interpreting Recorded Human History' in Douglass North, Daron Acemoğlu, Francis Fukuyama, and Dani Rodrik, eds, *Governance, Growth, and Development Decision Making* (Washington, DC: World Bank), 9–16.

North, D. C., Wallis, J., and Weingast, B., 2012, *Violence and Social Orders: A Conceptual Framework for Interpreting Recorded Human History* (New York: Cambridge University Press).

North, D., Weingast, B., 1989. 'Constitutions and Commitment: The Evolution of Institutions Governing Public Choice in Seventeenth Century England', *The Journal of Economic History*, XLIX (4), 803–32.

Nunn, N., 2008, 'The Long-term Effects of Africa's Slave Trades', *Quarterly Journal of Economics*, 123 (1), 139–76.

Nunn. N., and Wantchekon, L., 2011, 'The Slave Trade and the Origins of Mistrust in Africa', *American Economic Review*, 101 (7) (December), 3221–52.

Nye, J. S., 1967, 'Corruption and Political Development: A Cost-Benefit Analysis', *The American Political Science Review*, 61, 2 (June 1967). American Political Science Association, pp. 417–27. https://www.jstor.org/stable/1953254

Obama, B., 2014, 'Speech at the Open Government Partnership Meeting at the United Nations', *The Office of the Press Secretary* (on You Tube, The White House, 24 September).

Ofer, G., 1988, *Soviet Economic Growth: 1928–1985* (Los Angeles, CA: Rand/UCLA, Center for the Study of Soviet International Behavior).

Olson, M., 1971, *The Logic of Collective Action: Public Policy and the Theory of Groups* (Cambridge, MA; London: Harvard University Press).

Open Government Partnership, 2019, *Open Government Partnership Global Report: Democracy Beyond the Ballot Box* (First edn, I and II, Washington, DC: Open Government Partnership).

Open Government Partnership, 2022, *The Skeptic's Guide to Open Government* (Washington, DC: Open Government Partnership).

Ostrom, E., 1990, *Governing the Commons: The Evolution of Institutions for Collective Action* (Cambridge: Cambridge University Press).

Ostrom, E., Walker, J., and Gardner, R., 1992, 'Covenants With and Without a Sword: Self Governance Is Possible', *American Political Science Review*, 86 (2), 404–17.

Oxford University Press, 1999, *Concise Oxford Dictionary* (Oxford: Oxford University Press, 10th edn).

Pace, R., 1993, 'First-Time Televiewing in Amazônia: Television Acculturation in Gurupá, Brazil,' *Ethnology*, 32 (2) (University of Pittsburgh, Spring), 187–205, www.jstor.org/stable/3773772.

Pandey, R. and Ford, D., 2011, 'Gender Quotas and Female Leadership', background paper, *World Development Report 2012—Gender Equality and Development* (Washington, DC: World Bank).

Pascale, R., Sternin, J., and Sternin, M., 2010, *The Power of Positive Deviance: How Unlikely Innovators Solve the World's Toughest Problems* (Kindle version, Boston, MA: Harvard Business Press).

Paul, S. 2012, *A Life and its Lessons—Memoirs* (Bangalore: Public Affairs Centre).

Peltzman, S., 1993, 'George Stigler's Contribution to the Economic Analysis of Regulation', *Journal of Political Economy*, 101 (5), 818–32, www.jstor.org/stable/ 2138597).

Pempel, T. J., 'Bureaucracy in Japan', 1992, *PS: Political Science and Politics*, 25 (1) (March), 19–24.

Persson, A.,, Rothstein, B., and Teorell, J., 2012, 'Why Anticorruption Reforms Fail—Systematic Corruption as a Collective Action Problem', *Governance* 26 (3), 449–471.

Pettit, P. 1999, *Republicanism: A Theory of Freedom and Government* (UK: Oxford University Press).

Picard, L. 1987, *The Politics of Development in Botswana: A Model for Success* (Boulder, CO: L. Rienner Publishers.

Platteau, J.-P. 2000, *Institutions, Social Norms, and Economic Development* (London and New York: Routledge).

Posner, E. 2000, *Laws and Social Norms* (Cambridge, MA: Harvard University Press); Quoted in Basu, *Republic of Beliefs*.

Pritchett, L. and Woolcock, M., 2004, 'Solutions When the Solution is the Problem: Assessing the Disarray in Development' (World Development, 32.2, 191–212).

Putnam, R. 1993, 'What Makes Democracy Work?', *National Civic Review*, 82 (2), 101–7.

Putnam, R. 2000, *Bowling Alone: The Collapse and Revival of American Community* (New York: Simon and Schuster).

Putnam, R., Leonardi, R., and Nanetti, R., 1993, *Making Democracy Work: Civic Traditions in Modern Italy* (Princeton, NJ: Princeton University Press).

Quibria, M. G. 2006, 'Does Governance Matter? Yes, No or Maybe: Some Evidence from Developing Asia', *Kyklos* 59 (1), 99–114.

Quibria, M. G. 2014, 'Governance and Developing Asia: Concepts, Measurements, Determinants, and Paradoxes', *ADB Economics Working Papers Series* NO. 388.

Rajan, R, 2019, *The Third Pillar: How Markets and the State Leave the Community Behind* (India: Harper Collins).

Raychaudhuri, A., 2004, 'Lessons from the Land Reform Movement in West Bengal, India', a case study from *Scaling Up Poverty Reduction: A Global Learning Process and Conference* (Shanghai: World Bank, 25–27 May 2004).

Reagan, R., 1981, *President Ronald Reagan's Inaugural Address* (USA, 20 Jan. 1981).

Republic of Lebanon (2020) *The Anti-Corruption National Strategy (2020–2025)* (Beirut: Government of Lebanon).

Rizio, S., and Skali, A., 2020, 'How often do dictators have positive economic effects? Global evidence, 1858–2010', *The Leadership Quarterly*, 31 (3), (June).

Robinson, J., 1979, 'Morality and Economics: Commencement Speech: University of Maine, 1977' in Joan Robinson, *Collected Economic Papers*, 5 (Oxford: Blackwell Publishers).

Rodrik, D, 1995, 'Getting Interventions Right: How South Korea and Taiwan Got Rich', *Economic Policy*, 20, 55–97.

Rodrik, D., 2008, *Thinking about Governance, in Governance, Growth, and Development Decision-Making* (Washington, DC: World Bank).

Rodrik, D., Subramanian, A., and Trebbi, F., 2002, 'Institutions Rule: The Primacy of Institutions over Geography and Integration in Economic Development', National Bureau of Economic Research, *Working Paper 9305* (November), DOI 10.3386/w9305.

Rogers, E. M. et al. 1999, 'Effects of an Entertainment-Education Radio Soap Opera on Family Planning Behavior in Tanzania', *Studies in Family Planning* 30 (3),193–211, doi: 10.1111/j.1728–4465.1999.00193.x. PMID: 10546311.

Rosenthal, E. T., 2008, *Motivated by a Tax, Irish Spurn Plastic Bags* (New York: New York Times).

Rosenthal, E, 2011, 'Betty Ford's Momentous Contributions to Cancer Awareness', *Oncology Times*, 33 (15) (10 August), 7–8, doi: 10.1097/01.COT.0000403839.34558.e7.

Rotberg, R., 2004, 'Strengthening Governance: Ranking Countries Would Help', *The Washington Quarterly*, 28 (1), 71–81.

Rotberg, R, 2017, *The Corruption Cure: How Citizens and Leaders Can Combat Graft* (Princeton, NJ, and Oxford: Princeton University Press).

Rothstein, B., 2000, 'Trust, Social Dilemmas, and Collective Memories', *Journal of Theoretical Politics* 12 (4), 477–501.

Rothstein, B. and Teorell, J., 2008, 'What is Quality of Government? A Theory of Impartial Government Institutions', *Governance*, 21(2) 165–90.

Rothstein, B. and Teorell, J., 2015, 'Getting to Sweden, Part II: Breaking with Corruption in the Nineteenth Century', *Scandinavian Political Studies*, 38 (3), 238–54.

Rustagi, D., Engel, S., and Kosfeld, M., 2010, 'Conditional Cooperation and Costly Monitoring Explain Success in Forest Commons Management', *Science* 330/6006, 961–5.

Sachs, J., 2001, 'Tropical Underdevelopment', *Working Paper 8119*, National Bureau of Economic Research (USA).

Saisana, M. and Saltelli, A., 2012a, 'Corruption Perception Index 2012: Statistical Assessment', *Joint Research Centre Scientific and Policy Reports*. Report EUR 25623 EN, Technical Report (Luxembourg: European Commission, May).

Saisana, M. and Saltelli, A., 2012b, 'The WJP Rule of Law Index 2012: Statistical Audit', *Joint Research Centre Scientific and Policy Reports* (Luxembourg: European Commission).

Samuelson, P., 1954, 'The Pure Theory of Public Expenditure', *The Review of Economics and Statistics*, 36 (4) (November), 387–9.

Samuelson, W. and Zeckhauser, R., 1988, 'Status Quo Bias in Decision-Making', *Journal of Risk and Uncertainty*, 1 (1) (), 7–59.

Sansom, G., 1950, *The Western World and Japan: A Study in the Interaction of European and Asiatic Cultures* (New York: Alfred A. Knopf).

Schelling, T., 1960, *The Strategy of Conflict* (Cambridge, MA and London, England: Harvard University Press).

Sebedubudu, D., Khatib, L., and Bozzini, A., 2017, 'The Atypical Achievers: Botswana, Qatar, and Rwanda' in A. Mungiu-Pippidi. and M. Johnson (eds), *Transition to Good Governance: Creating Virtuous Circles of Anti-Corruption* (UK, USA: Edward Elgar Publishing), 31–56.

Sen, A., 1967, 'Isolation, Assurance, and the Social Rate of Discount', *The Quarterly Journal of Economics* 81 (1) (February.), 112–24.

Sen, A., 1977, 'Rational Fools: A Critique of the Behavioral Foundations of Economic Theory', *Philosophy and Public Affairs* 6 (4) (Summer), 317–44.

Sen, A., 1999, *Development as Freedom* (New York: Anchor Books).

Sen, A., 2002, 'Why Health Equity?', *Health Economy*, 11 (8), 659–66. Published online in Wiley Interscience (www.interscience.com) doi:10.1002/hec.762.

Sen A., 2006, *Identity and Violence: The Illusion of Destiny* (UK: Penguin).

Sen A., 2009, *The Idea of Justice* (New York: Allen Lane).Seth, M., 2002, *Education Fever: Society, Politics, and the Pursuit of Schooling in South Korea*, Hawaii Studies on Korea (Honolulu, HA: University of Hawaii Press).

Sharma, R., 2017, *The 10 Rules of Successful Nations* (UK: Penguin).

Shils, E., 1960, 'Political Development in the New States (II)', *Comparative Studies in Society and History*, 2 (3), 265–92. Published online (Cambridge University Press, 2009).

Shinada, M. and Yamagishi, T., 2007, 'Punishing Free Riders: Direct and Indirect Promotion of Cooperation', *Evolution and Human Behavior*, 28, 330–9.

Shliefer, A. and Vishny, R., 1993, 'Corruption', *The Quarterly Journal of Economics* (August), 599–617.

Shu, L., Gino, F., and Bazerman, M.H., 2009, 'Dishonest Deed, Clear Conscience: Self-Preservation through Moral Disengagement and Motivated Forgetting', *Harvard Business School Working Paper 09–078*.

Simon, H., 1947, Administrative Behavior: A Study of Decision-Making Processes in Administrative Organizations. (First Edition, New York: Macmillan).

Simon, H., 1957, Models of Man: Social and Rational, John Wiley.

Sinclair, T., 1962, *Aristotle: The Politics*, translated by T. Sinclair. Revised edn 1981. (UK: Penguin Books).

Smith, A., 1902 [1776]a, *An Inquiry into the Nature of and Causes of the Wealth of Nations* (New York: P. F. Collier and Son).

Smith, A., 1902 [1776]b, *The Wealth of Nations* (Kindle edn, New York: P. F. Collier & Son,).

Smith, A., 2016 [1759], *Of Sympathy, The Theory of Moral Sentiments* (Enhanced Media Publishing).

Sonoda, H., 1990, 'The Decline of the Japanese Warrior Class, 1840–1880', *Japan Review*, 1, 73–111. Available at www.jstor.org/stable/25790888, accessed 16 Apr. 2019.

Stigler, G.J., 1971, 'The Theory of Economic Regulation', *The Bell Journal of Economics and Management Science*, 2 (1), 3–21, https://doi.org/10.2307/3003160.).

Stiglitz, J., 2019, *People, Power, and Profits: Progressive Capitalism in an Age of Discontent* (UK: Allen Lane).

Stuntz, W., 2000, 'Self-Defeating Crimes', *Virginia Law Review*, 86 (8), *Symposium: The Legal Construction of Norms*, 1871–99.

Subbaraman, R., Shitole, S., Shitole, T., Sawant, K., O'Brien, J., Bloom, D., and Patil-Deshmukh, A., 2013, 'The Social Ecology of Water in a Mumbai Slum: Failures in Water Quality, Quantity, and Reliability', *BMC Public Health*, 13, 173, 7–9.

Sugden, R., 1989, 'Spontaneous Order', *Journal of Economic Perspectives*, 3 (4), 90–1.

Sunstein, C., 1996, 'Social Norms and Social Roles', *96 Columbia Law Review*, 903–68.

Tanzi, V. and Davoodi, H., 1997, 'Corruption, Public Investment, and Growth', *IMF Working Paper WP/97/139, 1-27*

The Telegraph (6 Dec. 2019), www.telegraph.co.uk.

Tennankore, K., Klarenbach, S., and Goldberg, A., 2021, 'Perspectives on Opt-Out Versus Opt-In Legislation for Deceased Organ Donation: An Opinion Piece', *Canadian Journal of Kidney Health and Disease* (June), 8, 1–6. https://doi.org/ 10.1177/ 20543581211022151.

Thaler, R., 2015, *Misbehaving: The Making of Behavioural Economics* (UK: Penguin Random House).

Thaler, R. and Benartzi, S., 2004, 'Save More Tomorrow: Using Behavioral Economics to Increase Employee Savings', *Journal of Political Economy*, 112 (1), S164–S187.

Thaler, R. and Sunstein, C. R., 2008, *Nudge: Improving Decisions About Health, Wealth, and Happiness* (New Haven, CT: Yale University Press).

Thaler, R., Sunstein, C. R., and Balz, J. P., 2014, 'Choice Architecture', *The Behavioral Foundations of Public Policy* (10 December), SSRN: https://ssrn.com/abstract= 2536504 or http://dx.doi.org/10.2139/ssrn.2536504.

Times Atlas of World History, Quoted in Putnam et al. (1993)

Titmuss, R., 2018 [1970], *The Gift Relationship: From Blood Donations to Social Policy* (Bristol: Policy Press).

Todd, P. and Gigerenzer, G., 2000, 'Precis of Simple heuristics that make us smart', *Behavioral and Brain Sciences*, 23, 727–80.

Transparency International, 2003 a, *Global Corruption Barometer*, https://www.trans parency.org/en/gcb/global/global-corruption-barometer-2003

Transparency International, 2003b, 'The Transparency International Global Corruption Barometer: A 2002 Pilot Survey of International Attitudes, Expectation, and Priorities on Corruption'. TI Center for Innovation and Research, Berlin. https://images.transparencycdn.org/images/2003_GCB_EN.pdf

Transparency International, 2004, *Global Corruption Barometer*. https://www.trans parency.org/en/publications/gcb-2004Transparency International, 2010, *Global Corruption Barometer*. https://www.transparency.org/en/gcb/global/global-cor ruption-barometer-2010-11

Transparency International, 2015, *Successful Anti-Corruption Reforms*. Anti-Corruption Helpdesk TI (Berlin). https://www.transparency.org/files/content/ corruptionqas/Successful_anti-corruption_reforms.pdf

Transparency International, 2017a, *Corruption in Service Delivery Topic Guide*, com-piled by the Anti-Corruption Desk, TI. https://knowledgehub.transparency.org/ assets/uploads/topic-guides/Topic_guide_service_delivery_2017.pdf

Transparency International, 2017 b, 'People and Corruption: Citizens' Voices from Around the World', *Global Corruption Barometer*. https://www.transparency.org/ en/gcb/global/global-corruption-barometer-2017

Transparency International, 2019, *Corruption Perception Index*. www. transparency. org/en/cpi, accessed 17 Sept. 2020.

Transparency International 2020, *Global Corruption Barometer*. Available at www. transparency.org/en/gcb/africa/africa-2019, accessed 25 Apr. 2023.

Transparency International, 2022a, *Corruption Perception Index (2022)*. www.trans parency.org/en/cpi/2022a.

Transparency International, 2022 b, *Corruption Perception Index 2022*. Available at www.transparency.org/en/cpi/2022 a.

Tridimas, G., 2011, 'Cleisthenes' Choice: The Emergence of Direct Democracy in Ancient Athens', *Journal of Economic Asymmetries*, June 2011. doi:10.1016/j.jeca.2011.01.002

UNDP, 2020a, *Human Development Report 2020*. Available at https://hdr.undp.org/en/2020-report, accessed 25 Apr. 2023.

UNDP, 2020b, *Human Development Composite Indices*, Human Development Report 2020, (New York: UNDP).

UNICEF, 2021, *Female Genital Mutilation (FGM)*. Available at https://data.unicef.org/topic/child-protection/female-genital-mutilation/, accessed 25 Apr. 2023.

Underkuffler, L., 2009, 'Defining Corruption: Implications for Action' in Robert Rotberg, ed., *Corruption, Global Security, and World Order* (Washington, DC: Brookings Institution), 27–46.

Uslaner, E. and Rothstein, B., 2016, 'The Historical Roots of Corruption: State Building, Economic Inequality, and Mass Education', *Comparative Politics*, 48 (January), 227–48.

Voigtländer, N. and Voth, H-J, 2012, 'Persecution Perpetuated: The Medieval Origins of Anti-Semitic Violence in Nazi Germany', *Quarterly Journal of Economics*, 127 (3), 1339–92. Available at SSRN: 2012, http://dx.doi.org/10.2139/ssrn.1824744, accessed 23 July.

Wade, R., 1985, 'The Market Rate for Public Office: Why the Indian State is not better at Development', *World Development* 13 (4), 467–97. https://doi.org/10.1016/0305-750X(85)90052-X

Wantchekon, L., Klasnja, M. and Novta, N., 2015, 'Education and Human Capital Externalities: Evidence from Colonial Benin', *Quarterly Journal of Economics*, 130 (2), 703–57.

Weber, M., 1946, *From Max Weber: Essays in Sociology* (New York: Oxford University Press).

Wechsler, H. et al., 2000, 'College Binge Drinking in the 1990s: A Continuing Problem, from Results of the Harvard School of Public Health 1999 College Alcohol Study', *Journal of American College Health* 48 (5, 199–210, doi: 10.1080/07448480009599305. PMID: 10778020.

The White House, Office of the Press Secretary, 2011, 'Fact Sheet: The Open Government Partnership', Briefing Room, 20 September.

Williamson, O. E., 1979, 'Transaction-Cost Economics: The Governance of Contractual Relations', *Journal of Law and Economics*, 22, 233–61.

Williamson, O. E., 1991, 'Economic Institutions: Spontaneous and Intentional Governance', *Journal of Law, Economics, and Organization*, 7, 159–87.

Winkler, D. and Yeo, B., 2007, Identifying the Impact of Education Decentralization on the Quality of Education (Washington, DC: EQUIP2, USAID).

World Bank, 1992, Governance and Development.

World Bank, 1993, *The East Asian Miracle: Economic Growth and Public Policy* (USA: Oxford University Press).

World Bank, 1997, *World Development Report 1997—The State in a Changing World* (New York: Oxford University Press).

World Bank, 2002, *World Development Report 2002—Building Institutions for the Markets* (New York: Oxford University Press).

World Bank, 2008, *Governance, Growth, and Development Decision Making*, Working paper by D.C. North, D. Acemoglu, F. Fukuyama, and D. Rodrik) (Washington, DC: World Bank).

World Bank, 2015, *World Development Report 2015—Mind, Society, and Behavior* (Washington, DC: World Bank).

World Bank, 2017, *World Development Report 2017—Governance and the Law* (Washington, DC: World Bank).

World Bank, 2018, World Development Report 2018, *Learning: To Realize Education's Promise* (Washington, D.C.: World Bank).

World Bank, 2020, 2021, 2022 World Governance Indicators www.info.worldbank.org/governance/wgi.

World Bank, 2022, The World Bank in Uruguay. Available at www.worldbank.org/en/country/uruguay/overview, accessed 25 Apr. 2023.

World Bank, n.d., *World Justice Project*. Available at www.worldjusticeproject.org, accessed 17 Sept. 2020.

World Bank, n.d., World Bank Open Data. Available at https://data.worldbank.org/, accessed 25 Apr. 2023.

World Health Organization, 2020, *World Malaria Report 2020* (Geneva: WHO).

You, J-I., 1998, 'Income Distribution and Growth in East Asia', *Journal of Development Studies*, 34, 37–65.

You, J-S., 2015, *Democracy, Inequality, and Corruption: Korea, Taiwan, and the Philippines Compared* (UK: Cambridge University Press).

You, J-S., 2016, 'Demystifying the Park Chung-He Myth: The Critical Role of Land Reform in the Evolution of Korea's Developmental State'. Available at SSRN: https://ssrn.com/abstract=2505810 OR http://dx.doi.org/10.2139/ssrn.2505810.

You, J.-S., 2017a, 'South Korea: The Odyssey to Corruption Control' in A. Mungiu-Pippidi and M. Johnson (eds), *Transition to Good Governance: Creating Virtuous Circles of Anti-Corruption* (UK, USA: Edward Elgar Publishing), 128–58.

You, J.-S., 2017b, 'Based on Ju, G. & Kim, M. (2006), *Understanding of Personnel Administration System in Korean Bureaucracy*' (in Korean) (Seoul: Gyongsewon).

Young, P., 1993, 'The Evolution of Conventions', *Econometrica*, 61 (1), 57–84.

Zuvich, A., 2016, *A Year in the Life of Stuart Britain* (England: Amberley Publishing).

Index

For the benefit of digital users, indexed terms that span two pages (e.g., 52–53) may, on occasion, appear on only one of those pages.

Tables, figures, and boxes are indicated by *t*, *f*, and *b* following the page number

Aam Aadmi Party (Common Persons' Party) 336
accountability 23, 32–33, 42, 46–47, 48, 51–52, 56–57, 61, 62, 63*f*–69*f*, 65, 70, 75, 91, 163, 231, 246, 283, 299–300, 301, 302, 308–9, 310, 330, 332, 334, 335, 337, 340–41, 343, 352–53, 356, 357, 367, 370, 372
  of public officials and State 52
  redressal mechanism 52
  responsibilities and 51–52
Acemoglu, Daron 113, 114, 118, 119–20, 121, 122, 293, 295, 338, 349–50
adult literacy 2, 66, 69–70
  governance and 67*f*
advanced countries 17, 60, 365, 372
Africa 68, 75, 85, 90, 365, 372, *see also* Botswana; sub-Saharan Africa
  trust levels within 191, 194–95, 206
African Development Bank 4
African Union Convention to Prevent and Combat Corruption 54
aging societies 15–18, 17*t*
Alatas, Syed Hussain 85–86
Alexander the Great 86–87
allocation of resources 6
altruistic behaviour 158
amoral familism 192–93, 328–29
anchoring effect 137–38
anti-corruption measures 53, 96, 100–2, 101*f*, 181–84, 230, 360–61
anti-Semitism 328–29
Arab Spring 35, 372
Aristophon 86–87

Aristotle 82–83, 328
  Politics 43, 328
Arrow, Kenneth 129
Asian Development Bank (ADB) 4, 52, 90–91
  policy on Good Governance 90–91
Asian economies *see* Bangladesh; China; East Asia; India; Japan; South Asia; South Korea
Asian financial crisis, 1998 346
Autocles 86–87
automatic thinking 131–33, 142, 204–5
  framework of understanding 134–36
  rules 134

bad equilibrium 150–51, 152, 155, 174–75, 196
  role of social norms 180–84
Banerjee, Abhijit 66, 86, 91, 213–14, 338
  Poor Economics 205
Banfield, Edward 192
  amoral familism 192, 329
  The Moral Basis of a Backward Society 192
  social and economic development of Italy 192–94
Bangladesh 15–16, 60, 77*f*
  relationship between government and civil society 70–71
Bardhan, Pranab 84, 91, 113
Basu, Kaushik 95, 172, 175
  'ink on paper' 172
  republic of beliefs 171
behavioural economics 8–9, 123–24, 199, 355, *see also* human behaviour

beliefs 8, 9, 12, 112–13, 114, 123, 127,
128, 147, 152–53, 182–83, 186, 195,
196, 199, *see also* mental models;
social norms
collective 129–30, 182, 190
explicit 131–32
monetary incentives, influence of 165
role in human behaviour 169–77
rule of law 171–77
self-efficacy 193–94
belief traps 195–96
biases 42, 55, 132, 204
present 141
status quo bias 138–41
Black Death pogroms, Germany 194
'black swan' events 375
Botswana 60, 62, 77f, 275–82, 288–
89, 363
bounded rationality 129–30, 134, 144
Brazil 20t, 33–34, 43, 60, 77f, 340–41
burden of disease 3

Canada 20t, 61, 77f, 138–39, 283
corruption control 100–2, 101f
economic output and income
levels 19
governance 61
HDI ranking 60, 61
caste discrimination in India 190–91
Chanakya 87–88, 327–28
Arthashastra 43
Charles I 237, 239
Charles II 239, 240, 241
childbirth (per 100,000 live births) in
sub- Saharan Africa 2–3
China 15–16, 20t, 33–34, 60, 61–62, 69,
77f, 207–8, 252, 304, 346
choice architecture 142–43
Christian VI 231
Chung-hee, Park 270
Cicero 81, 82
citizen engagement 312–13
citizens of republic of beliefs 196
Citizen's Report Card 310
civic society 35, 39, 372
Clayton Act, 1914 321
Clean India (Swachh Bharat) 187

climate change 28–31, 368–69
damages to public property and
infrastructure 30
environmental issues 29–30
fighting against 35
global warming 28, 29
storm-related deaths 29–30
weather-related disasters 29–30
Coase, Ronald 106–7, 123–24
Code of Hammurabi 88
cognitions 130, 199
broader framing and reflective
thinking 204–5
depletion from poverty 200–2, 203
intention-action divide 202–4
cognitive depletion 203, 218
cognitive tax 200–2
child's education 200
sugar-cane farmers in
India 200, 201–2
cognitive tax on the poor 200–2
collective action problems 113, 153–56,
183, 190, 197, 208
collective actions 147–48, 153, 167–68,
209–10, 295–96, 306–7, 359
collective cooperation 210–13
collective human behaviours 199
influence of social norms 182, 196–97
commitment 111–12
common pooled resources (CPR) 161
communication (voice), go elsewhere
(exit), and loyalty, importance
of 343–45
communications revolution 371
community 10, 327, 351, 353, 361
challenges of governance 335–38
decentralizing powers 330–31
information-sharing, feedback, and
consultation mechanisms 332–34
local 328
in planning and investment
decisions 328
as a self-governing political
entity 328
social, economic, and environmental
challenges 330–31
voices of 329–30

community-driven development
(CDD) 328
conditional cooperation 162–67
conditional cooperators 158–62, 163,
185, 196–97, 210
confirmation bias 196
contracting out services 311
cooperation 112, 158–61, 162–67
conditional 162–67
role of economic incentives and social
preferences 163–67
coordination 112–13
corruption 5, 7, 11, 12, 33*f*,
33–34, 309
in advanced regions 33–34
aggregate indicators 98
ancient times 81, 88
anti-corruption laws 183
bribery 90
as challenge for poor countries 86
changing perceptions about 89–92
Code of Hammurabi 88
as collective action problem 183, 184
control of 53, 96, 100–2, 101*f*,
181–84, 230, 360–61
as a culture-specific
phenomenon 85–86
distinction between 'immoral' and
'corrupt' transactions 84
effect in basic public-service
delivery 94–95
effect on economic growth, poverty,
and inequality 92–95
in EMDEs 33–34
as enabler of development 90, 91
experiential surveys 98–100
extortion by errant officials 88
for getting illegal water
connections 94
ills of 88–89
impact on government's ability to
mobilize revenues 94
large-scale 34
Lockheed Affair 88
meaning and definition 82–83
measures of 95–100
official statistics on 96

perception surveys 96–98
petty 34
in piped-water-supply schemes 335
principal-agent relationship in 84
private gain 84
in rent seeking activity 92
social norms in fighting 181–84
in sub-Saharan countries 33–34
as a tax hike 92–93
as tax on profits 92
understanding 81–85
Corruption Perception Index (CPI) 96–
97, 263–64
counter norms 208, 209–10, 218, 359
COVID-19 pandemic 11, 14–
15, 368–69
impact on lives of people 14–15
rise of unemployment and
poverty 14–15
vaccines against 15
Cromwell, Oliver 239–40
crony capitalism 321
crowding in 167
crowding out 167
Crown Game 151–53, 174
cultural context 212
cultural relativism 86
cultures 8, 85, 86, 102, 162, 181, 212,
358, *see also* beliefs; social norms

Dae-jung, Kim 346
Debreu, Gerard 129
decentralization 330–31, 335,
337, 352–53
school autonomy 337–38
de jure and de facto measures 53–56
de jure indicators 55
outcome indicators 55
democracies 32–33
demographic changes 15–18
advanced regions 17, 18
East Asian countries 15–16
position of women 18
by region (1950–2020) 16*f*, 17–18
social preferences for larger
families 18
South Asian countries 16–17

demographic dividend 18
Deng Xiaoping 346
Denmark 6, 60, 61, 77*f*, 223, 246,
    352, 359
  institutions and governance 122–23
  journey to 'Denmark' 234–35
  professionalization of judiciary and
      bureaucracy 230–31
  property rights 230, 234–35, 246
  social-development 1
  social hierarchy 229
  system of petitions (*suppliker*) 231
  trajectory of 234–35
development 3–4, 12, 105, 169,
    356–57
  citizens as agents of 48, 50–51
  community-driven 328, 335
  corruption as an enabler of 90, 91
  economic 3, 5, 71, 106, 107, 192, 270,
      271, 273, 296
  as freedom 45–46
  human 26–27, 46, 60, 70, 95, 113, 297
  impact of governance on 62–72
  impact of policies 5–6
  institutional 114–16, 199
  social 66–67, 71, 107, 113, 357
  State's capability in 306
dictator game 158
discrimination 2
dominance 293–94
'double whammy' effect 319
dowry system 197
Duflo, Esther 66, 213–14
  Poor Economics 205

Ease of Doing Business Indicators 54
East Asia 75, 372
Easterly, William 6, 45–46
economic and social deprivation 3–4
economic efficiency 105–6
economic growth 3, 6, 46
  capital investments and 4–5
  developing countries 4–5
  poverty-reduction strategy 6
economic incentives 164–65,
    166, 212–13
  effect on behaviour 163–67, 211–13

economic output and income
    levels 18–22
  average per capita income by regions,
      2019 21*t*
Econs 8–9, 127, 131, 133, 144, 157, 195
education 366, 368
  India 338
  Latin America 27
  during Meiji era 259–60
  South Korea 272
  during Tokugawa shogunate 252–53
Einstein, Albert 129
The Elusive Quest for Growth 6
emerging economies) 13, 368–69, 372
  access to basic infrastructure 27–28
  access to justice 36
  challenges in urban management 25
  climate change impacts 28, 30–31
  COVID-19 pandemic impact 14–15
  economic output and income
      levels 19
  environmental issues 29–30
  HDI for 26, 27
  income inequality 22
  infrastructure services to
      citizens 27, 28
  per capita incomes 21–22
  share in global economic output 19
  social media 35–36
  urbanization 25
empirical expectations 186
endowment effect 140, 144
enlightened despotism 233, 234–35
'equilibrium fiction' 195
ethical universalism and
    particularism 118
Europe 3–4, 61, 75, 228, 233, 239,
    303, 304, 372. *see also* advanced
    countries; Denmark; Great Britain
extractive institutions 118–21, 125, 223,
    236, 242, 253–55, 279, 360

Federal Reserve Act, 1913 321–22
female genital cutting (FGC) 186–87,
    189, 195–96, 197, 208, 209
First Northern War, 1657 227
focal-point e 148–50

foot binding 207–8
Forbes, Naushad 307
   *The Struggle and The Promise:
      Restoring India's Potential* 307
Ford, Betty 214
freedom 1, 47, 51, 56–57, 66, 73, 96–97,
      233–34, 281–82, 293, 294, 295, 300,
      313, 338, 353, 356–57, 361, 365, 375
   'intrinsic' and 'instrumental'
      values of 45
free-rider problem 153
French Revolution 233
French Revolution in 1790s 233
Friedman, Milton 130
Fukuyama, Francis 47, 115–16, 223,
      294–95, 306

game theory 148
Gandhi, Mahatma 123
Gandhi's *swaraj* (self- rule)
      movement 328
gender discrimination 328–29
gender role attitudes 194
Germany 3–4, 20*t*, 233–34, 363
*The Gift Relationship: From Blood
      Donations to Social Policy*
      (Titmuss) 164
global average
   adult literacy rate 2
   life expectancy 2
   per capita income 1
Global Climate Risk Index 2021 29–30
Global Corruption Barometer 99, 100
global economy, transformation of 372
Glorious Revolution (1688–1689) 122–
      23, 241–44
good choice architecture 142–43
   human organ donations 143
   nudges 142, 143
good development 7, 11–12, 45, 116,
      121, 357
good equilibrium 167–68, 174–75, 181
   role of social norms 180–84
good governance 5–6, 7, 11–12, 105,
      221, 356–57, 374
   accountability 51–52
   basic elements of 48–52, 357

benefits 45, 66, 357
economic growth and 68
efficient and effective use of national
      resources 67–68
participation 50–51
predictability 48–49
role of state 295–98
transparency 49–50
governance 356, 357
   correlation between income growth
      and 64*f*, 64
   country-wise 61
   definition and interpretations 46–47
   de jure and de facto measures 53–56
   for economic growth 46
   effects of per capita income on 65
   impact on incomes and other
      development outcomes
      62–72, 63*f*
   indicators 63*f*
   intrinsic and instrumental
      values 45–46
   legal aspects of 47
   meaning of 43–47
   as a measure of state capacity 47
   multidimensional nature of 46–47
   need for 41–43
   niti and *nyaya* 44
   percentile rankings and ratings
      values 75*f*, 77*f*
   profiles of 59–62
   region-wise 61
   rules of engagement 43
   social development and 66–67
   sustainable improvements in 362
governance matters 67–72
Great Britain 235–46
   England's first parliament 236–37
   Glorious Revolution, 1688 236,
      248, 316
   Great Rebellion of 1642 239–41
   Habeas Corpus Act 243
   impositions 237–38
   inclusive political and economic
      institutions 244–46
   Industrial Revolution, 1700s 236
   judicial system 245

Great Britain (*cont.*)
  'King in Parliament' 242–43
  Magna Carta (the Great
    Charter) 235, 236, 247
  Parliament, role of 242–44
  pluralism and centralization
    in 236–37
  political reforms in 247
  property rights and institutions 238,
    243, 245
  public and private capital
    markets 245–46
  Star Chamber 239
  tensions between monarch and
    Parliament 242, 247
Greif, A. 175
group-minded individuals 147

hard autocracies 32
Harpalus affair 87
Havel, Vaclav 171
  The Power of the Powerless 170
Henry III, King 236
Henry VIII, King 237
Hirschman, Albert
  Exit, Voice, and Loyalty: Responses to
    Decline in Firms, Organizations,
    and States 343–44
  importance of communication
    (voice), go elsewhere (exit),
    loyalty 343–45
HIV/AIDS 133–34, 204, 276
Hobbes, Thomas 162–63, 293–94, 296,
  313, 338
Hobbesian despotic Leviathan 295
'homo economicus' (Econ) 129, 131
Hong Kong's Independent Commission
  Against Corruption 309
horizontal teaching systems 214
human behaviour 130, 358–59
  altruistic behaviour 158
  beliefs, role of 169–77
  cognition and motivation 130
  collective action and social dilemmas,
    challenges of 153–56

conditional cooperation 162–67
cooperation 158–61, 162–67, 178–79
Crown Game 151–53
emotions and morals 129–30
focal-point effect 148–50
influence of social norms 177–84
Island Game 150–51
managing the commons 161–62
Meeting Game 149–50
moral disengagement 166
rationality 129–30
reciprocity 157–58, 178–79
role of economic incentives and social
  preferences 163–67
shifting behaviour 184–86
social interactions 180–84
socially enforced behaviour 178
state of equilibrium 150–53
willpower 141
human capability 273, 297, 364
human capital 4, 6
Human Development Index (HDI) 26–
  27, 26*t*, 60
human predispositions 147
human sociality 147–48
human thinking 128, 130, 190
  anchoring effect 137–38
  automatic and reflective
    system 131, 132–33
  bias of present 141
  cognitive challenges 133–34
  endowment effect 140
  framework of understanding 134–36
  options and consequences of
    actions 142–43, 145
  phenomenon of loss aversion 138–41
  status quo bias 140–41, 144
Hume, D. 162, 171
Huntington, S. P. 90
Hypereides 86–87

IMF 36–37, 94
impartiality 100
inclusive economic institutions 118–21,
  125, 230, 360

feedback dynamics 120–21
incentives and opportunities 118–19
plurality of members 119
stability of 121
inclusive institutions 68–69, 119,
120, 121, 123, 125, 223, 234,
236–37, 243–44, 247, 248, 270–71,
276–77, 280–81, 288–89, 355,
356, 359–61
inclusive localism 334, 336, 353, 361
inclusive political institutions 119–20,
121, 247, 272–73
Index of Public Integrity (IPI) 263–64
India 15–16, 33–34, 60, 61–62, 304
Indianapolis 331
individual rights 108
Indonesia 15–16, 20t, 27–28, 77f, 340–
41, 347
inequalities 2, 306, 368
between- countries 22
in Brazil 38
in China 22, 38
intra-country 22–23, 368
in Latin America 38
infant mortality 66, 103
Bangladesh 69–70
governance indicators and 66, 67f
in selected 20 countries 67f
Inflation Reduction Act, 2022 28
information, framing and salience
of 134–36
information-sharing 332–34, 371
infrastructure gap 27, 28
infrastructure services to citizens 27
institutional strengthening 110, 116
institutions 127, 213–14, 357–58, see
also inclusive economic institutions
bargaining process 115
challenges of institutional
reforms 121–23
commitment 111–12
constraints 108
context-specific 116–18
cooperation 112
coordination 112–13

definition 111–12
distinction between organizations
and 110–11
enforcement 108
ethical universalism and
particularism 118
extractive 118–21
formal 112–13, 114, 117–18,
357–58
functions of 111–13
importance of 113–16
incentive structure of society 108–9
inclusive 68–69, 118–21, 123, 125,
223, 234, 236–37, 243–44, 247, 248,
270–71, 276–77, 280–81, 288–89,
355, 356, 359–61
informal 112–13, 114, 357–58
institutional capacities 115–16
institutional failures 113
limited- and open-access orders of
societies 116–18
political 114
political power structures and
development of 114–16
role in economic and social
development 113
as rules of the game 109
intention-action divide 141, 204
interactive rationality 148
Inter-American Development Bank 4
Intergovernmental Panel on Climate
Change (IPCC) 28, 368–69
'invisible hand' 129, 147
I Paid a Bribe 95
Island Game 150–51
isolation paradox 177
Italy 20t, 192–93, 206, 329, 336–37
civic traditions 337
economic output 19

Jan Lokpal Bill (Citizen's Ombudsman
Bill) 99–100
Japan 18, 61, 77f, 271–72, 273, 359,
363, 366
Japanese miracle 250

Japan (*cont.*)
  Meiji Restoration (1868–1912) 122–
    23, 257–63
  Tokugawa shogunate
    (1603–1868) 250–57
judicial institutions 300–2
judicial reforms 302
justice 36–37, 57, 87, 108, 123, 297,
    300–1, 314, 338, 352
  access to 36–37, 340, 352
  power of State to ensure 295,
    306, 313–14
  social 44, 296–97
  World Justice Project (WJP) 36–37

Kahneman, Daniel 131–32
  Thinking, Fast and Slow 137
Kalmar Union 225
Kattendyke, Willem van 260–61
Kaufmann, D. 56, 58*b*, 59*b*, 65, 66–
    67, 91
Kaufmann, Kraay, and Mastuzzi
    (KKM) 56
Kaula Bandar 94
Khama, Seretse 280–81, 288–89, 364
King, Jr, Martin Luther 45–46,
    123, 328

Latin America 4–5, 41, 337, 366–67, *see
    also* Brazil; Uruguay
lawlessness syndrome 308–9
laws 188, 197
  beliefs *vs* 171–77
  as 'commands' 173–74
  implementation of 174–77
  as ink on paper 172, 174–77
  role in human behaviour 172–74
  sanctioning and expressive
    powers 188
  shift of equilibrium 175–76
  suggestive or expressive power 175–76
  implementation of 174–77
leadership 345–49, 364
  autocratic leaders 347–48
  commitment to reforms 346–47

  in market and community 348
  transformational leaders 348
Leviathan 293–94, 295
  Shackled 338–43, 363
liberal democratic regimes 209, 233–34,
    247, 283–84, 302, 362, 365
liberalization 270, 304–5, 346
limited-access orders of societies 116–
    18, 223, 233, 234, 359–61, 362, *see
    also* open-access orders of societies
Lockheed Affair 88
loss aversion, phenomenon of 138–41
Louis XIV of France, King 240

Machiavelli 82–83
Maghribi traders 175
malaria 3
managing the commons 161–62
Mandela, Nelson 123
markets 10, 315–17, 351, 361
  impact of corruption on 319
  institutions supporting 317–20
  quality and safety of products sold
    in 321–22
  related institutions 291
Marshall, Alfred 105
Marshall Plan 3–4, 303
Matsuhito, Emperor 257
matsyanyaya 44
Meeting Game 149–50
meeting game 149–50
Meiji Restoration (1868–1912) 257–63,
    272, 364, *see also* Japan
  centralization of power and social
    changes 258
  civil servants 262
  constitutional and absolute
    monarchy 259
  economic institutions 259
  education system 259–60
  fiscal constraints 258–59
  land reforms 258
  Land Tax Revision Act of
    1873 258, 262
  modernity and military power 257–58

private property system 258
punctuality 260–61
rule of Shoguns and daimyos 262
rules for admission to the naval
    academy 261–62
social norms 260–61
social structures 261–63
taxation system 259
transformative institutional
    changes 257–59, 262
mental models 9, 190–96, 199, 206–
    10, 359
ability to adapt to new
    opportunities 194
catching them young 214
changing 213–15
effect on levels of social capital 192
effects of long-term staying power
    of 191–95
environment- and
    society- specific 191
influence of past collective
    experiences 194
intergenerational transfers 191–96
power and persistence of 207
specific behaviours 190–91
television, impact of 214–15
use of 190
Mexican debt crisis 304
microfinance 70–71, 205
middle classes 23, 233, 366–67
    percentage of people classified 24t
Middle East 75
mistrust 194–95
monopoly of violence 120
Montesquieu 3
The Moral Basis of a Backward Society
    (Banfield) 192
moral disengagement 166, 211
Morgan, John 320
mugs story 139
multiple equilibrium 150
Mungiu-Pippidi, Alina 90, 100, 118,
    121–22, 225–26, 234, 281–82,
    284, 289

Myerson, Roger 148
Myrdal, Gunnar 91

Narayan, Deepa 43
Nash equilibrium 150–53
national defence 296
National Police Act 55
New Institutional Economics
    (NIE) 106, 123–24
The New Localism: How Cities Can
    Thrive in the Age of Populism (Katz
    and Nowak) 330
newly industrializing countries
    (NICs) 366–67
Nigeria 27, 33–34, 43, 60, 77f, 223
niti and nyaya 44
normative expectations 186
'norm entrepreneurs' 189–90
norms 8, 9, 206–10, see also
    social norms
    cascades 209
    changing 207–10
    counter 208
    cultural context of 212
    of punctuality 180–81
    tipping point 208
North, Douglass 106, 110–11
North America 3–4, 61, 75, 372, see also
    advanced countries
Northern Seven Years' War
    (1563–1570) 227
Nudge (Thaler and Sunstein) 185
nudges 142, 143, 206
Nye, J. S. 83, 84, 90

Oceania 75, 372, see also advanced
    countries
open-access orders of societies
    116–18, 223, 233, 234, 261–63,
    264, 282–83, 359–61, 362,
    see also limited-access orders of
    societies
Open Government Partnership
    (OGP) 340–43
organizational strengthening 110

Organization for Economic
    Co-operation and Development
    (OECD) countries 21–22
organizations
    influence on institutions 110–11
    social interactions 110–11
    types 110
ostracism 175, 180, 193, 340
Ostrom, Elinor 108–9, 161, 193–94, 334

Pacific Railway Act, 1862 320
Panchayati Raj Amendment
    Act 213–14
participation 50–51, 357
    in decision- making process 51
    deliberations and decision- making
        processes 51
    intended beneficiaries 51
particularism 118
Perry, Matthew C. 256
Pettit, Philip 293
Philip II of Macedon, King 86–87
Philippines 15–16, 43, 60, 69, 77f, 85,
    101f, 161, 271, 340–41, 345
    land reforms 271
physical and human capital 71–72
physical security 111–12
Pittsburgh 330–31
Plato 82–83, 327–28
    Republic 43
pluralism 119–20, 224–25, 233, 234–35,
    236–37, 243–45, 246, 247, 270–71,
    272–73, 279, 363
political and economic
        institutions 299–300, see also
        inclusive economic institutions
political corruption 320
polluted cities 31t
population trends and aging
    advanced countries 18
    East Asia 15–17
    Germany 18
    Japan 18
    South Asia 16–17
    sub-Saharan Africa 17

populism 112
Populists 321
Posner, Eric 180
poverty 1–2, 3, 95, 107, 133, 200–2, 203,
    205, 206, 218, 255, 276, 282, 306,
    329, 357
    effect of corruption on 34, 86,
        92–95
    effect of good governance on 46, 276
    income 41, 46, 218
The Power of the Powerless (Havel) 170
Pradhan, Sanjay 341
predictability 48–49, 357
    in public policy 49
    of rule-based system 49
predictability 48–49
'principal-agent' relationship 183
Prisoner's dilemma 154–56
private gain 84
The Problem of Corruption 85–86
procrastination 218
Progressive movement 321
Public Affairs Centre (PAC) 310, 333
public goods 296–97
Public Goods Game 158–59, 167
public infrastructure 296
public-private partnerships 310–11
Pure Food and Drug Act, 1906 321–22
Putin, Vladimir 346

quality of life 6

Rajan, Raghuram 10, 116, 350
    The Third Pillar (Rajan) 292
Rao, Narasimha 346
Rational Fools 155
'REACH' (Reaching Everyone for Active
        Citizenry @Home) 333
reciprocity 157–58, 163–64, 165, 178–
    79, 210–11
recycling 167, 188–89, 209–10
reflective thinking 132–34, 135–36,
    138–39, 142, 205, 218
reforms
    leadership commitment to 346–47

opportune time for 346
The Third Pillar (Rajan) 292
regulatory capture 322
Rhee, Syngman 266
Robinson, James 96, 113, 114, 118, 119–
20, 293, 295, 338, 349–50
Rockefeller, John 317–18, 320
on rationalization and
competition 318
Standard Oil Company 318,
320, 321
Rotberg, Robert 82
Rousseau 82–83
rule of law 171–77
The 10 Rules of Successful Nations
(Sharma) 345–46
rules of the game 48, 107–8, 109, 110,
114, 117–18, 125, 130, 299
rural-urban migration 24–25, 367–68

Sachs, Jeffrey 3
Samuelson, W. 140
Schelling, Thomas 148
focal-point effect 148–49
The Strategy of Conflict 148
schooling, importance of 297–98
self-efficacy beliefs 193–94, 329
self-interest 147
self-perception of identity 194
Sen, Amartya 42, 44, 45, 177, 260,
273, 293
Shackled Leviathan 338–43, 363
Sherman Antitrust Act of 1890 321
Singapore 2–3, 77f, 345, 360–61,
363, 366
Singh, Manmohan 346
slave trade 191, 194–95
Smith, Adam 320
*An Inquiry into the Nature and Causes
of the Wealth of Nations* 317
invisible hand 129, 147
view of human nature 162
The Wealth of Nations 108
smoking 141, 179–80, 185, 188,
209–10

social development 1, 11–12, 13, 66–67,
70, 71, 103, 106–7, 113, 262–63,
272, 356, 357
social dilemmas 153–56, 157, 161,
163, 167–68
social indicators 2
social injustices 45
social media 35–36, 372
influence of 372
for social activism 372
social norms 199, 358–59, 364
in fighting corruption 181–84
influence on collective
behaviour 182, 196–97
influence on human
behaviour 177–90
role in individual and social
behaviour 177–84
to shift behaviour 184–90
in social interactions 180–84, 196
social preferences, effect on
behaviour 163–67, 212–13
Solon's reforms 338–40
cancellation of debt servitude 339
Hubris Law 340
judicial reforms 339–40
land reforms 339
pro-people reforms 339–40
State's powers 338–39
South Asia 61, 75
South Korea (Republic of Korea) 60,
77f, 363
bureaucracy 268–69
civil-service examinations 269
economic institutions 270
education system 267–68, 272
fight against corruption 263–64
Goryeo era (918–1392) 264–65
governance 61, 263–64
Government's pledge of 'land to the
tiller' 266–67
inclusive political and economic
institutions 270–71
Korean War (1950–1953) 263,
265, 272

South Korea (Republic of Korea) (*cont.*)
  land reforms 265–67, 268,
    270–71, 272
  meritocracy 269
  political institutions 270
  recruitment process 269
  share of global GDP 19, 20*t*
  social structures 264, 265
  state autonomy 269–70
  yangban or landed aristocracy 267
Soviet Union 68
State 10, 329–30, 351, 361
  authoritarian 318
  authoritarian tendencies 323
  balance between community
    and 335–38
  capability 306–13
  capture 319–20
  competitive pressures 310–12
  continuum of capability 307
  contracting out services 311
  expanding role of 303–4
  expectations of 302–5, 308–9
  generalized institutional framework
    of 298–302
  institutional capabilities 322–23
  involvement in economy 304–5
  laws, rules, and regulations 308–10
  public-private partnerships 310–11
  quality and safety of products sold in
    market 321–22
  role in good governance 295–98
  rules of engagement with local
    governments 335
  in shaping society's well-being 313
  top-down 327–28
status quo bias 140, 144
Stigler, George 322
The Strategy of Conflict (Schelling) 148
sub-Saharan Africa 61, 75, *see also*
    Botswana
Sunstein, Cass 129
suppliker 231
Swing Riots in 1830 350

System 1 and System 2 of thinking 131

Tae-woo, Roh 272–73
Tagore, Rabindranath 1, 36, 375
Takayoshi, Kido 259–60
tax-collection institutions 319
taxes, effect on international trade 319
technological breakthroughs 369–70
Temple of Hibis 88
Thaler, Richard 129
Thinking, Fast and Slow (Kahneman) 137
Thirty Years' War (1618–1648) 227
Thucydides 82–83
tipping point 188, 208, 209, 233–34
tit for tat strategy 158–61, 162
Titmuss, Richard
  explanation for avoidance of blood
    donation 166
  *The Gift Relationship: From Blood
    Donations to Social Policy* 164
  on state or market-oriented provision
    of health services 164
toilet ownership 187
Tokugawa shogunate (1603–1868) 250–
    57, 272, *see also* Japan
  Act of Seclusion 1636 252
  agricultural production 252
  consolidation of power 251–52
  daimyos 254
  decline of 255–57
  economic growth 254
  economy 252
  education and living
    standards 252–53
  feudal structure of society 253–55
  hans (domains) 251
  property rights 253–54
  samurai 251, 254–55
  self-imposed isolation 256
  shogunate (or *bakufu*) 250
  shugos 250
  Temple schools (the *terakoya*) 253
  Tokugawa Ieyasu 250–51
  Treaty of Kanagawa 256

tragedy of the commons 153
transaction costs 106–7, 109
transparency 49–50, 210, 357
  challenges in ensuring 50
  in process of policymaking and
    implementation 50
Transparency International (TI) 56,
    91, 263–64
  Corruption Perception Index 309
  Global Corruption Barometer 94–
    95, 99
trust 83, 165, 179, 191
Trust Game 165
Tunisia 61
Twende na Wakati (Let's Go with the
    Times) 214–15

ultimatum game 157–58
unbounded rationality 133, 144, 217–18
unfreedoms 42, 171
United Nations Development
    Program 26
United States 68
  American Marshall Plan 303
United States Steel Corporation 320
universal ethics 118
urbanization 24–26, 367–68
Uruguay 289
  clientelism 283–84
  corruption 283
  electoral reforms 286
  ethical universalism 285
  fundamental institutional
    reforms 285
  governance 283
  guerrilla movement (the
    Tupamaros) 286
  Human Development 282
  income levels 282–83
  inequality in 282–83
  'multiple simultaneous voting system
    (MSV)' 284
  open-access orders of societies 282–
    83, 287

Partido Colorado, 'Red' (PC)
    and Partido Nacional, 'Blanco'
    (PN) 283–84
  partisan control 283–84
  pension reforms 286
  political plurality 286–88
  poverty level 282
  privatization 286
  'Public Enterprises Law' 286
  tradition of democracy 283–84
  transparency 283

vaccines against COVID-19
    pandemic 15
Valdemar IV, monarch 224–25
Vietnam 27–28, 61, 69, 77f,
    101f, 160–61
violence against women 196
'voice' 56–57, 61, 62, 63f–69f, 65, 71, 75,
    283, 343–45
voting rights 350, 351

'Warre' 338
Washington Consensus 5
Weber, Max 120
  ideal bureaucracy 262
Western 'Slacktivism' 35
WGICC 97, 98, 100
Why Nations Fail (Acemoðlu and
    Robinson) 113
William of Orange 240–41
Wolfensohn, James 90–91
World Bank 4, 36–37, 43, 46, 54–55,
    56, 90–91, 275, 283, 334,
    337, 366–67
  2019 Doing Business Report 54–55
World Economic Forum 56
World Governance Indicator (WGI) 97
world in 2022 13
  differences between advanced and
    developing countries 13
  per capita incomes 13
World Justice Project (WJP) 36–37
  Rule of Law Index 97

World Justice Project Rule of Law Index
  (WJI) 97
World Trade Organization
  (WTO) 330
Worldwide Governance Indicators
  (WGI) 56–57, 58*b*
  clusters and component
    indicators 56
  control of corruption 57
  economic and social interactions 57

government effectiveness 57
regulatory quality 57
rule of law 57

Yew, Lee Kuan 347
Yoritomo, Minamoto 250
Yoritomo, Shogun 250
Yunus, Muhammad 205

Zeckhauser, R. 140